PUBLIC ADMINISTRATION

PUBLIC ADMINISTRATION
A READER

Edited by

Bidyut Chakrabarty
Mohit Bhattacharya

OXFORD
UNIVERSITY PRESS

OXFORD

UNIVERSITY PRESS

Oxford University Press is a department of the University of Oxford.
It furthers the University's objective of excellence in research, scholarship,
and education by publishing worldwide. Oxford is a registered trademark of
Oxford University Press in the UK and in certain other countries

Published in India by
Oxford University Press
22 Workspace, 2nd Floor, 1/22 Asaf Ali Road, New Delhi 110002, India

First Edition published in 2003
Oxford India Paperbacks 2006
25th impression 2021

ISBN-13: 978-0-19-567902-1
ISBN-10: 0-19-567902-4

Typeset by Jojy Philip
Printed in India by Manipal Technologies Limited, Manipal

dedicated to
our children in the
hope that the future
will be better-administered

Acknowledgment

The volume seeks to present the readers and scholars in the discipline an integrated anthology of updated theoretical advances and key issues in Public Administration. As a social science, Public Administration has in recent times been evolving as a critique of administration in its bid to adjudge the discipline's coping ability in a fast changing scenario of proactive institutional mechanism and procedure. The authors were instinctively goaded by the desire to harness systematically the fruits of research and observations that would benefit scholars and researchers in the discipline. We are grateful for advice from many colleagues, as also quite a few authors who gave ready permission to include their contributions in the present volume. We look forward to receiving their comments from users and to update it in future in keeping with the growth of the discipline.

We are thankful to OUP for agreeing to our proposal.

Acknowledgment to Publishers

The publishers wish to thank the following for permission to include the articles/extracts in this volume:

Routledge and Kegan Paul for Nicos Mouzelis, 'The Ideal Type of Bureaucracy' in his *Organisation and Bureaucracy: An Analysis of Modern Theories*, 1975.

Indian Political Science Association for O.P. Dwivedi, William Graf, and J. Nef, 'Marxist Contributions to the Theory of Administrative State', in *The Indian Journal of Political Science*, 45(1), January–March 1985.

Indian Institute of Public Administration for V. Subramanian, 'Administration in the Eighties: Major Trends and Challenges', in *Indian Journal of Public Administration* XXVI(3), July–September 1980.

John Wiley and Sons for Richard Bately, 'The Consolidation of Structural Adjustment: Implications for Public Administration', in *Public Administration and Development*, vol. 14, 1994.

Economic and Political Weekly for Niraja Gopal Jayal, 'The Governance Agenda: Making Democratic Government Dispensable', 22 February 1997 and N. Mukarji, 'Changeful Society and Changeless Governance', 15 July 1989.

Sage Publications Inc for Richard C. Box, 'Running Government like a Business: Implications for Public Administration Theory and Practice', in *American Review of Public Administration*, 29(1), March 1999.

Blackwell Publishing for Gerry Stoker, 'Governance as Theory: Five

Propositions' in *International Social Science Journal* (on Governance), March 1988.

University of Chicago Press for L.I. and S.H. Rudolph, 'The State and its Permanent Government', in *In Pursuit of Lakshmi: The Political Economy of the Indian State*, 1987.

Sage Publications, India for Mohit Bhattacharya, 'Bureaucracy and Politics in India', in Zoya Hasan et al. (ed.), *The State, Political Processes and Identity*, 1989 and Kuldeep Mathur, 'Strengthening Bureaucracy: State and Development in India', in *Indian Social Science Review*, 1, 1, 1999.

Contents

Contributors

B.B. Mishra
Former Professor of History, University of Delhi, India

Nicos P. Mouzelis
Professor of Sociology, London School of Economics and Political Science, University of London, UK

Ramesh K. Arora
Professor and Director, Department of Public Administration, University of Rajasthan, Jaipur, India

O. P. Dwivedi
Professor Emeritus of Political Science, University of Guelph, Canada

William Graf
Former Chair of Politics, University of Guelph, Canada

J. Nef
Associate Professor of Political Science, University of Guelph, Canada

V. Subramaniam
Former Visiting Professor, Australian Graduate School of Management, University of New South Wales, Kensington, New South Wales, Australia

Richard Batley
Professor of Development Administration, School of Public Policy, University of Birmingham, UK

Niraja Gopal Jayal
Professor of Law and Governance, Jawaharlal Nehru University, New Delhi, India

GERRY STOKER
Professor of Political Science, University of Starthclyde, Glasgow, UK

RICHARD C. BOX
Associate Professor of Public Administration, University of Nebraska-Omaha, USA

L. I. RUDOLPH
Professor Emeritus of Political Science, University of Chicago, USA

S. H. RUDOLPH
Professor Emeritus of Political Science, University of Chicago, USA

P.C. ALEXANDER
An Indian Administrative Service officer, former Governor of Maharashtra, India

BIDYUT CHAKRABARTY
Professor and Head of the Department of Political Science at the University of Delhi, New Delhi, India

MOHIT BHATTACHARYA
Former Professor, Indian Institute of Public Administration, New Delhi and former Chairman, Municipal Administrative Reforms Committee, Kolkata, India

MADHAV GODBOLE
Former Home Secretary, Government of India

NIRMAL MUKARJI
Former Cabinet Secretary, Government of India

KULDEEP MATHUR
Former Professor, Centre for Political Studies, Jawaharlal Nehru University, New Delhi, India

JAYTILAK GUHA ROY
Associate Professor of Criminal Justice, Indian Institute of Public Administration, New Delhi, India.

Preface to the Paperback Edition

Public administration is government in practice. Seeking to unravel the dynamics of governance, public administration is perhaps the only discipline in social sciences that is being constantly redefined. In other words, public administration is a contextual response to governance. Since the context is important, one has to grapple with the ideological inputs whereby 'the art of governance' is articulated. Starting with the Wilsonian conceptualization of public administration as unalloyed professional enterprise, the discipline has become far more complex than is usually admitted. The reason lies in the fact that the government of the day is invariably influenced by the prevalent socio-economic and political milieu. One therefore cannot ignore the ambience in which public administration is conceptualized. Linked with this is the idea that the nature of public administration differs from one context to another. So, there cannot be a universal design. Despite the theoretical importance of the Weberian 'ideal form of organization', it would be wrong to undermine the 'spatial' nature of public administration. Models of administration are therefore contingent on the socio-historical circumstances. Whatever is relevant today may not remain so in the days to come.

Based on the contextual nature of public administration, the Reader is primarily concerned with the theoretical advances in the field that may not be apparent unless one is drawn to the tricky interplay of social, economic, and political circumstances. Public administration is not merely governance but also a process in which administration is meaningfully articulated. Following the onset of globalization, the traditional bureaucratic model appears to have lost its significance presumably because of the growing importance of the non-state actors in administration. The instrumental view of administration does not therefore appear to be tenable for reasons connected with 'the pluralization of state'. Given the increasing role of transnational forces even in domestic administration, the state-centred theories of bureaucracy seem to be inadequate in addressing the radical metamorphosis of public administration both in the developed and developing countries. One can thus safely argue that while the twentieth century was the age of organization where bureaucracy symbolized the core values of public administration, the twenty-first century has ushered in an era of 'network-based organization', drawn on neo-liberal values.

Globalization is a force that cannot thus be easily dispensed with. Government is being 'reinvented' not only structurally but also ideologically in an environment where neo-liberal values seem to have triumphed. State retreats and government withdraws form areas that traditionally remain its domain. Globalization has led to 'marriage' between corporate discipline and entrepreneurial spirit with government discarding it traditional image of 'a doer'. Seeking to accommodate 'the market impulse', the government has become 'an enabler'. Globalization thus restricts the national governments and limits its policy options. A new situation has emerged and the governmental functions are redefined within the neo-conservative theoretical parameters. The corporate state has become a reality resulting in an obvious shrinkage of the traditional state system. The state is increasingly being guided by neo-liberal values endorsing globalization of capital. The distinction between public and private administration does not appear to be critical in conceptualizing public administration. Citizens are customers and those involved in public administration are functionaries seeking to approximate to the 'corporate' culture. Accountability in public bureaucracy is ascertained not only internally but also through various external agencies, including citizen's charter. Public administration is now 'governance' which is nothing but checklists of certain activities designed both to stabilize and also to consolidate neo-liberalism. The neo-liberal thought found favour with the Western donor agencies such as the World Bank and the IMF that were engaged in the funding of the development projects of the 'debt-ridden' Third World. The convergence of thought in regard to 'change' reached its apogee in the newly emergent phenomenon of 'structural adjustment programme', facilitated by the free flow of fund, goods, and services as dictated by the new conditionalities laid down by the WTO, and by the new IT revolution (internet, fax, and web-based communication). In other words, the structural adjustment programme led to economic reforms in the developing countries that largely 'delegitimized' the role of 'the hegemonic state'. And the conditional loans to the developing countries by the transnational agencies make them dependent on the global capital. This appears to be a vicious circle from which there is no escape for the developing countries presumably because the alternative ideological power-centres are too weak to be effective partners in sustaining the drive for development. Furthermore, the drive towards 'depoliticizing development' systematically obscures 'power', 'class', and 'politics'. Critical to development are activities around 'civil society'—that, by implication, identifies development as a mere techno-economic effort which takes place outside the political arena. This is an argument that clearly undermines the role of ideology in development especially in the developing countries where public administration is critically 'partisan' for historical reasons.

The impact of all these on government and public administration has been forcefully and systematically argued out in the World Development Report, 1997(World Bank 1997). The Reader has devoted considerable space to elucidate this momentous ideological and institutional turning point in the evolution of public administrative thinking on 'reform', or another word that has been coined recently, 'innovation'. Although differing on contextual parameters such as 'developing' country situation, organized private sector, more firm regulatory framework, etc., the worldwide search for governmental reform today exhibits certain striking similarities.

II

There are challenges as well especially in the developing countries where public administration can never be said to be derivative of western models. A cursory look at the Indian administration confirms that despite having adopted the 1991 New Economic Policy it has features which are not strictly neo-liberal but drawn on the Nehruvian socialistic pattern of society. This is why the contextual model is theoretically viable and practically meaningful. Rooted in peculiar historical circumstances in which colonialism remained most decisive, the post-colonial government in India sustained several significant administrative structures, including the All India Services that safeguarded the alien interests during the British rule. Given their role in the context of 1947 partition riots, these administrative structures became organic to the India's public administration despite their imperial origin. Despite its imperial legacy, the steel frame was retained in independent India. When the matter was introduced in the Constituent Assembly for discussion, there was no unanimity among the members. Critical of its role in the freedom struggle, members like, M. A. Aayyangar and S. L. Saksena vehemently opposed the continuity of the All India Services in free India. There were some members who defended the dismantling of the Services because of the heavy financial burden which the government had to bear on account of their salary. Some of them were keen to have a written assurance from those in the Service expressing their willingness to serve the country 'sincerely, honestly and incorruptibly' because they were created and nurtured in opposition to the interests of the nationalists. That the Service was retained more or less *in tact* was due to Vallabhbhai Patel's insistence on its continuity for practical considerations.

The Constituent Assembly debates are very useful in grasping what finally defended the continuity of the steel frame in otherwise unfavourable circumstances. Not only does the discussion in the Assembly draw our attention to the mindset of the founding fathers, it is also very significant in grasping the nature of the emerging public administration in India under the stewardship of those who fought the British and won freedom.

While accepting the 'steel frame' of the British bureaucracy presumably because of its structural utility, the founding fathers sought to radically alter its nature by locating its functioning within a system of democratic governance. So, bureaucracy metamorphosed substantially in view of the involvement of the people in the decision-making processes. And, the administrator had to articulate these characteristics in his/her deeds. All this involved 'close contacts and touch with the people and winning over the people to his (sic) side'. It was 'a normal approach of a politician when he wants to win over the people to his side to do something with their help'. So administration was not merely routine jobs, it was also a creative response to human problems in which people had a decisive role. This was a revolutionary step for two reasons: *first*, instead of doing away with the prevalent bureaucratic set-up, the post-colonial leaders sought to adapt the structure to the requirement of democratic values and ethos which free Indian represented. *Secondly*, the steel frame of the past transformed its nature radically to fulfill the goal of the new nation that emerged after a long struggle against the British. Interestingly, for the prevalent bureaucracy, the transition from an imperial to a qualitatively different regime in free India was smooth and it was rather easier for those who took charge of administration immediately after Independence to initiate reforms in administration without difficulty.

With the adoption of the socialistic pattern of society these structures had obviously undergone radical changes By the 1990s, the scene was however different and India's bureaucracy responded, though in a guarded manner, to the neo-liberal values challenging the state-directed planned economic development. Government is being 'reinvented' but with a caution presumably because of the ideological pressure, exercised by forces critical of globalization and neo-liberalism.

The recent changes in Indian public administration owe, to a significant extent, to inputs from both the external and internal sources. Administrative changes are generally articulated in the reports of Reforms Commission, appointed regularly by the government of India. The Fifth Pay Commission, 1997 has however gone beyond the conventional bounds of a pay commission and performed the role of an administrative reform commission touching on the vital issues of governance in India. Although this pay commission has set the new agenda of 'good governance' into action, the Fourth Pay Commission, 1982 had also suggested steps to improve 'efficiency' in public administration primarily in terms of enhanced salary and other benefits. What is unique about the Fifth Pay Commission is its articulation of the changed role of government in response to global inputs. The government needs to be downsized and debureaucratized. The government should confine itself primarily to 'core functions' that cannot be performed by the market. Everything must be left to private initiative. So, not only has the Fifth Pay Commission (1997) suggested a new pay structure for civil service, it has also made recommendations of far reaching nature affecting its size, efficiency, morale and motivation, training and recruitment, and general operation procedures. The 1998 *Action Plan for Effective and Responsive Government* is a clear articulation of the proposed measures to attain the goal set by the Fifth Pay Commission. Product of the 1996 Chief Secretaries Conference, the Plan seeks to (a) make administration accountable and citizen-friendly, (b) ensure transparency and right to information, and (c) take measures to cleanse and motivate civil services. The Action Plan clearly indicates that the vertical structure of hierarchy is 'unsuitable for either speedy decision-making or empowerment down the line to encourage bright young talent to take decisions and be accountable for them'.

III

There is no doubt that globalization has radically altered public administration all over the globe. Its impact has not been uniform. In the developed countries, public bureaucracy redefines its role accommodating the neo-liberal thrust on administration. The transition from one ideological *raison d'être* to another is not as thorny as it is in the developing countries. Reasons are not difficult to seek. *First*, historically public administration flourished under the state patronage in most of the developing countries that had a long colonial past. Even after decolonization, public bureaucracy continued to remain perhaps the most decisive 'cog' in the entire governmental machinery. *Secondly*, by following the path of state-directed centralized planed development, these post-colonial states sought to provide an alternative to the western capitalist route that never appeared to be an effective challenge to the rampant poverty and other related problems. Whatever the justifications, the centralized planning failed to bring about economic development to the extent it was expected. Arguments were thus marshalled against 'protected' economy and bureaucratically-designed public administration. And, globalization seems to have created an occasion to try-out other alternatives since the non/anti-capitalist path of development did not appear to be adequate. In the changed context, centralized bureaucracy became a stumbling block to change and reform. As a result, under the 'new public management regime', many developed and developing countries have shifted from 'process-oriented' to 'result-oriented' performance of public agencies with increasing focus on outcome rather than inputs. On the face of it, the result-oriented administration may look quite attractive; but such mode of governance may not always uphold the 'publicness' of public administration. In other words, since the result-oriented public administration tends to focus on 'what' is being achieved regardless of consequences, it is likely to undermine its nature as 'a benevolent guardian'.

Apart from re-conceptualizing public bureaucracy, economic reforms have also contributed to our search for alternatives to the Weberian pyramidic structure of power. Decentralization—both the Gandhian and non-Gandhian forms—provides significant inputs to administrative reforms and innovations especially in the context of 'democratic surges' at the grassroots. The Weberian theoretical format has no clue to this system of governance in which hierarchy is replaced by the Gandhian notion of 'an oceanic circle'. Drawn on peoples' participation, governance structured around the theoretical ideas of the *panchayati raj* system provides a creative solution to the administrative *impasse* due to well-entrenched bureaucratization. This is undoubtedly a serious theoretical discourse seeking to redefine the goal, and thus nature of an administration that is apparently reluctant to change due to historically nurtured social, economic, and political prejudices. In a way, globalization is thus a significant input in our search for appropriate explanatory models of governance.

IV

As evident, public administration has been undergoing some major changes in terms of both thematic variety and conceptual dimension. Hence a companion volume on *Administrative Change and Innovation*[1] has been recently brought out to capture the expanding scope of the discipline. Synoptically, four interconnected themes have emerged in recent years as 'new' directionality in the discipline: 'globalization', 'network' administration, 'governance', and 'democratization-participation'. The *first theme* refers to a new emergent world order based on deep and wide interconnectivity among nations. This phenomenon has been compelling nations to reorient their public administration to manage externalities and strike a balance between domestic needs and international linkages. The *second theme*, which is closely related to the first and the third, symbolizes a novel transformation of public administration from its traditional insular and hierarchic status to a 'network' profile with linkages protruding in different directions, as most problems tend to elude its erstwhile monopolistic grip. The *third theme* of 'governance' that essentially extended the ambit of domestic public administration was given considerable space in the present anthology. What is presently being experienced is the need for its 'rescoping' in terms of complex linkages with a variety of external actors in an intensely globalized situation. The *fourth theme*, which has also been touched upon in this anthology, is being resurrected more stridently in recent years as a reaction to both globalization and the neo-liberalist trend in administrative repositioning. Democracy, not so much as a form of government, but as a structural and processual feature of public administration is assuming considerable significance contemporaneously. There is a

[1] Bidyut Chakrabarty and Mohit Bhattacharya (eds), *Administrative Change and Innovation: A Reader*, Oxford University Press, New Delhi, 2005.

resurgence of people-as-actor syndrome today to safeguard a beleaguered 'legitimacy' of government under the New Public Management dispensation as also to assert real popular control over government in terms of decentralization, openness, transparency, and accountability. Thematic richness and diversity of public administrative issues would possibly call for a new venture altogether in the form of another anthology. Meanwhile, we would be expecting a much warmer reception to this paperback edition that might inspire us to prepare ourselves for the proposed new experiment.

V

The literature on the subject is expanding. Originally, the idea of bringing out a 'Reader' in public administration was to present to a variegated group of scholars and practitioners a rounded and fairly comprehensive anthology on both theoretical and practical aspects of the evolving discipline of public administration. It would however be difficult, if not impossible, to dwell on each and every relevant issue. Our effort was to cast the net as wide as possible to present an anthology of contributions which are significant from the point of view of the discipline as well the practice of public administration. The articles which we incorporated in the Reader are both innovative and provocative: innovative because these selected articles dwell on those issues that figure prominently in public administration which is far from Weberian; provocative since they raise questions which are relevant in conceptualizing public bureaucracies around the globe in a context where neo-liberal politico-economic values appear to have prevailed over other contrasting ideological strands. So, this is an anthology that serves twin-purposes of dissemination of knowledge and laying foundation for further research. The task was made easier because the contributors analysed various dimensions of public administration with references to forces that emanate from wider social, economic, and political milieu. In order to grasp the complex unfolding of contemporary public administration, the experts who wrote for the Reader highlighted the linkages between the structures of administration and the ambience in which the process of administration is articulated. Appreciative of inter-disciplinary borrowings, the Reader is thus a serious intervention in relocating public administration both as a discipline and as a practice. Apart from this obvious intellectual purpose, when we compiled the volume, one of our aims was to make the Reader available to the students at an affordable price. With the publication of a cheap paperback edition, our aim is now fulfilled. A cheaper paperback edition of the volume is sure to enhance its accessibility to a still larger circle of readers. We compliment the Oxford University Press for having brought out a paperback edition of the Reader. We are also thankful to our students and well-wishers for their support. And, of course our families that always stood by us deserve special mention.

Delhi   BIDYUT CHAKRABARTY
July 2005   MOHIT BHATTACHARYA

Preface

The main purpose of writing this book is to compile a volume of articles/excerpts that are useful in comprehensively grasping the historical evolution of the discipline and its current manifestations. Given its emphasis on both historical and existential perspectives, this compilation is unique in its own right. Drawing on the analytical character of Public Administration as a discipline, this collection identifies new areas of research which is, so far, largely confined to description of the structures of administration without reference to their socio-economic and cultural roots. Since its primary concern is to critically understand the system of administration in its complexity, the volume revolves around two ideas: (a) to bring together major theoretical works in Public Administration and other related fields in Social Sciences without which the importance of Public Administration as an explanatory device shall highly be restricted; and (b) to test the validity of these theoretical premises in the context of India that itself is a microcosm of those decolonized countries, placed under similar socio-economic and political circumstances.

Intellectually, the Reader provides a very useful design underlining both the theoretical and descriptive aspects of the discipline of Public Administration; it is also certain to draw the attention of those interested in the growth and development of Public Administration as an independent subject. The substantive coverage in terms of bureaucratic structure and operation follows the conceptual paradigmatic presentations to illuminate bureaucratic operations and practices. Major theoretical advances in administrative theory since the Weberian formulation, having relevance for India and the 'third world' have been garnered together as a conceptual backdrop for subsequent discussions on the structure, processes and behaviour of bureaucracy.

It is true that Public Administration owes a great deal to the writings of Max Weber. The idea of 'an ideal form of organization' happens to be one of the most formidable concepts in Public Administration and the concept seems to be the guiding force in most of the post-Weber writings. Notwithstanding the theoretical significance of the Weberian ideal form of organization one tends to gloss over the complexity of modern bureaucracy if one accepts the concept uncritically. For instance is bureaucracy always a 'rational' instrument or an instrument without 'personality'? If it is the former, then bureaucracy is an institution and if it is the latter, then bureaucracy is merely a device. The Weberian conceptualization is, therefore, riddled with this kind of tension which is vivid and runs through in the writings of Max Weber.

The Reader has three parts—each with a distinct focus. Part one has articles on the theoretical advances in the discipline since Weber's formulation. While B.B. Mishra traces the origin of public administration in the complex evolution of the concept of bureaucracy in the European context, Nicos Mouzelis has identified unique features of authority and power in Weber's formulation of 'ideal form of organization'. Fred Riggs' conceptualization of 'administrative ecology' is a contextual formulation seeking to capture the rapidly changing 'third' world reality. Ramesh Arora provides a very lucid analysis of this model that has provoked new debates in the field of Public Administration. The article by O.P. Dwivedi and others is illustrative of a trend in public administration that draws upon Marx and the Marxist conceptualization of bureaucracy. Part two deals with the transformation of public administration in the context of changes ushered in by globalization. V. Subramaniam's paper is relevant because of its focus on what finally led to the growth of a new paradigm in public administration since the 1968 Minnowbrook conference. This is now clear that most of the changes in contemporary public administration had their roots in the 1980s when 'public' in public administration was being thoroughly redefined.

The selected pieces in Part two are thus directed towards unfolding the important dimensions of 'government in action'. An attempt has been made to bring out the theoretical contours of the widely publicized concept of 'governance' highlighting its wider connotation that is ordinarily associated with government. By locating governance in the neo-liberal agenda of the state, Niraja Gopal Jayal has dealt with the concept in a manner which is both intellectually refreshing and analytically challenging especially in the context of a

developing country, like India. Richard Box, in his theoretically stimulating article, focuses on the argument concerning the relative merit
of privatization as a mechanism of development primarily in the
context of developing nations. Richard Batley's article on the impact
of structural adjustment on public administration in developing countries is theoretically most provocative since it has brought out the
difficulty of the prevalent 'administrative state' of adjusting to an
externally-induced direction. Gerry Stoker's article on governance is
structured around five propositions underlining the significant
dimensions of 'governance' as an approach to study public
administration.

Part three is about the Indian public administration with reference
to its growth taking into account both the colonial past and its aftermath. Beginning the discussion with the historical context in which
founding fathers unanimously agreed to retain the 'steel frame' on
practical considerations, the Rudolphs have laid the background of
growth of bureaucracy in India that had a colonial past. This part
contains those representative pieces which are useful in grasping the
radical metamorphosis of public administration in India that is clearly
different from her neighbours due to unique historical circumstances
supportive of parliamentary democracy. Since there is a clear continuity given the inherent Weberian tendencies in Indian public
administration it is difficult, if not impossible, to demarcate precisely
the phases of the evolution of public administration in India. However, articles are clustered around a sequence that clearly shows the
growing importance of specific themes and hence their significance
in grasping the changes in public administration in contemporary
India. P.C. Alexander traces the historical roots of Indian civil service
while striving to grasp the 'continuity and change' in Indian bureaucracy. That the role of bureaucracy needs to be contextualized is what
provokes Mohit Bhattacharya, Madhave Godbole and Kuldeep
Mathur. By linking the constantly changing role of bureaucracy with
the contemporary socio-political context of India, these authors have
firmly established that public administration is generally ideological.
N. Mukarji pursues the argument a little further by underlining the
hiatus between the structure of governance that is largely stagnant
and the society, which is constantly changing. The article on voluntary associations sheds light on the Indian experience of the role of
voluntary organizations in development both as an instrument as
well as a conceptual framework to understand the development
process where the role of the state is pre-eminent. In his piece, Jaytilak

Guha Roy has brought out the human rights dimensions of public administration. It is an area that is increasingly becoming a significant part of Indian bureaucracy. This part is not at all exhaustive but given the limited space, we have selected those articles, which are clearly representative of the trends in today's public administration and are thus relevant in articulating its constantly changing nature in most of the developing countries where bureaucracy in the Weberian sense and form has flourished due to peculiar historical circumstances.

Public Administration
Theory and Practice

A s an aspect of government activity, administration has been co-existing with every political system as the action part of government for the fulfillment of the objectives set by the political decision-makers. Functioning of the machineries of government has attracted the attention of scholars and observers since the time of recorded history. Kautilya's *Arthasastra*, the *Mahabharata*, and the *Ramayana* contain many insightful observations about the organizations and working of government. In the history of western political thought, Aristotle's *Politics* and Machiavelli's *The Prince* are important contributions to both political and administrative issues and ideas.

Public Administration as a specialized academic field deals essentially with the machinery and procedures of government as these are used in the effective performance of government activities.[1] Administration has been defined as a cooperative human effort toward achieving some common goals. Thus articulated, Public Administration can be found in various institutional settings like a business firm, a hospital, a university, a government department and so on. As an aspect of this more generic concept, Public Administration is that species of administration that operates within a specific political setting. It is a

---

[1] Ernest Barker thus defines administration as 'the sum of persons and bodies who are engaged, under the direction of a government in discharging the ordinary public services which must be rendered daily if the system of law and duties and rights is to be duly served'. Ernest Barker, *The Development of Public Services in Western Europe, 1660–1930*, Oxford University Press, Oxford, p. 3.

means by which the policy decisions made by the political decision makers are carried out. In other words, it is 'the action part of government, the means by which the purposes and goals of government are realized'.[2]

The basic concerns of Public Administration as a field of study, therefore, include (a) structures of public organizations dealing mainly with the way the executive organizations are formed, readjusted and reformed, (b) administrative processes underlining the dynamic aspects of organization such as communication, control and decision-making, (c) bureaucratic behaviour with emphasis on the interpersonal and inter-group relationships in organizational settings and (d) organization–environment interactions covering the influential and meaningful relationships that are found to exist between Public Administration and its surrounding socio-political and economic milieu. The study of structures, processes and behaviour has been greatly facilitated by the emerging sub-discipline of organization theory. Its impact on Public Administration as an academic field has been considerable in recent times.[3]

The 'public' aspect of Public Administration[4] lends special character to it. The adjective can be looked at formally to mean 'government'. So, Public Administration is government administration, the focus being specifically on public bureaucracy. This is the meaning commonly used in discussing Public Administration. What is crucial in Public Administration is that it is an agency of the public. Central to this approach is the idea of the public 'as an active participant in change, rather than as a passive and docile recipient of instructions or

[2] John J. Corson and Joseph P. Harris, *Public Administration in Modern Society*, Mc-Graw Hill, New Delhi, 1963, p. 12.

[3] Public Administration is not a study of the administrative structures in isolation, instead, it is a study in which the importance of the socio-political and economic background is sought to be assessed to grasp the nature and type of administration of a particular country. For details, see Ferrel Heady, *Public Administration: A Comparative Perspective*, Prentice-Hall, New Delhi, 1966.

[4] Although 'public' constitutes an important dimension of Public Administration there is no standard definiton of public. While dealing with this aspect, Dwight Waldo preferred to define 'public' in terms of such words as *government* and *state*, as is often done. An attempt to understand these words in turn leads to 'an inquiry into such legal and philosophical concepts as sovereignty, legitimacy and general welfare. Or, one might take quite a different empirical track and attempt to define "public" simply by the test of opinion. In a particular society what functions or activities are believed to be public?' Dwight Waldo, 'What is Public Administration?', in A. M. Willms and W. D. K. Kernaghan (eds), *Public Administration in Canada: Selected Readings*, Methuen, London, 1968, pp. 2–16.

of dispensed assistance'.[5] The role of the public is significant since public policies are the articulation of priorities that emerge from social values and affirmations. 'Public' in Public Administration has also been expanded to include any administration that has considerable impact on the public. Hence, the Calcutta Electric Supply Corporation, though a private company, can easily be an appropriate theme for discussion in Public Administration. Given the growing complexity of Public Administration, its wider connotation serves a useful purpose. It would, therefore, not be proper to maintain the distinction between 'public' and 'private' as rigidly as it was construed earlier. In a situation in which 'public' is being appropriated for 'private' ends, the narrow meaning of 'public' is not adequate to explain the reality, shaped by the apparently not visible social forces and interests. Hence what is required, as Kuldeep Mathur argues, is the following:

an examination of the genesis of institutions of public administration because it reflects those social and political forces that dominate at a particular time. The effectiveness of achieving aims of public policy will depend on the motives of those groups or interests that brought these organizations into being. This perspective demands that we look beyond the boundaries of organization and take into account wider societal forces which give rise to specific interests that lead to the establishment of organizations.[6]

Research on rural power structure in India has, for instance, demonstrated how 'public' resources have in many instances been used for 'private' purposes and the local institutions like the panchayats and cooperatives have been captured by the rural power elites. In such circumstances, the public administrative systems remain more a legal facade since in reality the system is manipulated to promote private interests. The study of Public Administration will therefore remain exclusively institutional and formalistic unless these 'hidden, behind-the-scene social forces and interests are laid bare to reveal the real nature of the administration'.[7]

[5] Amartya Sen, *Development as Freedom*, Oxford University Press, Delhi, 2000, p. 281.

[6] Kuldeep Mathur, 'Whither Public Administration', in Kuldeep Mathur (ed.), *A Survey of Research in Public Administration, 1970–9*, Concept, New Delhi, 1986, p. 4.

[7] Mohit Bhattacharya has brought out this dimension of Public Administration in rural India in his study of administration in rural India especially in those areas where 'a power elite' has appropriated the local government to advance its personal interests. See his 'Research and Teaching in Public Administration', in Mohit Bhattacharyya (ed.), *Restructuring Public Administration*, Jawahar Publishers, New Delhi, 1997, pp. 112–13. The role of the power elite in local administration in West Bengal has amply been

IMPORTANT DIMENSIONS OF PUBLIC ADMINISTRATION

Public Administration as a discipline has been evolving over the years since the Wilsonian call for specialized study of 'government' to make it less 'un-business like'. Woodrow Wilson's 1887 article entitled 'The Science of Administration' was written at a time when there was a crying need to eliminate corruption, improve efficiency and streamline service delivery in pursuit of public interest. His advocacy that 'there should be a science of administration' has to be seen in the historical context. Writing against the background of widespread corruption, 'science' meant to Wilson a systematic and disciplined body of knowledge which he thought would be useful to grasp and defuse the crisis in administration. While commenting on the domain of the administrators, Wilson argued that the administrators should concentrate on operating the government rather than on substituting their judgment for that of elected officials. So, there is a dichotomy between politics and administration[8] although Wilson later revised his stance by underlining that Public Administration was innately political in nature. According to him, '[a]dministration cannot be divorced from its connection with the other branches of Public Law without being distorted and robbed of its true significance. Its foundations are these deep and permanent principles of politics'.[9]

If Wilson is the pioneer of the discipline Max Weber is its first theoretician who provided the discipline with a solid theoretical base. His 'ideal' type of bureaucracy continues to remain fundamental in any conceptualization of organization. Weber's formulation has been characterized as 'value neutral'; it simply provides a conceptualization of a form of social organization with certain

---

documented by Dwaipayan Bhattacharyya in his study of the Left Front rule in West Bengal. See his *Agrarian Reforms and Politics of the Left in West Bengal*, unpublished Ph.D. dissertation, University of Cambridge, Cambridge, 1993.

[8] The dichotomy does not appear to be a real one since 'social processes', argues Peter Self by drawing upon Karl Mannheim, 'include a rationalized sphere of settled procedures (administration) and a non-rational matrix (politics) which flows into this settled sphere'. In simpler words, 'politics is an area of change and indeterminancy and administration is one of stability and routine'. Peter Self, *Administrative Theories and Politics: An Enquiry into the Structure and Processes of Modern Government*, S. Chand, New Delhi, 1981 (reprint), p. 151.

[9] Arthur S. Link, *The Papers of Woodrow Wilson*, vol. 7 (1890–92), Princeton University Press, New Jersey, 1968.

'ubiquitous' characteristics. It can be examined from three different points of view which are not, of course, mutually exclusive. First, bureaucracy can be viewed in terms of purely structural characteristics. In fact, the structural dimension has attracted the most attention in the discussions on bureaucracy. The features like division of work and hierarchy have been identified as important aspects of structure. Secondly, bureaucracy has been sought to be defined in terms of behavioural characteristics. Certain patterns of behaviour form an integral part of bureaucracy. According to Weber, 'the more the bureaucracy is "dehumanized" the more completely it succeeds in eliminating from official business love, hatred, and all purely personal, irrational and emotional elements which escape calculation. *This is the specific nature of bureaucracy and its special virtue'* (emphasis added).[10] Thirdly, bureaucracy has also been looked at from the point of view of achievement of purpose. This is an instrumental view of bureaucracy. As Peter Blau suggests, it should be considered as an 'organization that maximizes efficiency in administration or an institutionalized method of organized social conduct in the interests of administrative efficiency'.[11]

What is distinctive in Weberian formulation is the attempt to construct 'an ideal type' or a mental map of a 'fully-developed' bureaucracy. The ideal type is a mental construct that cannot be found in reality. It is an abstraction and as such exaggerates certain features and de-emphasizes certain others to convey 'an image' or 'an idea'. It will, therefore, be theoretically misleading to argue that Weber's ideal type is nothing but a comment on civil services. It refers, in fact, to the sociological concept of 'rationalization of collective activities'. As a form or design of organization, it assures predictability of behaviour of members, associated with the organizational activities. The bureaucratic form, according to Weber, is the most efficient organizational form for large scale, complex administration, developed so far in the modern world. It is superior to any other form in decision, precision, stability, maintenance of discipline and reliability.

The evolution of Public Administration has been ably documented in many books and there is no point in repeating the successive stages of its evolution.[12] However, it seems fair to suggest that the literature

[10] Max Weber, 'Bureaucracy', in H. H. Gerth and C. Wright Mills (eds), *From Max Weber: Essays in Modern Society*, Oxford University Press, Oxford, 1946, p. 215

[11] Peter M. Blau, *Bureaucracy in Modern Society*, Random House, New York, 1956, p. 60.

[12] While recounting the evolution of Public Administration within the framework

that is available on it has tended to focus around two different visions of Public Administration. The first, termed as 'a discretionist' vision characterizes Public Administration as almost an independent or autonomous agent for the advancement of government actions that promote 'public interest'. By defining public interest in accordance with their own properly informed and ethically guided notions, civil servants should, according to this vision, discharge their duties. The second, which might be described as 'an instrumentalist' vision, identifies Public Administration almost entirely as an instrument of the political will of a community, as expressed through its elected political leaders. As mere instruments, the civil servants, according to this vision, must ascertain and perform their assigned functions following directions of the elected representatives of the people.[13] Our objective here is to identify some of the salient dimensions of the discipline that have already emerged in recent times. Obviously, this exercise is a highly selective one and the criterion for selection is the explanatory strength of a new thrust that has produced a major impact on methodological and/or substantive aspects of the discipline. It needs to be emphasized at the outset that there is no unanimity

---

of western civilization, Leonard D. White argued that two great systems of administration developed. One is *'Anglo-American,* based on a deep-seated preference for self-government in local communities, wide citizen participation, dispersion of authority, well-established responsibility of the administrative system to the legislative body and the responsibility of officials to the civil society at the instance of private citizen. This system prevails in Great Britain, in the Dominions, and in the United States. The other is the *French,* derived like the Anglo-American from the Middle Ages and formulated by Napoleon based on the dominance of national over local authorities, on the professionalism of the public service and its psychological separation from the body of citizens and on the responsibility of officials to a separate set of administrative courts. The French system which the Prussian closely resembled prevails not only in the country of its origin, but in Belgium, Holland, Spain, Italy, the Balkan countries, near East including Turkey, South and Central America including Mexico and with variɛ ions in the Latin countries. The Russian and the Chinese administrative systems are indigenous to their peoples, developing their own forms and character in response to national habits and performance'. Leonard D. White, *Introduction to the Study of Public Administration,* Macmillan, New York, 1955 (fourth edition), p. 5.

[13] Although the distinction between discretionist and instrumentalist visions of Public Administration is analytical, it is useful because it has raised points still remarkably germane to contemporary disagreements about the role of Public Administration. The issues that differentiate the two visions were best articulated in a lively written debate between Carl Friedrich (1940) and Herman Finer (1941). For details of the debate, see, Michael W. Spicer, *The Constitution and Public Administration: A Conflict in World Views,* Georgetown University Press, 1995, Chapter 5 (Visions of Public Administration), pp. 54–66.

among the scholars about the boundaries of the discipline and its theoretical frameworks. The principal thrusts of Public Administration have in recent times been as follows:

(a) the normative concern;
(b) the inter-theoretical linkages;
(c) the post-Weberian debate over bureaucracy-democracy relationship;
(d) the radical critique of development administration; and
(e) a general Marxist orientation toward public administration analysis.

The discipline has, however, moved beyond the above areas of interests in response to governmental practice. More specifically, the New Right Movement has spawned New Public Management; and the good governance philosophy—a la the World Bank—has reoriented Public Administration toward the multiple actors in governance beyond the traditional monopoly of formal government.

The Normative Dimension

Despite Herbert Simon's effort to formulate positivistic decision-making theory,[14] the normative questions have in recent times been reasserted to illuminate the meaning of 'efficiency' in public administration. The resurgence of 'value' questions could be traced back to the post-behavioural era in Political Science. It is, however, the emergence of the philosophy of 'neo-liberalism' that has provided a powerful base for the sitting of Public Administration in 'public interest' philosophy as propounded by such philosophers as John Rawls and Robert Nozick. Especially Rawls' monumental work, *A Theory of Justice*[15] has profoundly influenced the ethical dimension in Public Administration analysis. Generally speaking, however, normative research in this field is highly underdeveloped. Evaluation of administrative behaviour calls for standards against which alone can moral claims in the exercise of bureaucratic discretion be judged. In this connection, the two opposite schools of administration suggested by Donald P. Warwick—administrative Darwinism and Weberian Idealism—are of some significance.[16] In the first school, the officials are

[14] Herbert Simon, *Administrative Behaviour: A Study of Decision-Making Processes in Administrative Organizations*, Free Press, New York, 1997 (fourth edition, the original work was published in 1945).

[15] John Rawls, *A Theory of Justice*, Harvard University Press, Cambridge, 1971.

[16] Donald P. Warwick, 'The ethics of administrative discretion', in Fleishman et al.

portrayed as players in games of self-interest, and in the other, there is a combination of conformity with directives from above and an internalized understanding of proper behaviour for career officials.

Inter-Theoretical Bridge Building

Public Administration analysis has in recent times shed much of its analytical and uni-disciplinary myopia. This is in keeping with the general trend in the Social Sciences to evolve a culture of shared epistemology, as disciplinary parochialism has been found to be an impediment to meaningful social explanation. Three distinct inter-theoretical linkages that have been attempted recently can be identified as:

(i)   politics–administration union;
(ii)   economics–administration confluence and the political economy paragidm; and
(iii) organization theory and administration inter-mixing.

The first inter-theoretical linkage has a fairly long tradition that can be traced to the earlier debates over politics-administration dichotomy. With more and more 'policy science' orientation in Public Administration, politics came to be reunited with administration. But the real thrust toward 'political and value-loaded' Public Administration came from the 'New Public Administration' Movement starting from the 1968 Minnowbrook Conference.[17] Public Administration is, it was asserted, just another expression for the study of politics. It is ultimately a problem in political theory. Relating administration to the 'political' was the central focus of the New Public Administration School. Articulating this new approach, Peter Self thus argues, *the political approach* is concerned with the rules of accountability and the control of administrative power, while *the managerial approach*, as conventionally followed in Public Administration, is concerned with the rules of effective work organization and task performance.[18]

The second inter-theoretical linkage brings Public Administration within the purview of economic analysis. The study of public sector

---

Public Duties: The Moral Obligation of Government Officials, Harvard University Press, Cambridge, 1981.

[17] For details of the New Public Administration School that came into being following the Minnowbrook Conference in 1968, see Frank Marini (ed.), *Toward a New Public Administration*, Chandler, 1971.

[18] Peter Self, *Administrative Theories and Politics: An Enquiry into the Structure and Processes of Modern Government*, S. Chand, New Delhi, 1981 (reprint), pp. 81–5.

bureaucracy by A. Downs,[19] G. Tullock[20] and W. A. Niskanen[21] has exploded the myth of 'neutral' and 'rational' bureaucracy and the real life bureaucracy has been revealed as one of self-aggrandizement, resource manipulation and generally antithetical to 'public' interest. The contribution of economics to organization theory has also been noteworthy.

The study of the economics of information, as in Arrow's examination of the motives for vertical integration[22] has influenced organizational structuring including incentives structuring. J. K. Galbraith's *Economics and the Public Purpose*[23] marks a novel distinction between the 'market system' and the 'planning system'. The organizations in the market system have been found to be behaving differently from those in the planning system. The allocative and distributive decisions in the former are impersonally determined while similar decisions in the latter are made by the procedures themselves. Galbraith's *The New Industrial State* coined the term 'technostructure' to refer to the power of knowledge in the hands of the specialists.[24] This is a conceptual innovation in organization study.

Internal organizational forms have been more elaborately treated by O. E. Williamson whose name is associated with the U-Form and M-Form structure.[25] In the former, each operating unit performs a specialized function for all product lines; while in the latter, operating divisions or quasi-firms exist to perform all specialized functions for a single product.

A major inter-theoretical confluence has been termed the 'political economy' paradigm. As M. N. Zald puts it, '[p]olitical economy is the study of the interplay of power, the goals of power wielders and the productive exchange system'.[26] While discussing decision making and resource allocation, this new paradigm focuses on both political

[19] A. Downs, *Inside Bureaucracy*, Little Brown, Boston, 1967

[20] G. Tullock, *The Politics of Bureaucracy*, Public Affairs Press, Washington, D.C., 1965

[21] W. A. Niskanen Jr., *Bureaucracy and Representative Government*, Aldin-Atherton, Chicago, 1971.

[22] K.J. Arrow, 'Vertical Integration and Communication', *Bill Journal of Economics*, vol. 6, no. 1, 1975.

[23] J. K. Galbraith, *Economics and the Public Purpose*, Houghton Miffin, New York, 1973.

[24] J. K. Galbraith, *The New Industrial State*, Mentor Books, New York, 1967

[25] O. E. Williamson, 'Managerial Discretion, Organizational Forms and Multi-Division Hypothesis', in Marris and Wood (eds), *The Corporate Economy*, Macmillan, London, 1971.

[26] M. N. Zald, *Organizational Change: The Political Economy of the YMCA*, University of Chicago Press, Chicago, 1970.

and economic dimensions. It has spawned the two important concepts of 'organizational constituents' and 'internal polity'. The first
concept refers to the fundamental normative structure of agreements
and understandings, defining limits, goals, responsibilities and rights
of participants. The second concept illuminates the political character
of the organizational milieu where the distribution of resources and
the process of conflict resolution are important determinants of
allocative and distributive decisions.

The strength of the political economy approach lies in the fact that
the political dimension highlights the process through which authority is distributed giving rise to power differentials, and the economic
dimension focuses on the allocative process, but at the same time
incorporates such variables as power and authority. The paradigmatic shift is in part due to an ever-growing intellectual hostility to
Parsonian functionalism and its associated positivism. By contrast, a
phenomenological orientation lays emphasis on the inter-subjective
and symbolic dimension of organizational structure and roles.[27]

Organization Theory-Administration Intermixing

Public Administration has traditionally been an ally of organizational theory. Advances in organization theory—open system analysis,
contingency theories, socio-technical system analysis, organic–
mechanistic distinction—have found ready acceptance in administrative theory. Analysis of complex organizations falls into two broad
categories: the structural analysis and the interactive perspective.
The structuralists such as Blau and Perrow have viewed organizations as coherent systems and the participants in them as passive
instrumentalists. By contrast, the interactive perspective
views organizations as aggregates and organizational members as
proactive and initiative-taking.

Current debates in organization theory that have relevance to
Public Administration revolve round the 'goal paradigm' and the
'rational model'. The new issues centre around the concepts of 'power'
and 'action'. The action approach lays emphasis on the process through
which particular organization patterns are created and maintained.
Approaches such as 'the political economy' model,[28] strategic

---

[27] Guy B. Adams, 'Prolegomenon to a Teachable Theory of Public Administration',
in Thomas Vocino and Richard Heimovics (eds), *Public Administration Education in
Transition*, Marcel Dekker, New York, 1982.

[28] M. N. Zald, *Organizational Change: The Political Economy of the YMCA*, University
of Chicago Press, Chicago, 1970.

contingency theories[29] and research dependency theories[30] have all accepted power as a key variable. It has been argued that consensus has been an overplayed concept. Organizational change and the behaviour associated with it can be understood by examining power or compliance relationship and the real processes of conflicts of their resolution.[31]

Another intervention that deserves attraction is a steady attempt to construct a radical organization theory based on Marxist thought. Conventional organization theory has been criticized as system-maintaining and capitalism-serving. Its basic weakness lies in its inability to relate the internal organizational structure to the more general social structure in which organizations are embedded. Labour, it has been argued, is forced to conform to organizational controls as dictated by the overarching capitalist mode of production.[32] Conventional organization theories explain this phenomenon as inter-personal and inter-group relationships, ignoring the wider social setting of such relationships. Often, academic support is lent to such controls by recommending reorganization of controls with the help of behavioural science recipes.[33]

Radical organization theory is the outcome of a conjunction of organizational analysis and political radicalism. It is 'radical' as it aims to study the structure of capitalism and use knowledge explicitly in the interests of the exploited majority. 'The analytical starting point', as suggested by the radical organization theorists, 'should be the totality of contemporary capitalism. However within this totality, the need for an understanding of existing organizations is underlined, since it is here, within these legally constituted facilities, that capital and labour meet, that the labour process takes place and that productive and non-productive labour interact. It is organizations which represent the point of production, the meeting place of deep-seated contradictions, the initial focus of class-based conflict.[34]

[29] D. J. Hickson et al. 'A Strategic Contingency Theory of Intra-Organizational Power', *Administrative Science Quarterly*, vol. 16, 1971.

[30] J. Pfeffer and G. R. Salancik, *The External Control of Organizations: A Resource Dependence Perspective*, Harper and Row, 1978.

[31] P. F. Driggers, 'Theoretical Blockage: A Strategy for the Development of Organizational Theory', *The Sociological Review*, vol. 18, Winter, 1977.

[32] S. Clegg and D. Dunkerly (eds), *Critical Issues in Organizations*, Routledge and Kegan Paul, London, 1977.

[33] K. J. Benson, 'Organizations: A Dialectical View', *Administrative Science Quarterly*, vol. 22, no. 1, March, 1977.

[34] Gibson Burrell, 'Radical Organization Theory', in David Dunkerly and Graeme Salaman, *The International Yearbook of Organization Studies*, 1980.

As shown above, it is difficult to conceptualize organization as a functional category in terms of a single paradigm. Instead, there are various dominant trends exhibiting diversity, heterogeneity, competition and changing fashions [that tally] well with the poly-paradigmatic status of Public Administration as a discipline.[35]

The post-Weberian Debate Over
Bureaucracy–Democracy Relationship

The Weberian paradigm has dominated Public Administration since its inception, despite a variety of criticisms against it. An analysis of Weberian conceptualization of bureaucracy has led to a new perspective to both the theory of bureaucracy and the debate over bureaucracy–democracy relationship. For instance, the political writings of Weber have been excavated to point out Weber's critical comments on the politics of bureaucracy and the tendency of bureaucracy to transform itself from 'instrument' to 'institution' at the cost of the politicians.[36]

As a reaction to over-bureaucratization in the wake of rapid expansion of governmental activities and dissatisfaction with bureaucratic inefficiency, at least four major innovative streams of thought have emerged. The first of these is the public choice school. Far from accepting bureaucracy as 'rational' and 'efficient', the protagonists of this school have been highly skeptical about its structure and actual operating behaviour. The arguments of Downs, Tullock and Niskanen are, in this context, based on the assumption of administrative egoism. The bureaucrats are, in their view, 'individualistic self-seekers' who would do more harm than good to public welfare unless 'their self-seeking activities are carefully circumscribed'.[37] This explains the tendency toward bureaucratic growth that brings in more and more rewards for the officials and *quid pro quo*.

Vincent Ostrom questions the efficiency of bureaucracy as the organization for efficiently supplying public services. As he argues:

The theory of public goods is the central organizing concept used by [these] political economists in conceptualizing the problem of collective action and of Public Administration. This contrasts with the theory of bureaucracy as

---

[35] Dwight Waldo, 'Revisiting the Elephant', *Public Administration Review*, November–December, 1978.

[36] David Beetham, *Max Weber and the Theory of Modern Politics*, George Allen and Unwin Ltd, London, 1974.

[37] S. K. Das, *Civil Service Reform and Structural Adjustment*, Oxford University Press, Delhi, 1998, p. 7.

the central concept in the traditional theory of Public Administration. When the central problem in Public Administration is viewed as the provision of public goods and services, alternative forms of organization may be available for the performance of those functions apart from an extension and perfection of bureaucratic structures. Bureaucratic structures are necessary but not sufficient structures for a productive and responsive public service economy.[38]

As evident, Ostrom's argument is an attack on the Wilsonian paradigm that has seen Public Administration in terms of bureaucracy and has striven for bureaucratic efficiency through principles of hierarchical organization, the cost calculus and the exclusion of politics. Herbert Simon's challenge, as he explains, 'was to the foundations of Public Administration theory and to the notion that perfection in hierarchical organization is most efficient; [nevertheless, it retained] the organization as the primary focus'.[39] In contrast with the 'bureaucratic' or 'governmental' view of Public Administration, Ostrom favours the public choice tradition relying on the individual as the unit of analysis and utilizing the methods that have proven effective in economics. Drawing upon the theory of externalities, common properties and public goods to define the structure of events relevant to Public Administration, Ostrom's argument is a direct attack on the structured authority of bureaucracy since civil servants are 'utility maximizers' who seek to promote their own self-interest. This is in stark contrast with the theories which view bureaucracy as impersonal and possibly the best instrument for the pursuit of 'public' interest. Most public choice theorists converge on the main point that government has grown much larger than what the general public wish it to be, because it has grown to meet the preferences of politicians, bureaucrats and interest groups. Basically what the public choice proponents seek to do is to point out inconsistencies in the classical model of representative democracy and to suggest an alternative basis for decision making in government or public choice.

The central issue in public choice model is how to limit government and to check the natural tendency for over-government. One favoured strategy has been to bring about constitutional reforms placing limits on government growth. Another strategy has been to

---

[38] Vincent Ostrom, *The Intellectual Crisis in American Public Administration*, University of Alabama Press, Tuscaloosa and London, 1974.

[39] David John Farmer, *The Language of Public Administration: Bureaucracy, Modernity and Postmodernity*, The University of Alabama Press, Tuscaloosa and London, 1995, p. 118.

reduce the influence of interest groups on government policy. Still another strategy is to decentralize political power. Individuals would then have the option to 'exit' by moving to another jurisdiction when dissatisfied with the mix of taxation and services provided in their area.

To mitigate the evils of bureaucratic monopoly, Niskanen[40] suggests the following steps:

(a)   stricter control on bureaucrats through the executive or the legislature;
(b)   more competition in the delivery of public services;
(c)   privatization or contracting-out to reduce wastage; and
(d)   dissemination of more information for public benefit about the availability of alternatives to public services, offered on a competitive basis and at competitive costs.

The public choice school has been successful in pointing out that there are alternatives available for the delivery of services to the citizens. The role of 'market' as a competing paradigm has challenged the hegemonic position of the state. Also the power of bureaucracy has been similarly slashed, opening up possibilities of non-bureaucratic citizen-friendly organizational options. It is not, however, a state versus market debate, as it is often made out to be. The real issue is how to make the state more democratic and citizen-friendly and not to relegate it to the background altogether and install the 'new god' of market in its place. The assumptions of the public choice school are not above board, nor are the arguments in favour of the market always justified. Again, the situations may differ from country to country and their prescriptions to check governmental overgrowth may not be of universal relevance. For instance, the state-led development activities in the Third World are not everywhere amenable to public choice prescription. It is probably true that the growth and complexity of government and perhaps a decline in the force of social opinion and sanctions have given increased opportunities for politicians and bureaucrats to pursue their own gain at the general expense. '[B]ut the extent to which they actually do', argues Peter Self, 'is another matter which is unlikely to be settled by formal models of behaviour based upon simple assumptions'.[41]

[40] William A. Niskanen, *Bureaucracy and Representative Government*, Aldine-Atherton, Chicago, 1971.
[41] Peter Self, *Modern Theories of Government*, George Allen and Unwin, London, 1985, p. 31.

Drawing upon the arguments on the tension between bureaucracy and democracy, alternative democratic structures have been discussed by Vincent Ostrom, Douglas Yates[42] and Eva-Etzioni-Halevy.[43] Yet, the discussion converges on one fundamental point that the old recipe for democratic government—effective administrative action within the guidelines of collective political leadership—is 'in principle as sound as ever'.[44] Whether structural adjustment, the new World Bank prescription for market-friendly development, would be able to further the cause of democracy by reducing the role of the state and discouraging redistributive policies remains an open question. Writing in the African context, Goran Hyden has drawn our attention to the 'de-institutionalization of Public Administration' due to the over-arching influence of the all pervading 'patrimonial administration', a type of non-policy government run through patronage and personal loyalty rather than policies and procedures. Elaborating the argument, he further states:

[t]he patrimonial tendencies in African politics have not disappeared with recent democratic reform. While the form of governance may have changed in most African countries, its content remains much the same. The public service remains subject to the interference by political spoils considerations with the consequence that it is secretive and private rather than open and public in orientation towards the citizenry. Efforts in recent years to reform the public services have [virtually] focused more on form than content.[45]

Claus Offe has refreshingly reviewed Weberian bureaucratic theory. In legal–bureaucratic administration, as Offe points out, 'efficiency means the reliable subsumption of action under promises'. The structural mode of welfare state administrative policy is just the opposite. 'Efficiency is no longer defined as "following the rules", but as the "causing of effects"'. This changed perspective has implications for personnel policy and organizational structure. As Offe argues, '[w]elfare state administrative policy becomes dependent on extralegal legitimations, that is, upon the substantive realization of some

[42] Douglas Yates, *Bureaucratic Democracy: The Search for Democracy and Efficiency in American Government*, Harvard University Press, Cambridge, 1982

[43] Eva-Etzioni-Halevy, *Bureaucracy and Democracy: A Political Dilemma*, Routledge and Kegan Paul, London, 1986.

[44] Peter Self, *Administrative Theories and Politics: An Enquiry into the Structure and Processes of Modern Government*, S. Chand, New Delhi, 1981 (reprint), p. 299.

[45] Goran Hyden, 'Democratization and Administration', in Ales Hadenius, *Democracy's Victory and Crisis* (Nobel symposium No. 93), Cambridge University Press, Cambridge, 1997, p. 253.

values (rather than compliance to rules) and upon the resulting processes of empirical consensus formation'.[46]

The other point made by Offe relates to the need for co-production of results in a welfare state by administration and its clients. Outcomes of administrative action are not, thus the outcomes of authoritative implementation of pre-established rules. Weber's bureaucratic theory, under such circumstances, becomes irrelevant to the welfare state situation. To quote Offe:

Under conditions of developed, welfare-state capitalism, the rationality of bureaucratic action does not guarantee, but rather perhaps conflicts with, the functional rationality of the political system. Bureaucratic domination is not, as Weber supposed, the irrevocable structural feature of all future societies. Rather, it turns out to be tied to a specific historical phase and contingent from the standpoint of functional rationality.[47]

The other post-Weberian development of great significance is the impact of 'critical theory' on Social Sciences in general and Public Administration in particular. Jurgen Habermas, a major exponent of the critical perspective has argued that 'access to a symbolically structured object domain calls for procedures that are logically distinct from those developed in the natural sciences'. It has been Habermas' dominant concern to demarcate critical social theory based on the interpretative (social action depending on the agent's definition of the situation—the *verstehenden* approach) from strictly empirical–analytic science.

Rejecting the positivistic and goal-determined approach of Parsonian structural-functionalism, Habermas offers an alternative social system analysis incorporating the historic–hermeneutic and critical dimensions.[48] Following this cue, a critical theory of Public Administration would seek replacement of the stifling effect of techno-administrative domination of the bureaucracy. From this standpoint, impersonalization of human beings and the managerial manipulation of man are built into a positivistic approach to organization and administration as revealed in mainstream Public Administration. A critical theory of public organization would instead plead for debureaucratization and democratization of administration through free flow of communication and exposure of inherent contradictions

---

[46] Claus Offe, *Disorganized Capitalism: Contemporary Transformation of Work and Politics*, Polity Press, Cambridge, 1983.

[47] Ibid.

[48] Jurgen Habermas, *Communication and the Evolution of Society*, Heinemann, London, 1979.

in hierarchical relationships. Inspired by the critical approach, a movement toward improving the quality of organizational life by breaking barriers of communication and encouraging participative and shared organizational existence, has become almost a sub-discipline in organization and administrative theory.[49]

Radical Critique of Development Administration

The theoretical advances—from the heyday of development administration to 'deadlock' in development administration—led to the rise of a sub-discipline in Public Administration which emerged at one stage almost as an alternative paradigm for the 'Third World' situation. The sub-optimization criticism came from within the developmentalists as Fred Riggs, Lucian Pye and Eisenstadt and others cautioned against bureaucracy—reinforcing devices that might undermine and weaken political institutions and processes. As Riggs argued, '[t]he existence of a career bureaucracy without corresponding strength in the political institutions does not necessarily lead to administrative effectiveness.'[50] Without firm political guidance, the argument further continues, bureaucrats have weak incentives to provide good service whatever their formal, pre-entry training and professional qualifications. They tend to use their effective control to safeguard their expedient bureaucratic interests—tenure, seniority rights, fringe benefits, toleration of poor performance, the right to violate official norms—rather than to advance the achievement of programme goals. The debate also continued between technological-managerial school[51] and the ecological school. While the former relied on 'planning' and 'managed' development by organizational changes and personnel manipulation, the latter advocated wider sociological understanding of administration which was conceived more in terms of a dependent variable.

[49] Drawing upon the critical theory, the following studies have made a serious intervention in the study of administrative theory. Bert King et al. (eds), *Managerial Control and Organizational Democracy*, John Wiley & Sons, London, 1978; J. Richard Heckman and Greg R. Oldham, *Work Redesign*, Addison-Wesley Publishing Co, London, 1980

[50] Fred W. Riggs, 'Bureaucrats and Political Developments', in Jason L. Finkle and Richard W. Gable (eds), *Political Development and Social Change*, John Wiley & Sons, London, 1971.

[51] For instance, the works by A. Waterson and Denis A. Rondinelli deserve mention. See A. Waterson, *Development Planning: Lesson of Experience*, Johns Hopkins University, Baltimore, 1965; and Dennis A. Rondinelli, *Development Projects as Policy Experiments: An Adaptive Approach to Development Administration*, Methuen, London, 1983.

Another school of thought has questioned the strategy of development administration by characterizing it as the 'First' World's diplomatic effort to steal the tide of insurgency and communist movement in the 'Third World'.[52]

Development administration has also been criticized as 'ideological' and 'Eurocentric'. The model of modernization and development seems an export model of civilization that is incompatible with life in most Third World countries. Hence, there has been a persistent demand for a 'non-ethnocentric' theory of development and an alternative conception of Third World development.[53]

A more universalistic conception of 'development' has been conceived in global terms by a team of social scientists. To them, development has a wider connotation; it is 'social transformation' and therefore civilizational in scope. Viewed from this perspective, the present crisis of the Third World forms an integral part of the acute global crisis today. It is the expression of a crisis of the 'system' as such, a crisis rooted in the dynamics of the system's own development.[54]

From this perspective, the theory of development–underdevelopment complementarity is the logical step. The phenomenon of underdevelopment, according to the dependency theorists, has its roots in the exploitative relationship, forged by the First World. Pioneered by Gunder Frank,[55] the dependency theory has wider significance for Third World development within the framework of a capitalist world economy. For development administration, the implication is that the underdevelopment–dependency movement conceives bureaucratic behaviour in 'class' terms. By contrast, conventional development administration looks at bureaucratic behaviour as an outcome of organizational structure and hence is manipulative.[56]

Autonomous state action through development administration seems to have reached a virtual *cul de sac*. As Wallerstein has argued

[52] O. P. Dwivedi and J. Nef, 'Crises and Continuities in Development Administration', *Public Administration and Development*, January-March, 1982.

[53] Howard J. Wiarda, 'Toward a Non-Ethnocentric Theory of Development: Alternative Conceptions from the Third World', *The Journal of Developing Societies*, July, 1983.

[54] Herb Ado et al. *Development as Social Transformation: Reflection on the Global Problematique*, Hodder & Stoughton, London, 1985.

[55] Andre Gunder Frank, *Capitalism and Underdevelopment in Latin America*, Monthly Review Press, New York, 1967; and also by him, *Latin America: Underdevelopment or Revolution*, Monthly Review Press, New York, 1969.

[56] David Hirschmann, 'Development or Underdevelopment Administration: A Further Deadlock', *Development and Change*, vol. 12, 1969.

the Third World states are in the institutional vortex of the capitalist world economy. Hence the Third World's insular development effort has its limitations. In his opinion:

It is the fact that the states of the capitalist world economy exist within the framework of an inter-state system that is the *differentia specifica* of the modern state, distinguishing it from other bureaucratic politics. The inter-state system constitutes a set of constraints, which limit the abilities of individual state machineries, even the strongest among them, to make decisions. The ideology of this system is sovereign equality, but the states are in fact, neither sovereign nor equal.[57]

A General Marxist Orientation Toward Public Administration Analysis

Within the liberal political framework, the pluralist perspective has generally dominated both the fields of Political Science and Public Administration. Although in Political Science, Marxist analysis has made considerable headway in recent times, in Public Administration analysis similar efforts are rare. One argument has been that the base–superstructure model has meant that Public Administration is a derivative of economic base and hence lacking in autonomy. Administrative theory is, thus, subsumed in the theory of state. There is an alternative 'structuralist' version that visualizes autonomous administrative action within the parameters of capitalist interest-serving. While examining the prospect of a new Public Administration based on Marxist analysis, it has been optimistically observed,

The two versions of the state in mature Marxist political theory—fundamentalist and relative autonomy—have two kinds of implications for any theory of Public Administration. The fundamentalist notion of the class state yields a reductionist theory of bureaucracy as an appendage of the dominant class embedded in capitalist political economy. By contrast, Nicos Poulantzas, Claus Offe and others have sought to reconstruct Marxist political theory by pointing out the relative autonomy of the state in real life from the powerblock and the hegemonic faction. Such a reconstruction of Marxist theory of the state has opened up new possibilities of Marxist theory of Public Administration.[58]

[57] Immanuel Wallerstein, *The Politics of the World Economy: The States, the Movements and the Civilizations*, Cambridge University Press, Cambridge, 1987.

[58] O. P. Dwivedi et al., 'Marxist Contribution to the Theory of the Administrative State', *The Indian Journal of Political Science*, vol. 46, no. 1, January–March, 1985. This argument has also been reiterated by Mohit Bhattacharya in his, 'Public Administration

At the micro level, urbanization and urban development, local government and local finance have been studied fruitfully from the Marxist perspective.[59] Urban question refers to the organization of 'the means of collective consumption as the basis of daily life of all social groups: housing, education, health, culture, commerce, transport etc.' While extending these facilities, the state, as an expression of a class society, acts generally in favour of 'the hegemonic fraction of the dominant fraction of the dominant classes'.[60]

In this connection, Patrick Dunleavy's brief but bold attempt to carve out a 'radical' approach to Public Administration deserves attention. Basically drawing on some forms of 'unorthodox, democratized neo-Marxist and radical forms of social political thought' derived from the works of Max Weber, Dunleavy proposes to chart out the future development of Public Administration.[61] While the effort, no doubt, looks promising, Dunleavy seems to have chosen essentially incompatible partners—Marx and Weber. Also, there is a streak of institutional conservatism in his project as his 'radical' approach rules out the prospect of institutional collapse. In effect, his radicalism emerges in rectifying the iconoclastic garb.

Any attempt to build a theory of Public Administration on the basis of Marxist analysis calls for systematic empirical investigations into the web of relationships between the bureaucracy and the class structure and the mode of production. Actions such as policy-making and implementation need to be closely observed before any sound generalizations could be reached for the purposes of reliable theory building. Alongside this, doubts have been expressed about the suitability of the Marxist model for explaining 'underdevelopment' in the Third World. Goran Hyden, for instance, calls for a more insightful study of the indigenous processes of development of peasant economies under conditions of pre-capitalist mode of production.[62]

---

in India: A Discipline in Bondage', *Indian Journal of Public Administration*, April–June, 1986.

[59] The major works in this perspective are: (a) Manuel Castells, *The Urban Question: A Marxist Approach*, Edward Arnold, London, 1977; (b) Cynthia Cockburn, *The Local State: Management of Cities and People*, Pluto Press, London, 1977; (c) James O'Conner, *The Fiscal Crisis of the State*, St. Martin's Press, New York, 1973

[60] Manuel Castells, *City, Class and Power*, Macmillan, London, 1978, p. 3.

[61] Patrick Dunleavy, 'Is There a Radical Approach to Public Administration?' *Public Administration*, vol. 60, Summer, 1982.

[62] Goran Hyden, *Beyond Ujjama in Tanzania*, University of California Press, Berkeley, 1982.

PUBLIC ADMINISTRATION AND GLOBALIZATION

Issues arising out of globalization have radically altered the nature and scope of Public Administration. No longer confined to the analysis of the structure of administration, the discipline has to respond to the challenges of the 'new economic order' that appeared to have decisively influenced, if not determined, Public Administration. In the context of globalization, national economies are becoming more and more 'open' and subject to supra-national economic influences. As economies lose their discrete, self-contained character and become enmeshed in global networks and processes, they become less and less amenable to national control and management. In a nutshell, the ideology and practice of globalization privileges voluntarism and the market as the underpinnings of the new economic order.[63]

Public Administration today is reflecting in large parts the changing nature of practice of governments especially in the developed worlds. The practices of traditional Public Administration are under increasing attack from neo-liberal economists, interest group theorists and rational choice scholars who have provided the intellectual inputs to the politicians determined to reduce the size and scope of the public sector. This is scarcely surprising since the theoretical changes have tended to emphasize the significant extent to which Public Administration is political and is part of the overall process of determining 'who gets what'. Approaches to Public Administration are also embedded in wider conceptions of the state, the relationship between State, market and of citizenship. Changes in the ideological climate are, therefore, likely to have a decisive impact on Public Administration and this is what is evident now.

Waves of reforms have swept through the public sector over the past several decades under societal pressures and demands—both national and international. These changes have been piecemeal and fragmented without being integrated into clear 'visions' regarding planned change in Government. The *market model* of governance has been holding the centre stage since the 1980s. Drawing upon the basic thrust of this model, several new models were constructed to articulate the emerging trends in governance.[64] For instance, the *participatory*

[63] For details, see Gerald Caiden, 'Globalizing the Theory and Practice of Public Administration', in Jean-Claude Gracia-Zemor and Renu Khator (eds), *Public Administration in the Global Village*, Praeger, West Port, CT, 1994, pp. 49–59.

[64] B. Guy Peters, 'Models of Governance for the 1990s', in Donald F. Kitt and H. Brinton Milward (eds), *The State of Public Management*, The Johns Hopkins University Press, Baltimore, 1996.

model that concentrates on the participation of lower echelons of workers and even the clients and citizenry has been a direct rebuttal of the traditional hierarchic bureaucratic model in Public Administration. Similarly, the idea of *flexible government* goes against the conventional model of permanent employment. Public organizations with much less full-time employment and increasing level of part-time and temporary workers have steadily come into existence at many places depending on the nature of labour market. Rooted in the movement towards 'reinventing government', the idea of 'deregulatory government' rests on the assumption 'that if some of the constraints on action [in the form of bureaucratic formalities] were eliminated, the Government could perform its current functions more efficiently and it might be able to undertake new and creative activities to improve the collective welfare of the society'.[65] By emphasizing that public interest would be better served by a more active and interventionist public sector, this model further adds that collective action is part of the solution and not part of the problem for contemporary societies, as being alleged by public choice theorists.

The debate directs our attention to a more flexible and open-ended vision of governance. 'As long as democracy is valued', as it has been ably put, 'the big questions of Public Administration must go beyond the big questions of Public Management'.[66] Public Administration diminishes its role in society if understood primarily in terms of managing public agencies. The Minnowbrook I and the Blacksburge Manifesto have both raised this issue of democratic governance in public interest. What is relevant in the context of the 'Third World' is that Public Administration is being crippled in the name of structural adjustment invoking more and more the market model of governance in utter disregard of the crucial development role of the state in developing societies. The interests of Public Administration are no longer people-related; these are instead capital-related. And, here lies the perils of externally induced administrative 'reform' through which most of the 'Third World' countries are passing today.

In terms of administrative theory-building, the current emphasis on 'public management' via the market model of governance needs to be viewed in a proper historical perspective. Historically, two contrasting visions have guided the pursuit of administrative analysis:

---

[65] David Osborne and Ted Gaebler, *Reinventing Government: How the Entrepreneurial Spirit is Transforming the Public Sector*, Prentice-Hall, New Delhi, 1992, p. 28.

[66] John J. Kirlin, 'The Big Question in a Democracy', *Public Administration Review*, September–October, 1996.

(a) the managerial vision and (b) the democratic vision. In liberal democracies, both public bureaucracy (and managerialism) and democratic polity have gained in importance almost simultaneously due to specific historical circumstances in which they have emerged. But the analysts since the articulation of Wilsonian paradigm and later the POSDCORB formulation have often tempted to overemphasize 'managerialism' with its predilection for efficiency, economy and effectiveness. The other more central pursuits of Public Administration—like achieving a democratic polity, improving the instruments of collective action and creating conditions for good citizenship and increasing societal learning—are of no concern for the 'public management' advocates. A major flaw in the managerial perspective is its inordinate interest in organizational concerns and measures of organizational performance. The interests of a democratic polity and maintenance of a legal order are substituted by the concern of organizational survival. There is in this move a misplaced emphasis on 'instrument' at the cost of 'purpose'. Public Administration as 'management' undermines, if not altogether bypasses, the overarching perspective of a democratic polity. Sustained capacity of the political system for collective action, effective citizenship and developing and nurturing the civic infrastructure for protecting citizens' rights and promoting collective life are of vital significance for any public administrative system in a democracy. The new management 'cult' poses peculiar problems for the 'Third World' Public Administration, as it tends to strengthen bureaucracy further, impeding the development of alternative people's institutions so necessary for both generating social capability to govern and creating more democratic spaces outside of central bureaucratic administration. Under the pressure from the external donor agencies momentous changes have been taking place in the 'Third World' public administration. On the one side, the structural adjustment policy tends to 'downsize' government and allow the 'market' more freeplay; the 'governance' concept, on the other hand, has mooted to move away from the traditional model of organization of formal government and recommend instead plurality of societal actors. In this the observation of Arturo Israel is of considerable relevance: the problem is actually to enhance 'the quality of government not so much to reduce its size'.[67]

Under the changed circumstances, the traditional concept of Public

[67] Arturo Israel, 'The Changing Role of the State: Institutional Dimension, Policy Research and External Affairs', Working Paper, Country Economics Department, *The World Bank*, August, 1990, p. 17.

Administration revolving around a sheltered bureaucracy is no longer viable. For instance, in the recently posed 'public choice' perspective, the question has been raised as to why bureaucratic form of organization should have the monopoly to provide public goods and services. It has been alleged that bureaucratic failures, numerous in reality, affect the society badly both immediately and from the long-term perspective as well. There are various options available for the delivery of public goods and services and society may benefit from the many suppliers syndrome. It is not necessary that government should always assume the role of a direct provider of goods and services; instead, governments operate indirectly as 'enablers' allowing non-government agencies to operate directly in a wide range of social activities. Contracting out and 'privatization' in many forms are now the hallmarks of what is commonly known as 'the New Right' philosophy of governance.

Since hierarchy is essentially power-oriented, rather than work-oriented, rigid, rule-bound and hierarchic Public Administration, as critics point out, does not satisfy the requirements of dynamic situations demanding speedy action. In this respect, many of the flexible organizational designs and practices pioneered by the private sector should be profitably introduced in Public Administration with appropriate modifications. The public–private distinction should not be fetishized as a matter of orthodoxy. In the larger interest of societal development, the two sectors should mix freely and collaborate whenever necessary and feasible. Even healthy competition between them should be welcome to improve quality of performance and to accelerate the pace of work. The publication of *Reinventing Government*[68] in 1992 is a watershed in the growth of New Public Administration in the sense that it has sought to redefine the functions of government. The authors argue in favour of 'entrepreneurial government' that is certain to bring about radical changes by (a) improving public management through performance, measurement and evaluation, (b) reducing budgets, (c) downsizing the government, (d) selective privatization of public enterprises and (e) contracting out in selective areas.

As evident, with changes in the role of government globally, Public Administration is currently engaged in an act of soul-searching. Some of the major theoretical concerns in the discipline, as it has

[68] David Osborne and Ted Gaebler, *Reinventing Government: How the Entrepreneurial Spirit is Transforming the Public Sector*, Prentice-Hall, New Delhi, 1992.

shaped now in response to inputs from both the developed West and non-Western societies, are as follows:

(a) application of Public Choice theory to Public Administration seeking to assess the relative importance of both market and State as contending providers of public good;

(b) decentralization and democracy—underlining participation and empowerment of people at the grassroots;

(c) the inadequacy of the Weberian notion of 'rational bureaucracy' in the post-colonial states which is being assailed as 'self-aggrandizing, priority-distorting and budget-maximizing';

(d) organizational pluralism striving to ensure absolute 'freedom' of the individuals in choosing without interference. As a consequence, suggestions are being offered for 'load-shedding' of Government, privatization, decentralization and empowerment and also encouragement of NGOs in the voluntary sector. Organizational pluralism is being articulated in the advocacy of enhanced social capacity as against governmental capability. Government through the agency of Public Administration is being treated as just one form of governance. The concept of governance opens up possibilities of government through non-bureaucratic agencies, other than formal government;

(e) 'performance partnership' in the form of different levels of government coming together corresponding to public-private joint venture. And, networking of government, NGOs and private agencies is being suggested and pursued;

(f) small government in terms of downsizing and grassroots people's efforts is another idea being broached now. In this context, decentralization of government and people's own efforts are being more and more advocated. Another kindred suggestion is the reconceptualization of government's role. Also, re-examination and assertion of 'Public Interest' has led to a revival of interest in this core concept. Neo-institutional device in the form of institutional capacity-building is being advocated and institutional studies are gaining in importance;

(g) transparency of governance and open citizen-friendly administration via 'citizen's charter' are now being advocated. Also the 'gender' issue has been brought to the fore, arguing that Public Administration has virtually been a male preserve. Alongside the discourse of bureaucratic rationality, there is the need for the juxtaposition of the discussion of 'domesticity' connoting feelings, emotions, and human warmth.

This paradigm shift in Public Administration analysis in the developed West has its ripple effect on the 'Third World' as well. In the post-colonial Third World, radical socio-economic transformation within as short a time span as possible has been the basic agenda items of governments in a situation of relative absence of a socially responsible private sector. Also, there has been a general skepticism about the role and efficacy of an essentially control-oriented, people-avoiding and rule-bound 'colonial' bureaucracy. The idea, therefore, gains ground that public organizations have to be people-oriented as distinguished from structure-oriented under the changed circumstances in which 'governance' has acquired a completely different meaning as opposed to its traditional connotation.[69]

Governance, in spite of being one of the most widely used concept in contemporary Public Administration, has been one which has been either simplistically decoded or then misunderstood and abused. This has obviously been reflected in its practical implications and therefore it is extremely necessary to delimit its scope before engaging in any discussion on its implications in Indian administration. Governance can be defined as 'the manner in which power is exercised in the management of a country's social and economic resources for development'. Subsumed in this broad approach is economic governance by which is meant 'sound development management'. There are four key components of governance, viz.,

[69] Governance is not synonymous with the government, the latter being endowed with formal authority. Governance refers to activities backed by shared goals which may or may not derive their legitimacy from the government. Other sources of legitimacy for activities and goals are civil society and the market. Thus, governance encapsulates government, but goes beyond it and encompasses non-governmental mechanisms to meet the needs and aspirations of citizens. See J. N. Rosenau, 'Governance, Order and Change in World Politics', in J. N. Rosenau and Ernst-Otto Czempiel (eds), *Governance without Government: Order and Change in World Politics*, Cambridge University Press, Cambridge, 1992, pp. 1–16. The governance perspective provides a reference point which challenges many of the assumptions of traditional Public Administration. Articulating this new approach, Gerry Stoker thus draws our attention to the following five propositions as integral to governance perspective: (1) governance refers to a set of institutions and actors that are drawn from but also beyond government; (2) governance identifies the blurring of boundaries and responsibilities for tackling social and economic issues; (3) governance identifies the power dependence involved in the relationships between institutions involved in collective action; (4) governance is about autonomous self-governing networks of actors; and (5) governance recognizes the capacity to get things done which does not rest on the power of government to command or use its authority. It sees government as able to use new tools and techniques to steer and guide. Also, Gerry Stoker, 'Governance as Theory: Five Propositions', in *International Social Science Journal*, No. 155, March, 1998, pp. 13–28.

accountability, transparency, predictability and participation. While accountability and transparency converge on the right of citizens to information regarding government transactions, predictability refers largely to the system of law and justice encompassing the laws of contract and property and the system of judicial settlement of disputes without loss of time and at affordable costs for all concerned. The fourth criterion of governance is participation, the process through which the public at large can function as a watchdog over governmental activities and the use of public resources as well as provide 'a feedback to the government on the ability and efficiency of public services'.[70]

The concept of governance is inextricably linked to the working of the nation–state as it involves all those activities of social, political and administrative actors which can be seen as purposeful efforts to guide, steer, control or manage societies. The weedy growth of a nation-state in the twentieth century, primarily because of the growth of its commitments and activities, combined with a perception of its limited or diminishing effectiveness, has led in the 1980s to a global crisis of confidence in the state. The crisis was prompted by the dismal performance of states in sub-Saharan Africa, statist failures in the Soviet block and deteriorations elsewhere. These concerns have thereby brought into focus the states' governing capacity. Seeking to explain the governing capacity of a nation-state, Gunar Myrdal introduced the concepts of 'hard state' and 'soft state'. While a hard state sets priorities and executes them because the actual administration is based on 'rational' bureaucratic principles, in a soft state, the administrators habitually circumvent laws and regulations, officials and politicians often collude to thwart implementation of public policies and corruption is rampant. Thus, in a soft state, the political accountability of the rulers to the people, the accountability of the bureaucrat to his/her boss, the law and the people, and the rule of law which enables individuals/groups to redress grievances either against each other or the state—all get eroded.[71] This defines an inability on the part of the states to govern themselves leading thereby to 'mis'-governance—a term which has gained currency simultaneously with 'good' governance.

---

[70] S. Swaminathan, 'Governance in Crisis', *Hindu*, 5 May 1999.

[71] For a detailed discussion of the soft state, as it has emerged in most of the post-colonial nation-state, see Pradeep Khandwalla, *Revitalising the State: A Menu of Options*, Sage, New Delhi, 1999.

There is no standardized recipe for good governance. In fact, it is a result of effective learning by the state to cope with the many challenges and crises it comes across during its evolution. The first element of good governance is a respect for the rule of law. It is this feature which gives India the status of a progressive open-minded society. It is the impartiality of the working of the rule of law that gives dignity to the weak and justice to the underprivileged. It is the rule of law that protects individual freedom and civil liberties and frees the human spirit in its search for excellence. It is the duty of civil society to ensure that the rule of law is maintained, that power is not unduly concentrated and that all civil liberties and human rights are protected'.[72] The second feature of good governance is to have special care for the disadvantaged and the weak. In order to protect the underprivileged, the state is required to undertake steps to uphold the basic human rights and values. These include civil and political rights such as the right to life, liberty and security, to hold property, the right not to be discriminated against, the right to vote, to freedom of speech and freedom of press and protection from arbitrary invasion of privacy, family or home. In the contemporary world, it has also been emphasized that the scope of human rights cannot exclude crucial social, economic and cultural rights, including most prominently the right to development and rights of minority and disadvantaged groups, such as religious or linguistic minorities, women, children and tribes. A third equally important aspect is that good governance implies tolerance and broad-mindedness, which allows us to accept and embrace unity and diversity. Such an arrangement provided not only for cultural expression of pluralities but also for multiple and overlapping governances within its fold. A multicultural society like India is illustrative here because the nation-state that emerged in the aftermath of decolonization held together 'the diverse social and cultural entities ... not within a single state, as we understand the term today, but in a single political–civilizational system'.[73] The numerous cultural and social entities that constitute India do not live in isolation nor do they enjoy complete autonomy *vis-à-vis* each other. They share 'a symbolic meaning system', which ensures 'fluidity of cultural expressions among them at different levels'.[74]

---

[72] I. K. Gujral, 'Governance of India', *Mainstream*, 14 August 1999, p. 7.

[73] D. L. Sheth, 'The Nation-State and Minority Rights', in D. L. Sheth and Gurpreet Mahajan (ed.), *Minority Identities and the Nation-State*, Oxford University Press, New Delhi, 1999, p. 31.

[74] Ibid., p. 30.

PUBLIC ADMINISTRATION IN INDIA

Historically, Public Administration as a practice in India has been bearing the imprint of British colonial administration which is of immediate scholarly interest. The pre-British, particularly Mughal, administrative forms and functions were, to some extent, absorbed by the imperial rule. But, what continues even today is, in most parts, the lingering structure of colonial administration. The secretariat organization and practices, the district administrative structure, and the superior civil services have continued uninterrupted even after Independence; and not much change has really been effected in the long phase of post-Independence administrative life of the nation. Eminent historians have ably dealt with historical account of administrative evolution.[75] The aim of this reader is to (a) identify theoretical advances in the discipline of Public Administration keeping in view their relevance to Indian administration and (b) focus on significant contributions to Indian administrative thought that serve to illuminate and critically analyse the structures and processes of the multi-level complex of Indian administration including its impact on society, polity and economy.

Bureaucracy in India—its structure, role, behaviour and interrelationships—has evolved over a long period in history since the designing of the system about the middle of the nineteenth century.[76] The Macaulay Committee Report, 1854 is a watershed in the growth of bureaucracy in India. By recommending a civil service based on the merit system, the committee sought to replace the age-old patronage system of the East India Company.[77] Defending the idea of a generalist administrator—'all rounder'—the committee 'portrayed the ideal administrator as a gifted layman who, moving from job to job irrespective of its subject matter, on the basis of his knowledge

[75] Ashok Chanda, *Indian Administration*, Allen and Unwin, London, 1967, pp. 15–42; B. B. Mishra, *The Bureaucracy in India*, Oxford University Press, 1977; B. B. Mishra, *Government and Bureaucracy in India, 1947–76*, Oxford University Press, Delhi, 1996, pp. 1–36; David C. Potter, *India's Political Administrators, from ICS to IAS*, Oxford University . ess, Delhi, 1996 (reprint).

[76] For a detailed account of the civil service in India during the British rule, see Philip Mason, *The Men who Ruled India*, Rupa & Co., Calcutta, 1997 (reprint).

[77] As the report underlined, '[h]enceforth, an appointment to the civil service of the Company will not be matter of favour but matter of right. He who obtains such an appointment will owe it solely to his own abilities and industry'. The Macaulay Committee Report (1854) in *The Fulton Committee Report*, vol. 1, HMSO, London, 1975, p. 125.

and experience in the government'.[78] The efficiency of the members of the ICS as administrators may have been exemplary, but there is no doubt that they were motivated primarily by imperial interests and hence 'the interests of the country were too often postponed to the interests of the [Crown]'.[79] Furthermore, there was a Weberian aspect to the ICS. Drawn from the well-off sections of the society, the civil servants came from some of the best universities and were chosen on the basis of a competitive examination. Those within the ICS were therefore secluded from the rest given their exclusive class, caste and educational backgrounds. In other words, they had the special status within the society that Weber felt was essential to a true bureaucracy. Given their peculiar characteristics the British officials in India formed a most unusual kind of society with no organic links with the society they were to serve.[80] The Indian Civil Service held a pivotal position in the system of administration that flourished during the colonial rule. Recognizing its immense importance in sustaining the empire, Lloyd George thus declared in the House of Commons in 1922 that '[t]hey are the steel frame of the whole structure. I do not care what you build upon it—if you take the steel frame out, the fabric will collapse'.[81]

In independent India, the Indian Administrative Service (IAS)

[78] Quoted in *The Fulton Committee Report*, ibid., p. 125.

[79] George Trevelyan, *The Competition Wallah*, London (second edition), 1907, pp. 6–7; quoted in Bernard S. Cohn, *An Anthropologist Among the Historians and Other Essays*, Oxford University Press, Delhi, 1990. p. 545. Given their stake in the British administration, it is but natural that whatever they did, they were simply acting in the imperial interests and in the process preserving or enhancing their superior positions. However there is a school of thought defending that the imperial logic never appeared crucial in administration since 'the ICS [was] Jeremy Bentham's prototype of the benevolent social guardian committed to achieving the common good'. For details, see Eric Stokes, *The English Utilitarians of India*, Oxford University Press, Oxford, 1959, p. 159.

[80] While explaining the nature of the British civil servants Bernard S. Cohn developed this argument further by drawing upon their post-recruitment training first at the Haileybury School and later in Oxbridge colleges that hardly took into account the rapid socio-structural shifts in India during the colonial rule. Bernard S. Cohn, *An Anthropologist Among the Historians and Other Essays*, pp. 500–53.

[81] Lloyd George was quoted in Philip Mason, *The Men who ruled India*, Rupa & Co, Calcutta, 1997 (reprint), p. xv. Duffrin was probably more categorical in appreciating the role of the Indian Civil Service. According to him, '[t]here is no service like it in the world. If the Indian Civil Service were not [as they are], how could the government of the country go on so smoothly? We have 250 million subjects in India and less than 1,000 British civilians for the conduct of the entire administration'. Duffrin's statement was quoted by Jagmohan in his 'Riveting the steel frame of the ICS', *Hindustan Times*, 1 November 1998.

succeeded the ICS.[82] Despite its imperial roots, the Indian political leaders chose to retain the structure of the ICS presumably because of its efficient role in conducting Indian administration in accordance with prescribed rules and regulations supporting a particular regime. However, during the discussion in the Constituent Assembly, the house was not unanimous as regards the fate of ICS. The argument opposing its continuity was based on its role as an ally of imperialism. 'The Civil Service as the Steel Frame ... enslaved us [and] they have been guilty of stabbing the nation during our freedom struggle. [W]e should not, therefore,' as the argument goes, 'perpetuate what we have criticized so far'.[83] Vallabhbhai Patel was probably most vocal in defending the ICS and its steel frame. Since they were 'patriotic, loyal, sincere [and] able', Patel was not in favour of tampering with bureaucracy especially when the country was reeling under chaos towards the close of the British rule. As early as 1946, he convened the provincial Premier's Conference to evolve a consensus on the future of which was then All India Services (AIS). In view of their long association with Public Administration, officers belonging to the AIS 'are most well-equipped to deal with new and complex tasks'. Not only 'are they useful instruments, they will also serve as a liaison between the Provinces and the Government of India and introduce certain amount of brashness and vigour in the administration both of the Centre and the Provinces'.[84] Later while speaking in the Constituent Assembly, he categorically stated that, '[y]ou will not have a united India if you do not have a good all-India service' which had the independence to speak out its mind and enjoyed a sense of security. He also attributed the success of the Constitution to the existence of an all-India service by saying that, 'if you do not adopt this course, then do not follow this Constitution ... . This Constitution is meant to be worked by a ring of service which will keep the country intact'. 'If you remove them', Patel thus apprehended, 'I

---

[82] For a succinct account of the evolution of the Civil Service in India both during the British rule and its aftermath, see B. Shiva Rao et al., *The Framing of India's Constitution (select documents)*, Vol. V, IIPA, New Delhi, 1968, Chapter 23 (pp. 708–23).

[83] Shibban Lal Saksena's statement in *the Constituent Assembly Debate*, 10 October 1949, Vol. X, Lok Sabha Secretariat, New Delhi, 1999 (third print), p. 46. Prominent among those who criticized the decision to retain the ICS was M. Ananthasaynam Ayyanger who failed to understand the logic of providing 'guarantee to those persons who have played into the hands of others [and] cared only for money and the salaries they got'. Ayyangar's statement in the debate, 10 October, 1949, ibid., p. 42.

[84] Quoted in S.R. Maheshwari, *Indian Administration*, Orient Longman, New Delhi, 1984 (reprint), p. 211.

see nothing but a picture of chaos all over the country'.[85] Even
Jawaharlal Nehru who was very critical of the ICS for its role in
sustaining the imperial rule in India,[86] seemed persuaded and supported its continuity for 'the security and stability of India, ... including coping with the slaughter and its aftermath in Punjab, crushing
opposition in Hyderabad, and containing it in Kashmir'.[87] Patel's
views were translated in Article 311 of the Constitution of India that
stated that no civil servant shall be dismissed or removed or reduced
in rank except after an enquiry in which he has been informed of the
charges and given a reasonable opportunity of being heard in respect
of those charges.[88] So, an instrument that consolidated the imperial
rule in India 'with so slight use of force'[89] survived in completely different political circumstances[90] primarily because there was continuing

[85] Vallabhbhai Patel's speech in the Constituent Assembly, See *The Constituent
Assembly Debates*, Vol. X, 10 October, 1949, pp. 48–52. Seeking to persuade his col-
leagues in the Constituent Assembly, he further argued, 'if these service people are
giving you full value of their Services and more, then try to learn to appreciate them.
Forget the past. We fought the Britishers for so many years. I was their bitterest enemy
and they regarded me as such ... What did Gandhiji teach us? You are talking of
Gandhian ideology and Gandhian philosophy and Gandhian way of administration.
Very good. But you come out of jail and then say, 'These men put me in jail. Let me take
revenge', that is not the Gandhian way. It is going far away from that'. Ibid., p. 52.

[86] As late as 1934, Nehru characterized the Indian Civil Service as 'neither Indian
nor civil nor service [and] it is thus essential that the ICS and similar services disappear
completely'. Jawaharlal Nehru, *An Autobiography: With Musings on Recent Events on
India*, John Land the Bodley Head, London, 1941 (reprint), p. 445.

[87] Jawaharlal Nehru's speech in the Constituent Assembly. See *The Constituent
Assembly Debates*, vol. 1, 1947, pp. 793–95.

[88] For a detailed discussion in the Constituent Assembly during the preparation
and final acceptance of Article 311, see B. Shiva Rao (ed.), *The Framing of India's
Constitution: A Study*, IIPA, New Delhi, 1968, pp. 713–23.

[89] While explaining the continuity of the steel frame for almost two hundred years,
Philip Mason stated, the administration in India 'had the immense advantage over
those in the later African territories that it was possible to set up the framework of
government before the invention of the electric telegraph and close control of England.
Use was made of Akbar's machinery and whatever local institutions could be adapted.
The whole was controlled by a cadre of district officers, rigorously picked, but trained
almost wholly by doing what in fact they were learning to do. Since they were so few
they had let their subordinates do their own work. Confidence that they would be
backed up from above was the hall-mark of their profession and they acquired a
confidence in themselves and a confidence that they would be obeyed, which meant
that they were obeyed. Few administrations can have ruled so many with so slight use
of force. Everything was done through Indians and by Indians to whom power was
delegated'. Philip Mason, *The Men Who Ruled India*, Rupa & Co., Calcutta, 1997 (reprint), pp. 345–6.

[90] P. C. Alexander, himself an IAS, thus argues, '[t]he new civil service for all

support for it first from the British government and then the Congress government. Furthermore, its continuity did not pose any threat to the dominant classes that reigned supreme following the 1947 transfer of power in India. The new civil service for all practical purposes was, as a former bureaucrat comments, therefore 'the continuation of the old one with the difference that it was to function in a parliamentary system of government, accepting the undoubted primacy of the political executive which in turn was responsible to the people through their elected representatives in the legislature'.[91] Besides its structure, which is more or less, an expansion of the steel frame, the continuity is at a deeper level. While the colonial civil servants had a paternalistic attitude towards the people, and ruled largely by negative discretionary powers, '[t]heir successors, noting the vast unmet development needs of the people, substituted positive discretionary powers of patronage and subsidies, reinforcing the colonial syndrome of dependency on the *mai-baap* state'.[92]

Apart from its functional utility, the fact that the steel frame was retained more or less *intact* was because as B. P. R. Vithal, himself an IAS officer, said, 'the Congress leaders who took office ... shared the social background of the senior civil servants whom they inherited from the colonial state'.[93] Thus, for example, Nehru felt at ease while working with senior civil servants. Similarly, Rajagopalachari felt more at home with the ICS officers who were placed with him when he was the Prime Minister of Madras (1937–39) than with certain elements in the Congress party. The political processes subsequent to Independence gave rise to changes in the class composition of the political executive that was far-reaching and rapid than changes in the social composition of the civil services. While the political executives, trained in vernacular, came largely from rural and semi-urban areas, those in the steel frame were generally urban-based and educated in English. The growing disparity between the class background

---

practical purposes was the continuation of the old one with the difference that it was now to function in a parliamentary system of government accepting the undoubted primacy of the political executive'. See P. C. Alexander, 'Civil Service: Continuity and Change', in Hiranmory Karlekar (ed.), *Independent India: The First Fifty Years*, Oxford University Press, Delhi, 1998, p. 62.

[91] Ibid.

[92] R. Sudarshan, 'Governance of Multicultural Polities: Limits of the Rule of Law', in Rajeev Bhargava et.al, *Multiculturalism, Liberalism and Democracy*, Oxford University Press, New Delhi, 1999, p. 111.

[93] B. P. R. Vithal, 'Evolving Trends in the Bureaucracy', in Partha Chatterjee (ed.), *State and Politics in India*, Oxford University Press, Delhi, 1997, p. 224.

of the political executive and the civil servants led to frequent friction between the administrators and politicians in the Westminster parliamentary system of governance when the latter had assumed a leading role in building a new nation.

Following Independence, government functions have also expanded in scope and content. With the introduction of the parliamentary form of government and the setting up of people's institutions right down to the village level, there has been an inevitable rise in the level of expectations and performance have widened. People's institutions were set up with the objective of creating self-governing institutions at the village level. The objective remains distant forever. Similarly, Independence and Five Year Plans were perceived by people as synonymous with economic and social equality and well-being, and freedom from want and oppression. In the early days of the planning era, people did not crib much about the shortage which they confronted with fortitude because the future held hope and promise for them. With the passage of time, they felt their hopes were 'belied' and they were 'nowhere near the promised land of honesty, plenty and happiness'. The ethos of self-governance, decentralization and community-development were flagged in with considerable élan and fanfare. For example, the three-tier Panchayati Raj system and the urban local bodies were conceived of as a properly meshed network of institutions to accelerate the development process.[94] The Seventy-Third and Seventy-Fourth Amendments (1992) to the Constitution seek to advance the concept of 'self-governance' by providing for (a) regular elections, (b) minimal suppression of Panchayati Raj bodies through an administrative fiat and (c) regular finances through statutory distribution by state finance commissions. The aim, argues Kuldeep Mathur, 'is to reduce the margin of political and administrative discretion and to allow the decentralized institutions to gather strength on the basis of people's involvement'.[95] But, due to

---

[94] For an interesting, though slightly dated account of the panchayati system in West Bengal, Uttar Pradesh and Karnataka, see Atul Kohli, *The State and Poverty in India: The Politics of Reform*, Cambridge University Press, Cambridge, 1987; and for studies of urban government of Delhi, see Ajoy K. Mehra, *The Politics of Urban Development: A Study of Old Delhi*, Sage, New Delhi, 1991.

[95] Kuldeep Mathur, 'Strengthening Bureaucracy: State and Development in India', *Indian Social Science Review*, vol. 1, no. 1, January–June, 1999, p. 22. According to Mathur, [t]he success of the Seventy-Third and Seventy-Fourth Amendments making decentralized structures part of the Constitution has yet to be seen—not only because they were only instituted in 1993, but also because the states have shown little evidence of implementing the requirement through their own statutes'.

various reasons, the political process became what may be termed as 'reversed' and highly centralized and personalized systems of government developed both at the Central and State levels. There has been a massive erosion of institutions, whether they are the Parliament and parliamentary institutions, or the party system and democratic procedures in the running of parties, or the judiciary, or indeed the press. Describing the crisis and erosion of institutions as 'the natural and expected consequences of a political process that has undermined both the role and authority of basic institutions',[96] Rajni Kothari has sought to grapple with a peculiar reality in which public administration appears to be largely delinked with the basic institutions of democratic system that has flourished in India following Independence.[97]

Indian historical experience, both during the British period and its immediate aftermath, has led to the emergence of a public administration that was ill-suited to the needs and aspiration of the people. The reasons are not difficult to seek as studies have shown that the bureaucrats who have been brought up and trained in the colonial administrative culture are wedded to the Weberian characteristics of hierarchy, status and rigidity of rules and regulations and concerned mainly with the enforcement of law and order and collection of revenues. For the colonial regime, this structure was most appropriate while it is completely unfit to discharge the functions in the changed environment of an administration, geared to the task of development. As the government becomes the main institution for development in the democratic set-up that India adopted following Independence, the role of the officials has undergone changes. Their sole objective is to 'emphasize results, rather than procedures, teamwork rather than hierarchy and status, [and] flexibility and decentralization rather than control and authority'.[98] Seen as 'the

[96] Rajni Kothari, *State against Democracy: In Search of Human Governance*, Ajanta, Delhi, 1988, p. 287.

[97] The process, known as 'deinstitutionalization' invariably leads to a non-policy government that 'operates by means of spoils and preferments that take into account the particular situations of persons and communities'. Very common in the sub-Saharan Africa, 'such government tends to be "private government" both in the sense that government offices are treated as private property and in the sense that spoils, unlike policies, must be managed in a discreet and even clandestine fashion. They cannot be advertised, nor can they be publicly debated'. See Goran Hyden, 'Democratization and Administration', in Axel Hadenius (ed.), *Democracy's Victory and Crisis* (Nobel symposium no. 93), Cambridge University Press, Cambridge, 1997, p. 252.

[98] Anil Bhatt, 'Colonial Bureaucratic Culture and Development Administration:

development administrator', the bureaucrat is therefore characterized by 'tact, pragmatism, dynamism, flexibility, adaptability to any
situation and willingness to take rapid, ad-hoc decisions without
worrying too much about procedures and protocol'.[99]

Taken together, the pre-Independence and post-Independence career of Indian bureaucracy—particularly the higher echelons at the
central and state levels—makes interesting reading both socio-his-
torically and managerially. Historical writings on Indian bureaucracy are numerous. By contrast, analytical studies of the bureaucracy
in operation in India are rather scattered and ill-defined. The proposed anthology will trace the track record of the bureaucracy both
historically and operationally covering the pre-Independence and
post-Independence phases.

The Recent Trends in Administrative Reforms in India

Reforms in administration in India in the 1990s have been basically
driven by the measures on economic liberalization. Good governance has suddenly entered the vocabulary of Public Administration. The concept of governance was for the first time highlighted in
a World Bank document on the sub-Saharan Africa. It however received an adequate attention in a 1992 report, entitled *Governance and
Development*, that defines governance as 'the manner in which power
is exercised in the management of a country's economic and social
resources for development'. From its lending experience in many
developing countries, the bank came to realize that 'good governance is central to creating and sustaining an environment which
fosters strong and equitable development, and it is an essential
complement to sound economic policies'. Three distinct aspects are
identified in the conceptualization of governance: (a) the form of
political regime (parliamentary or presidential, military or civilian,
authoritarian or democratic); (b) the process by which authority is
exercised in the management of a country's economic and social
resources; and (c) the capacity of government to design, formulate
and implement policies, and in general, to discharge government
functions. The first aspect falls outside the bank's mandate. The focus
of governance is therefore directed towards the second and third
aspects.

Portrait of an Old-Fashioned Indian Bureaucrat', *Journal of Commonwealth and Comparative Politics*, vol. 17, 3, 1979, p. 259.

[99] Ibid., p. 281.

Recounting its wide experience, the bank document narrates vividly the problems of governance. For instance, despite technical soundness, programmes and projects have often failed to produce the desired results. Laws are not enforced properly and there are often delays in implementation. Privatized production and market-led growth do not succeed unless investors face clear rules and institutions. In the absence of proper accounting systems, budgetary policies cannot be implemented or monitored. Many a time, procurement systems encourage corruption and distort public investment priorities. Again, the failure to involve beneficiaries and others affected in the design and implementation of projects has often led to substantial erosion of their sustainability. Against this background of malgovernance, the bank has attempted to focus on some of the key dimensions of governance, such as, public sector management, accountability, the legal framework for development and information and transparency.

Good governance leads, as the bank document underlines, to sound economic, human and institutional development, though it cannot be achieved overnight. What is required is constant effort on the part of the citizens. The bank document thus insists that '[a]lthough lenders and aid-agencies and other outsiders can contribute resources and ideas to improve governance, for change to be effective, it must be rooted firmly in the societies concerned and cannot be imposed from outside'. More pronounced political meaning of governance appeared in the directives of the Organization of Economic Cooperation and Development (OECD) countries, laying down conditionalities for receiving economic assistance. The OECD documents sought to link development assistance with (a) participatory development, (b) human rights and (c) democratization. The key components of governance were identified as:

i) legitimacy of government; (ii) accountability of political and official elements of government; (iii) competence of governments to make policy and deliver services; (d) respect for human rights and Rule of Law (including individual and group rights and security, a legal framework for economic and social activity and participation).

What emerges from the combined effort of the aid-giving countries and international funding agencies is that entitlement to aid would depend on whether a client country has a liberal democratic state with a pluralist polity in which legislatures are constituted through free and fair elections.

The Indian response was clearly articulated in the 1996 conference

of Chief Secretaries which suggested several corrective steps to arrest
the present drift in civil service before it was too late. What was
suggested in the conference had its root in the arguments, put forward by Rajiv Gandhi, the former prime minister, in favour of 'responsive administration'. In his series of speeches at the workshops
of district magistrates and collectors that spanned for almost two
years between 1987 and 1988, Rajiv Gandhi argued that:

[the] paternalistic model of [our] administration is not suitable for a society
where the main thrust of administration is on development. It was agreed
that the regulatory functions of administration should not be seen as an end
in themselves, as they tended to be in colonial times, but as a means of
reinforcing and sustaining the processes of broad-based development. [A]
more representative and more responsive administration would be better
placed to relate the purposes of administration to the larger goals of our
national life—democracy, socialism, secularism and non-alignment.[100]

The other point that was also hammered is 'the dependency syndrome' of the people. Bureaucracy continues to remain 'a doer' and
not 'a enabler'. The people in general wait for the government to do
'the simplest things which they can do themselves'. The system has
become 'so top-heavy and top-oriented' that at every level, people
look to the level above for a solution. What is therefore needed is 'to
push the administration down, not just in the administration but also
sometimes out of the administration to the community'. By involving
people in both planning and executing developmental programmes
at the grassroots, the administration will become both 'responsive'
and 'representative' in character.[101]

If Rajiv Gandhi's detailed exposition was an attempt to diagnose
the administrative ills, the 1996 conference of the Chief Secretaries
sought to provide policy-prescriptions to defuse the crisis in Indian
administration. In the agenda note entitled 'For An Effective and
Responsive Administration in India', it was admitted,

the public administration and the civil service at all levels are passing through
difficult times in terms of eroded credibility and effectiveness of the civil
service, growing public perception of an unholy nexus between certain
elements among politicians and civil servants and criminals (as elaborated in
the Vohra Committee Report[102]), and increasing criticism of the low level of

---

[100] Rajiv Gandhi, 'Responsive Administration', (speech on 18 June, 1988 at
Coimbatore), *Times of India*, 19 June 1988.

[101] For details, see Rajiv Gandhi's speech at Hyderabad, 13 February 1988, Government of India Press, New Delhi, 1989, p. 10.

[102] The Vohra Committee, under the chairmanship of N. N. Vohra, Home Secretary,

honesty, transparency and accessibility to the political and bureaucratic elements in charge of administration.[103]

The imperative need was for governments at all levels to reinvent themselves and redefine their roles and responsibilities and bring about reforms in all areas which have an interface with people. The public image of the bureaucracy, it was candidly confessed, was one of inaccessibility, indifference, procedure-orientation, poor quality and sluggishness, corruption-proneness and non-accountability for result. The need of the hour was therefore 'to assure the people of India of an efficient, open, responsible, accountable, clean and dynamically adjusting administration at all levels'.[104] Immediate steps should be taken to restore people's confidence in the capacity and fairness of administration. Very significantly, the conference recognized that 'governance has to extend beyond conventional bureaucracies to involve actively citizens and consumer groups at all levels, to empower and inform the public and disadvantaged groups, and to ensure service and programme execution through autonomous elected local bodies'.[105] There were, thus, three important aspects of this new agenda for Civil Service reform: (a) there was a crisis in administration which was not people-sensitive or citizen-friendly; (b) there was an urgent need to bring about reform in administration to make it people-sensitive, efficient and cost-effective; and (c) there was also need for a change in the mindset so that governing could be conceived *afresh* as 'governance'—a wider term than mere formal 'government'—opening, in the process, possibilities of inclusion of other actors, such as citizens, consumer groups, elected local bodies or those who are linked with the administration in some way or the other.

In view of the above well-directed designs for Civil Service Reform,

---

Government of India, was appointed on 9 July, 1993 to take stock of all available information about the activities of crime syndicates/mafia organizations which had developed links with and were being protected by government functionaries and political personalities. Its report that was submitted in 1997 contained direct references to the growing criminalization of politics and the nexus between politicians, bureaucrats and those involved in the activities of crime syndicates/mafia organizations. See *The Vohra Committee Report*, Ministry of Home Affairs, Government of India, 1997.

[103] *An Agenda for Effective and Responsive Administration* (the agenda paper circulated in the conference of Chief Secretaries of States and Union Territories), Department of Administrative Reforms and Public Grievances, Ministry of Personnel, Public Grievances and Pensions, Government of India, New Delhi, November, 1996, p. 1.

[104] Ibid., p. 1.

[105] Ibid., pp. 1–2.

the recommendations of the Fifth Pay Commission are another milestone in this direction. True to the spirit, expressed in the 1996 Chief Secretaries conference, the Fifth Pay Commission has recommended: (a) downsizing the government through corporatization of activities which involves 'manufacturing of goods or the provision of commercial services'; (b) transparency, openness and economy in government operation through 'privatization of activities where government does not need to play a direct role' and also 'contracting out of services which can be conveniently outsourced to the private sector'[106] and (c) contractual appointment in selected areas of operations 'for the purpose of maintaining a certain flexibility in staffing both for lateral entry of experts, moderating the numbers deployed depending on the exigencies of work and ensuring availability of most competent and committed personnel for certain sensitive/specialized jobs.'[107]

The Central government has been advised to go for a thirty per cent reduction in the strength of the Civil Services, as the Pay Commission felt that it would be unwise to let the government sector continue as 'an island of inefficiency' and 'inertia'. The normal procedure of voluntary retirement after completing twenty years should be continued. Alongside this, the Commission recommended a special scheme of voluntary retirement in the departments where surplus manpower has been identified. In such cases, there should be a provision for selective retirement of persons, the initiative always resting with the government and for 'a golden handshake'.

The other significant recommendation of the Commission concerns 'openness' in administration. Defending the repeal of 'the Official Secrets Act of the old colonial days', the Commission insists on openness which 'means giving everyone the right to have access to information about the various decisions taken by the Government and the reasoning behind them'.[108] Except what is detrimental to the interests of the nation, the security of the state or its commercial, economic and other strategic interests, may not be made public, 'nothing should be held back just to subserve the interests of individual bureaucrats and politicians'.[109] Every important government decision involving 'a shift in policy' should invariably be accompanied

---

[106] *The Report of the Fifth Pay Commission*, vol. 1, Government of India Press, New Delhi, 1997, pp. 122–3.

[107] Ibid., p. 175.

[108] Ibid., p. 150.

[109] Ibid., p. 151.

by a White Paper 'in the nature of an explanatory memorandum'. As an integral part of Civil Service Reform, the Commission insisted on the formation of 'an efficient grievance redressal machinery [that] has to be effective, speedy, objective, readily accessible and easy to operate'.[110] Drawing upon the examples of Canada, UK and Malaysia where effective grievance redressal cells have been functioning efficiently, the idea of a Citizens' Charter—defining the rights of the customers of government schemes and services—was mooted by the Commission. The recognition by the Commission of a citizen's right to information and the procedures suggested in this connection are of seminal importance from the point of debureaucratizing government and making it citizen-friendly. The issues, raised by the Pay Commission figured prominently in the 1997 Conference of Chief Ministers where an action plan was adopted to (a) make the administration accountable and citizen-friendly, (b) ensure transparency and right to information and (c) adopt measures to cleanse and motivate civil services.[111]

The latest in government-citizenship relationship is the concept of Citizens' Charter. Under the Charter, citizens have been brought at the centre of all the government activities changing the prevalent concept of treating the citizens as passive recipients of government service. The idea behind the Charter is tapping citizens' responses to the actual working of government organizations. Normally, the Charter would cover all public services and aim at demanding from the government and service organizations (post office, railways etc., for instance) accountability, transparency, quality and choice of services, provided by them to the people.

The Citizens' Charter was first introduced in Britain in 1991 to streamline the administration and also make it citizen-friendly.[112] Many government departments and service organizations have been brought under its purview since its formulation. As citizens are at the centre of public administration, the Charter insists on the following key elements to fulfill its aim:

(a) *standards*: setting, monitoring and publication of standards of the services

[110] Ibid., p. 157.

[111] *Times of India*, 25 May, 1997. For details of the recommendations, see *Annual Reports, 1997–98*, Ministry of Personnel, Public Grievances and Pensions, New Delhi, 1998, pp. 65–9.

[112] For a detailed discussion of the Charter and its evolution in Britain, see Norman Lewis, 'The Citizens' Charter and Next Steps: A New Way of Governing?', *Political Quarterly*, vol. 64, no. 3, July–September, 1993, pp. 316–26.

that individual users can reasonably expect; (b) *information and openness*: full, accurate information, readily available in a plain language about the performance of those, involved in delivery; (c) *choice and consultation*: the public sector should provide choice wherever practicable, and there also should be regular and systematic consultations with those for whom the service is slotted; (d) *courtesy and helpfulness*: courtesy and helpful service from those involved in public administration; (e) *putting things right*: in case, there is delay in delivery of services, the Charter stipulates for a full explanation with an apology; (f) *value for money*: efficient and economical delivery of public services within the resources, the nation can afford.[113]

As evident, the Charter is not at all, a list of new principles of governance; instead, it has merely reiterated those norms which ideally should constitute the foundation of Public Administration. It is, therefore, an attempt to bring back the basic values of Public Administration that are eroded due to various socio-political reasons, connected with the evolution of the British political system.

So the primary issue is to restore 'publicness' of Public Administration. The Charter is a significant influence in the latest efforts, undertaken by the Government of India, to make administration citizen-friendly, open, transparent, sensitive and accountable. By 2000, forty-nine Citizens' Charters have been finalized by the various departments and agencies of the Government of India. The Ministry of Food and Consumer Affairs, Government of India have prepared model Charters for public hospitals by the Department of Health and for the Targeted Public Distribution System (TPDS).[114]

THE CITIZENS' CHARTER AND GOOD GOVERNANCE

As a strategy, the Charter is revolutionary especially when the public institutions are in decline. What is remarkable in this effort is the emphasis on disseminating information to the public and laying down some of the basic principles which should be the concern of organizations involved in the delivery of public service. Apart from the listed steps which public administration `ould take into account to attain 'good governance', the Charte. .. equally important in

---

[113] UK Foreign and Commonwealth Office, *Raising the Standards: Britain's Citizens' Charter and Public Service Reform*, Citizens' Charter Unit, Her Majesty's Government, London, 1992, p. 6—quoted in R. B. Jain, 'Citizens' Charter—An Instrument of Public Accountability', *Indian Journal of Public Administration*, July–September, vol. XLIV, no. 3, 1998, p. 367.

[114] *Annual Reports, 1999–2000*, Ministry of Personnel, Public Grievances and Pensions, Government of India Press, New Delhi, pp. 68–71.

conceptualizing some of the changes in government as a process. First, the governance agenda, as set by the World Bank, subsumes a set of state–society regulating disciplinary procedures. There is an underlying belief that accountability of government through checks and balances available under a liberal democratic system would ensure that state activity meets the needs and expectations of society. So, the right kind of state and the right kind of society are both posited as the ultimate objectives of the overarching neo-liberal agenda. Secondly, as suggested earlier, the World Bank's 'good governance' has been linked to the problem of sound development management in the 'Third World' countries. And very explicitly, the bank dictates terms and conditionalities for being eligible for the Bank's assistance though '[t]here is little clear guidance as to how well or badly a government must perform before it is granted or disqualified from funding'.[115] 'Governance', in this context, stands for establishment and operation of social institutions complementing the activities, undertaken by Public Administration. Concretely, it manifests itself in formal rules and regulations, decision-making procedures, and programmatic activities that serve to define social practices and guide and regulate the interactions of participants in such practices. In real life, there are many forms of community organizations or voluntary, collective self-approaches through which a group of people organize themselves to achieve common purposes, such as irrigation, water distribution, resolution of local disputes and community defence. Governance, as conceptualized by the World Bank, is also a way of crafting social institutions as a matter of public concern. So, governance has reintroduced the debate on relative importance of formally constituted government or the existing communitarian life, embedded with mechanisms for collective problem-solving. Finally, by striving to go beyond the institutionalized administration, 'governance', as a practice, has created conditions under which 'governance without government' can prosper. It is, therefore, a theoretical device to relocate the significance of various community organizations

---

[115] Bob Currie, 'Governance, Democracy and Economic Adjustment in India: Conceptual and Empirical Problems', *Third World Quarterly*, vol. 17 no. 4, 1996, p. 803. Since there is no clarity, governance remains, as Currie argues, 'a particularly difficult variable to operationalize. At present, good governance is seemingly defined in terms of a check-list of criteria (transparency, accountability, public sector management etc.) that government must broadly satisfy in order to justify receiving loans. However it is not made explicit which, if any, of these are prioritized and how they should be measured and compared. Governance is not a binary variable and cannot be defined in terms of "on/off" or "present/absent" criteria'.

in many parts of the world through which local communities have sought to solve collective problems in their own way. This had led to two specific kinds of responses with immense theoretical significance for the discipline of Public Administration; (a) it has shifted our attention away from the formal organizations which have failed due to various socio-political reasons; and (b) it has also resurrected interests in community organizations as forms of collective problem-solving mechanisms in civil society. So, governance, conceptualized as a device to revitalize the collective institutions, which are 'non-governmental', provides a theoretical cue challenging privatization as the only solution of a whole range of problems affecting the growth of the non-Western societies.

CONCLUDING OBSERVATIONS

Public administration is contextual. It has grown differently in different countries due to peculiar socio-economic and political circumstances in which it is grounded. Given the specificity of administration in India and other Third World countries due to historical reasons public administration of these decolonized countries cannot be properly grasped by those theories, rooted in developed countries of the West. In other words, the theories and concepts of a stable state in a milieu of institutionalized system may not necessarily be appropriate to grasp the developing state system undergoing a tortuous and occasionally uncertain process of institutionalization.[116] So, both as a discipline and an activity, Public Administration has to take into account the peculiar characteristics of the prevalent socio-economic and political reality of these countries to meaningfully explain its distinctive nature. A New Public Administration, with its unmistakable identity can, for instance, grow in India only by a creative encounter with the prevalent reality.

Economic liberalization has set a new agenda for Public Administration. First, not only has the role of the state been restricted, reductions in the size of state bureaucracies and contracting out work have

[116] Kuldeep Mathur therefore argues, '... public administration continues to be weak as an academic and social science discipline. The weakness primarily emerges from its inability to develop theoretical and conceptual approaches that offer a better understanding of the contemporary scene in India. It continues to be heavily influenced by the western social science paradigms which have in a way provided it professional but not academic strength'. See his, 'Whither Public Administration', in Kuldeep Mathur (ed.), *A Survey of Research in Public Administration, 1970–9*, Concept, New Delhi, 1986, p. 17.

also been placed higher on the strategic agenda. The move towards liberalization is accompanied by a fresh look at the role of the state. It has increasingly been argued that the state should gradually withdraw from many aspects of policy implementation—that can conveniently be transferred to the private sector. The state should ideally be 'a provider' by ensuring that essential goods and services are delivered but not aiming to be the sole 'deliverer' or 'producer'. In other words, in the changed milieu, as the state moves from a concern to do towards a concern to get things done, the managerial focus has increasingly been shifted from the formal processes to results.

Secondly, the concept of organization has undergone sea-changes under the impact of globalization. The conventional ideas about organization seem, under the changed scenario, rather dated and are unable to capture the essence of today's reality. For instance, information technology has radically altered our views about 'boundaries' between firms and also within firms. Although evident in many advanced 'First World' firms, sophisticated information and communication platforms are now available to link the members of an organization to a common source of organizational memory and a fully distributed relational network. These developments are slowly pulling down the rigid walls around organizational layers and functions.

Thirdly and more importantly, 'hierarchy', the distinguishing feature of bureaucracy, has received a battering due to 'downsizing' and 'delayering' of organization. The career track of workers is no longer clear and certain, and there is no clear path for advancement within organizations. What is thus likely to emerge following reforms in administration is in contrast with bureaucratic hierarchy that has traditionally provided a clear career path and concrete expectations for workers at all levels. It has been a fundamental tenet of bureaucracy that the organization would reward those who fulfilled their organizational obligations which were set forth in formal policies and job descriptions. It was a kind of organizational commitment to workers to secure their loyalty and cooperation. Since the 1980s, the picture turned out to be different. There were more and more temporary workers with a higher percentage of professionals, whose morale was low and organizational loyalty much decreased.

What has been described so far has been confined mostly to private firms in the US and Europe. But the trend was noticeable in their overseas units in other parts of the globe as well. Different kinds of organizational restructuring took place, and even then, in a highly competitive global scenario the firms were still being asked to respond even more quickly to deliver still higher quality products and services and to bring about substantial cost reduction. Organizational changes were initiated by cutting down many management layers and expanding span of control. The traditional organizational format that has been sanctified by the principles of classical organizational theory seems to be fast-disappearing.

Finally, the ruling authority as part of structural adjustment vigorously pushes privatization. Its support is 'rooted in its ideological desire to shrink government—particularly, programmes like education, transportation, medical care and housing—which foster a redistribution of goods and services to those at the bottom of the social order'.[117] This ideological goal is being pursued rather easily probably because it is being articulated as a pragmatic concern for 'government efficiency'.[118] Although those advocating privatization are generally in favour of a greater role for the market and lesser role for the state there are also neo-liberal and neo-conservative elements within their advocacy. The former has been primarily concerned with the promotion of individual liberty while the latter with the restoration of traditional values. This has, *inter alia*, led to a new theoretical quest for the role of women and other underprivileged sections of society in bureaucracy that has generally remained the preserve of the privileged. Far from being 'rational' bureaucracies, it has been argued, they have been found, in real life, mirroring the prejudices of the larger society. Not until 1869, the Blacks were, for instance, not allowed to work in the American federal bureaucracy. Outright discrimination against women came to an end in federal bureaucracy as late as 1967. So, the 'merit myth' of bureaucracy is merely theoretical with no connection with the reality. In India, the constitutional provisions guaranteeing 'equality before law' and 'equality of employment opportunities' mark a watershed in the history of civil services. Despite such constitutional provisions, two problems that persist in

[117] Elliot D. Sclar, 'Public Service Privatization: Ideology or Economics?', *Dissent*, Summer, 1994, p. 330.

[118] This is a new ethic that has, argues Niraja Gopal Jayal, accompanied the neo-liberal shift in the agenda of the state. This ethic endorses the virtues of individualism, as opposed to considerations of the common good. Through its emphasis on efficiency, this new agenda accords 'respectability to the idea of competition as bringing forward the best, and simultaneously discounts welfarist initiatives as slowing down progress by subsidizing the undeserving and unproductive. In such a Darwinist environment, the collusion between government and business also becomes normal and accepted'. Niraja Gopal Jayal, 'Changing Conceptions of Political Morality', *Indian Journal of Public Administration*, July–September, 1995, p. 272.

India are (a) the lower representation of women at all levels of government and (b) gender-inequalities within the service. In 1989, for instance, women constituted, in the Union Government both at gazetted and non-gazetted levels, only 6.6 per cent of the total workforce. The scene in 1995 was not very encouraging because the share of women had gone up to only 10 per cent, a mere increase of 3.4 per cent. Even in case of the Indian Foreign Service and Indian Police Service, as the 1992 figure shows, the share of women was a meagre 1.6 per cent. Given the women representation, it seems that bureaucracy in India reflects the biases of a larger societal context and is responsible for creating, maintaining and reproducing the same.[119]

The other dimension attracting enormous attention is 'transparency' or 'openness' in governmental transactions. Recently, the government of Rajasthan has announced that the villagers could apply for and obtain on payment photocopies of the documents containing details of expenditure on works done in the area and use them as evidence if they so liked. Giving wide publicity to 'planned' and actually executed public works should be the duty of government. Two landmark cases need to be mentioned in this context. In the state of Uttar Pradesh versus Raj Narain (1975), 4 SCC 428, Justice Mathew held that to cover with the veil of secrecy, the common routine business is not in the interest of the public. Such secrecy can seldom be legitimately desired. It is generally desired for the purpose of parties and politics of personal self-interest or bureaucratic routine. The responsibility of officials to explain and to justify their acts is the chief safeguard against oppression and corruption.

In the other case of S. P. Gupta versus Union of India, 1982 Justice Bhagwati argued that the concept of an open government is the direct emanation from the right to know which seems to be implicit in the right of free speech and expression guaranteed under Article 19 (1a). Therefore, disclosure of information with regard to the functioning of government must be the rule and secrecy an exception justified only when the strictest requirement of public interest so demands.

Drafted under unusual circumstances such as defence of imperial rule, countering espionage and anti-people policies generally, the Official Secrets Act, 1923 which is still the law of the land, stands

---

[119] The details of women's share have been taken from the survey on 'Gender and Civil Service in India' that was conducted in 1997 by the Government of India. For details, see Sarojini Thakur. *Increasing Awareness for Change: A Survey of Gender and The Civil Services*, Department of Administrative Reforms and Public Grievances, Government of India, New Delhi, p. 1.

today as a gross insult to constitutional democracy in India. The Act makes it a penal offence for any person holding office under the government willfully to communicate any official information to any other person other than the person to whom he is authorized to communicate. As S. Maheshwari has observed, '[t]he Official Secrets Act has thus kept the people in the dark about what has been happening within the government. It was the catch-all provisions of this statute which encouraged the political leadership to pursue courses of action highly detrimental to public morality'.[120] Successive attempts have been made to amend the Act of 1923 without much success. Recently, the Fifth Pay Commission (1996) in its report stressed the need for framing a new law on Right to Information in keeping with the needs of our democratic polity. To quote the Commission, '[t]he effort is to satisfy public demands as far as is reasonable and practicable. Transparency also has to be fully compatible with the constitutional and parliamentary system of the country, and the cost of sharing information should be commensurate with the benefit to the public. It may also not be practicable to give information about any proposal under considerations while it is yet to be finalized, as this is likely to bring into play several pressure groups with attendant increase in corruption. Thus, what we need in the country today is a limited openness in government functioning, which would make available *ex-post-facto* information about various, but not all government decisions to the citizens of this country. While anything that is detrimental to the interests of the nation, the security of the state or its commitment, economic and other strategic interests, may not be made public, nothing should be held back just to subserve the interests of individual bureaucrats and politicians'. After dithering over the issue for years, the Central government has finally introduced the Freedom of Information Bill, 2000 in Parliament on 25 July. It has to be seen in what form ultimately the bill comes out of parliamentary scrutiny and finally becomes an act since, according to Madhav Godbole, 'the bill, as presented in Parliament, hardly does justice to bring transparency to issues of governance'.[121]

[120] S. R. Maheshwari, 'Secrecy in Government in India', *Indian Journal of Public Administration*, October–December, 1979.

[121] Madhav Godbole, 'Unending Struggle for Right to Information', *Economic and Political Weekly*, 12 August 2000, p. 289. Godbole further observed that 'through five years of dithering over the Bill on the Right to Information, the position of the Central Governments which have been run by two United Fronts, the BJP and its allies, has remained the same. [It] is disconcerting that in this important area of governance, the

We may add at this stage the cautionary remarks of Donald C. Rowat, an authority on the subject of administrative secrecy. As Rowat has observed that a law on the subject will not succeed unless it contains three key provisions: (i) there must be an unequivocal declaration that the general principle is to open public access to documents; (ii) the types of matter which may legitimately be kept secret should be identified narrowly and specifically and (iii) the law should provide a right of appeal to an independent authority such as the courts or an ombudsman or preferably both. Again Rowat is right in suggesting that governments rarely surrendered any of their own powers voluntarily. 'Since a monopoly over information gives them power, such a law will not be adopted without strong pressure from all segments of society that suffer under traditional system of discretionary secrecy'.[122]

The concept of governance, as discussed earlier, has led to the recognition of the role of multiple agencies in organizing and undertaking public business. In addition to formal government, the role of non-governmental organizations and community-based organizations has been acknowledged as supplementary public agencies. Another significant development is decentralization and empowerment of localities for local resources and knowledge-based authentic grassroots governance. The Seventy-Third and Seventy-Fourth Constitutional Amendments (1992) signal momentous changes in terms of grassroots people's empowerment whose full potentialities are yet to be realized. The new instrumentalities like the Lokpal/Lokayukta for dealing with people's grievances against top functionaries in government still remain a distant dream. Corruption in many forms continue to plague the Indian public system, but its ability to successfully deal with corruption at different levels has fallen short of the requirement. The other instrumentality is the 'Human Rights' institution at the national and state levels which are quite recent in Indian public administration. There are both international and domestic pressures to uphold human rights and ensure effective 'rights regimes' at all levels in the interest of steady democratization of the public sphere.

Thus Public Administration has undergone a sea-change in

---

interests of bureaucracy and the ruling elite seem to converge against the empowerment of the common man'.

[122] Donald C. Rowat (ed.), *Administrative Secrecy in Developed Countries*, Macmillan, Surrey (UK), 1979, p. 18.

response to new inputs from the contemporary socio-economic and political scene. It is therefore difficult, if not impossible, to grasp the nature of public administration in terms of Weberian conceptualization underlining its rigid, rule-bound and hierarchic characteristics. Instead, the preferred form of administration is one, which is accessible, transparent and accountable, and the citizens are consumers. Furthermore, the notion 'public' in public administration has acquired new dimensions where the public–private distinction is more analytical than real since there is a growing support for both cooperation and healthy competition between these two sectors in the larger interests of societal development. So Public Administration, if conceptualized in its orthodox mould, is both an inadequate tool of analysis and also inappropriate to meaningfully articulate governance in which government is merely an actor in the complex web of public administration. By drawing attention to the changes in the theoretical domain of Public Administration—reflective of the metamorphosis of the realities where Public Administration is located—the Reader is both a comprehensive review of the available literature and also a quest for 'new' directions in the unfolding and consolidation of the discipline.

PART I

MAJOR THEORETICAL ADVANCES

CHAPTER ONE

Conceptual Development in the West*

B.B. Mishra

In common parlance, the terms bureaucracy and civil service, are interchangeably used to connote more or less the same phenomenon. Strictly, in a technical sense, they are however substantially different for civil service refers to a cadre of 'public servants' at a higher level ignoring those involved in running public administration at a lower level. In other words, the term 'bureaucracy' is wider than 'civil service'. Dwelling on the conceptual development of the phenomenon, called bureaucracy, B.B. Mishra seeks to trace its multifacetedness in its growth and functioning.

MODERN BUREAUCRACY—A MIDDLE CLASS CONCEPT

Originating from the institution of absolutism, bureaucracy found, in the Industrial Revolution of the eighteenth century, a suitable incentive for growth and, in the subsequent progress of the capitalist economy, its opportunity to attain maturity. The period of absolute monarchy in the West and the phase of national sovereignty that followed as a result of social and economic development, were two important landmarks in the emergence of the modern concept of bureaucracy. Though mutually conflicting, absolutism and national sovereignty agreed in postulating a concept of the state as something *sui generis* and separate from both, as something in the nature of a

* B.B. Mishra, *The Bureaucracy: A Historical Analysis upto 1947*, Oxford University Press, New Delhi, 1977.

service-rendering and legal organization designed to secure the protection of rights and enforcement of duties independently of any particular form of government. Such a conception of the state was a prior condition for the development of modern bureaucracy.

French in origin, especially in the thinking of the eighteenth century physiocrats, the term 'bureau' signified a chest of drawers, a writing table, an office or even a department for transacting business. And when applied to government, the addition of the suffix derived from the Greek word for 'rule' imparted to the composite term 'bureaucracy' a meaning which signified a body of officials invested with the exercise of power in their own right, a collective designation for officials organized on a constitutional basis and discharging definitive functions independently of a king or any other head of state. Indeed, bureaucracy emerged as a middle class concept, the basis of obedience to its authority being law, a contractual principle—not personal loyalty, which was the foundation of an aristocracy entitled to obedience through traditionally recognized social position based on birth. Bureaucracy is in fact the antithesis of aristocracy.

Bureaucratic Development in England

The history of modern administration may be said to have begun roughly around 1660, when the Restoration in England marked the end of royal absolutism and the King acted through his Privy Council and its ancillary organizations. The year 1661 witnessed the beginning of the personal rule of Louis XIV in France. With the aid of Colbert he shaped into the French administrative system the inherited institutions of the past which came to endure even after the modification introduced by Napoleon between 1799 and 1804. It was in 1660 again that Frederick William, the Great Elector, brought to his troubled dominions in northern Germany a period of peace and administrative reorganization.

The middle-class concept of bureaucracy was preceded by a twofold development, the disintegration of the aristocracy and the emergence of bureaucratic absolutism. The period between the end of the fifteenth century and the middle of the seventeenth was a period when the feudal system was being permanently subdued. The social and political vacuum so arising from the decline of the baronage was being steadily filled by the increasing power and influence of monarchy and its supporters, the rising middle class.

There was however no uniformity in the growth of administration. The administrative system of each country was determined by its own historical tradition, its own geographical situation and above all, its own social system, including the character of the social classes from which administrators were drawn, their position and their standing in the social hierarchy, and the nature of the society itself on which administration had to act. A common feature, however, was the decline of feudalism which created conditions favourable to bureaucratic state administration.

This transformation from feudalism to a bureaucratic state did not initially proceed from economic factors, for the system of economic production did not undergo any radical change during the early phase of the period. To begin with, it was the result of a far-reaching revolution taking place in military skills and organization, more especially in the field of firearms. The baronial castle could easily be pulled down once the use of canon became common. The heavy cavalry of the nobility became likewise a liability, with infantry adopting the arquebus after it had attained a fair degree of perfection. Changes in military science and technology not only brought military success but also changed the nature and form of political organization from feudal to bureaucratic.

The second and perhaps most important factor which brought about this transformation was the growth of a new social class, the bourgeoisie in the broad sense of the term. A product initially of royal favour and patronage, this class held a position in between the common people and the descendants of the old feudal aristocracy. It consisted mainly of the people engaged in trade and commerce on the one hand and the learned professions on the other. The bourgeoisie heralded the emergence of the bureaucratic state.

The early English middle class, culturally speaking, combined moderate means with liberal and scientific education to a degree barely possessed by other classes in society. It took advantage of the subdivision of administrative tasks and their gradual separation from the royal household which had already started towards the end of the fifteenth century. The Exchequer (Finance) and the Chancery (General Administration) were, for instance, two departments which had grown out of the King's Household even before the reign of Edward III.[1] The proliferation of offices and their separation from the King's Household were significant developments; for these were steps away from the personal service of a ruler in the direction of

[1] See T.F. Tout, 'The Emergence of Bureaucracy' in Robert K. Merton (ed.), *Reader in Bureaucracy*, pp. 68–79.

what later grew into public service. Under Edward III, however, this distinction between private and public service had not yet appeared. It proceeded later from the growth of the middle class and the extended employment of this class in government departments which were increasingly being separated from the royal court to satisfy the new demands of growing trade and commerce. Towards the end of the fifteenth century, for example, clergymen were being steadily replaced by laymen educated and trained in the universities as jurists and humanists. The lay education which the bourgeoisie promoted with royal assistance made the middle class better fitted for appointment to administrative posts growing outside the royal court as a result of social and economic development.

By virtue of their literary, legal and scientific education the members of the rising middle class were being sharply distinguished from the lower orders of society. But if they could successfully detach themselves from the lower classes so as to form a distinct social layer, with prospects even to mingle with the aristocracy, the credit went not a little to the absolutism of the Tudor monarchs. They promoted trade and commerce; maintained peace and tranquillity; pried the nobility loose from its grip on landed property, and made cross-fertilization possible between rural and urban classes. While the loss of ancient sovereign rights forced many noble families to move close to the royal court for lucrative positions, some of the larger business houses became owners of rural properties. Due to a rise in economic status the middle class also sometimes moved up and mingled with the more well-to-do sections of society. However, the progress of cross-fertilization did not obstruct the growth of class consciousness. The cultural habits of the middle class and its value system based on liberal and lay education obliged it to draw apart from the nobility in spite of occasional overlapping with the aristocratic layer.

The Civil War in the reign of Charles I further weakened the nobility, but the failure of Cromwell's constitutional experiments led to popular reaction against the Commonwealth and the Restoration(1660) appeared as a compromise, a break from despotism, but not yet a step towards democracy. It represented the Aristotelian notion of a mixed government, a blending of monarchy, aristocracy and democracy. The Glorious Revolution (1688–9)and the Act of Settlement (1701) were essentially a confirmation of the principle recognized in 1660. Together, these contributed on the basis of a new conception of popular sovereignty to a new stability of power relationships, a sort of working partnership of the bourgeoisie and the aristocracy.

This new conception, at least in theory, was supposed to invest every individual with the exercise of sovereign power, which in practice meant involvement in the election of a representative assembly or parliament. It differed from the earlier conception which identified popular sovereignty with the 'natural' leaders of society, such as the barons and heads of corporations and communes, who alone were recognized as the legitimate representatives of the people. Theoretically, the new concept left no room for any intermediate sovereignty between the Crown and Parliament on the one hand and the individual citizen on the other. Having a much wider social base, the bourgeoisie was to step in politically to supplant the nobility.

The settlement of 1688–9, however, made a compromise. It left with the aristocracy the virtual monopoly of the government machinery, which in practice meant control over Parliament and the civil service. But while using that machinery full respect had to be shown to the interest of the middle class which was now dominant. That compromise was a necessity; for no class at the time was in possession of unchallengeable supremacy and the bourgeoisie saw in the agrarian and urban proletariat a far more serious source of danger than from the aristocracy.[2]

However, the arrangement of 1688–9 did not signify any recognition of intermediate sovereignties. These were all replaced by the sovereignty of laws of the Crown in Parliament. The Crown extended its approval to a series of parliamentary enactments that followed. The Habeas Corpus Act, the Bill of Rights and the Act of Settlement were all unanimous in emphasizing the obligation of the Crown to govern in accordance with the laws enacted by Parliament. The absolute monarchy which had earlier provided incentive to the growth of the bourgeoisie, thus came to yield place to the sovereignty of law, an artifact of the bourgeoisie.

In terms of administrative development, British bureaucracy did not become as formal and theory-bound as its counterparts in France and Germany. An important reason was that the English Crown did not at the time create two efficient instruments of despotism, a standing army and a stable centralized bureaucracy. This was partly from consideration of economy and perhaps partly from a sense of security against foreign invasion which the insular position of the country ensured. While the armed military recruited in each country satisfied the periodic requirements even of the Tudor kings, 'the will of

[2] See Donald J. Kingsley, *Representative Bureaucracy*, p. 21.

the central government depended for its execution on the voluntary co-operation of a hierarchy of part-time, unpaid officials; Lord and Deputy Lieutenants, Sheriffs, Justices of the Peace, High and Petty Constables, Overseers of the Poor and Churchwardens'.[3] They were local notables who served in civil offices in an honorary capacity, as these offices imparted prestige to their holders and lustre to the families to which they belonged. Bureaucratic regimentation could not grow in local administration because of the hold these unofficial elements retained over a long period of time.

And as far as the central stipendiary civil servants of the King were concerned, even under Charles I they were 'his own, and not yet those of some institutional abstraction, the Crown or State'.[4] All major offices, many in the middle ranks and some minor posts, were in the King's gifts. Below the top level this sometimes involved an actual personal choice by the sovereign. But it so happened that he often gave formal approval to the choice already made by the head of the department concerned, or by other ministers. Even the personal choice of the King was often swayed by the importunities of suitors or court favourites.[5] The degree of bureaucratization was in these circumstances reduced on account of the varied influences that went into the selection even of the stipendiary office-holders. The alleged absolutism of the English King was in fact not absolute. His bureaucracy was therefore not as bureaucratic as it might have been.

There was yet another important development in England, the separation of administrative and political functions. Earlier, the King's civil servants exercised both functions. Before the eighteenth century there existed in fact no distinction between civil servants and politicians. The King's office-holders also held seats in Parliament. They were expected to support him with zeal and fervour at all times. It is true that in the first half of the seventeenth century some of the King's servants, especially those in the law courts and in the departments, were beginning to be recognized as public servants of the Crown. They were being distinguished specifically from the private servants of the sovereign. The idea of loyalty to the State, to the 'Commonwealth' or the public good, as distinct from service to the King, was slowly engaging men's minds. Pym and his supporters in Parliament, for instance, were actually thinking in these terms when in the course of the Civil War they emphasized that they were not fighting

---

[3] C.E. Aylmer, *The King's Servants: The Civil Service of Charles I, 1625–42*, p. 7.
[4] Ibid., p. 3.
[5] Ibid., p. 60.

against the King, but against his evil counsellors who led him astray. But the idea had not yet taken root. The religious foundations of monarchy were still strong and the person of the monarch was still regarded as inviolate. It was not practicable to treat the King's servants as public servants unless he himself had to a great extent been depersonalized and in some degree also depoliticized. The civil servants of the Stuart Kings naturally continued to act more or less as royal servants, lending support to their masters in administration as well as Parliament.

To protect its political independence Parliament enacted after the Glorious Revolution a series of measures to exclude certain office-holders from the House of Commons, and ultimately disenfranchising the bulk of the civil service by the time Anne became Queen. This principle of exclusion extended to government contractors in 1782 and to clergymen of the established church in 1801. In 1782, 50,000 customs and revenue officers were disenfranchised. Thus it was not until the opening of the nineteenth century that the permanent separation of administrative staff from the political branch of the government became fairly advanced. The gradual emergence of the distinction between administrators and politicians was in fact the result of the exclusion of 'placemen' (as a later generation described permanent royal officials) from the House of Commons in the latter part of the eighteenth century and the early nineteenth century. The evolution of ministries in the modern sense of the term was closely related to this distinction between non-political offices, which did not change hands with changes in ministry, and the political, which did.

The Parliament which was effecting this separation between administration and politics was however still aristocratic in complexion, although it was acting in the interest of the middle class. It was not until the Reform Act of 1832 that the middle class started asserting itself for a direct and effective share in political power. Even so, over two decades elapsed before a competitive system could replace 'patronage' as a mode for the selection of a Permanent Civil Service. This was first done under the Northcote–Trevelyan Report (1853). The service introduced under the recommendations of this Report marked the beginning of a bureaucracy where the mercantile element of the bourgeoisie acquired gradual ascendancy.[6]

[6] The higher administrative posts had by 1911 become the preserve of the upper middle classes, the sons of merchants being more successful than those of any other occupational group or category. The parents of only two per cent of the successful candidates had by then come to be classed as landed proprietors. During 1836–54, on

Thus the distinctive feature of development in England was that, while the feudal aristocracy was slowly transformed into an instrument of bourgeois interest and representative government, the bourgeoisie had the patience to wait and complete that transformation without the rigour of an intervening period of bureaucratic absolutism. There were eruptions of violence which even led to a full scale civil war, but that was an exception rather than the general rule. The process of change remained on the whole peaceful, and no organized ideological backing was needed to promote change on the basis of class antagonism.

This brief narrative of the growth of administrative services in Britain indicates that modern bureaucracy is a middle class, bourgeois concept. Analyses of similar developments in Western Europe support this thesis. Bureaucracy emerged as an antithesis of feudalism, a result of economic progress and intellectual development, which together dictated the necessity of reorganizing the services on a principle and in a manner consistent with the requirements of a growing organization rather than those of a static feudal estate. Its rise and growth represented a change-over from purely personal service of the sovereign to a public service, of the State, a legal, impersonal and institutional abstraction disengaged from the social privileges founded on the legitimacy of right by birth. This transition from the 'personal' to the 'public' involved a whole gamut of social change from feudalism through bureaucratic absolutism to political democracy. But the middle class, bourgeois character of bureaucracy remained by and large unaffected in the civil service, although recruitment to it under the system of 'patronage' tended to exclude the commercial element.

In spite of variations in the formal structure of the political systems of various countries, there developed over the years a general sense of co-operation and reciprocity of control between the bureaucratic and the elective elements of government, for both were inspired by the same source, modern commerce and industry, although, historically, the former chiefly sprang from the centres of higher education, while the latter grew for the most part from the centres of economic production. In spite of different historical sources, therefore, capitalism and the public services developed great similarity in

---

the other hand, out of 22 successful candidates only one was the son of a merchant, while the fathers of more than 70 per cent were either officials or landed proprietors. See Donald J. Kingsley, op cit., p. 65.

their respective norms of organization.[7] Functionally, however, they differed considerably. The impersonality of governmental bureaucracy and the peculiar procedural norms that went with it, were two important features which together constituted what might be called the independent variable in bureaucratic analysis. It is this independent variable that lent to it a professional character, rule-bound, value-free and service-oriented. In this sense, bureaucracy became identifiable with what might be called 'public administration'. It was indispensable to the functioning of all public offices (irrespective of their political complexion) 'according to principles entirely different from those applied under the profit motive',[8] which characterizes commercial transactions in terms of money and market value.

BUREAUCRACY VIEWED POLITICALLY

In its technical sense, bureaucracy was once viewed as a purely administrative organization, separate and distinct from the decision-making body, the political executive. This distinction proceeded from the exclusion of the King's servants from Parliament. But since it was in practice a social group invested with the exercise of power, its action could not be free from political criticism. The term 'bureaucracy' naturally acquired a pejorative connotation—a hierarchy of civil servants operating in a manner inimical to freedom as well as free enterprise. Indeed the bureau system came to be identified with controls, queues, form-filling, 'red tape' and petty tyranny. An officer in the new bureaucratic system was required to execute in writing everything which in earlier days might have been done by word of mouth. All orders had to be reduced to writing as a legal safeguard against the guise of the newly emerging abstraction of 'public service' and bureaucratic impersonality, individual officers had enormous powers over ordinary citizens.

The exercise of power by bureaucracy in its own right led to its being viewed as a class of power elites, a political dimension which with the growth of industry, urbanization and a working-class population, acquired an added importance in Britain in the second half of the nineteenth century. This growth called for an extension in the scope of state activity against 'poverty' and provided for social security in order to check political unrest. It involved not only bureaucratic interference to readjust capital-labour relationships, but also

---

[7] See Mouzelis, *Organization and Bureaucracy.*
[8] Ludwig von Mises, *Bureaucracy*, p. 47.

the necessity for speed and efficiency to effect that readjustment in favour of social justice. In other words, it meant an augmentation in the executive power of the state, and involved the risk of impairing the independence of Parliament and the liberty of individuals.

While politicians were guided in their attitude by practical considerations of power politics, political thinkers were swayed by abstract notions of liberty. In his *Principles of Political Economy* (1848) John Stuart Mill, for example, expressed himself against concentrating in a dominant bureaucracy all the powers of organized action existing in the community. For he feared that over governance might stultify political life in England in the same way as on the Continent. In *On Liberty* (1859) he further elaborated his views by pointing out that the extended function of the state involved the creation of more careers under a government which in turn monopolized the talent of the whole nation. In his *Considerations on Representative Government* (1861) Mill viewed bureaucracy as no less than rule by officials, which clashed with the principles of representative government. 'The work of government', he observed. 'has been in the hands of governors by profession, which is the essence of bureaucracy'.[9] The bureaucratic form of government, he added, accumulates experience, acquires well-tried and well-experienced maxims, and makes provision for appropriate practical knowledge in those who have the actual conduct of affairs'.[10] This approach to bureaucracy, which emphasized its control to carry on administration, was responsible for its being treated as the ruling class.

The Civil Service Reform of 1870 actually invested the British bureaucracy with a degree of control which took it nearer to its Continental counterpart. The whole trend was towards permanent officials taking the management of affairs into their own hands, even at the cost of Parliamentary independence. The Reform Bill of 1884, which extended the franchise to workers, had the support even of the Tory Party; the reasons were obviously political, for the Tories wanted to 'ransom' the working class in a bid to snatch power from the Liberals. These developments led Herbert Spencer to make a vehement attack on state intervention in the regulation of the capital–labour relationship.[11] He viewed the new trend as a violation of the freedom of contract which the Liberals themselves had earlier promoted as an article of faith and a matter of principle. That principle, however, was

[9] *Considerations on Representative Government*, p. 113.
[10] Ibid., p.114.
[11] See H. Spencer, *Man Versus the State*.

in its origin a product of nascent capitalism, which recognized no intermediate sovereignty between the ordinary citizen and the modern state of its making. But times had changed. New 'intermediate sovereigns' had now emerged. These included political parties, business and labour organizations, pressure groups and bureaucracies organized into committees and boards. There had been a considerable shift in the decision-making function away from constitutional bodies to these extra-constitutional agencies, irresponsible but yet acting as pockets of political power. Politicians had to reckon with them. Spencer's was therefore a cry in the wilderness. The state control of industries and labour relations tended to open up a variety of careers for a developing bureaucracy. The members of the educated middle class elite were naturally tempted to favour the extension of that control as a lever to power and to augment employment opportunities.

The power approach to bureaucracy involved class antagonisms in its very nature. The use of the term bureaucracy in an abusive sense was mainly a result of class or group interests, the privileged class complaining of loss of privilege, the business classes of interference in free trade, the scientists of ignorance, the common people of inordinate delays and 'red tapism'.

THE HEGELIAN CONCEPT

Unlike the pejorative approach of English philosophers who were concerned with the question of individual liberty, Hegel invested bureaucracy with a sublime mission transcending all considerations of freedom. Consistent with the Prussian tradition of absolutism, in his *Philosophy of Right* (1821) he raised the concept of bureaucracy to abstract heights, a transcendent entity, a mind above individual minds. He defined it as 'State formalism' of civil society, as the State's consciousness', as the State's will', as 'State power', as a corporation.[12] Though only one social class, Hegel considered bureaucracy to be the universal class, a synthesis uniting the particularism of civil society with the general interest of the state, the paradigm for mediation between the particular and the universal, between civil society and the state. The exercise of power, according to him, was a mission to be performed for God or society. Public officials shared in that mission

---

[12] David McLellan, *Karl Marx: Early Texts*, p. 68. See also *Philosophy of Right*, para. 205.

by executing decisions made by the sovereign about the nature of 'general interest'.

Hegel was a supporter of the *bureau* system which Germany had adopted after 1806. He pointed out that public servants were to discharge specific duties on the principle of division of labour in separate departments organized hierarchically under ministers. For a proper execution of the general interest Hegel recommended special education for officials and adequate financial support, so that they could subordinate their private interest to the common weal of the state.

Hegel's concept of bureaucracy was indeed based on the abstract philosophy of law. He did not draw that philosophy from an analysis of existing social and political organizations. On the contrary, he recognized law as an expression of objective morality, a metaphysical entity that determined political organizations *a priori*. In other words, he treated objective reality as a product of that metaphysical entity. His conceptual frame for bureaucracy was no more than a metaphysical superstructure raised over the legal foundations of the Prussian code. All that this superstructure aimed at was the subordination of bureaucrats to what he considered the universality of the state, thereby divesting them of their claim to being treated as an independent unit. In spite of its being a dominant class in society, Hegel did not conceive of bureaucracy as an element distinct from the state. Due to their identification, at least in theory, with 'general interest', both were to be treated as one and the same entity.

The Marxist View

Like Hegel, Marx also did not recognize bureaucracy as an independent object of analysis. But his premise was different. It proceeded from his economic interpretation of politics, where power was supposed to flow from the position of a class in the economic order of society. Basic to his political analysis was this class and its relationship to economic production in society, not the state which, according to Marx, was not an independent entity which possessed its own 'intellectual, ethical and libertarian basis'.[13] He pointed out that the state merely reflected the economically determined power relationships existing in a given society at a given period of time. He naturally treated bureaucracy as an instrument of the economically

---

[13] L.S. Fener (ed.), *Marx and Engels: Basic Writings on Politics and Philosophy*, p. 127.

dominant class, an agent of government functioning under the direction of that class or of the group controlling the power of the purse, not as an integral part of a transcendent Hegelian state which, in spite of its claim to be one with civil society, remained allied with the nobility and military class. In his class approach to power relationships Marx saw no place for the independence of officials. To him they posed no separate problem for analysis.

Marx's opposition to the Hegelian concept of bureaucracy was directed specially against the manner in which the separate entities of the state (representing general interest) and society (a conglomeration of private interests) were sought to be reconciled and reunited to secure the general interest through such devices as the system of hierarchic authority, the independence of corporations, the devolution of power to local bodies and, finally, through the morality and selfless character of public officials themselves. Marx dubbed as ineffectual each of these mechanisms to ensure the unity of state and society. 'Bureaucracy identifies the interest of the state with particular private goals in such a way as to make the interests of the state into a particular private goal opposed to other private goals.'[14] He therefore recommended that the state should become the real, not the apparent, general interest, so that its bureaucratic organ might be obliged to serve the common weal.

This was not to deny the state the independence it had acquired. What Marx objected to was the manner in which it functioned. In *The German Ideology* (1846) he clearly acknowledged the separate identity of the state, but not on the Hegelian model of moral objectivity. He held that the state so identified was 'nothing more than the form of organization which the bourgeoisie necessarily adopt ... for the mutual guarantee of their property and interests'.[15] In order to set the state free and make it truly representative of the general interest it was essential to convert it by force 'from an organ superimposed upon society into one completely subordinate to it'.[16]

Here again there was a difference, but not a negation of the state as an independent unit. The concept of objective morality apart, while Hegel recommended his own set of mechanisms to enable the state and bureaucracy to serve the common weal, Marx recommended the use of force as an alternative. Marx's early writings[17] in fact make it

---

[14] Quoted in Shlomo Avineri, *The Social and Political Thought of Karl Marx*, p. 24.
[15] K. Marx and F. Engels, *The German Ideology*, p. 78.
[16] Quoted in Shlomo Avineri, op cit., p. 51.
[17] See David McLellan, *Karl Marx: Early Texts*.

clear that he was not unaware of the growth and significance of the state and bureaucracy, especially in France, where, as he wrote even later in *The Civil War in France* (1871), 'the state power which nascent middle class society had commenced to elaborate as a means of its own emancipation from feudalism' came to be 'transformed' in the course of time 'into a means for enslaving labour by capital'.[18] He had earlier in *The Eighteenth Brumaire* expressed a similar grievance against French bureaucracy for its attempt to reduce men to mere objects of manipulation. 'Every common interest', he said, 'was straightaway severed from society, counterposed as a higher *general* interest, snatched from the activity of society's members themselves and made an object of government activity, from a bridge; a schoolhouse and the communal property of a village community to the railways, the national wealth and the national university of France ... it was the instrument of the ruling class, however much it strove for power of its own.'[19] Marx thus admitted that bureaucracy was an important factor in government and that, in spite of its limitations, it strove for power in its own right. Mill's comments pointed more or less in the same direction.

In his *Critique of Hegel's Philosophy of Right* (1843) Marx had even earlier referred to the fixity of bureaucratic principles, attitudes and traditions. In it he devoted a full section on bureaucracy which, he said, 'holds in its possession the essence of the state, the spiritual essence of society'. He added:

The general spirit of bureaucracy is secret, mystery, safeguarded inside itself by hierarchy and outside by its nature as a closed corporation. Thus public political spirit and also political mentality appear to bureaucracy as a betrayal of its secret. The principle of its knowledge is therefore authority, and its mentality is the idolatry of authority. But within bureaucracy the spiritualism turns into a crass materialism, the materialism of passive obedience, faith in authority, the mechanism of fixed and formal behaviour, fixed principles, attitudes, traditions. As far as the individual bureaucrat is concerned, the aim of the state becomes his private aim, in the form of a race for higher posts of careerism. ... Bureaucracy must therefore make it its job to render life as material as possible. ... The state only continues to exist as separate fixed spirits of bureaux whose connection is subordination and passive obedience.[20]

It is clear then that Marx was aware not only of the existence and growth of the state, but also of the distinction that existed between

[18] *Selected Works*, p. 518, cited in Shlomo Avineri, op cit., p. 50.
[19] Shlomo Avineri, op cit., p. 50.
[20] David McLellan, op cit., pp. 69–70.

the state and its bureaucracy, a non-political administrative organization possessing certain fixed principles of conduct.

Three years later, in 1846, *The German Ideology* noticed bureaucracy growing in the German states and acquiring an abnormal degree of independence in the exercise of authority. Marx attributed this to the absence of any single dominant group being able to impose its rule on society. Obviously the so-called economically dominant group was not also able to rule. It is true that the bureaucracy noticed in *The German Ideology* served the interests of the bourgeoisie. But it did so not as an appendage of that class, but as an independent administrative instrument. For, a couple of years later Marx himself admitted that the liberal Prussian government established in Berlin after the March insurrection of 1848 represented the bourgeoisie far more effectively by replacing the old bureaucracy 'which did not wish to sink to the level of maidservant to a bourgeoisie to which it was once a despotic schoolmistress'.[21]

These early comments of Marx leave no room to doubt that he was fully conscious of the growth of bureaucracy and its distinction from the state in both functional and structural terms. A common feature underlying both the Hegelian and the Marxian concepts was their recognition of the principle of contract-based law, which not only kept on enlarging its operational area in the regulation of social and political relationships, but provided the middle class bureaucracy with a new basis of legitimacy to justify obedience to its authority. However, the basic difference between Hegel and Marx was the fact that while the former invested law with a divine mission as the basis of bureaucratic action, the latter related it to society and later came to view it as an instrument of class rule. In *The Civil War in France* (1871) Marx finally pointed out that in a classless society there would be no place for appointed officials, the executive power being in that situation vested in the people themselves. He was perhaps thinking in terms of restoring society to its functional independence, not by reversing history, but by an elimination through violent means of the bourgeoisie whose bureaucracy, as he thought, had steadily been arrogating to itself functions originally performed by society. For, writing as late as 1871, he reiterated more or less the same argument against bureaucracy in the *Critique* of 1843:

Every minor solitary interest engendered by the relations of social groups was separated from society itself, fixed and made independent of it and

---

[21] Cited in Martin Albrow, *Bureaucracy*, p. 71.

opposed to it in the form of state interest, administered by state priests (bureaucrats) with exactly determined hierarchical functions.[22]

Though fully aware of the existence, and probably even of the independence, of bureaucracy, especially in his earlier writings, Marx did not go beyond giving it casual significance, and his discussion of bureaucracy was probably a reaction to Heinsen's ideas. In his anxiety to advance the dialectic of class antagonism as a principle of social action Marx took steps to controvert Karl Heinsen, the German socialist whose study of Prussian bureaucracy, published only a couple of years after Marx's *Critique:* attributed the existence of classes not to the interaction of the productive forces in society, but to the existence of political privileges and monopolies.[23] According to Heinsen it was politics that determined social stratification, not economics. He not only identified bureaucracy with bureaux, but asserted, on the basis of his *political* thesis, that it had acquired for itself unlimited power for the preservation of its independence as an instrument of administration. If Marx allowed this thesis to go unchallenged, the whole premise of his economically dominant class as the prime mover of history would fall through. That perhaps was why from *The German Ideology* (1846) onwards he started relegating bureaucracy to the background by reducing the importance annexed to it in his *Critique* three years earlier. The acceptance of bureaucracy as an independent entity would indeed have forced the introduction of a third dimension, dislocating his action-oriented scheme of a bourgeois–proletariat class war.

THE POWER-ELITE CONCEPT

The first outstanding advocate of the power-elite concept of bureaucracy was Gaetano Mosca, who held that bureaucracy signified rule by officials. His argument was that no social development was possible without a 'poiitical class', the ruling minority, which rendered any theory of democracy more or less nugatory. In fact, his analysis of politics in realistic terms made him sceptical about the effectiveness of parliamentary government insofar as its control over bureaucracy was concerned.

Like Marx, Mosca accepted the dominant-class theory as well as

---

[22] Cited in Shlomo Avineri, op cit., p. 50.
[23] See L.S. Fener (ed.), *Marx and Engels: Basic Writings on Politics and Philosophy,* p. 456.

the existence of class antagonism. But his was a power-based politically dominant class,[24] not an economic class. In other words, the eternal class struggles that went on were not between the bourgeois minority and the proletarian majority, but between an old minority defending its actual predominance and a new and ambitious minority determined to wrest power either with the object of fusing with the former or dethroning and replacing it. These class conflicts were mere struggles between successively dominant minorities, a continuous process of history, which would never cease, as Marx imagined, on the establishment of a classless society.

In *The Ruling Class* Mosca propounded his thesis in historical perspective:

In all societies—from societies that are very meagrely developed and have barely attained the dawnings of civilization, down to the most advanced and powerful societies—two classes of people appear—a class that rules and a class that is ruled. The first class, always the less numerous, performs all political functions, monopolizes power and enjoys the advantages that power brings, whereas the second, the more numerous class, is directed and controlled by the first, in a manner that is now more or less legal, now more or less arbitrary and violent, and supplies the first, in appearance at least, with material means of subsistence and with instrumentalities that are essential to the vitality of the political organism.[25]

Independent of a political organization, this ruling class might, according to Mosca, become subject to pressures arising from the discontent of the masses who are swayed by a variety of emotional confabulations constituting a threat to its power. But even when discontent or passion succeeds in the overthrow of a ruling class, there has to emerge another organized minority from 'within the masses themselves to discharge the functions of a ruling class. Otherwise all organizations, and the whole social structure would be destroyed'.[26] In fact, Mosca believed that this ruling class was the directive social group without which society could not exist. It is true that its elements were subject to frequent partial renewal. Even so, it constituted the only durable factor in human history. In support of this argument, Mosca tracked the transformation of society from one phase to another in different countries, and pointed out that while in

[24] Mosca believed that a politically dominant class must under all circumstances rest upon a major social force. See J.H. Meisel, *The Myth of the Ruling Class*, pp. 94–5. Meisel discarded that theory.

[25] *The Ruling Class*, p. 50.

[26] Ibid., p.51.

the feudal, agricultural phase the warrior, military barons were the dominant ruling class, enjoying exclusive ownership of land and control over administration, the growth of commerce and industry replaced military valour by wealth as 'the characteristic feature of the dominant class'. The men who came in the second phase were to rule 'the rich rather than the brave'.[27]

However, the basis of legitimacy for obedience to a ruling class was not merely its *de facto* possession of power, but a certain principle generally called the principle of sovereignty; a 'political formula', as Mosca called it, which answered a real need in man's social nature. According to the level of civilization, this formula might be based on theocracy or secularism, the divine right of kings or the divine right of elected assemblies, democracy and human dignity or class conflict and proletarian dictatorship. Social groups were divided according to their belief in, or opposition to, one or the other of these and several other foundations of loyalty to political authority. The political formula of a ruling class, as Mosca pointed out, flowed from the special beliefs and the strongest sentiments of the social group in which that formula or principle was current, or at least from the beliefs and sentiments of the particular portion of that group which enjoys political pre-eminence.

Mosca never bothered to define bureaucracy. Instead, he proceeded to divide all governments into two main categories, the feudal and the bureaucratic. He defined the former as a political organization 'in which all the executive functions of society—the economic, the judicial, the administrative, the military—are exercised simultaneously by the same individuals'.[28] The Europe of the Middle Ages offered the most familiar example where 'the medieval baron was simultaneously owner of land, military commander, judge and administrator of his fief, over which he enjoyed both a pure and mixed sovereignty'.[29] In the bureaucratic state, on the other hand, not all the executive functions 'need to be concentrated in the bureaucracy and exercised by it', Mosca defined it as a political organization with an extensive number of public services receiving their 'salaries' from the government for the performance of 'public duties' demanding 'a greater specialization' of functions, 'a far greater discipline in all grades of political, administrative and military service'.[30] The

---

[27] Ibid., p. 57.
[28] See J.H. Meisel, *The Myth of the Ruling Class*, pp. 196–206.
[29] Mosca. *The Ruling Class*, p. 81.
[30] Ibid., pp. 81–5.

bureaucratic organization being essentially rule-bound, the personal qualities or the supreme head of the state were not as significant as in a feudal system, 'Under a bureaucratic organization', as Mosca pointed out, 'society is influenced less by the given individual leader than by the ruling class as a whole'.[31]

Though conceptually undefined, bureaucracy was identified with a body of public officials who not only formed an integral part of the ruling class, but who also defined the characteristic features of public administration in the modern state. Since he did not attribute to his ruling class a monolithic character and rejected the Marxian notion of an identity of interest among those similarly situated in a social class, he conceived of bureaucracy as not altogether destructive of liberty, except in a situation where it monopolized both wealth and military power. To prevent it from becoming absolute, Mosca recommended the mechanism of the vote, which reflected the varied interests and talents of society.

Vilfredo Pareto, the ablest exponent of Mosca's theory, elaborated the principle of minority rule by a reference to what he called the substitution of one group of the dominant classes by another. His in fact was a theory of the circulation of elites, propounded in his *Theorie de la circulation des elites*. It was a theory of replacement of one group of elites by another, applicable more to a purely representative government where a constitutional opposition like that in England, for example, aimed at such a circulation, a substitution of the party in power without altering the basic structure of the government. In this sense Pareto even regarded socialism as a means to the creation of a new working class elite.

In his *First Lectures in Political Sociology* Robert Michels held the same view as Pareto, with the reservation however that the circulation of elites was a continuous process of interaction, the old elements attracting, persisting and even assimilating the new. Discussing the relative position of the elite and the proletariat, Michels wrote:

Does an elite exist in the proletariat, and if it exists, does it remain in the bosom of the proletariat? Experience shows us that there is an elite, but that it does not remain in the proletariat. The educated worker elevates himself from his social stratum. The very fact that he emerges makes him change his social membership. As the superior stratum of the middle class aspires to enter into nobility in an aristocratic country, so the proletariat aims to form a part of the middle class.

[31] Ibid., p. 85.

Michels called this process of intermixture the 'law of imitation, the impulse towards 'social capillarity' by which inferiors move towards superiors in a free society, promoting freedom of movement in social space.[32]

Quoting researches on the origins of illustrious men, Michels showed that 30 per cent of the celebrated men came from the official class, 25 per cent from the nobility, 27 per cent from the liberal professions and only 10 per cent from the less wealthy classes. In terms of the degree of elite circulation, these figures might vary from class to class and from country to country. But the principle of social mobility arising from a continuous process of interaction between groups or classes could not ordinarily be challenged.

And since bureaucracy, besides being an administrative organization, was also a social class, the principle of elite circulation applied to it as well as to any other group or class. Like Mosca, Michels assumed that the immediate concern of bureaucracy was the exercise of power. But the latter was conscious of both the political and organizational aspects of bureaucratic functioning. He believed that it was an instrument through which the politically dominant class exercised control over the rest of society. It was not a force in its own right. He therefore discussed it in the context of political parties whose oligarchical and bureaucratic character was a matter of practical and technical necessity.

The Marxist theory of the state, of its being an instrument of the ruling class, was admitted by Mosca and his school. But the possibility of a classless social order emerging from the socialization of the means of production was considered utopian, contrary to historical experience. Even if it was assumed that on the seizure of political power by the proletariat, private property would become transformed into public property; that no social differences or class antagonisms would remain and that the proletariat would in that situation put an end to the state, the result would be the ending of the dominant class. But who would administer the social wealth so created? The answer was bound to be a bureaucracy, far more extensive than the one required in a capitalist system. It may be argued that an elected party cadre could bridge the gap. But since salaried officials are not peculiar in modern times to the state alone, the suggested alternative would necessarily involve the creation of a large, complex party organization, with full-time paid employees, possessing specialized

[32] *First Lectures in Political Sociology*, pp. 80–1.

skills and functioning under the control of leaders who, by virtue of their education and ideological commitment, may in turn be expected to manage a hierarchy of government and party officials. Professionally, both the leadership and the officials, even if elected, would in terms of power categories and cultural standards be differentiated from the general membership of the party, remaining outside the portals of power, or more especially from the mass of the people who, in a monolithic political system, may not have the freedom to choose an opposition party. There is in fact no escape from bureaucracy as part of a ruling class. Functionally, it is indispensable. Under a socialist system or one-party dictatorship its role tends to be all the more pervasive.

Drawing data from history, therefore, Robert Michels not only built on Mosca's minority-rule thesis in relation to the functioning of parties, but extended the operation of that principle to all other organizations including bureaucracy. In his *Political Parties*, for instance, he highlighted the oligarchical nature not only of parties, but of all large-scale modern organizations.

The principle that one dominant class inevitably succeeds another, and the law deduced from that principle that oligarchy is, as it were, a preordained form of the common life of the great social aggregates, far from conflicting with or replacing the materialist conception of history, completes that conception and reinforces it. There is no contradiction between the doctrine that history is a record of a continued series of class struggles and the doctrine that class struggles invariably culminate in the creation of new oligarchies which undergo fusion with the old. The existence of a political class does not conflict with the essential content of Marxism, considered not as an economic dogma but as a philosophy of history: for in each particular instance, the dominance of a political class arises as the resultant of the relationships between the different social forces competing for supremacy, these forces being of course considered dynamically and not quantitatively.[33]

Proceeding from the Marxian premise that the state is no more than a mere agent of the ruling class, Mosca and his followers not only denied the possibility of a state without classes, but also emphasized, in the light of their general political formulations, that the eternal process of class conflict, besides being basic to the understanding of historical movements, was really advantageous to society. Consistent with their political views, both Mosca and Michels agreed that bureaucracy was a necessity in the modern state, but that

[33] *Political Parties*, p. 407.

the scope of its activity should be limited. However, while Mosca restricted his analysis of bureaucracy to the limited field of public administration, Michels extended its scope to all modern organizations which, he thought, were invariably subject to 'the iron law of oligarchy'. This element of determinism in his approach to bureaucracy constituted an advance over Mosca's concept. But the concept of both remained essentially simple, limited to a body of salaried officials hierarchically organized on the basis of specialization and functional differentiation. It was of course linked with the sociology of power, administration and authority. But their concept was not developed in any depth or refinement. It was Max Weber who did both, digging deeper and doing the refining.

THE WEBERIAN CONCEPT—A SYNTHETIC APPROACH

The Weberian concept of bureaucracy was based on a sociological analysis which united in a single frame of reference both political and organizational dimensions. The contributions of Max Weber were in this respect by far the most outstanding. He not only formulated his concept theoretically and established the connection of bureaucracy as an administrative organization with politics and society, but imparted to his technical definition a degree of clarity and sophistication never attained before. In his technical definition he was concerned exclusively with the mode of administration and the type of administrators. It had nothing to do with the pejorative aspect of bureaucratic administration.

Weber's starting point was his theory of organization, a central issue applicable not only to bureaucracy, but to all other modern organizations, social or economic. From his broad organizational premise where he analysed the conceptual distinctions of power, administration and authority, he proceeded to the analysis of bureaucracy in two parts, the first dealing with the general concept, and the second with the pure or rational type known also as the 'ideal type'. From the analysis of the pure type he went on to democracy where, unlike Michels who held that bureaucracy and democracy were opposite and mutually exclusive categories, Weber attempted to show that, since the specific nature of modern administration and the control of the apparatus of the modern state were conceptually distinct, the two systems could very well coexist. He suggested the application of a number of checks to make this co-existence a practical proposition.

Organizational Analysis

Weber's analysis of organization formed part of his exposition of basic sociological concepts.[34] It comprehended within its scope such differing institutions as the state, the political party, the church, the sect and the firm. He used the term *Verband*, the German equivalent of the English term 'organization', which Henderson and Parsons later translated as 'corporate group'. The idea of a corporate group is that admission to it is limited by the rulers, and social relationships within the group are ordered and enforced by the action of specific individuals whose regular function is to maintain that ordering. The organizational or corporate group concept is also inclusive of a chief or 'head' *(Leiter)*, usually with an administrative staff. The existence of such a corporate group in fact results from the presence of a person in authority, 'the governing authority composing the incumbency of a directing position or participation in the functions of the administrative staff'.[35]

The existence of a set of rules governing action or behaviour was, according to Weber, basic to the concept of an organization. It was necessary to distinguish between what was and what was not organizational behaviour. These rules governing corporate action formed part of a system of order which Weber preferred to call an 'administrative' order regulating `not only the action of the administrative staff, but also that of the members in their direct relations to the corporate group'.[36]

Connected with administrative order was the important question of a conceptual distinction between power and authority employed to enforce obedience to that order. According to Weber, a person could be said to have 'power' if 'within a social relationship' he 'will be in a position to carry out his own will despite resistance'.[37] It was a broad and comprehensive concept, sociologically amorphous. It signified that 'all conceivable qualities and all conceivable combinations of circumstances may put him in a position to impose his will in a given situation'.[38] The concept of 'authority', on the other hand, was more precise and definite. It was a special instance of power, where 'a command with a given specific content will be obeyed by a given

[34] See A.M. Henderson and T. Parsons (tr.), *The Theory of Social and Economic Organizations*.
[35] Ibid., p. 146.
[36] Ibid., p. 150.
[37] Ibid., p. 152.
[38] Ibid., p. 153.

group of persons'.[39] The existence of authority or 'imperative control', as Weber put it, implied 'the actual presence of one person successfully issuing orders to others', even independently of the existence of an administrative staff. In fact, 'every form of authority expresses itself and functions as administration', while every form of administration in some way requires authority, since its 'direction demands that some sort of power to command is vested in someone'.[40]

In terms of the theory of organization, Weber was one of the leading founders of the Structuralist school, which represented a synthesis of the classical (formal) approach and assumed that the most efficient organization would be the most satisfying to its participants; and the human relations (informal) approach which held that the most satisfying organization would be the most efficient. While the classical school emphasized increasing productivity and economic rewards as satisfying to both the management and the workers, the focus of the human relations school was on non-economic social incentives, with increasing workers' participation as a condition for efficiency and greater output. The interests of both schools were however limited to industrial and business concerns. The Structuralists were the first to enlarge the scope of their analysis by an extension of the area of inquiry to such establishments as hospitals and prisons, churches and armies, political parties and the bureaucracy. In so doing, they did not interfere with the formal or 'rational' elements of analysis dealing with power to control, especially in relation to the administration of political organizations. Although Max Weber, for instance, recognized that the use of physical force was neither the sole, nor even the more usual, method in such organization, 'the threat of force, and in case of need its actual use, is the method which is specific to political associations and is always the last resort when others have failed'.[41] The Structuralists in fact entered into a serious dialogue with the human relations school, the object being to control the participants in a manner which might maximize effectiveness and efficiency, and minimize the unhappiness which the need to control tended to produce. The Structuralist recognition of informal or non-rational methods to secure organizational discipline followed from this dialogue, and were all designed to make a formal system of order persuasive and conformtable to the values acknowledged by the participants.

[39] Ibid., p. 152.
[40] Quoted in Martin Albrow, *Bureaucracy*, p. 39.
[41] Henderson and Parsons (tr.), op cit., p. 154.

The main source of irritation, as Weber pointed out, was the manner in which power was exercised in a formal organization. Compliance could be deeper and more effective if only the exercise of that power was seen as legitimate by those subject to it. Like Michels, he also referred to the theory of minority power in modern organizations. But while explaining the inevitable rule of oligarchy, he opened up a whole new perspective on organizational discipline by stressing that obedience to command was a function of belief in legitimacy, a belief that the orders given were justified and that it was right to obey. This belief constituted the foundations of all authority. It lent prestige to the person exercising it.[42]

Norms of Authority

Consistent with different forms of belief in the legitimacy of authority, Weber formulated different authority structures, such as 'charismatic authority', 'traditional authority' and 'legal authority'. Obedience to charismatic authority was justified on the ground of a certain quality by virtue of which the individual leader 'was set apart from ordinary men and treated as endowed with supernatural, superhuman, or at least specifically exceptional powers or qualities'.[43] This obedience was paid to the leader as personal trust and part of a spiritual and moral duty. His followers were personal disciples. He owed no obligations to them, such as were essential to the holder of office. Authority was referred to as traditional when the orders of superiors were obeyed on grounds that this was the way things were always done. Its basis of legitimacy was 'the sanctity of the order and the attendant powers of control as they have been handed down from the past'.[44] Here, as in the case of charismatic authority, the nature of the loyalty paid was personal. Obedience was to the person concerned, not to any officer. And this he enjoyed by virtue of his traditional status according to traditionally transmitted rules, not of charisma, or even of enacted rules which characterized legal authority. The person exercising traditional authority was not a 'superior', but a personal 'chief'.

The administrative staff of the person in traditional authority, as Weber pointed out, does not consist primarily of officials, but of personal retainers. Those subject to authority are not members of an association, but are either his traditional comrades or his subjects.

[42] Ibid., p. 382.
[43] Ibid., p. 358.
[44] Ibid., p. 341.

What determines the relations of the administrative staff to the chief is not the impersonal obligation of office, but personal loyalty to the 'chief'.[45]

The basis of legal authority, on the other hand, was 'a belief in the legality of patterns of normative rules and the right of those elevated to authority under such rules to issue commands'.[46]

General Concept of Bureaucracy

Of the three categories, legal authority alone was considered 'rational', a quality which constituted the most important feature of a modern organization, the fountain source of Weber's general concept of bureaucracy. This con cept did not recognize all officials as part of bureaucracy. Those who happened to be elected, were specially excluded. To him bureaucracy signified a collective term for a body of appointed officials. This of course was in line with the views of Mosca and Michels. Weber additionally specified certain general organizational features of legal authority. These included a set of five beliefs, constituting its foundation, and eight fundamental forms of rational legal authority characterizing an organized administrative staff peculiar to bureaucratic structure.[47]

The set of five beliefs were:

1. That a legal norm can be established either by agreement or by imposition with a claim to obedience on the part of the members of a corporate group or organization.

2. That the law is a system of abstract rules covering all possible cases of conduct within the organization, the administration of law being the application of these rules to particular cases.

3. The fundamental sources of authority in the legal type is the authority to the impersonal order of an officer holding a specifically legitimized status under the rules with powers to issue commands.

4. That the person who obeys authority does so in his capacity as a member of the corporate group and what he obeys is only the law.

5. That the members of the corporate group, in so far as they obey person in authority, do not owe this obedience to him as an individual, but to the impersonal order. In other words, there is an obligation to obedience only within the sphere of the rationally delimited authority which, in terms of the order, has been conferred upon him.

[45] Ibid., p. 341.
[46] Ibid., p. 328.
[47] Ibid., pp. 329–32.

Weber's five beliefs were thus founded on the legitimacy of enacted rules and the impersonality of a command issued by a person invested with authority. He ignored the importance of the man who issued an order under the rules. For he believed that no order would be considered legally rational if it was to be influenced by the person issuing it and not by the abstract rules under which it must be issued. Weber in fact allowed law to supersede man.

The eight fundamental principles of rational legal authority, on the other hand, included the organization of official functions on a continuous rule-bound basis; a specified sphere of competence and of distinct functions based on a systematic division of labour; the principle of hierarchy, with a lower office under the control and supervision of a higher one; trained personnel for the conduct of business; complete separation of members of the administrative staff from the ownership of the means of production or administration, with a clear separation likewise in principle of the property belonging to the organization and controlled within the sphere of office, and the personal property of the official available for private use; a complete absence of appropriation of official position by the incumbent; the formulation and recording in writing of all acts, decisions and rules; and the ideal type being the purest form of legal authority or 'imperative co-ordination'.

The Ideal Type

The five concepts of legitimacy and the eight principles of rational-legal authority together constituted Weber's general concept of bureaucracy, applicable to all forms of modern corporate groups, political, religious or otherwise. These applied equally to the bureaucratic administrative staff based on what Weber called the imperative co-ordination of the 'ideal type', capable of leading itself to generalization. He associated with this type certain additional characteristics which, though overlapping in some cases, imparted a focus of its own. He pointed out that the purest ideal type of legal authority was that which employed a bureaucratic administrative staff, where the authority even of the supreme head of the organization holding a position by election or appropriation, consisted in a sphere of legal competence. The whole administrative staff under that supreme authority consisted of individual appointed officials.[48] These officials were personally free and subject to authority only in respect of their

[48] See Henderson and Parsons (tr.), op cit., pp. 333–4.

impersonal official obligations. They were organized in a well-defined hierarchy of offices[49] filled by a free contractual relationship. Their appointment was preceded by selection, made on the basis of technical qualifications tested by examination and guaranteed by diplomas certifying them. The officials so appointed were to be remunerated by fixed salaries, mostly with a right to pensions and the grading of salaries according to rank in the hierarchy. Weber insisted that the office in a legally rational system must be treated as the sole, or at least the primary, occupation of its holder, for it constituted a career, with a system of promotion according to seniority, or achievement, or both. The ideal type of bureaucracy was in fact to be governed by strict and systematic discipline and control in the conduct of the office.

These features constituted the essentials of the pure bureaucratic administration, known also as monocratic. Weber treated these as completely indispensable, the choice only being that between bureaucracy and dilettantism. He believed in the inevitability of the bureaucratic process which in effect meant the growth of the several 'rational' features. He made it clear that even socialist organization could not alter the fact except by reversion through decentralization to small-scale organization in every field of human activity. The extended functions of the state under a socialist system would in fact demand a still higher degree of formal bureaucratization than in capitalism, the father of the rational bureaucratic system.

When Weber spoke of the purely rational type as by far the best form of administration, he had in mind certain peculiar advantages that followed specially from it—precision, speed, reliability, discipline, continuity, operational uniformity, discretion, and provision for the reduction of friction. However, one of the main criticisms directed against his legal-dominance theory is that he emphasized more the office than the officer. Herbert A. Simon, for instance, contends that there are certain obvious limits to rationality which seriously affect 'efficiency'. These include limits on the ability of the office-holder to perform and make correct decisions; the speed of his

---

[49] Weber's conception of hierarchy was based on the principle of appointment. 'There is no such thing', he said, 'as a hierarchy of elected officials in the same sense as there is a hierarchical organization of appointed officials. In the first place election makes it impossible to attain a stringency of discipline even approaching that in the appointed type. For it is open to a subordinate official to compete for elective honours on the same terms as his superiors, and his prospects are not dependent on the superior's judgement, Appointment by free contract, which makes free selection possible, is essential to modern bureaucracy,' Ibid., p. 335.

mental processes; his values, ideas and purpose, which influence decisions, and his loyalty to the organization; and, above all, the extent of his knowledge of matters related to his job.[50] Weber was aware of the limitations of men, not only in terms of decision-making but more so in terms of applying a decision to an individual case. What was basic to his conception of bureaucracy, however, was the idea of calculability, a logical sequence of the rule of law, which took into account this reservation. For he said:[51]

[The calculability of decision-making] and with it its appropriateness for capitalism. ... [is] the more fully realized the more bureaucracy 'depersonalizes' itself, i.e., the more completely it succeeds in achieving the exclusion of love, hatred, and every purely personal, especially irrational and incalculable, feeling from the execution of official tasks. In the place of the old-type ruler who is moved by sympathy, favour, grace and gratitude, modern culture requires for its sustaining external apparatus, the emotionally detached, and hence rigorously 'professional', expert.

Max Weber thus used the efficiency of the pure type in a relative sense. This efficiency increases only to the extent that it 'depersonalizes' the execution of official tasks. The idea of administrative impersonality too had its limitations and Weber seemed to have taken note of that also. For he drew a line between discretionary activity in modern administration and the personally motivated favours meted to individuals in the name of discretion under pre-bureaucratic systems. The former was based on the rule of law, on the supremacy of the impersonal objectives ascertainable by rational discussion and grounds for justification. Unlike the latter, it was not arbitrary. Weber in fact rejected the principle of decision-making which differed from case to case. Under a monocratic system there was no recognition of social and economic differentiation in so far as the exercise of authority was concerned. It was to be exercised according to rules, and everyone subject to that authority was legally equal.

This conception of legal equality tended to bring about a corresponding change in the system of education, a national system providing for equal eligibility for education to ensure equal eligibility for administrative appointments. In short, educational degrees and diplomas came to replace social and economic privilege as the basis of recruitment. However, the increasing importance of technical expertise from which the power of modern bureaucracy proceeded, tended

[50] See R.K. Merton (ed.), *Reader in Bureaucracy*, pp. 51–8.
[51] Cited in Reinhard Bendix. *Max Weber: An Intellectual Portrait*. pp. 423–4.

to bring in its train a problem of human culture in that the importance of the cultivated man seemed to wane before the expert. Classical literature, which earlier fostered the cultivation of the mind, was yielding place to science and technology. The inequality which earlier arose from social and economic gaps came to be substituted by another kind of inequality proceeding from increasing specialization. The problem which a modern bureaucratic organization was thus called upon to resolve was how best to strike a balance, to have the best of both worlds by means of a happy integration of technology and culture.

Weber did not fail to recognize that increasing bureaucratization meant corresponding accession to the power of officials. He also realized that the source of that power was the exercise of control on the basis of knowledge, not only of the art and science of government, but more so of the factual data acquired through experience in the service. Even so, he did not identify bureaucracy with rule by officials. Conceptually, he considered them separate and distinct from the political apparatus of the modern state. He was aware of the tendency on the part of officials to accumulate power and control the action of leaders. In order to check such a tendency he suggested the use of a number of mechanisms. These included decision-making on the principle of collegiality; the separation of powers; the association of amateur elements with public administration; democratic decentralization as a form of direct democracy; and, above all, a representative form of government which, though by no means ideal, steered a middle course between mass irrationality and bureaucratic tyranny. Weber believed that elected non-bureaucratic heads fulfilled an important function in lending emotional or non-rational psychological support to bureaucratic rationality, reinforcing abstract commitment to organizational rules.

Democracy has limitations, arising from the operation of political parties through which it functions. As Mosca and Michels pointed out, the internal structure of parties is oligarchic. Maurice Duverger agrees with them in the criticism of party-based democracy:

Their internal structure is essentially autocratic and oligarchic: their leaders are not really appointed by the members, but co-opted and nominated by the central body; they tend to form a ruling class, isolated from the militants, a caste that is more or less exclusive. ... Parties create opinion as much as they represent it; they form it by propaganda; they compose a prefabricated mould upon it. ... Growing centralization is increasingly diminishing the influence of members over leaders. ... Parliamentary representatives themselves are compelled to an obedience which transforms them into voting machines controlled by the leaders of the party. Thus there arise closed, disciplined, mechanized bodies, monolithic parties ... [which] become totalitarian.[52]

Schumpeter went further and observed that democracy 'does not mean and cannot mean that the people actually rule in any obvious sense of the terms "people" and "rule". Democracy means only that the people have the opportunity of accepting or rejecting the men who are to rule them. ... Democracy is the rule of the politician.'[53]

Though agreeing with his predecessors' premises, Duverger draws a conclusion which lends support to the case for democracy. He points out, and rightly so, that while the representative system made it possible to form a ruling class from amongst the people to replace the old, political parties were necessary to have democratic opinion effectively represented. These in addition created new elites which rendered the notion of representation really meaningful: democracy in that case became 'a government of the people by an elite springing from the people'.[54] Though essentially a minority, no ruling party could afford for all time to ignore the views and interests of the people, the fountain source of all alternative power elites.

The functioning of the ballot box in a free and fair away has indeed enormous potential for peaceful change. The success of democracy, especially in developing societies, depends however on a cultural reorientation of both the elected representative and bureaucracy. It calls for a spirit of understanding on the part of both, so that flexibility is not sacrificed to rules nor rules sacrificed to flexibility. It is difficult to adjust politics to administration and *vice versa*, requiring not only sophisticated skill but also moral quality. Politicians and bureaucrats must learn to live together in mutual respect. That perhaps is why Schumpeter advised the pursuit of politics as a career,[55] like administration.

A SUMMING-UP

Briefly, the term bureaucracy signifies two main things, a type of administrative organization and a form of rule or system of government. The first is technical in approach, the second political.

[52] Duverger, *Political Parties*, pp. 422–3.
[53] *Capitalism, Socialism and Democracy* (2nd ed., 1947), pp. 284–5.
[54] Duverger, op cit. p. 425.
[55] *Capitalism, Socialism and Democracy*, p. 285.

Technically, a bureaucracy is an impermeable and complex hierarchy, its emphasis being on the principles of organization, recruitment, education, training, conditions of service, rules of business, and so on. In other words, it deals with the machine and the whole structure of rules designed to keep the machine together.

Politically, on the other hand, bureaucracy is a form of government with officials either acting as rulers themselves, or co-existing with elected executives, but connected conceptually in all cases with the exercise of authority as members of a class of power elites.[56] It has to deal with man, a social being with a bundle of complexes, psychic and sociological, and its dealings extend to society as a whole.

A bureaucracy which unites in its functioning both technical and political dimensions thus presents a difficult problem for analysis. The problem is not only to strike the highest common denominator in the formulation of rules, which by itself is an impossible task in view of the existence of social and economic antagonisms; but even if rules are well drawn, their execution is bedevilled by the interplay of varied interests, values and other irrational elements injected through the agency of individuals and groups into the rationally planned and established bureaucratic machine. These difficulties become all the more pronounced because of the organizational complexities resulting from the 'Parkinsonian' capacity of administration to keep on expanding.

However, all that needs to be emphasized here is that, independently of its pejorative features, bureaucracy or, in other words, a body of full-time professional administrators organized hierarchically in departments, has come to stay as an indispensable instrument of all governments. The issue is not whether or not bureaucratization is dispensable. The question is that of emphasis. Should the emphasis be on the technique of administration, on its mechanical, impersonal and professional aspects having immediate relevance to speed, economy and efficiency, or should it be on bureaucracy as a class of power-elites exercising control over society either for its own sake, or for the sake of an ideology, or a combination of both? If the emphasis is on the technique, it is clear that modern administration is the result of a long process of change, especially since the eighteenth and nineteenth centuries. Max Weber not only elaborated the formal, technical aspect of bureaucracy, but also raised it to the height of theoretical

---

[56] See Harold D. Lasswell and A. Kaplan, *Power and Society: A Framework of Political Inquiry*, pp. 205–6, 209–10.

sophistication. But if focus is shifted to the analysis of power, bureaucracy gets immediately involved in a maze of controversy, the central theme being the manner in which power is distributed and exercised. It divides government and society into groups based on religion, language, economic interests and so on, each competing for a share in power which not only gives status and prestige, but also opens out prospects for better living standards. The social pressure so generated tends to weaken the foundations of the competitive system on which selection is ordinarily expected to be made in a rule-bound bureaucracy.

This situation applies specially to developing societies in a multicultural country with considerable imbalance in the educational and economic development of regional and cultural units. In Western countries, however, modern administration came to function professionally as a more or less separate entity, in spite of changes in the political complexion of government. This ensured continuity in their administrative processes and administrative policy. The continuity so ensured imparted to their bureaucratic system a non-committed impersonal character. This in turn enabled civil servants in the West to function anonymously and to exercise a considerable degree of independence in their own right despite changes in society and politics. Bureaucracy remained a merit-based non-committed institution.

The principle of political non-commitment however did not apply to the Soviet Union. With the Communist Party under Lenin and his followers the old bureaucracy acquired a strong pejorative overtone. It was viewed as a hangover of the capitalist state, hostile to socialism and Soviet rule. It was believed that once the final stage of social evolution was reached with the coming into being of a true communist society, the state would wither away and so would its administrative bureaucracy. In other words, 'the government of persons [would be] replaced by the administration of things and the direction of the process of production'.[57] It was perhaps assumed that human activity in a communist society would remain limited to the process of production in fields and factories and that other activities would keep moving automatically. But this was no more than a dream, a result of ideological obsession.

In *The State and the Revolution* (1917) Lenin pointed out that the old bourgeoisie state had to be smashed and followed by a dictatorship of the proletariat before the withering away of the state. He envisaged

[57] Engels cited in Aylmer, op cit. p. 457.

the establishment of a new state after the revolution with a highly centralized government of the proletariat organized into Soviets, of workers and soldier deputies. He did not rule out the presence of officials. He simply wanted to see that they did not become bureaucrats, 'privileged persons divorced from the people and standing above the people'.[58] But he could not prevent officials from becoming bureaucrats in the technical sense of the term. For no process of production, much less socialist or communist, could be administered without the involvement of an organized human agency. Even politically, the influence of the old bureaucracy did not go. In 1920, the Ninth Congress of the Communist Party of the Soviet Union attacked what it called bureaucratic centralism.[59] The allegation was repeated in 1921 when demands were made for the expulsion of non-proletarian elements from the administration and the suppression of bureaucracy from the Party itself.[60] Lenin himself admitted his failure to smash the old apparatus and tried to explain it away as a survival of the bourgeois hangover.[61] But there was no escape. In a report to the Sixteenth Congress in 1930 Stalin referred to the emergence of communist bureaucrats and assured the Congress that he would take steps to rid both the Party and government of bureaucratic tendencies.[62] Even so, these tendencies have continued.

Ironically, the most serious of all recent attacks on the communist bureaucracy has come from Milovan Djilas, an ex-communist and former Vice-President of Yugoslavia. In *The New Class* he describes the Communist Party itself as a bureaucracy, a ruling class that exercises power of a particular type, 'a power which has become an end in itself'.[63] Instances are common where social classes maintain ownership without a monopoly over power, or power without a monopoly over ownership. The case of the Soviet Union is one where power and ownership of state property are both united in the Central Committee of the Communist Party.

As regards personnel administration, the policy governing placement depends not only on the norms set by the Ministry of Finance and on the procedures laid down by the Ministries concerned, but

[58] *Collected Work*, xxv, pp. 486–7.
[59] See R.V. Daniels, *The Conscience of the Revolution: Opposition in Soviet Russia*, pp. 115–18.
[60] Ibid., p. 145.
[61] See A.G. Meyer, *Leninism*, p. 214.
[62] See J. Stalin, *Leninism*, ii, pp. 372–3.
[63] *The New Class*, p. 167.

also on the Central Committee of the Communist Party. Agencies of the Party specifically mark out such positions as have to be filled only with its prior approval. These agencies also prepare rosters of persons whom they consider trustworthy for specified jobs. The Soviet Union is in fact a party state where the Communist Party also uses and disposes of state property, not by free vote or consent but by an appeal to ideology and force.

As a large-scale organization the Party itself is highly bureaucratized, with provision for paid workers who are given political as well as professional training. In 1962 between 150,000 and 200,000 persons, or some four per cent of its membership, were paid Party workers; the actual number was probably higher, since many held temporary assignments in various institutions. Through higher Party schools first established in 1946, this cadre of activists has become increasingly professionalized; by 1956 there were 29 Party schools officially rated as institutions of higher education, offering a four-year curriculum.[64]

The Communist bureaucracy is thus not only a bureaucracy of public service, but also of political life, an example of administration and politics being fused together, a committed bureaucracy, but a bureaucracy none the less. It presupposes the existence of a party state as an absolute condition.

[64] *International Encyclopaedia of the Social Sciences*, p. 212.

CHAPTER TWO

The Ideal Type of Bureaucracy*

Nicos P. Mouzelis

Weber's ideal type of bureaucracy has been, especially since the war, the starting point and the main source of inspiration for many students of organization. At the same time it has been the object of criticism and long controversies. As such, it is important to analyse and criticize it in some detail and to pay particular attention to the way in which it has been used by modern students of bureaucracy. The first section of this chapter comments on the Weberian characteristics of bureaucracy, especially on the way in which they were used in recent organization literature. The second section is mainly an assessment of the logical status and the methodological functions of the ideal type. In the third section, different modern uses of the term bureaucracy and their links to the ideal type are briefly discussed.

SOME COMMENTS ON THE CHARACTERISTICS OF BUREAUCRACY

The ideal type of bureaucracy is a conceptual construction of certain empirical elements into a logically precise and consistent form, a form which, in its ideal purity, is never to be found in concrete reality.[1] The detailed way in which this form is constructed will be examined in the second section. For the moment, we shall only be concerned with the empirical elements which refer to the various characteristics of bureaucracy. Indeed, the characteristics contained in the ideal type, although transformed and exaggerated in a certain

---

* Nicos P. Mouzelis, *Organisation and Bureaucracy: An Analysis of Modern Theories*, Routledge & Kegan Paul, London, 1975 (reprint).
[1] Cf. M. Weber, *On the Methodology of the Social Sciences*, Glencoe, III, 1949, pp. 90–3.

way, correspond, more or less, to concrete features of existing organizations. Briefly, the main characteristics of the bureaucratic type of organization are:

- High degree of specialization
- Hierarchical authority structure with limited areas of command and responsibility
- Impersonality of relationships between organizational members
- Recruitment of officials on the basis of ability and technical knowledge
- Differentiation of private and official income and fortune and so on.

Now, if one tries to see what lies beyond the above characteristics, how they are linked with one another, one finds a common, all pervasive element; the existence of a system of control based on rational rules, rules which try to regulate the whole organizational structure and process on the basis of technical knowledge and with the aim of maximum efficiency.

Bureaucratic administration means fundamentally the exercise of control on the basis of knowledge. This is the feature of it which makes it specifically rational.[2]

So from this general point of view, what makes an organization more or less bureaucratic is not simply the existence of rules, but the quality of these rules. Feudal administration also controlled organizational action through rules.[3] But the decisive difference between it and a bureaucracy is that these rules were not based on technical knowledge and rational thinking but on tradition. The above point must always be kept in mind when one deals with the ideal typical features of bureaucracy. This will become clearer by a brief discussion of the ways in which some of the above characteristics have been used by modern writers.

The Nature of Bureaucratic Hierarchy

Modern theorists of bureaucracy, basing their views on Weber, often use the hierarchy characteristics as one of the most decisive criteria for finding out to what degree an organization is bureaucratized. For example, Stanley Udy Jr., wanting to make this criterion operational, decided that from the hierarchical point of view, an organization

---

[2] Weber, *The Theory of Social and Economic Organization*, p. 311.

[3] 'Traditional Authority is bound to the precedents handed down from the past and to this extent is also oriented to rules', ibid., p. 322.

should be labelled bureaucratic if it had three or more levels of authority.[4] Other authors use the term hierarchy in general as a feature of bureaucratic organization, without specifying in what sense, a hierarchy constitutes a bureaucratic characteristic.[5] In this way, they imply that any kind of hierarchy is a bureaucratic characteristic, an implication which is not correct, at least in the Weberian sense.

Actually hierarchy in general (in the sense of levels of authority) is to be found in any administration which has a certain degree of magnitude and complexity. The feudal type of administration had a complicated hierarchical system. 'There is hierarchy of a social rank corresponding to the hierarchy of fiefs through the process of sub-infeudation ... '[6] But the difference between the two kinds of hierarchies, according to Weber, is to be found in the type of authority relations. In the feudal case the relationship between inferior and superior is personal and the legitimation of authority is based on a belief in the sacredness of tradition. In a bureaucracy, authority is legitimized by a belief in the correctness of the rules and the loyalty of the bureaucrat is oriented to an impersonal order, to a superior position, not to the person who holds it (cf. chapter 2, section 2). So what makes an administration more or less bureaucratic from the hierarchical point of view is not the number of levels of authority, or the size of the span of control; the decisive criterion is whether or not the authority relations have a precise and impersonal character, as a result of the elaboration of rational rules.

Hierarchy and Discretion

Another point for comment on the hierarchical characteristics of Weber's model is the problem of discretion: the relation between initiative and discipline. Monroe Berger,[7] who bases his analysis of the Egyptian bureaucracy on Weber's concept, uses as one of the criteria of bureaucratization of an organization the high degree of discretion that an official has in the performance of his duties,

[4] 'Bureaucracy and rationality in Weber's organisation theory: an empirical study', *American Sociological Review*, vol. 24 (1959), pp. 791–5.

[5] For example M. Berger in constituting a bureaucratic scale, has used hierarchy as one of the criteria of bureaucratization. He defines it in such general terms as emphasis upon the prerogatives of position, upon authority and obedience. But one could object that a feudal administration or any other type of administration has also a hierarchy emphasizing prerogatives and obedience (cf. M. Berger, *Bureaucracy and Society in Modern Egypt*, Princeton, 1957, p. 49).

[6] Weber, *The Theory of Social and Economic Organization*, p. 344.

[7] Berger, p. 49.

discretion being defined as an emphasis upon personal judgement and initiative, acceptance of responsibility and full use of discretionary powers within the rules. It is indeed very problematical if this characteristic can be called bureaucratic in a real or in an ideal sense.

On the one hand it is true that Weber in his discussion about hierarchy in the ideal model, left room for both centralized and decentralized systems of authority.

Hierarchies defer in respect to whether and in what cases complaints can lead to a ruling from an authority at various points higher in the scale, and as to whether changes are imposed from higher up or the responsibility for such changes is left to the lower office, the conduct of which was the subject of complaint.[8]

Moreover, it is clear that by the strict delineation of the areas of command, the bureaucrat, outside his official role, is much more free and independent of his superior than any other type of official.

But on the other hand, within the area of the office and concerning the ways in which a bureaucrat performs his duties, there is no doubt that for Weber's ideal type his discretion is minimized by strict procedural rules. These rules, aiming at the avoidance of any arbitrary action, imposing strict discipline and control, do not leave much room for initiative and discretion. 'In the great majority of cases he (the bureaucrat) is only a simple cog in an ever-moving mechanism which prescribes to him an essentially fixed route of march.'[9] Moreover, one arrives at the same conclusion if the problem is placed in the larger context of Weber's philosophy of history. The trend towards increasing bureaucratization in the modern world is very closely linked with a decrease in individual freedom (cf. chapter 2, section 2).

So we must conclude that although he does not explicitly elaborate this point, Weber not only does not include the concept of discretion in his ideal type, but rather he does the contrary. In order to rationalize and make an administrative machine efficient, one has to control and guide administrative behaviour by strict rational rules—thus limiting individual initiative to a minimum.

Administration and Organization

Does the ideal type of bureaucracy refer to the organization as a whole or simply to its administrative apparatus? If one takes into

[8] Weber, *The Theory of Social and Economic Organization*, p. 303.
[9] Gerth and Mills, p. 228.

consideration all the characteristics formulated by Weber, it becomes clear that some of them refer only to the administrative apparatus of an organization. For example such characteristics as insistence on written documents and files could only apply to an office, to the clerical staff of a factory, not to its workers. But when Weber uses the ideal type for the examination of concrete historic cases, he often gives bureaucracy a more inclusive meaning. This is evident, for instance, when he speaks about the bureaucratization of the factory or of the political party.[10]

The lack of distinction between organization and administration in Weber's work can be explained by the fact that he formulated his concept of bureaucracy within the context of his political sociology— i.e. having in mind the governmental apparatus. Moreover, in many cases, it is difficult to distinguish organizational members who belong to the administrative staff and those who do not. The same difficulty arises when one tries to delineate the boundaries of an organization. For instance to what extent the shareholders or the clients of a firm are part of the organization.[11] In modern literature the term bureaucracy seems to be used in the same indiscriminate manner. Sometimes it refers only to the administrative apparatus of an organization; at other times it refers to the organization as a whole.[12]

I think the best conceptual clarification of this problem was given by Parsons who distinguished three levels or subsystems in the hierarchical structure of every organization: the technical, the managerial and the institutional. The first sub-system is concerned with all those technical activities which contribute directly to the performance of the organization's goal (e.g. the processing of raw material in a factory, the actual teaching in a school). The managerial system administers the internal affairs of the organization and mediates between the technical subsystem and its immediate environment by procuring the necessary resources and by finding 'customers' for the disposal of organizational products. Finally the institutional subsystem operates as a link between the technical-managerial subsystem, and the larger society. Thus for instance, in a business organization the plant would correspond to the technical subsystem, the office or administration to the managerial and the board of directors to the institutional. Parsons

---

[10] Cf. Gerth and Mills, pp. 209ff.

[11] For an interesting discussion of this problem cf. A. Etzioni (ed.), *A Comparative Analysis of Complex Organizations*, N.Y., 1964, pp. 15–19.

[12] Cf. for example, A.W. Gouldner, *Patterns of Industrial Bureaucracy*, Glencoe, Ill., 1954.

thinks that these distinctions are justified by the fact that each sub-system has different functions to perform and consequently different structural arrangements by which it tries to cope with such problems. Therefore at the points of articulation between them 'we find a qualitative break in the simple continuity of "line" authority'.[13]

In the light of the above distinctions it is clear that most of the literature on bureaucracy examines mainly the managerial subsystem of an organization. It is also clear that such distinctions must be kept in mind in order to broaden the scope of organizational studies and in order to promote comparative research on the similarities and systematic differences between subsystems of various organizational types.

THE MODE OF CONSTRUCTION OF THE IDEAL TYPE

Many criticisms of Weber's concept of bureaucracy are rather irrelevant, as they make the assumption that the ideal type has the same logical status as a simple classificatory type, or as an empirical model. For example the ideal type has been criticized for not focusing on other crucial aspects of organizational reality (informal organization, dysfunctional consequences, etc.).[14] To such a criticism, Weber could reply that it was not his intention to construct a model of bureaucracy which would approach as much as possible to concrete reality. Rather, he tried to identify the administrative characteristics typical of a certain kind of organization. Thus he was not obliged to use all or the most important organizational aspects, if and in so far as these aspects existed in other types of administration as well. For example, the feudal type of administration also had rules (traditional rules) and as a consequence even in this case, there was an informal organization deviating from the traditionally prescribed rules. The same

---

[13] Cf. Parsons, p. 65.

From this point of view organizations do not differ only according to their goals but also according to the way in which they articulate their various subsystems with each other and with the larger societal environment (for instance the break in authority and generally the interrelationships between the technical and the managerial subsystem in an army and in a school are quite different).

For a more detailed exposition and discussion of Parson's contribution to the theory of organizations cf. chapter 7.

[14] Cf. for example P. Selznick, 'An Approach to the Theory of Bureaucracy', American Sociological Review, vol. 8 (1943), p. 47; and his 'Foundations of the Theory of Organization', American Sociological Review, vol. 13 (1948), pp. 25–35; also cf. R. Merton, Social Theory and Social Structure, 2nd ed., 1957, Glencoe, Ill., pp. 50–4.

could be said about other important aspects of an organization like decision-making, dysfunctions and so on.

Other critics have pointed out that some of the ideal type's characteristics are not to be found in organizations which are manifestly bureaucratic in Weber's sense; consequently they are not essential and they should not be included in the concept of bureaucracy.[15] Such criticisms consider the ideal type of bureaucracy as a simple logical class which should group under its denomination all concrete organizations having certain specific characteristics. But Weber has explicitly stated that the ideal types cannot 'be defined by *genus proximum* and *differentia specifica*, and concrete cases cannot be subsumed under them as instances'.[16]

The only way to make a valid criticism of Weber's concept of bureaucracy is to consider it as what it was meant to be (in ideal type) and to analyse it on this level. But before such an analysis, because of the numerous misunderstandings and misuses of the concept, it is necessary to point out in some detail what the ideal type is not meant to be:

(a) The term 'type' has been used in various ways and has had many meanings in the social sciences.[17] The first meaning which is most obviously dissociated from Weber's ideal type, is when the term is used in the sense of average. When one speaks of the ideal type of bureaucracy, there is certainly no implication of a typical bureaucracy in the same sense in which we would speak of an average firm or a typical student.

(b) Moreover, as was said above, the ideal type is not a logical class or a simple type. A simple classificatory type, as a logical class, has as a function to group under its heading various concrete phenomena, taking as criteria of classification certain common and specific properties.[18] Thus the ideal type of bureaucracy must not be seen as comprising a fixed number of specific characteristics determining which organizations must be put in the bureaucratic pigeonhole and which must be left outside.

(c) Neither is the ideal model of bureaucracy an 'extreme type'

---

[15] Udy, pp. 791 ff.

[16] Weber, *Methodology of the Social Sciences*, p. 93.

[17] Cf. C. Hempel, 'Problems of Concept and Theory Formation in the Social Sciences', in *Science, Language and Human Rights*, American Philosophical Association, Philadelphia, 1952, p. 66.

[18] The various racial typologies in physical anthropology are good examples of this kind of classification.

which has as a function the ordering of various concrete phenomena along a qualitative or quantitative continuum. Such types, which are very often used in psychology, and sociology,[19] are constructed by the exaggeration of certain properties of concrete phenomena. They thus constitute extreme poles of a scale and they are useful in so far as they help in the comparison of concrete instances along a continuum.[20]

Although the ideal type of bureaucracy has been used in this sense (cf. section 3), it was not meant by Weber to be simply an extreme type. Weber's construct, more than a classificatory or an ordering type, was meant to be an analytic tool contributing directly to the explanation and interpretation of social phenomena.

(d) But in spite of such claims, Weber does not consider the ideal type as a theoretical model, that is as a set of interconnected hypotheses which can be validated or rejected by empirical research.[21]

In order to see how an ideal type differs from a theory or a model, we must try to analyse in detail the various steps taken for the construction of the former:

- The first step is the selection and conceptualization of empirical data, this selection being determined by Weber's interest in finding the typical aspects of a certain type of administration. So for example many of the ideal characteristics of bureaucracy, despite their purity, were selected in an inductive way, by taking, into consideration real organizations in which such features were more or less present.[22]

- The second step consists in exaggerating such selected features to their logical extreme.[23] For example, in the ideal type of bureaucracy, the hierarchical relations between bureaucrats are one hundred per cent impersonal. In reality this is never the case.

[19] Cf. J. McKinney, 'The Typological Tradition', in J.S. Roucek (ed.), *Readings in Contemporary American Sociology*, Paterson N.J., 1962, p. 557.

[20] So, for example, Riesman's types of other-directed and inner-directed people, although in their extreme formulations do not correspond to any real concrete instances, they are useful for ordering concrete individuals as more or less near the one or the other pole (cf. David Riesman et al., *The Lonely Crowd*, Yale, 1952).

[21] Cf. Weber, *Methodology of the Social Sciences*, p. 90. Also cf. T. Parsons *The Structure of Social Action*, 1937, pp. 601 ff. and C. Friedrich, 'Some Observations on Weber's analysis of Bureaucracy', in R.K. Merton et al. (eds), *Reader in Bureaucracy*, Glencoe, 1963, p. 28.

[22] cf. Weber, *Methodology of the Social Sciences*, p. 90.

[23] The term 'ideal' refers precisely to this sort of exaggeration of empirical features. Of course this use of the term differs from its everyday usage (the latter referring to an actual thing which serves as a standard of imitation).

• Finally, the selection and exaggeration of empirical elements and their formation into an ideal type is not done in an arbitrary way. These elements are interconnected in such a way that they form a whole portraying an inner consistency and logic. These interconnections are not theoretical statements making hypotheses about interrelationships between concrete phenomena. Thus their validity cannot be judged by experimentation but by the following criteria:

(a) The criterion of objective possibility requires that the constructed type must be an empirically possible one. In our example, this would mean that, even if the type of bureaucracy is never to be found in its ideal extremism, it must not contradict any of the 'known laws of nature'.[24]

(b) Moreover, the ideal construction must not only be objectively possible, but also 'adequate at the level of meaning'.[25] Very crudely, that means that it must also make sense to us, give us the feeling of consistency and plausibility. It is this kind of intuitive understanding, of empathic knowledge[26] which plays a great role in the construction and comprehension of the ideal type.

In the case of bureaucracy, it is the meaning of rationality, grasped in the above intuitive manner, which links together the various ideal characteristics and which gives consistency and logic to the whole construct. An ideally rational organization, in the Weberian sense, is an organization performing its tasks with maximum efficiency. Thus the selection and exaggeration of the various empirical elements and their interconnections were established in such a way, that a perfectly efficient organization would result if ever such an extreme type existed in reality. In other terms, to the empirical elements which Weber incorporated into his ideal type and to their combination he attached the attribute of rationality. And this evaluative assumption is not a hypothesis to be checked by further research. It is simply the meaning of bureaucracy which is caught when this type of organization is imagined, in isolation from all alien elements which, in the real world, distort its ideal rationality.

The issue at this point of the discussion is to see to what extent it is

---

[24] Cf. Weber, *Methodology of the Social Sciences*, p. 91.

[25] D. Martindale, 'Sociological Theory and the Ideal Type', in L. Gross (ed.), *Symposium on Sociological Theory*, N.Y., 1959, p. 72.

[26] Cf. T. Abel, 'The Operation called Verstehen', in H. Feigl and M. Brodbeck (eds), *Readings in the Philosophy of Science*, N.Y., 1953.

possible to construct a conceptual model of a perfectly rational organization, by specifying in detail and *a priori* (that is without previous empirical research) the characteristics and their combination which, if ever realized, should give the maximum degree of efficiency. Or in other words, to what extent is it possible, assuming the members of an organization to be acting in the most efficient way in the accomplishment of their tasks, to find out by the imagination only what the structural characteristics of such an organization should look like? The answer to such a question must be in the negative. Although in different cases an ideal typical formulation may be very useful, in this particular case it does not seem to have been successful. Indeed, the way in which Weber constructed the ideal type of bureaucracy does not satisfy even his own criteria of validity for such a type.

Concerning first the criterion of meaningful adequacy, it does not necessarily make sense to someone that a type of organization having the Weberian characteristics to an extreme degree should yield maximum efficiency. One could equally well imagine such an organization as being extremely inefficient. For example, some of these characteristics, even from a common sense point of view, seem to promote administrative inefficiency rather than efficiency (e.g. promotion by seniority).

As to the criterion of objective possibility, in the light of the empirical research done since Weber, one can argue that a perfectly rational-efficient organization having Weber's ideal characteristics is not objectively possible, in the sense that it runs against the *known laws of nature*—in this case, against recent empirical findings. Such findings rather indicate that the more accentuated some characteristics of the ideal type are, the more inefficient the organization becomes. In one sense, a great part of the literature on bureaucracy since Weber is a systematic exposition of the dysfunctional aspects and the unintended (mainly undesirable) consequences of strict bureaucratic control (cf. chapter 3). For the moment a few examples will be sufficient. Consider for instance, the problem of the efficiency of rules. Although to a certain degree the elaboration of precise and strict rules avoids indeterminacy and arbitrariness, on the other hand, especially when there is an effort to control by procedural rules even the details of each bureaucratic activity, and thus reduce seriously the initiative of the official, the results are rigidity and inefficiency of the whole organization.[27]

---

[27] Cf. chapter 3, introduction.

Moreover, it has been shown that ideal characteristics are not always compatible with each other. Consequently, when present in an organization, they become the source of friction and inefficiency. Among many writers, Parsons[28] and Gouldner[29] point out an inherent contradiction in the ideal type between hierarchical position and technical knowledge: 'On the one side, it was administration based on expertise: while on the other, it was administration based on discipline'.[30] In the ideal type both hierarchical authority and expert knowledge are present, but the eventual conflict between them is ignored, as it is not compatible with the assumption of ideal rationality.

In consequence it is clear that the characteristics included in the ideal type, when approximated in reality, do not necessarily yield maximum efficiency. Their efficiency or inefficiency is always determined by the specific organizational situation, mainly by the existing technology, the objectives and the societal environment of the organization. As a consequence; it is radically impossible to construct ideally, outside a concrete context, a type identifying the mechanisms which should bring maximum efficiency.

For Weber the ideal type is a conceptual tool which helps us to understand better social phenomena, by analysing the discrepancy between their ideal form and their concrete state. In our case the problem should be to compare the ideal type of bureaucracy with a real administration, find out the differences, and try to explain them.[31] Even if a conceptual construction of an ideal bureaucracy were possible, in order to make the comparison, we ought to know something about concrete bureaucracy. But to do this, we have to use a non-ideal model, that is a model which attempts to describe, explain and approach, as much as possible, the real situation.

So the ideal type, in any case, cannot be a substitute for theory and model building in the social sciences. Finally, if one should insist on building up a construct approaching the ideal type of bureaucracy,

---

[28] Cf. his introduction in Weber's *The Theory of Social and Economic Organization*, pp. 58–60, footnote 4.

[29] Gouldner, p. 22.

[30] I.e. The conflict between the professional specialist and the administrator (the staff and 'line' controversy in management theory—cf. chapter 4).

[31] As H. Becker, another proponent of ideal types points out, the constructed or ideal type has a negative utility. It draws our attention to the investigation of all those factors which distort the ideal form of social configurations and make social reality so different from them, cf. *Through Values to Social Interpretation*, Durham, N.C., 1950, pp. 259–64.

one should begin the other way round. One should construct a realistic model, learn something about actual efficiency or inefficiency of real organizations and then try, on the basis of this knowledge to speculate on the hypothetical form of an entirely rational model. Thus one does not need an ideal type in order to understand reality, but rather one needs some knowledge of reality in order to construct an ideal model (at least in the study of bureaucracy).[32]

But on the other hand, the contradictions of the ideal type have not seriously handicapped Weber's insights and contributions to the study of organizations. This is because Weber has not used the ideal type in the way he said one should use it. As in other instances, there is a discrepancy between Weber's methodological writings and the actual method that he uses in his historical analyses.[33] Martindale has pointed out that Weber does not so much compare ideal to real phenomena in order to establish and investigate their discrepancy—rather, he uses the ideal type as a tool for the historical comparison of two or more real situations. In this context the type helps to isolate 'the factors on which the comparison becomes critical'.[34] Moreover, as Andreski remarks there is nothing very ideal about the way Weber talks about bureaucracy or feudalism. 'He moves on the level of abstraction which is not very far removed from observable reality.'[35]

Thus Weber does not use the concept of bureaucracy for a microanalysis of the internal structure of an organization.[36] He uses it in his cross-cultural general analysis, mainly in order to distinguish various types of domination and their corresponding administrative apparatus. On this macroscopic level, where details and minor variations become irrelevant, the concept of bureaucracy, used as an extreme type, is useful and adequate. Even the assumption concerning the rational superiority of the bureaucratic type of administration, when

[32] The above remarks do not apply to all kinds of ideal types. For example, what J. Watkins calls individualistic ideal types are logically acceptable and methodologically useful for the explanation of specific cases (cf. 'Ideal Types and Historical Explanation' in Feigl and Brodbeck, p. 275). These types consist in the construction of the rational behaviour of an actor by deducing it from a set of given premises postulating the actor's preferences and information—e.g. the economic man construct in economics.

But the ideal type of bureaucracy cannot be considered as a similar construct.

[33] Cf. Gerth and Mills, p. 57.

[34] Martindale, p. 88.

[35] S. Andreski, 'Method and Substantive Theory in M. Weber', *British Journal of Sociology*, vol. 15 (1964), p. 4.

[36] After all, Weber devotes only a few pages in his vast work to the discussion of the characteristics and internal structure of bureaucracy.

considered as a hypothesis assessing the comparative efficiency of various historical types of administration, is very plausible. Indeed, in spite of all the dysfunctions of the organizational control by rational rules, one could hardly imagine a big modern corporation functioning without such rules. As a matter of fact the complexity and size of modern administrative tasks make the bureaucratic type of organization, when compared with the feudal or the patrimonial, by far the most efficient.

CHAPTER THREE

Riggs's 'Administrative Ecology'*

Ramesh K. Arora

Fred W. Riggs, who is perhaps the most innovative contemporary theorist in comparative public administration, has been concerned primarily with conceptualizing on the interactions between administrative systems and their environment. The main locus of his interest has involved 'developing'[1] or transitional societies. It is to explain the 'administrative ecology' of such societies that he has constructed 'prismatic-sala' models. In order to provide a background for these models, certain key elements of the ecological and the structural–functional modes of analyses will be discussed briefly in this chapter. This analysis will be followed by an introduction to certain basic components of early Riggs's typology of 'Agraria' and 'Industria'; then the essential characteristics of his 'fused-prismatic-diffracted' typology will be given. Some critical comments will also be offered on these models. It may be stressed that Riggs is an example of those comparative public administration writers who are seriously interested in the ecological perspective. An analysis of his work will allow a fuller examination of the emerging emphasis upon ecology.

Riggs has concluded that Weber's ideal-type construct of bureaucracy, because of its assumptions of a relatively autonomous administrative system, is not particularly relevant to the study of developing societies, where the administrative structures do not have

---

* Ramesh K. Arora, *Comparative Public Administration (An Ecological Perspective)*, Associated Publishing House, New Delhi, 2000 (reprint).

[1] The terms 'developing' and 'developed' are being used in the general sense of 'modernizing' and 'modernized' respectively, unless specified otherwise. The fundamental emphasis in the terms is on the socio-economic change, though sometimes, 'political development' is also implied by them.

the same degree of autonomy from other social structures as do their counterparts in many of the developed societies. Administrative structures which are in close and continuous interaction with many portions of the general social system adopt a highly multifunctional character in the developing countries. It is even likely that these structures perform less of the strictly 'administrative' and more of a variety of 'extra-administrative' functions. There may even be cases when the 'manifest' administrative function is entirely lost sight of in practice. In such situations, it would be most difficult to evaluate an administrative sub-system on the basis of its departures from the strict norms of the ideal-type bureaucracy. The 'real' bureaucratic systems in the developing states are so removed from either the legal–rational model or the purely traditional type that to study them with the aid of such 'pure' dichotomous constructs will provide misleading results.[2] Therefore, Riggs has argued, there is need to develop new conceptual constructs to study societies which have a *mixture* of 'primitive' and 'modern' structural characteristics.[3]

The 'overlapping' and 'heterogeneous' structures in the developing societies, Riggs has further observed, are difficult to encompass within the conceptual framework of Weber's bureaucratic model which appears to be based on the assumption of a continuous trend of certain broad social structures (especially the administrative ones) toward universal 'bureaucratization'.[4] Eugene Litwak has claimed that Weber's bureaucratic model 'is most efficient when the organization deals primarily with uniform events and with occupations stressing traditional areas of knowledge rather than social skill.'[5] In this context, Karl Deutsch has commented that Weber did not provide

---

[2] See, for example, Monroe Berger, *Bureaucracy and Society in Modern Egypt* (Princeton: Princeton University Press, 1957). Since it did not account for the environment in which an administrative system works, Berger concluded, Weber's ideal-type bureaucracy does not fit the Egyptian case.

[3] Fred W. Riggs, *Administration in Developing Countries: The Theory of Prismatic Society* (Boston: Houghton Miffin Co., 1964), hereafter referred to as *Administration*, p. 73.

[4] See, Reinhard Bendix, *Max Weber: An Intellectual Portrait* (Garden City, New York: Doubleday, 1962), hereafter cited as *Portrait*, p. 459; H.H. Gerth and C. Wright Mills have observed: 'We nevertheless feel justified in holding that a unilinear construction is clearly implied in Weber's idea of the bureaucratic trend'. *From Max Weber: Essays in Sociology*, edited with an introduction by Gerth and Mills (New York: Oxford University Press, 1946), hereafter cited as *Essays*, p. 51.

[5] Eugene Litwak, 'Models of Bureaucracy which Permit Conflict', *The American Journal of Sociology*, LXVII (1961), p. 177.

any 'dynamic' ideal-types, although in Weberian analysis 'change' is dealt with in discussions of historical systems.[6]

It has also been pointed out that a widely under-emphasized aspect of Weber's bureaucratic analysis is the linkage between the 'macroscopic' and the 'microscopic' via middle-range levels of analysis. Except for studying in some detail the interaction between the political system and its administrative sub-systems, Weber did not analyse extensively the linkages of the economic and socio-cultural systems with the bureaucracy. Although he related ' bureaucratization' with the emergence of a money economy and with the nature of capitalism,[7] and also referred to the effect of bureaucracy in levelling socio-economic differences in a society,[8] Weber's analytical treatment of the interaction among the phenomena is found to be 'less developed'.

Further, Talcott Parsons has noted that even though 'all of the most important technical elements of Weber's analysis of authority are of generalized significance for the whole field of social relationships', Weber tends to 'treat the sphere of the organization of authority as *analytically* autonomous in a way which obscures this continuity of patterns throughout the social system as a whole.'[9] Parsons has also criticized Weber for not employing systematically the concept of generalized social system at all main levels.

In addition, it has been argued that international patterns between authority systems and other social structures are under-stressed in Weberian analysis. Thus, Alvin Gouldner has pointed out that the ideal-type model is 'theory relatively innocent of spatio-temporal cautions,' and that it gives the impression that bureaucracy 'has existed in an essentially similar form, regardless of great differences in the social structures in which it was enmeshed'. Weber's bureaucratic model, Gouldner has observed, has been created only out of elements 'which may be constant, regardless of varying social structures'.[10]

While considering the above criticism of Weberian analysis, it appears that several scholars who profess to believe in the 'idea of ecology' overlook the efficacy of the 'ecology of ideas'. There seems to be a tendency among some writers to pay only lip-service to Weber's

[6] Karl Deutsch, *The Nerves of Government* (New York: Free Press, 1966), p. 46.

[7] Bendix, *Portrait*, p. 383.

[8] *Essays*, pp. 224–8; 230–2.

[9] 'Introduction', in *Theory*, p. 76. Emphasis original.

[10] Alvin W. Gouldner, 'On Weber's Analysis of Bureaucratic Rules', in Robert Merton, *et al.* (eds), *Reader in Bureaucracy* (New York: Free Press, 1952), p. 48.

contribution to the socio-administrative analysis, and then to criticize him for what he did not do. Long check lists are often prepared to point out what is missing in Weberian analysis. This way, not only is Weber's real contribution disparaged, but injustice is also done to scholarly analysis by evaluating a writer outside a 'proper' perspective. In fact, however, Weber must be studied in the context of the time he was writing his ideas, of his methodology of ideal-types, of the heuristic character of his analysis, of his discussion of historical systems, and, most importantly, of his place in the evolution of social thought.

Discovery of 'limitations' of Newton's law of gravity was not possible until the major development of his ideas had led to the discovery of new unexplainable anomalies. To criticize him now for not taking into account the theory of relativity would reflect no more than an extremely anti-ecological bias. Paradoxically, however, Weber's bureaucratic analysis is often evaluated from the standpoint of all the advances which organization theory, systemic analysis, and development theory have made in the last thirty years or so. Thus, it should be stressed that Weber set out to explain 'bureaucracy' as he defined it—which did not include the institutions of current 'developing' nations. In conceptualizing bureaucracies, he was looking at societies where the process of modernization was not highly pronounced nor rapid. Consequently, he did not chart the possible kinds of changes which occur in 'developing' social systems. In fact, there were not many 'developing' nations of the kind we find today. Furthermore, Weber's bureaucratic analysis should be understood in the context of his ideal-type model, which is, methodologically, a 'static' system construct.

It should be clear, then, that in evaluating Weber's analysis, two complementary approaches can be adopted: (1) to examine it from the perspectives of his methodology and of the period in which he wrote his ideas; and (2) to view it from the angle of the *present* needs of social analyses, while recognizing that most of Weber's limitations are not simply inherent 'weaknesses' but emerge in the context of present-day requirements. Therefore, the need is, as Weber himself would have stressed, to move further in constructing new conceptual categories to meet the challenges of the rapidly changing empirical reality. It is in this context recently that ecological–developmental perspectives have been given greater emphasis in the study of public administration.

THE ECOLOGY OF PUBLIC ADMINISTRATION

The basic premise of the ecological approach in comparative public administration is that public bureaucracies may be regarded as one of the several basic institutions in a society. Thus, in order to understand bureaucracy's 'structures' and 'functions', one must study bureaucracy in the context of its interrelationships with other societal institutions. In systemic terms, the bureaucratic system is continually interacting with—i.e., affected by and feeding back upon—the political, economic, and socio-cultural sub-systems in a society. It is both a modifying influence upon these systems and a system which is modified by their activity.

The need to study the ecology of public administration has been emphasized by several scholars, such as John M. Gaus,[11] Robert A. Dahl,[12] Roscoe Martin,[13] and Fred W. Riggs.[14] Riggs, for example, has observed that only those studies are 'truly' comparative which are empirical, nomothetic, and ecological.[15] From this perspective, administrative process may be viewed as a system having an environment with which it interacts, and in which it operates.[16] This proposition is a corollary of the view that the 'larger society' is a 'system containing administrative institutions as a sub-system.'[17] Riggs has been primarily interested in analysing the interaction between the administrative sub-system on the one hand and the political, social, cultural and economic sub-systems of the society on the other. This speaks of his basic orientation, which is termed as *ecological*.[18] Behind such a perspective lies Riggs's belief that the nature of

[11] 'The Ecology of Government', in *Reflections in Public Administration* (University of Alabama Press, 1947), pp. 1–19.

[12] 'The Science of Public Administration', *Public Administration Review*, VII (1947), pp. 1–11.

[13] 'Technical Assistance: The Problem of Implementation', *Public Administration Review*, XII (1952), p. 266.

[14] Among others, see *Administration*, and *The Ecology of Public Administration* (Bombay: Asia Publishing House, 1961), hereafter referred to as *Ecology*.

[15] Riggs, 'Trends in the Comparative Study of Public Administration', *International Review of Administrative Sciences*, XXVIII (1962), p. 15.

[16] *Administration*, p. 19.

[17] Ibid.

[18] Keith Henderson has opined that Riggs's prime perspective could best be characterized as 'ecological'. *Emerging Synthesis in American Public Administration* (Bombay: Asia Publishing House, 1966), pp. 51–2. Ferrel Heady has labelled Riggs's theory-building as 'ecological oriented'. 'Comparative Public Administration: Concerns and

public administration in any country cannot be understood without grasping the social setting in which it operates.

A useful approach in the ecological analysis of different social systems is 'structural–functionalism'. Riggs has considered this framework of analysis appropriate to his ecological orientation in the study of administrative systems, for, in many ways, structural–functionalism involves a delineation of the *general* social context within which administration operates. Therefore, an overview of the structural–functional approach is pertinent at this point.

THE STRUCTURAL–FUNCTIONAL APPROACH

Various scholars, such as Talcott Parsons,[19] Robert Merton,[20] Marion Levy, Jr.,[21] Gabriel Almond,[22] and David Apter,[23] have used the structural–functional approach in social analysis. In structural functionalism, social structure is considered as 'any pattern of behaviour which has become a standard feature of a social system'.[24] Structures may be 'concrete', such as government departments and bureaus, or they may be 'analytic' i.e., constructs abstracted from concrete reality, such as structure of authority'.[25] Generally, analytic structures include some concrete referents.

Priorities', in Heady and Sybil L. Stokes (eds), *Papers in Comparative Public Administration* (Ann Arbor: Institute of Public Administration, University of Michigan, 1962), p. 4.

[19] See, among others, *The Social System* (Glencoe, Illinois: Free Press, 1957).

[20] *Social Theory and Social Structure* (Glencoe, Illinois: Free Press, 1951).

[21] *The Structure of Society* (Princeton, N.J.: Princeton University Press, 1952); 'Structural-Functional Analysis', *International Encyclopedia of Social Sciences*, VI, 21–9; *Modernization and the Structure of Societies* (Princeton: Princeton University Press, 1966).

[22] Almond and James Coleman (eds), *The Politics of the Developing Areas* (Princeton: Princeton University Press, 1960); Almond and G. Bingham Powell, *Comparative Politics: A Developmental Approach* (Boston: Little Brown, 1966).

[23] See, among others, *The Politics of Modernization* (Chicago: University of Chicago Press, 1965).

[24] Riggs, *Administration*, p. 20. Riggs, in introducing the structural–functional approach in comparative public administration, has drawn largely on Levy, *The Structure of Society*.

[25] Alex Inkeles, *What is Sociology* (Englewood Cliffs, N.J.: Prentice-Hall, 1964), p. 35. Riggs, while giving an example of 'bureau' as a structure, has observed that a 'structure is not composed of people and things themselves, but of their actions.' However, 'it (structure) does not include all their actions, but only those actions which relate to the goals and work of the bureau. The bureau also includes the relevant actions of "outsiders" with whom it interacts in the normal course of business, its *clientele* or

All social structures perform some 'functions'. In structural–functional terms, a 'function' involves 'a pattern of interdependence between two or more structures, a relationship between variables'. It refers to 'any consequences of a structure in so far as they affect other structures or the total system of which they are a part'.[26]

In social systems research, a one-to-one relationship between structures and functions should not be assumed; the functional effects of particular structures are a matter of empirical research.[27] A social structure may perform more than one function, and, likewise, a function may be performed by more than one structure. These premises allow the structural–functional analysis to obviate the misconceptions that (a) structures having resemblance to each other in different environmental settings perform similar functions; (b) the non-appearance of any particular structure implies the absence of some function(s); or (c) structures may be only unifunctional in character.[28] Even though not all kinds of functions are performed in *all* societies, the structural–functional approach assumes that there are some structures and functions which are 'requisite' or 'prerequisite' for the survival or health of a society.[29] Although various scholars have produced different sets of requisite functions of social systems, this does not lessen the utility of these concepts which provide 'categories to identify structures, which, though different, are analytically comparable'.[30] Thus, in comparative analysis, functional requisites provide a basis for comparative research involving different environmental settings.

"audience". They may be served or regulated by it; they may be the subject as well as the object of its activity.' *Administration*, p. 20. Emphasis original.

[26] For an analysis of the various meanings of functions, see, Robert Merton, 'Manifest and Latent Functions', in N. J. Demerath III and Richard A. Peterson (eds), *System, Change and Conflict* (New York: Free Press, 1967), pp. 10–75.

[27] Riggs, *Administration*, p. 20.

[28] Robert H. Jackson, 'An Analysis of the Comparative Public Administration Movement', *Canadian Public Administration*, IX (1966), p. 120.

[29] Recently, Levy has distinguished between structural and functional 'requisites' and 'prerequisites'. Requisites are essential for the continued existence or maintenance of a particular social unit, 'prerequisites' are the necessary conditions before a particular social unit comes into being. 'Structural-Functional Analysis', pp. 23–4. Talcott Parsons has not distinguished between the functional requisites and prerequisites. He has postulated four functional requisites of social structures: goal-gratification, adaptation, integration, pattern maintenance and tension management. See, among others, Parsons, Robert F. Bales and Edward Shils, *Working Papers on the Theory of Action* (Glencoe, Illinois: Free Press, 1953).

[30] Riggs, *Administration*, p. 22.

Riggs has identified five functional requisites for any society—economic, social, communicational, symbolic, and political.[31] The same set of functional requisites applies to an administrative subsystem. Riggsian analysis does not argue as to why only these functional requisites are chosen, nor does his analysis provide such categories a central place.

The present summary is an incomplete overview of the structural–functional approach. But even this overview makes it relatively clear that this particular mode of analysis:

1. focuses on the *interactions* among various components within a social system, and
2. analyses the interaction between the system and its environment.

These characteristics are indicative of the 'systemic–ecological' character of the structural–functional approach.[32]

In the field of public administration, it was first suggested in 1955 by Dwight Waldo that structural–functional analysis might provide some guidance in the construction of 'a model of what an administrative system is like as a general type'.[33] Waldo's suggestion was first followed by Fred W. Riggs when he came out with his 'agraria–industria' typology two years later.[34] Since then, Riggs has been the prime 'user' of the approach in comparative public administration, although other scholars have also been influenced by the comparative features and the 'value-neutral' premises of structural–functionalism. Basically, the approach has brought a consciousness that the institutions and practices of the administrative systems of the western nations are not necessarily the best in all cases. These various indigenous structures in non-Western nations, though seemingly dysfunctional from Western views, may prove 'functional' for their own particular social settings.[35]

[31] Ibid., p. 99. Also, see note 30, above.

[32] Oran Young also has considered the structural–functional analysis as a 'systemic' approach. See, *Systems of Political Science* (Englewood Cliffs, N. J.: Prentice-Hall, 1968), pp. 27–37.

[33] *The Study of Public Administration* (New York: Doubleday, 1955), p. 9.

[34] 'Agraria and Industria—Toward a Typology of Comparative Administration', in William J. Siffin (ed.), *Toward a Comparative Study of Public Administration* (Bloomington, Ind.: Indiana University Press, 1957), pp. 23–110.

[35] Lynton Caldwell. 'Conjectures on Comparative Public Administration', in Roscoe Martin (ed.), *Public Administration and Democracy* (Syracuse: Syracuse University Press, 1965), p. 232.

THE AGRARIA AND THE INDUSTRIA

In his agraria–industria models, Riggs distinguished between societies that are 'predominantly or characteristically industrial' and those in which the 'agrarian institutions predominate'.[36] The models were designed to provide 'a system of hypothetical categories for the classification and analysis of realities, including patterns of political and administrative transition'.[37] The polar types were abstracted from observed realities, with Imperial China and contemporary America providing the bases for conceptualizing the agraria and the industria respectively. Essentially, these ideal-types resemble the Weberian constructs of the traditional and the legal–rational authority systems, although unlike Weber, Riggs used an inductive approach in conceptualizing these models. The main structural features of the agraria were presented as follows:[38]

1. Predominance of ascriptive, particularistic, and diffuse patterns.[39]
2. Stable local groups and limited spatial mobility.
3. Relatively simple and stable 'occupational' differentiation.
4. A deferential stratification system of diffuse impact.

Conversely, a 'modern industrial society' was characterized as having the following structural features:[40]

1. Predominance of universalistic, specific, and achievement norms.
2. High degree of social mobility (in general—not necessarily vertical—sense).
3. Well-developed occupational system, insulated from other social structures.
4. 'Egalitarian' class system based on generalized patterns of occupational achievement.
5. Prevalence of 'associations', i.e., functionally specific, non-ascriptive structure.

Several scholars, including Riggs, found that the polar types of

---

[36] The basis of this conceptualization is found in F. X. Sutton, 'Social Theory and Comparative Politics', paper prepared for the SSRC Committee on Comparative Politics, Princeton, 1955 (mimeo).

[37] Siffin, 'Toward the Comparative Study of Public Administration', p. 9.

[38] Riggs, 'Agraria and Industria', p. 29.

[39] For an introduction to these Parsonian pattern-variables, see note 44 below.

[40] Riggs, 'Agraria and Industria', p. 29.

agraria and industria were not especially helpful in studying transitional societies. Although Riggs did construct a middle category of 'transitia', this category was less developed than the polar types of the agraria and the industria. The ideal-types lacked sufficient mechanism to analyse 'mixed-type' societies. Critics argued that the modern 'industrian' system never exists by itself, but always has an 'agrarian' system inside it.[41] These models also implied a unidirectional movement of a society—moving from an agrarian stage to an industrial stage. Moreover, from a researcher's viewpoint, the categories of the models were found to be too abstract and general, and most strikingly, the analysis of administrative systems was provided only a peripheral place in the whole scheme.[42] Riggs himself soon abandoned the agraria–industria typology in favour of a new scheme of constructs dealing with 'fused-prismatic-diffracted' societies. In spite of some of its limitations, the agraria-industria typology contributed significantly in the field of comparative public administration by paving the way for further ecological studies, to which Riggs's contribution is still predominant.

THE MODELS OF FUSED-PRISMATIC-DIFFRACTED SOCIETIES

In conformity with the concept of multifunctionality, social structures may be 'functionally diffuse' (if they perform a large number of functions), or 'functionally specific' (if they carry out certain prescribed limited functions).[43] Riggs has termed the functionally diffuse

---

[41] Almond, 'A Functional Approach to Comparative Politics', in Almond and James Coleman (ed.), *The Politics of the Developing Areas*, p. 23.

[42] For a critical appraisal of the agraria-industria typology, see, among others, F. J. Tickner, 'Comparing Administrative Systems', *Public Administration Review*, IX (1959), pp. 19–25; R. S. Milne, 'Comparisons and Models in Public Administration', *Political Studies*, X (1962), pp. 1–14; Robert Presthus, 'Behavior and Bureaucracy in many Cultures', *Public Administration Review*, XIX (1959), pp. 27–31.

[43] The distinction made between functional diffuseness and functional specificity is one of the five pattern-variables initially propounded by Talcott Parsons. A pattern-variable 'is a dichotomy, one side of which must be chosen by an actor before the meaning of the situation is determinate for him, and thus before he can act with respect to that situation'. Parsons and Edward Shils (eds), *Toward a Central Theory of Action* (Cambridge, Mass.: Harvard University Press, 1951), p. 77. Parsons has suggested that there are five, and only five basic pattern-variables, and they comprise:

1. The dilemma of gratification of impulse versus discipline: affectivity–affective neutrality;

2. The dilemma of private versus collective interests: self orientation–collectivity orientation;

societies as 'fused' and the functionally specific ones as 'diffracted'. The modal society intermediate between these two polar types is 'prismatic'.[44] The fused-prismatic-diffracted models are designed then to be 'ideal types not to be found in any actual society, but perhaps approximated in some, and useful for heuristic purposes and as an aid in the organization of data'.[45]

Using Parsonian pattern variable, Riggs has hypothesized that 'a diffracted system would rank high in terms of universalism and achievement orientation, a fused model high in particularism and ascription, with the prismatic model intermediate in these scales'.[46] Riggs has also developed intermediate categories of pattern variables. Thus, a prismatic society is characterized by 'selectivism' (intermediate category between universalism and particularism), 'attainment' (intermediate category between achievement and ascription), and 'poly-functionalsim' (intermediate category between functional specificity and functional diffuseness). Riggs has cautioned that correlations among these varianbles will be a matter of hypothesis alone and not of definition, i.e., only by empirical observations can the existence and degree of such correlations be identified.

The focus of Riggs's analysis is the study of certain key elements of the social structures in a prismatic society and their interaction with the 'sala', i.e., the administrative sub-system in such a society.[47] His treatment of the fused and diffracted societies is sketchy, and has relevance only to the extent that it aids the analysis of prismatic

---

3. The dilemma of transcendence versus immanence: universalism–particularism;

4. The dilemma of object modalities: ascription–achievement;

5. The dilemma of the scope of significance of the object: diffuseness–specificity, Ibid., pp. 80–4.

Riggs, in his analysis, has made use of only the last three of these pattern variables.

[44] *Administration*, p. 24. The terminology is drawn by analogy from optics—the prism causes the diffraction of undifferentiated fused white light into a rainbow spectrum of distinct colours.

[45] Riggs, *Models in the Comparative Study of Public Administration* (Comparative Administration Group, American Society for Public Administration, 1959) , p. 22.

[46] Riggs, *Administration*, p. 31.

[47] In Riggsian terminology, 'bureau' is the general term to denote the locus of administrative action in a society. A diffracted society has a diffracted bureau or office, having the characteristics of efficiency and rationality. A fused society has a fused bureau or a 'chamber'. The Spanish term 'sala' has a variety of meanings, such as a room, a pavilion, a government office, or a religious meeting; it represents an 'interlocking mixture of elements from the diffracted office and the fused chamber'. *Administration*, p. 268.

societies. Riggs's primary interest has been to illuminate administrative problems in transitional or developing societies.[48]

A summary of the basic characteristics of the prismatic-sala model of Riggs is in order.[49] Three such features have been identified by Riggs—'heterogeneity', 'formalism', and 'over-lapping'.

HETEROGENEITY

A prismatic society is characterized by a high degree of 'heterogeneity', which refers to the 'simultaneous presence, side by side, of quite different kinds of systems, practices, and viewpoints'.[50] The coexistence of fused and the diffracted traits is an indication and consequence of incomplete and uneven social change. There are, in a prismatic society, urban areas with a 'sophisticated' intellectual class, western style offices, and the modern gadgets of administration. On the other hand, there exist rural areas possessing traditional looks and outlooks, with village heads or 'elders' combining various political, administrative, religious, and social roles. This heterogeneity is a characteristic of the administrative structures as well. In a prismatic society, the sala exists along with modern 'bureau' and traditional 'courts' or chambers.

FORMALISM

'Formalism' refers to 'the degree of discrepancy or congruence between the formally prescribed and the effectively practiced, between norms and realities'.[51] The level of congruence between these elements

---

[48] In Riggsian analysis, a prismatic society may be 'transitional' if it is 'dynamic' in character. Likewise, transitional or 'underdeveloped' countries may possess strong prismatic characteristics. Ibid., p. 34. In spite of making an analytical distinction between these terms, Riggs, in providing concrete examples, has identified those societies as prismatic which are generally known as 'developing' or 'transitional'.

[49] The analysis is based on *Administration; Ecology;* The "Sala" Model: An Ecological Approach to the Study of Comparative Administration', *Philippine Journal of Public Administration*, VI (1962), pp. 3–16. This article is reprinted in Nimrod Raphaeli (ed.), *Readings in Comparative Public Administration* (Boston: Allyn and Bacon, 1967), pp. 412–32, and has also appeared under the title, 'The Ecological Approach: The "Sala" Model', in Heady and Stokes (eds), *Papers in Comparative Public Administration*, pp. 19–36.

[50] *Ecology* p. 91.

[51] Riggs, 'The "Sala" Model', *Philippine Journal of Public Administration*, p. 5. Also see, *Ecology*, pp. 91–2. By 'effective' behaviour, Riggs has referred to what *actually* happens, the unofficial conduct, the practice, the informal, the *real* behaviour of people, politicians, administrators, pressure groups, etc.

speaks of the degree of 'realism'; conversely, the discrepancy between them represents formalism. 'The greater the discrepancy between the formal and effective, the more formalistic a system.'[52] The fused and the diffracted societies have relatively high degree of realism,[53] while a prismatic society is characterized by a high degree of formalism. Actual official behaviour in prismatic societies does not correspond to legal statutes, even though the public officials may insist on following some of the laws literally. Often they insist on meticulously following some technical provision of laws and rules, while at the same time overlooking others—usually those that relate to general terms and objectives. Formalistic behaviour is caused by 'the lack of pressure toward programme objectives, the weaknesses of social power as a guide to bureaucratic performance, and a great permissiveness for arbitrary administration'.[54] The motivation for formalistic behaviour may come from an official's natural 'inclinations' or from the pay-off he gets in a particular situation. Thus formalism, generally, joins with the process of official corruption.

The policy implication of the realism–formalism dichotomy, according to Riggs is that formal reforms in administrative institutions in a diffracted society are likely to introduce changes in the administrative behaviour, while in a prismatic society, such reforms are likely to have only a superficial impact. Therefore, an attitude fostering realism should be nurtured among the public officials prior to bringing about any institutional changes in the administration of prismatic societies.

OVERLAPPING

Related to heterogeneity and formalism is the characteristic of 'overlapping', which refers to 'the extent to which formally differentiated structures of a diffracted society coexist with undifferentiated structures of a fused type'.[55] To the extent that structures perform their manifest functions in a diffracted society, substantial overlapping does not occur. Likewise, in a fused society, which has only one set of structures for almost all kinds of functions, the problem of overlapping

---

[52] *Ecology*, p. 92.

[53] Riggs has recognized that prismatic, characteristics may be found in the diffracted societies, for example in the United States local government. 'The "Sala" Model', p. 5.

[54] Ibid., p. 5.

[55] Ibid., p. 6.

does not arise, because in such a society, whatever is formal is also effective. In a prismatic society, on the other hand, although new or 'modern' social structures are created, in essence the older or undifferentiated structures continue to dominate the social system. New norms or values generally associated with the diffracted structures are paid lip-service only and thus are overlooked in favour of older values more appropriate to an undifferentiated society.[56] In the sala, overlapping may be judged by the 'extent to which what is described as "administrative" behaviour is actually determined by non-administrative criteria, i.e., by political, economic, social, religious, or other factors'.[57]

Overlapping in a prismatic society has several noticeable dimensions. These are conceptualized as nepotism, 'poly-communalism', the existence of 'clects', 'poly-normativism', lack of consensus, and the separation of 'authority' from 'control'.

NEPOTISM

In a diffracted society, the considerations of family loyalty are divorced from official behaviour. While in a fused society, the politico-administrative system has a patrimonial character and, therefore, provides dominant importance to kinship or family. On the other hand, in a prismatic society, the new formal structures are superimposed on the family and kinship. In addition, universalistic norms in administering the laws are often disregarded, while the official recruitment is determined by nepotism. Thus, patrimonialism is officially proscribed, but in fact practiced.

'POLY-COMMUNALISM' OR 'CLECTS'

In a diffracted society, almost everyone is 'mobilized' for 'mass communication'. Such a society has a 'national community' which exists with its own set of elites ('minority communities'). In a diffused society, on the other hand, mass media are absent, and hence there is a lack of mass mobilization. Each village or tribe exists as a relatively closed system. Between these two polar types falls the prismatic society where the rate of mass assimilation to the elite's symbol

---

[56] Thus, 'overlapping implies a social schizophrenia of contradictory formal (conscious) and informal (unconscious) behaviour pattern'. Ibid., p. 6.

[57] *Ecology*, p. 92.

system is likely to be slower than the rate of mobilization.[58] This situation produces a state of 'poly-communalism', or the simultaneous existence in a society of various ethnic, religious, and racial groups which live in a 'relatively hostile interaction' with each other. In such a poly-communal society, membership in various 'interest groups' is largely community based. Riggs has called these groups 'clects', which have characteristics of attainment orientation, selectivism, and poly-functionalism. Clects carry out relatively diffuse functions of a semi-traditional type, although they are organized in a 'modern' associational way.

Poly-communalism and clects influence the character of the sala. A public official in a prismatic society is likely to develop a greater sense of loyalty toward the members of his own community than toward the government. In matters of recruitment to the official positions and of the administration of rules and regulations, the dominant minority community gains disproportionate representation.[59] However, to protect the interests of other minorities a 'quota system' may provide a sort of proportional representation in the recruitment to official positions. But such an arrangement may lead to a mutual hostility among various communities, which in turn tends to generate non-cooperation among the several government agencies staffed by members of the rival communities.

Sometimes the sala, or one of its agencies, develops close relations with particular clects, or starts functioning like a clect itself. In these circumstances, the sala functions primarily in the interest of some particular groups, but it continues to pay lip-service to achievement and universalistic norms. As a consequence of this alliance between sala and clects, sala officials profit through kickbacks or rebates. This aspect of prismatic behaviour is closely related to the economic subsystem of prismatic society.

PRISMATIC ECONOMY—THE 'BAZAAR-CANTEEN' MODEL

In a diffracted society, prices are determined essentially by the market factors of supply and demand. Conversely, 'arena factors' (considerations which determine balance of power, prestige, and

---

[58] The concepts 'mobilization' and 'assimilation' have been borrowed by Riggs from Karl Deutsch, *Nationalism and Social Communication* (New York: Wiley, 1953).

[59] Riggs has noted that in the Southern region of the United states, the black community is disadvantaged in public employment. 'The "Sala" Model', pp. 7–8. This is an example of the prismatic characteristics existing in a relatively diffracted system.

solidarity) in the society dominate the economic system of a fused society, and the question of price scarcely arises. In a prismatic society, 'market' and 'arena' factors interact with each other and produce a state of 'price indeterminacy', where it is generally impossible to determine a common price for a commodity or service.

Riggs has studied the exchange relationship between public officials and their clients in terms of buyer–seller relationship. Thus, prices charged for public services in a prismatic society vary according to the nature of the relationship between a public servant and his clientele. Services are sold to the members of the 'inside' clects and of the dominant community at preferential (reduced) rates, and, conversely, at higher charges to members of the 'deviant' or minority community and of the 'outside' clects. In other words, the economic organizations in a prismatic society generally act like a 'subsidized' canteen, providing goods and services at lower rates to the members of privileged groups and to the politically 'influential' persons having access to the canteen. In addition, these economic organizations have characteristics of a 'tributary canteen'; they charge higher prices to members of the 'outside' groups.

Price-indeterminacy promotes a bazaar-like atmosphere in a prismatic society, involving considerable bargaining on the amounts of financial dealings with regard to such areas as taxes, fees, rebates, and bribes. Such practices influence considerably the whole set-up of the financial administration and, most particularly, that of budgeting, accounting, and auditing. Price indeterminacy also impairs the collection of government revenues, causing, among other things, low salaries for public officials. As a corollary to low emoluments through regular channels public officials feel more inclined and motivated to increase their income through illegitimate means. Thus, the norms of official conduct are affected by, and, in turn, affect, the economic subsystem of a prismatic society.

'POLY-NORMATIVISM' AND
LACK OF CONSENSUS

In a prismatic society, 'new' sets of norms and rules coexist with the traditional ways of behaviour. As a result of an overlapping of the formal and the 'effective' standards of conduct, prismatic society's social interactions are characterized by a lack of consensus on norms of behaviour. Such a situation of 'poly-normativism' or 'normlessness' affects the sala, where officials, although publicly claiming to follow objective, universalistic, and achievement-oriented practices, actually follow more subjective, ascription-oriented, and particularistic modes of conduct. They also respect the traditional rigid hierarchy of status. These officials claim to apply western rationalistic norms in their conduct, but still continue to cling to the traditional practices. In their desire to imitate the West and their own past simultaneously, the officials develop a 'mimetic' behaviour, which involves borrowing or appropriating what others have done.

A prismatic society's source of potential public officials is generally restricted to certain particular groups. Even when the officials acquire rank through achievement (via education or through a competitive examination), the opportunities for career-development and fringe-benefits depend largely on ascribed means, particularly support of one's superiors and seniority, in service. Even the citizen, in his relationship with the sala, is poly-normative—ready to disregard official rules for his own benefits, and yet stressing the idea that governmental conduct should be of a strict legal–rational character.

POWER DISTRIBUTION: AUTHORITY VS. CONTROL

The power structure of a prismatic society consists of a 'highly centralized and concentrated authority structure overlapping a control system that is highly localized and dispersed'.[60] There exists a separation of 'authority' ('officially sanctioned or legitimate power') and 'control' ('real' but 'unofficially permitted or illegitimate power').

The authority of the sala overlaps with the society's control structures which are based in poly-communalism, clects, and poly-normativism. Thus, the administrative function 'may be performed by concrete structures oriented primarily toward this function and also by other structures lacking this primary orientation'.[61] Such an overlapping influences the relationship between politicians and administrators. Generally, a prismatic society has what Riggs has called 'unbalanced polity' with bureaucrats dominating the politics-administrative system. This is so, despite the politicians' possessing formal policy-making authority. Thus, the sala officials have more extensive participation in decision-making processes than do their counterparts in a diffracted society. Such concentration of power in the hands of the bureaucrats tends to result in a lack of official

---

[60] 'The "Sala" Model', p. 14.
[61] *Administration*, p. 33.

responsiveness of public needs and wishes. Riggs has held that the strengthening of public administration in transitional societies is likely to block political development.[62]

To an important degree, the influence of political leaders (or those having 'authority') varies with their ability to reward or punish the administrators. A weak 'formal leadership' may not be able to reward bureaucrats adequately for the achievement of organizational goals and, therefore, might unintentionally motivate the sala administrator to devote most of his attentions to safeguarding and promoting his own material interests. Thus, the behaviour of the sala official ranges from an effectively dominant control over decision-making to the role of a sinecurist.

Whatever role a bureaucrat might play in a prismatic society, he influences considerably the level of output in the sala. Riggs has suggested that 'there is an inverse ratio between administrative output and bureaucratic power: the more powerful officials become, the less effective they are as administrators'.[63] The sala is characterized by nepotism in recruitment, institutionalized corruption, inefficiency in the administration of laws, and by the motives of gaining power and of protecting its own interests. The sala behaviour is 'basically wasteful and prodigal'.[64]

Much of the overlapping and formalism has to do with the character of development in a particular society. It would be pertinent to see how different sources of social change in a prismatic society induce some of its characteristics.

THE DILEMMA OF CHANGE IN A PRISMATIC SOCIETY

Riggs has observed that because of the relatively long time-span of their development, the western nations were able to adjust gradually their effective behaviour to the evolving prescribed behaviour. Consequently, these nations experienced less formalism, heterogeneity, and overlapping than is faced by the contemporary transitional societies. This difference in the pace of development is related basically to the sources of change in a particular society.

[62] *Administration*, pp. 226–7. In this context, by political development, Riggs has generally implied a 'balance' of power between the politicians and the bureaucrats; one gets a clear impression from his analysis that he favours effective political control over the bureaucrats.

[63] Ibid., p. 285.

[64] See, Ibid., pp. 260–85.

A prismatic society faces pressure for change from external sources as well as from internal ones. If change is caused primarily by external pressures (as under technical assistance programmes), it may be called 'exo-genous' change. Conversely, change that is stimulated predominantly through internal processes is 'endo-genous'. When both types of pressures for change are relatively equal in strength, the change they produce is 'equi-genetic'.

Riggs has hypothesized that the more exo-genetic the process of diffraction, the more formalistic and heterogeneous its prismatic phase; the more endo-genetic, the less formalistic and heterogeous.[65] Thus, greater formalism, heterogeneity, and overlapping are likely to exist in an 'exo-prismatic' society than in an 'endo-prismatic' one. This difference results because, with endo-genetic change, 'effective' behaviour precedes the creation of new formal institutions, but in an exo-genetic transformation the sequence is reversed. Paradoxically, in their bid to absorb the externally induced change in the shortest possible time, prismatic societies face the possibilities of higher formalism, heterogeneity, and 'the severity of revolutionary tensions'.[66]

APPRAISAL

A critical appraisal of certain salient characteristics of the prismatic-sala model in the overall context of the Riggsian typology of social and administrative systems is now possible.

Ecological models, such as those of Riggs, provide conceptual tools 'for identifying and analysing the contextual values that motivate administrative behaviour' in the developing countries.[67] A 'truly' ecological approach in public administration, however, would study the *interactions* between the administrative system and its environment and thus would analyse the way each of them affects the other's behaviour. In Riggs's analysis of the prismatic society, the major focus is upon the impact of the environment on the administrative structures. In his analysis, public administration appears to be a dependent variable, with little autonomy or independent capacity to control or modify its environment except as a result of external forces. This feature of Riggsian models becomes quite manifest in the analysis

[65] *Ecology*, p. 143.

[66] Ibid.

[67] Milton J. Esman, 'The Ecological Style in Comparative Administration', *Public Administration Review*, XXVII (1967), p. 278.

of the interaction between the sala and various socio-cultural and economic environmental structures. It is less manifest in Riggs's hypotheses on the relationship between the political system and its bureaucracy, for he makes much of the relative dominance of bureaucracy over the political system. In fact, however, the independent variables in his analysis lie *outside* bureaucracy in the social system. Since many prismatic societies in the real world have relatively autonomous administrative sub-systems capable of directing socioeconomic change, an analysis of prismatic societies should take into account the variation in the capabilities of administrative systems in different settings.

The major thrust of Riggs's models involves the structure of the environment of administrative systems and not the administrative systems themselves. His primary concern appears to be the input side of the administrative system, rather than throughput or output. The prismatic model is 'relatively more successful as a conceptualization of developing social systems than as an analysis of the place of administration in such systems'.[68] This is so mainly because Riggs has 'not fully worked out the implications of his theory for public administration'.[69]

As regards the structure of the environment of administrative systems, Riggs's models understate the possibility that various social structures may vary independently of each other. There are several cases, however, in the empirical universe where a 'developing' prismatic society has 'prismatic' socio-cultural sub-systems, but a relatively diffracted bureaucratic sub-system. For example, in India and Malaysia, largely as a result of their colonial experience, there is a considerable role-differentiation between the politicians and the bureaucrats, with the politicians generally being supreme. Although Riggs pays lip-service to the possibility of a variety of mixes, the major thrust of the prismatic model appears to be based on the assumption that there is a high degree of co-variation of certain structures, thus producing a limited set structural combination. There exists, therefore, a clear need to construct more 'mixed' type categories for the analysis of transitional societies, which would also take into account the degree of autonomy of each sub-system in a society.

[68] Jackson, 'An Analysis of the Comparative Public Administration Movement', p. 124.

[69] Richard A. Chapman, 'Prismatic Theory in Public Administration: A Review of the Theories of Fred W. Riggs,' *Public Administration* (London), XLIV (1966), p. 423.

The absence of such variously mixed analytical categories in Riggsian analysis has led to certain unfortunate causal implications. It is not necessarily true, for example, that formalism enhances the power of bureaucrats, or that increased power of administrators leads to administrative ineffectiveness. Nor can it be claimed that the subordination of bureaucrats necessarily makes the functioning of power centres more effective.[70] In fact, much would depend on the way a term such as 'power' is defined for various social environments. Likewise, Riggs's analysis conveys an impression of causality in his correlation of social and administrative structures.[71] One might argue that such impressions of causality are ingredients of the logical structure of Riggs's ideal-type constructs. Nonetheless, at various points of his analysis Riggs has discussed prismatic patterns and their interrelationships in a manner that suggests that these are accurate descriptions of patterns existing in the empirical universe.[72]

Riggs could have made his analysis more useful by hypothesizing more extensively on the interrelationships among certain structural conditions within a prismatic society. R.S. Milne has provided an example by specifying certain structural conditions which might cause or promote the emergence or existence of other structural characteristics. He has hypothesized that under two conditions bureaucrats may not be powerful in a prismatic model. First, if there is a tradition of civil service neutrality, and, second, if the politicians are powerful enough to be able to control the bureaucrats.[73] In Pakistan, the first condition obtains, but not the second; in India both prevail to a degree, while in the Philippines the second exists, but not the first. Thus, Riggs's analysis needs more analytical categories incorporating structural variation among different prismatic societies.

---

[70] Edgar L. Shor, Comparative Administration: Static Study versus Dynamic Reform, *Public Administration Review*, XXII (1962), p. 160.

[71] Ibid. In the summary of Riggs basic ideas in this chapter, terms such as 'likely' and 'generally' minimize much of the deterministic impression which the original works provide at several places. However, Riggs has argued that his model is an 'ideal-type', and does not represent 'reality'.

[72] Joseph La Palombara has observed that Riggsian analysis stresses that the diffracted and the fused societies are only ideal-types and thus appears to imply that all empirical systems are necessarily prismatic. 'Public Administration and Political Change: A Theoretical Overview', in Charles Press and Alan Arian (eds), *Empathy and Ideology: Aspects of Administrative Innovation* (Chicago: Rand McNally and Co., 1966), p. 93.

[73] *Concepts and Models in Public Administration* (New Delhi: Indian Institute of Public Administration, 1966), p. 18.

OVERLAPPING—A RESTRICTED CONCEPT

Another area requiring further examination is the concept of 'overlapping'. In Riggsian analysis 'overlapping' appears to be limited in its scope, as it is designed only to indicate the simultaneous existence of traditional institutions and those patterned after Western practices. It does not include certain other sources of overlapping found in transitional societies. John Montgomery has observed that one method of instituting administrative reforms in developing countries without a wholesale replacement of qualified personnel is 'to duplicate functions, placing the old bureaucracy in a competitive position or bypassing it altogether'. For example, 'semi-public corporations and similar devices can serve both to stimulate the bureaucracy and to develop controlled non-governmental capabilities for serving national purposes'.[74]

What is true of a developing or prismatic society may also be true of a 'relatively diffracted society' like the United States. Michael Crozier has observed that American administrators 'do not mind setting up two or three competitive agencies whose conflicts will certainly entail waste, but which also brings new ideas and interesting change'.[75] Thus the developed societies, despite having less multifunctionality of structures, are not different from the developing societies in regard to the phenomenon of overlapping considered broadly. Moreover, it should be noted carefully that overlapping *per se* is not dysfunctional to the process of administrative development. In some cases, as Crozier remarked, it might bring 'new ideas and interesting change'.

Thus, Riggs's ecological models should give greater recognition to the existence of overlapping in other contexts. An analysis of the sources of overlapping relatively diffracted societies could add to the heuristic utility of Riggs's models. Otherwise, the practice of associating the feature of overlapping largely with prismatic society, and at the same time enumerating the evils of overlapping, only reinforces the 'negative' image of prismatic societies (which, in essence, applies to all the developing societies of today).

---

[74] John D. Montgomery, 'Sources of Administrative Reform: Problems of Power, Purpose, and Politics' (Bloomington, Ill.: CAG, 1967), mimeo, p. 63, quoted in Milne, 'Differentiation and Administrative Development', *Journal of Comparative Administration*, I (1969), p. 222.

[75] *The Bureaucratic Phenomenon* (Chicago: University of Chicago Press, 1964), p. 253.

THE NEGATIVE CHARACTER OF THE PRISMATIC MODEL

In general, the prismatic model appears to have a western bias. The prismatic traits seem 'deviant' when viewed from the vantage point of a diffracted society. The negative character of the model is reflected, first of all, in the terminology used by Riggs to depict social behaviour in a prismatic society. Riggs uses terms like 'normlessness', 'ritualism', 'mimetic', 'donative expenditure', 'bazaar-canteen', subsidized canteen', 'myths', 'double talk', 'interference complex', and 'dependency syndrome' to characterize the functioning of a prismatic society. Unquestionably, such terms are value-laden. They emphasize only the negative aspects of the prismatic behaviour. The model implies that the 'negative' and 'negative alone' is the 'real' in a prismatic society. This prismatic terminology may be contrasted with terms like 'market imperfections' and 'frictions' used to understand deviant behaviour in a relatively diffracted society.

Terminology, however, is only one reflection of the apparent philosophy behind the prismatic model. As Michael Monroe observed recently: 'Riggs's theory appears to use developed nations, like the United States, as the standard for evaluating activities in the prismatic nations. In this way, development setbacks in the prismatic countries are explained as dysfunctional applications of diffracted norms to bewildered and unstable societies'.[76]

Riggs apparently has chosen to study only those actions of a prismatic society which appear to violate ideal standards of economy, efficiency, and morality of the West. He has not made complementary efforts to compare standards of morality, economy, and efficiency of the transitional societies with immorality, bad economics, and inefficiency in the developed nations.[77] Moreover, his model analyses essentially the negative aspects of the political, social, economic, and administrative sub-systems in developing countries. Logically, with an implicit idealized American comparative reference, the prismatic model emerges with largely a negative character.

Riggs has held that the United States comes very close to the diffracted model, although it has certain prismatic traits as found in

---

[76] 'Prismatic Behavior in the United States?', *Journal of Comparative Administration*, II (1970), p. 230. A part of the following discussion is based on this source.

[77] To a certain extent the analysts of comparative government lack the courage to compare unpleasant aspects of developed societies with similar as well as dissimilar observations abroad'. Ibid., p. 241.

the American local government. But such references to prismatic behaviour in the United States or in other relatively diffracted societies appear to be wholly peripheral in his scheme of analysis. Monroe, on the other hand, has provided convincing arguments that American social structures have a large number of prismatic characteristics. A few cases: violation of the letter and the spirit of the American Constitution in civil rights matters; indifference of public employees toward strike laws; corruption in high governmental circles; labour union activities which violate prescribed legislation; the discriminatory behaviour of the regulatory agencies; tax loopholes; weaknesses of the insurance system; the 'Mafia', politically backed private monopolies; bureaucratic overstaffing; phenomenal military budgets and anomaly of J. Edgar Hoover—the most 'powerful' bureaucrat.[78] In citing these instances, it is not intended to argue that American society is relatively prismatic. The purpose here is to indicate that Riggs has clearly understated the nature and the extent of prismatic traits in relatively diffracted societies. He has, in fact, assumed a close relation between the diffraction of social structures and legal-rationality in the behaviour of their participants. Thus, in Riggs's ecological models, with insignificant exceptions, prismatic behaviour consistently accompanies a medium level of differentiation, while diffracted behaviour is concomitant with a high level of differentiation. Riggs has presented several examples to support the first of three assumptions but has not carefully analysed the implications of the second assumption; thus the reasons for prismatic behaviour in a diffracted society are left undiscussed. As a consequence, Riggs appears to have evaluated the actual behaviour of prismatic societies in relation to the formally prescribed behaviour of diffracted societies. Analytically, this imbalance of emphasis overburdens the prismatic model with largely negative elements, implications, and inferences. If analytical categories of 'effective' social and administrative behaviour in a relatively diffracted society are created and then utilized to evaluate the functioning of the prismatic-sala system, then the image of social and administrative structures in the developing societies would not be as negative as Riggs's prismatic model would suggest.[79]

[78] Note another of Monroe's comments: 'Bureaucratic power may prove to be most socially maligned in a developed society where technology has given bureaucrats the communication and control capabilities to impose their will upon nearly all citizens.' Ibid., p. 238.

[79] Monroe has commented, 'A comparative analysis of formalistic or hypocritical

Further, Riggs has looked at both the formal and the actual norms and practices within a prismatic society. However, he appears to have considered the 'stated' goals and objectives as identical to the 'real' goals and objectives. Organizational analysis has demonstrated that formally 'given' objectives are often not the 'real' objectives. If the 'real' objectives of a social or administrative organization are not considered, findings will necessarily reflect a huge gap between assumed purposes and actual performance. Although it is difficult to study the 'real' goals of a social organization,[80] the alternative of considering the 'formal' goals for the 'real' ones is also risky. This dilemma is inherent in most cases of goal-analysis. Nonetheless, the image of prismatic society emerges as highly negative because of the identification of its 'real' goals with 'formal' ones.

The problem of negativism is increased in Riggs's model by the almost total neglect of the existence of diffracted behaviour in a prismatic society. Riggs has not considered 'adequately' significant variations in the effectiveness of different structures in a prismatic society. Jose Abueva has pointed out that in the Filippino bureau-cracy, at one extreme are 'decisional areas of known unmitigated cathexis and individual bargaining, such as patronage in semi-skilled and unskilled labour in public work projects'; while on the other end there are decisional areas where rules are applied and services ren-dered objectively and 'where official duties and obligations clearly transcend cathexis and bargaining as the form of exchange among ... those involved in official transaction.'[81] This is an example of the rather common occurrence of diffracted traits in a society which Riggs has considered as prismatic.[82] Riggs appears to have merely touched on this aspect of social behaviour in his ecological models. However, still another major limitation of these models is a relative neglect of the potentially positive consequences of a supposedly prismatic characteristic—'formalism'.

---

behaviour patterns in prismatic and diffracted contexts may demonstrate similar causes and perhaps call into question some of America's moral posturing', p. 234.

[80] For this and other difficulties in 'goal model', see, Amitai Etzioni, *Modern Organizations* (Englewood Cliffs, N. J.: Prentice-Hall, 1964), pp. 5–19.

[81] *Conditions of Administrative Development: Exploring Administrative Culture and Behavior in the Philippines* (Bloomington: Comparative Administration Group, 1966), pp. 54–5, quoted in Milne. Mechanistic and Organic Models of Public Administration in Developing Countries', *Administrative Science Quarterly*, XV (1970), pp. 63–4.

[82] For Riggsian analysis of Philippines as a prismatic society, see *Ecology*, pp. 98–143.

FORMALISM—POSITIVE AND NEGATIVE

In Riggsian terms, 'formalism' refers to 'the degree of discrepancy or incongruence between the formally prescribed and the effectively practiced, between norms and realities'. Riggs has stated that this 'distinguishing characteristics' of a prismatic system leads to official corruption, to arbitrary administration, and to obstacles in the achievement of programmed objectives. Thus, in Riggsian terms, formalism is dysfunctional for developing countries.[83]

Both structural–functional analysis and the ecological perspective suggest that a particular structure may be eufunctional or dysfunctional depending, among other things, on its environment. Riggs has not looked at this aspect of ecology when analysing 'formalism'. In a sense, Riggs's implication that formalism is dysfunctional in most or all circumstances represents a 'non-ecological' viewpoint. To counterbalance the Riggsian concept of 'negative' formalism, Valsan has recently presented a new concept of 'positive formalism'.[84]

Considering some empirical examples of public administration in India, the Philippines, and Stalinist Russia, Valsan found that formalism seemed to bring forth 'a positive and creative effect useful for development', by skipping several slow-moving routines of government. Such 'functional' formalism has been aptly termed by Valsan as 'positive formalism'. While the negative formalism leads to, what Riggs has called, 'negative development',[85] 'positive formalism helps positive development'.[86] Valsan has suggested that even in an 'atmosphere of negative formalism, where what is legal is given little respect, good leadership may "exploit" it for the sake of development thorough positive formalism'.[87] Interestingly, Milne has recommended that the training institutions in developing countries should *'teach and promote the virtue of practising positive formalism as much as*

[83] An example of this Riggsian viewpoint can be cited by referring to his analysis of the consequences of 'exogenous' change in a developing society. Riggs has remarked that the exogenous change 'accounts both for the more rapid course of transformation [and for] the higher *danger* of formalism and heterogeneity'. *Ecology*, p. 143. Emphasis added to underscore Riggs's assumption that formalism *is* dangerous.

[84] E.H. Valsan, 'Positive Formalism: A Desideration for Development', *Philippine Journal of Public Administration*, XII (1968), pp. 3–6.

[85] 'Negative development' refers to situations when 'undesired' changes occur in the areas of economic productivity, economic security, distribution of wealth, and non-economic values (such as social welfare). When 'desired' changes take place in these areas, it implies 'positive development', Riggs, *Administration*, p. 42.

[86] Valsan, 'Positive Formalism', p. 6.

[87] Ibid.

practicable'.[88] Although it may be difficult to develop 'formal' training in formalism, Milne's point emphasizes the value of positive formalism as a new dimension in comparative public administration. Thus, this concept creates an awareness that high administrative output is not always a function of 'realism' in bureaucratic behaviour.

DIFFRACTION, COORDINATION, AND PERFORMANCE

Riggs, in his search for a common variable in economic, political, socio-cultural, and administrative development, has found the degree of diffraction (or structural differentiation) a useful heuristic measure.[89] In his analysis, the central variable is 'increasing differentiation of structures rather than any consequences of that diffraction, whether it be productivity, capital formation, income distribution, personal security, or some associated political, social, or administrative variable'.[90] Thus, Riggs has not hypothesized or provided analytical categories concerning the relationship between the degree of diffraction and the level of development in a society, although he has stated that it might serve a heuristic purpose to identify these processes (of diffraction and development) with each other.[91]

Another area needing greater representation in Riggs's models is administrative coordination. Although Riggs has referred to the problems of 'poor coordination' in the context of developing countries in general,[92] in his diffraction-oriented ecological models, he has not related such problems to the internal organizational patterns in bureaucratic structures. Recently he has observed, however, that 'the more differentiated a system becomes, the more difficult and delicate becomes the task of coordinating highly specialized roles'.[93] But he has not developed this theme extensively. Paradoxically, most problems in prismatic societies can be seen from the perspective of lack of coordination—between the politicians and the administrators,

[88] Milne, 'Formalism Reconsidered', *Philippine Journal of Public Administration*, XIV (1970), p. 30. Emphasis added,

[89] *Administration*, p. 419.

[90] Ibid., pp. 421–2.

[91] Martin Landau has identified the concept of development with that of differentiation: 'the more developed the system, the greater the degree of specialization'. On the Use of Functional Analysis in American Political Science', *Social Research*, XXXV (1968), p. 57.

[92] *Administration*, pp. 253–5.

[93] *Thailand: The Modernization of a Bureaucratic Polity* (Honolulu: East West Center Press, 1966), p. 376.

between the generalists and the specialists, between planning agencies and the administrative organs, and between the central authorities and the decentralized administrative organs. Thus, a clear need exists to include an analysis of the problems of politico-administrative coordination within the structure of prismatic model.

Furthermore, Riggs's ecological models do not contain specific hypotheses on the relationship between differentiation and administrative performance. But outside the framework of these models, he has reflected on this subject. While dealing with the concept of 'administrative development',[94] he recognized that variations in performance level become increasingly significant as the degree of structural differentiation of a system increases.[95] The heuristic utility of Riggs's ecological models will certainly increase if they include some analytical categories hypothesizing interrelationships among the degree of diffraction, administrative coordination, and organizational performance. Adding more variables could make the tasks of a researcher more difficult, but the elements of coordination and performance are of crucial pertinence if Riggsian models are to become more *administration-oriented* than they are now.[96] A focus on administrative outputs will also help these models to become more developmental in perspective.

Some Aspects of 'Heuristicism' in Riggsian Models

The ideal-type models of Riggs, by underscoring the significance of 'administrative ecology', have influenced much research in comparative public administration.[97] 'Systemic' models which follow a

---

[94] The concept of 'administrative development' is introduced in Chapter VI.

[95] 'Administrative Development: An Elusive Concept', in J. D. Montgomery and W. J. Siffin (eds), *Approaches to Development: Politics, Administration, and Change* (New York: McGraw-Hill, 1966), p. 239. Milne has also underscored the inseparability of the elements of performance and differentiation in any concept of administrative development. See, 'Differentiation and Administrative Development', pp. 213–33.

[96] For suggestions to include psychological–cognitive, geographical, and ideological factors in ecological models, see Milne, *Concepts and Models in Public Administration,* pp. 16–18.

[97] Some works having an ecological approach in comparative public administration are: William J. Siffin, *The Thai Bureaucracy: Institutional Change and Development* (Honolulu: East West Center Press, 1966); Nghiem Dang, *Vietnam: Politics and Public Administration* (Honolulu: East West Center Press, 1966); and Riggs, *Thailand: The Modernization of a Bureaucratic Polity.* For an application of the prismatic-sala model to Japan, see, James R. Brady, 'Japanese Administrative Behavior and the "Sala" Model', *Philippine Journal of Public Administration,* VIII (1964), pp. 314–26.

macrosociological approach, as Riggsian constructs do, are essentially logical frameworks of analysis, designed to suggest certain relationships among the different variables they incorporate. The rigours of a 'scientific theory' should not be expected in these frameworks. It can be argued, nevertheless, that for aiding researchers, the concepts outlined in such models should be 'manageable' for research, and therefore they should be operationalized or made potentially operationable to the degree possible. This point becomes pertinent in Rigg's case because he has held that degrees of differentiation are potentially quantifiable. He observed: 'As the techniques become refined, it may be possible to locate individual countries—Thailand, Egypt, the Philippines, Mexico, Japan, Spain, Brazil, New Zealand, Ethiopia, the United States, China, Italy—on such a [diffraction] scale. We could imagine a central tendency for each country which could be located at a unique point in the scale of diffraction.'[98]

In their present form, the ecological models enable only qualitative and functional comparisons among various societies. But even such comparisons become less useful with reliance on impressionistic categories like 'more or less prismatic', 'highly prismatic', and 'typically prismatic'.[99] When efforts are made to measure diffraction, certain problems peculiar to public administration are bound to crop up. It is difficult to define, for example, the boundaries between 'policy-making' and 'policy-execution', and between 'discretion' and adherence to rules. In spite of these and other operational problems, the ecological models have brought new awareness of certain crucial kinds of interactions between the administrative system and its social environment.

CONCLUSION

The preceding analysis appears to have demonstrated that Weberian and Riggsian analyses somewhat complement each other in the study of cross-cultural administrative patterns. Weber described essentially the characteristics of bureaucracy which evolved as a result of certain kinds of socio-economic development (and which also contributed to

[98] *Administration*, p. 30. The assumption behind such a statement is that in any society, it is possible to find data on the degree of structural differentiation by studying the extent to which various organizational roles were exclusive or were permitted participation in other organizations in the same society.

[99] Other terms used by Riggs include: 'extremely fused', 'somewhat fused', 'quite diffracted', 'relatively fused', 'relatively diffracted', and 'highly diffracted'.

that development). Riggs, on the other hand, seems to be seeking explanation of why similar bureaucratic development does not emerge rapidly in present-day developing countries.

It is easy to discern Weber's influence on Riggs in the construction of ecological models. Like Weber, Riggs has provided three ideal-type constructs, which are essentially deductive in character. While the basis of Weberian categories is the type of legitimacy associated with an authority system, Riggsian typology is based on the criterion of structural differentiation, which differs from Weber's qualitatively distinct ideal-types. However, it appears that elements of Weber's legal–rational authority dominate in Riggs's diffracted society. More particularly, legal–rational authority system is characterized by a relative autonomy of structures, which is also a feature of a diffracted society. Likewise, it can be seen that a fused society (of Riggs) has several characteristics of Weber's traditional authority system. Both these systems have a role-differentiation of a simple sort.

Although no exact parallel of Weber's charismatic authority system is found in Riggs's typology, some characteristics of routinized charisma can be found in empirical 'prismatic' societies, such as India, Nepal, Ethiopia, and Iran. Nevertheless, empirical examples of charismatic authority are somewhat different today, in that most charismatic figures are obviously involved in modernizing programmes. Since Riggs has been interested primarily in contemporary administrative systems, he has not come out with a category of ideal-type charismatic leadership. Perhaps he has assumed that the fragmented administrative system in an emergent nation is not typically dominated by politicians even when there is a charismatic leader.

Weberian and Riggsian typologies differ in regard to the number of ecological elements incorporated in them. In Weberian analysis, the nature of the administrative staff is understood by reference to the character of the authority system. Weber linked several socio-cultural norms of the authority system with the character of the administrative staff. But his analysis of the impact of economic environment upon an administrative system is sketchy. Riggs's discussion of the socio-cultural and economic aspects of administrative ecology is much more extensive than Weber's. He has drawn upon contemporary structural-functionalism, and hence his analysis includes a more systemic approach on societal level. Both scholars, however, have paid considerable attention to interaction between the political system and its administrative sub-system.

Weber's analysis of the administrative staff within a legal–rational authority is extensive when compared to his treatment of administrative staff in a traditional and a charismatic authority system. Riggs, on the other hand, has been more interested in the working of the 'sala' in a prismatic society, and a discussion of the administrative patterns in the diffracted and the fused societies is only peripheral to his central concern of understanding the administrative problems of prismatic societies. In other words, Riggs, like Weber, has focused attention on nations at a certain stage of socio-cultural development—although he has chosen a different set of nations—and, therefore, has treated other nations only incidentally for purposes of comparison. Thus, the crux of Weberian analysis is legal–rational authority system and its bureaucracy, while that of Riggsian discussion is prismatic society and its 'sala'. Some of the major differences between Weberian 'bureaucracy' and Riggsian 'sala' can be seen as follows:

Bureaucracy	Sala
1. Organized in hierarchy of offices.	1. 'Heterogeneity'.
2. Defined competence of each office.	2. 'Overlapping'.
3. Selection of officials by achievement.	3. Attainment as the basis of recruitment; nepotism.
4. Administration by rule.	4. Formalism.
5. 'Universalism' and impersonal operations; officials are subject to authority only in official capacity.	5. Personalized norms in official behaviour.
6. Separation of public funds from private.	6. Widespread official corruption.

The problem in making such a distinction is that Riggs's ideal-type of sala system is by nature a composite one, and it is difficult to clearly specify in it all the counterparts of the characteristics of 'bureaucracy'.

Nonetheless, both typologies lack analytical categories to explain 'development' in social and particularly administrative systems. Weber's assumption of the unilinear development of bureaucratization is not very helpful for studying the crises of modernization. Riggs, likewise, chose not to analyse the impact of increasing diffraction upon development in his ecological models. Lack of developmental orientation in Weber's models can be explained by the fact that he was not looking at societies where the rate of modernization was pronounced. The 'third world' had not emerged before him, and, for that matter, the 'second world' had just begun to emerge before his death. On the other hand, Riggs's writings have been influenced by the emergence of numerous 'new' States. Outside of his ecological models, he has made substantial contributions to the nascent field of development administration. However, it is important that both the ecological and developmental perspectives should be included in comparative administrative models.

CHAPTER FOUR

Marxist Contributions to the Theory of the Administrative State[*]

O. P. Dwivedi, William Graf and J. Nef

The purpose of this essay is twofold. First, it explores the question of whether there is a specifically Marxist perspective in the analysis of bureaucracy and public policy; and second it examines the extent to which Marxist perspectives might contribute a broader under-standing of the phenomenon known as the administrative state. These themes are of substantial theoretical and practical relevance. For one thing they are at the core of the question of the socialist model of development and the transition to communism. On the other hand, a Marxist analysis and critique of the administrative state poses in very explicit terms the often complex relationship between, 'socialism' and 'democracy'. This being an exploratory essay, we shall be focusing on a few salient aspects to ensure that our analysis does not burgeon into an unwieldy conglomeration of partial de-scriptions. Therefore, the arguments presented here are necessarily tentative and suggestive, rather than comprehensive or definitive. In this essay, we have concentrated on the state bureaucracy rather than other types of bureaucratic organizations.

MARXISM AND THE STATE BUREAUCRACY

It is hardly fortuitous that Marxist scholarship until now has taken practically no interest in the study of public administration as such. This is so despite the fact that since the turn of the century at least, bureaucracy has emerged as a pivotal and central focal area within

[*] *The Indian Journal of Political Science*, vol. 46, no. 1, January–March 1985.

the political and social sciences. This apparent neglect is understandable, since any theory of public administration must rest upon a prior theory of the state. If the theory is left implicit and the bureaucracy is analysed as an institution-in-itself, then public administration as a scholarly subdiscipline is confined to the description and enumeration of catalogues of structures and functions, or the derivation of 'pathologies' and corresponding prescriptions for technical improvements. The *uncritical* approach, which takes as given the advanced capitalist context of bureaucratic operation, remains dominant in North American social science in particular. On the other hand, where theories of the state, and the premises underlying them, are made explicit, then the state bureaucracy can be better analysed and compared within this holistic framework. As Erik O. Wright observed in 1974:

What is needed is precisely a theoretical orientation that integrates these perspectives, that provides a systematic understanding of the relationship between social structure and the internal organizational process of the state.[1]

Until recently it could be said that Western Marxism had been hampered by the absence of an adequate theory of the state. That gap now appears to have been diminished by a spate of important recent studies.[2] But only very infrequently do these theories venture into an explicit examination of public administration. To undertake this task, then, one must in large measure *infer* such a theory of public administration from the large body of Marxist and neo-Marxist literature on the state. This literature at least contains numerous valuable *elements* of, and *insights* into an understanding and explanation of administration in general and the administrative state in particular. A central question here is whether those elements and insights coalesce into a discernible paradigm.

Even the 'early' Marx was concerned with the relationship between the state and bureaucracy. In his 1843 *Critique of Hegel's Philosophy of Right*—which, to be sure, was intended more as a critical analysis of the Hegelian dialectical method than as a general theory of the state—Marx advanced the proposition that, far from a 'universalistic', 'rational' institution 'above' particularist interests, the state

---

[1] Eric Olin Wright, 'To Control on the Smash the Bureaucracy: Weber and Lenin on Politics, the State and Bureaucracy', *Berkeley Journal of Sociology*, XIX (1974–75), p. 98.

[2] See, for example, N. Poulantzas, *Fascism and Dictatorship* (London: NLB, 1974); Ralph Miliband, *Marxism and Politics* (London: Oxford University Press, 1977); and Bob Jessop, *The Capitalist State* (London: Blackwell, 1981).

(bureaucracy) was in fact embedded in the conflict of interests and classes in capitalist society. The state bureaucracy, therefore, lacking any 'universal interest', turns out to be nothing more than one egotistic interest among many others.[3] The notion of the class nature of the state bureaucracy not only stands in opposition to subsequent Durkheimian and Weberian theories of the state, it also produces the important insight that the state is, in the last analysis, a partisan instrument in the enactment of intra-societal class struggles, rather than a neutral umpire of such struggles. State officials appropriate state power as their private property. Through this process they exercise both hegemony and domination in capitalist society. That is why, according to Marx, both private property and the abstract state must be abolished before the posited 'universal interest' and 'egalitarian democracy' of the dictatorship of the proletariat can be realized.[4] The partisan bureaucracy concept was later incorporated more systematically into the classic Marxian base superstructure model.[5] We stress here the resilient, heuristic quality of the Marxian model in contrast to cruder, deterministic variants of it which simply posited a general correspondence between the mode of production on the one hand and on the other the vast superstructure of state forms, law, religion, culture, etc. which was determined by the economic base. The problem arising from the viewpoint of the study of public administration is that the Marxist theory of the state in a sense precludes a nuanced examination of the operation of the state bureaucracy. For this is explained away by once positing (a) the class character of the bureaucracy and (b) the embedding of the bureaucracy in the capitalist political economy. Indeed, vulgar Marxism for too long was content with this superficial explanation. Only recent neo-Marxist scholarship has managed to revive and expand the analytical categories of the *relative autonomy* of the state and the *relative hegemony* of the state elite as operative categories. We will return to these presently.

MARXIST THEORY AND LENINIST PRAXIS

When after 1917 Marxist theory was confronted by historical reality, a major paradigmatic shift was required in the theory. This was

[3] See, Karl Marx, *A Contribution to the Critique of Hegel's Philosophy of Right*, Marx-Engels, *Collected Works*, vol. 3, 1843 (Moscow: International Publishers).

[4] See Karl Marx, 'On the Jewish Question', Marx-Engels, *Collected Works* (MECW), vol. 4, 1854.

[5] On this, see in particular, *The German Ideology and Capital*, vol. 3 both in MECW, op cit.

largely the contribution of V. I. Lenin, whose main concern lay much more in the realm of method than teleology, in strategy and tactics rather than values and end principles. In this respect, his is a very direct contribution to both a theory and strategy of power, including the tactics of revolution. It is also, therefore, a theory of the state as well as of management and organization.

Marxism–Leninism, as interpreted by Stalin, was hobbled from the outset by a series of contradictions which, *mutatis mutatndis*, have been imposed from the Soviet experience on to the praxis of all the Eastern European Soviet-type regimes. In the Soviet Union, there developed a conflict between a Marxist theory evolved in and for late capitalism (whose objective historical task was to create the *material preconditions* for communism), and a praxis conditioned by the historical reality of underdevelopment, the overriding imperative of modernization and the corresponding need to 'telescope' socioeconomic change. The imperative was reinforced by tendencies toward internal centrifugality (separatism, reaction), abetted and fostered by the presence of counter-revolutionary troops in the Soviet sphere. This in turn necessitated the rapid creation of a massive bureaucratic (democratic centralism) and military (Trotsky's Red Army) state apparatus which, in line with this situationally given 'primacy of politics', would in some measure have to persuade, guide and coerce a non-proletarian population toward mobilization and integration. This alone was a formidable undertaking in a predominantly rural 'traditional' society in which, therefore, the means of production were unevenly developed and perhaps a mere five per cent of the population could be classified as urban workers. Thus socialism not only had to take root under conditions of extreme want and scarcity, it had to socialize the entire production process virtually overnight. All of this—in the absence of a mass popular basis of support and of an adequate infrastructure—had to be accomplished by the Bolshevik state *on behalf of the people and in the name of the revolution*. In a very real sense, then the Soviet revolution was, above all other things, an administrative revolution.[6] The late Issac Deutscher, in this context, spoke of a confusion of means and ends.

As national wealth was being accumulated, the mass of consumers, who are also the producers, were exposed to continued and even aggravated want and poverty: and bureaucratic control over every aspect of national life substituted itself for social control and responsibility. The order of priorities

---

[6] See, Neil Harding, *Lenin's Political Thought* (London, 1981).

was as it were reversed. The forms of socialism had been forged before the content, the economic and cultural substance, was available: and as the content was being produced the forms deteriorated or were distorted.[7]

Yet the Leninist–Stalinist model of an administered revolution also represents a (historically and temporally fixed) resolution of the contradiction in Marx himself between means and ends, form and content. For the central goal of socialism for Marx—especially the 'early' Marx—was human emancipation. From Proudhon, Marx developed the notion that, once private ownership of the means of production and with it the division of labour in society could be eliminated, so too would all relations of domination and subordination disappear. Perfect freedom as species–being would be the result. Thus, in the *18th Brumaire* and *the Civil War in France* respectively, Marx counterposes the particularist, over-bureaucratized Second Napoleonic Empire with the Paris Commune which, briefly, had managed to do away with the bureaucratic machine and establish a system of voluntary interaction. Here the Marxist antibureaucratic aims are in close proximity to those of the anarchists. In both cases, society is to triumph over the state as a precondition for general emancipation.

However, Marx (the 'later' Marx of *Capital*, for instance) also clearly recognized that these revolutionary goals must be prepared for and executed on the basis of organization and administration. Both the elimination of capitalist exploitation, including the 'integration' of the exploiter class, and the reorganization of production and distribution would require a strong, albeit provisional, state: the dictatorship of the proletariat. Socialism presupposed a firm material base of security and welfare for all, in contrast to capitalism which could only exacerbate social inequality and progressively disassociate the non-owners from the means of production. Unlike anarchist prescriptions, which aimed at smashing the state *per se* and instantly establishing a system of voluntary cooperation, the Marxian, state, in the transitional period, would arrogate ownership and control over the means of production and distribution to itself. It would consolidate the productive forces through comprehensive, rational planning and through furthering the division of labour and specialization of function. The Marx and Engels of the *Communist Manifesto* thus advocate the socialization and nationalization of credit and banking,

---

[7] Issac Deutscher, *The Unfinished Revolution: Russia 1917–1967* (London: Oxford University Press).

transport and communications, all instruments of production and the labour allocation system under the aegis of the state. Only then, on the foundation of a highly developed, all-encompassing state, could the conditions for its eventual withering away be assured. Neil Harding sees this aspect of Marxian theory as 'technocratic Marxism' which he defines as:

... necessarily wedded to the twin principles of centralization within the state and subordination within the workplace. It had grandiose aspirations not merely for the size of individual productive units but for the planning and direction of the entire national and international economy. This would require, on an exalted plane, authoritative directions on the social division of labour and allocation of resources. Only a centralized authority could dictate, as it would have to, the measure or labour and consumption.[8]

Stalinist Leninism, in the particular Russian context of scarcity and underdevelopment, thus represented the (situationally inevitable) decision for technocratic Marxism not only over, but against emancipatory Marxism.

The role of party organization—the vanguard theory—is at the centre of Leninism. An organizational principle, democratic centralism, is elevated to a fundamental principle governing party life. Moreover, Leninism formulates and elaborates a theory of state power and the management of the dictatorship of the proletariat. Lenin shared much of Marx's distrust for bureaucracy. He sees the state and its bureaucracy as a 'special organization of force: it is an organization of violence for the suppression of some clases',[9] that is the basic structure of capitalist rule. In so doing, he recognized the distinct class character, as opposed to the instrumental nature of the state administration.[10]

Thus, Lenin's interpretation of the conspiratorial and largely superfluous and parasitic nature of bureaucracy in the main reflects Marx's own view. In his view, there is a built-in opposition between socialist—and even bourgeoisie—democracy and bureaucracy.[11] Only after the revolution could this apparatus by stages lose its coercive and exploitative character and be absorbed by society. The question

[8] Neil Harding, 'Socialism, Society and the Organic Labour State', in Neil Harding (ed.), *The State in Socialist Society* (London: Macmillan, 1984), p. 14.

[9] V. Lenin, *Selected Works* (Moscow: International Publishers, 1969), pp. 267 and 280.

[10] V. Seymour Wilson, *Canadian Public Policy and Administration Theory and Environment* (Toronto: McGraw-Hill Ryerson Ltd., 1981), p. 23.

[11] Eva Halevy–Etzioni, *Bureaucracy and Democracy: A Political Dilemma* (London: Routledge and Kegan Paul, 1983), p. 79.

of democratization as debureaucratization is central to Lenin's early thinking. The implicit model here is the just mentioned experience of popular rule by the committee during the ill-fated Paris Commune of 1871.[12] The organizational model is purposefully vague but it nevertheless contains a number of specific characteristics:

(1) election and recall of functionaries at any time;
(2) pay not to exceed that of workman; and
(3) immediate introduction of control and supervision by all to avoid bureaucratic complacency and ossification.

These features were to be instrumental in the establishment of the Soviets as people's committees charged with making the structures of government accountable to the popular will.[13]

Lenin draws a sharp distinction between 'bureaucrats' and 'technicians'. While he see the former 'staff' as entrusted only with relatively simple and superfluous tasks of control and accounting, he has a positive view of the technico-administrative groups as contributing to the productive process.[14] Thus, the sphere of production is real and material, while that of control is essentially a mystification of the entire apparatus of the state.

In this sense, 'Marx sees bureaucracy—unlike Weber—not as a techno-logical imperative necessitated by modern technology and mass administration ... (but as) ... a specifically *political* imperative for the stability of capitalism and the domination of the bourgeoisie'.[15] Bureaucratic transactions, like capitalist financial transactions, are not real necessities but a form of fetishism and alienation. It is precisely these—rather than the technico-administrative functions—that Lenin argued could be immediately transferred to the hands of the workers.

The operation of this mode, however, was a different question. In the process of transformation, he subsequently advocated a gradual transition towards abolishing the bureaucracy using heavy external and technical controls over the bureaucracy. Finally, as the requirements of modernization, defence and more survival set in, the Soviet leadership—Lenin included—had to come to grips with the 'reality' of bureaucracy both in the civil service and in the newly created Red

---

[12] Wright, op cit., p. 85.
[13] Lenin, *Selected Works*, vol. II (Moscow: Foreign Language Publications House, 1947), p. 343.
[14] Wright, op cit., p. 93.
[15] Ibid., p. 92.

Army. Management by committee and armed militias of peasants and workers could not be a match for the combined political, economic, bureaucratic and military might of the West.

Perhaps Leninism's greatest contribution to the theory of the administrative state is the application of Marxist principles to the task of induced development. It is in this task of modernization, as a categorical imperative of the new Soviet state that a sharp contrast emerges between Leninist theory and practice. Fully cognizant of the problems, just alluded to, of trying to distribute poverty in a less developed social formation at the periphery of the international capitalist system, Lenin saw the primary task of the Soviet state as economic development through socialist accumulation. The NEP and the central planning mechanism become fundamental tenets of applied Marxism–Leninism. Indeed, Lenin, and most certainly Stalin, consolidated a complex administrative state whose core *raison d'être* was modernization and the inducement of accelerated socio-economic change. Efficiency was emphasized through material incentives, long-range planning and rational management. At the level of the basic units of production, a form of 'scientific' organization of labour—*Stakhanovism*, a socialist variant of Taylorism—was instituted. In a word, Leninist Marxism and bureaucracy became inextricably linked in a distinct Soviet model. This included the following features;

(1) subordination of the functionaries to the party apparatus,
(2) central planning, budgeting, coordination and control,
(3) democratic centralism and verticality of decision-making,
(4) centralization of organization,
(5) expansion of state role into the spheres of production,
(6) scientific reorganization of the labour force in order to maintain productivity, including techniques of social engineering and social psychology, and
(7) specialization.

Stalinism, in a sense, was the specific application and indeed realization of these authoritarian principles in the Union of Soviets, the replacement of the democratically elected soviets with a centralist, driving bureaucracy. The 'Soviet model' constitues a concrete developmental experience which has profoundly affected state-socialist strategies of management and development, In both Eastern Europe and Asia its influence has been decisive, especially in the initial stages of socialist reconstruction and industrialization.

Subsequent theoretical debates about Marxist–Leninist principles in Western Europe and elsewhere have thus been impelled to take account of, and come to terms with Stalinism. These 'communist' tendencies are fundamentally a critique of the Soviet model and entail a restructuring of Marxist thought. They can be grouped into three main lines: (a) Western European reformulations, including its three main tendencies to explain the nature of the state: 'the character of its leading personnel, the pressures exercised by the economically dominant class, and the structural constraints imposed by the mode of production.'[16] (b) Eastern European revisions, ranging from the New Class postulated by Djilas, the Third Way advocated by Sik, and the immanent critique of Marxism–Leninism undertaken by Bahro; and (c) Third World reactions and new challenges based mainly on concepts of imperialism, neo-colonialism, dependency and various theories of the state its internal and its external linkages, as well as strategies of social revolution. Though all three are squarely in the Marxist tradition, their orientations, starting points and problematics do differ in important ways. For this reason, a brief separate analysis of each will be purposeful here.

WESTERN REFORMULATIONS

After World War II, Western Marxist scholars began making significant contributions to the theory of the administrative state. For many Marxist scholars the analysis of Western 'post-industrial' societies required a drastic revamping of Marxist–Leninist orthodoxy. There was also an increasingly open criticism of Stalinism and a revitalization of the debate over socialism and democracy rooted in the works of Luxemburg, Kautsky, Gramsci, and to a lesser extent, Trotsky. Last, though not least, there was a renewed critique of capitalism and bureaucracy under the new conditions of bourgeois welfarism.

Mainstream Marxism—the Leninist experience notwithstanding— still held on to an essentially instrumentalist view of the state and its functionaries. The state was viewed as determined by the base, as 'the committee for managing the common affairs of the whole bourgeoisie'. The realities of Western Europe and North America—the emergence of the administrative state and the military industrial complex, the differentiated social class structure, etc.—added new dimensions to the debate on state power.

The works of Louis Althusser, Ralph Miliband, Nicos Poulantzas,

---

[16] Ralph Miliband, *Marxism and Politics* (London: Oxford University Press, 1977).

Jurgen Habermas, James O'Connor, Claus Offe and Allan Wolfe, among others, pointed increasingly to a type of state enjoying relative autonomy from the power bloc and the hegemonic faction. Marx's analysis of Bonapartism and subsequent works by Antonio Gramsci pointed to the importance of the suprastructure—ideological, social and political—as well as the specificity of class configurations to an understanding of the direction of historical events. Western scholars like those mentioned above further developed these directions in Marxist analysis. As Miliband has put it:

> to view higher civil servants as mere executants of policies in whose determination they have had little or no share is quite unrealistic. This not to say that 'bureaucrats' are necessarily 'hungry for power', that they run the country ... The true position lies somewhere in between these extremes.[17]

Especially under conditions of institutionalized class struggle as it obtains in advanced bourgeois society, the purely repressive function of the state became less relevant in Marxian analysis. More important were the processes of direct accumulation and legitimation on the part of the state itself. This is not to say—and Poulantzas stresses this—that the state is somehow divorced from society. On the contrary, it is this ostensibly contradictory nature of the capitalist state, combining general legitimation with particularist accumulation, that provides it with a distinctive quality as manager and organizer of class hegemony.

It is around the notions of relative autonomy, institutionalized class struggle, hegemony, accumulation and domination that a Western Marxist theory of the state has been reconstructed. This has created a space as well for a (still rather implicit) Marxist theory of administration. As Vincent Wilson has pointed out, there are three fundamental areas where neo-Marxist theories of the state (as Western reformulations are often referred to) have been substantial.

(1) One has been a generalized or macro-theory of bureaucracy and the administrative state in general. Here, modern bureaucracy emerges as the key mechanism for the management of conflict among contending factions within the limits of bourgeois legitimacy but with a significant degree of relative independence from civil society.

(2) Another contribution has been in the field of the micro-theories of complex organization. Here, the most substantial Marxian

---

[17] Ralph Miliband, *The State in Capitalist Society* (London: Weidenfeld and Nicolson, 1969), p. 119.

conceptualization has been the theory or alienation under large-scale capitalist production.

(3) A third important contribution of western Marxist scholars towards a theory of public administration has been in the field of decision-making and public policy studies.[18] Standing in sharp contrast to bourgeoisie approaches to public policy—such as 'public choice' theories—Marxism has emphasized the essentially systemic, historical and conflictual nature of the policy process. Moreover, it has pointed to the need to blend theoretical analysis with a praxis of social transformation.

To sum up, Marxist contributions to a theory of public administration in the Western World have involved two central aspects. One has been a critique of the bourgeoisie administrative state and its functioning under conditions of post-industrialization. Another theme has been a critique of Marxist orthodoxy, especially the Soviet experience. The debate has been linked to the kind of policy debates and alliance strategies within the European and American left, especially the options offered by Euro-communism. It must be recalled however, that the debate described here, as will be shown in the case of Eastern Europe, has been *from within* the Marxist paradigm. It has not even hinted at the abandonment of Marxism altogether as some 'end of ideology' advocates have suggested.

Eastern European Revisionists

By the end of World War II, Stalinized Marxism–Leninism had certainly realized its primary goal, economic and military modernization, but the subordination of society to the immensely enlarged and pervasive state had clearly rendered democratization and participation into even more remote objectives. In a word, the Paris Commune model of emancipation had yielded to the organized dictatorship of the proletariat foreseen by the *Communist Manifesto*, but without the material preconditions and emancipatory goals assured by the latter. Marxist socialism was finally reduced to an issue of state ownership: the greater the scope and powers of the state, the closer the Soviet Union was said to approximate 'real' socialism. Domination and subordination, individual freedom from, e.g., alienation, the withering away of the state—these issues were simply reduced to irrelevance.

---

[18] Cf. Barbara Stallings, *Class Conflict and Economic Development in Chile 1958–1973* (Stanford: University Press, 1978), *Passim.*

In the wake of the advancing Red Army at the close of the war, it was this bureaucratic, economistic model of state socialism that was transplanted on to the People's Democracies of Eastern Europe. There, an initial policy of 'national roads to socialism' was increasingly supplanted against the background of an intensifying Cold War, by a uniform strategy of Stalinist homogenization. Naturally, the transplantation of a bureaucratic structure into countries at a higher stage of development (GDK, CSSR), with strong nationalist traditions (Poland, Hungary), or with different constellations of national and subnational power (Yugoslavia) involved a certain amount of friction and resistance and, not surprisingly, produced substantial opposition. Out of this opposition, but mainly from within the Marxian tradition, there developed a series of 'revisionist' critiques of bureaucratic state—socialism.

Intra-Marxist revisionist critiques of 'actually existing socialism' generally start from the telling empirical observation that certain phenomena have persisted in these societies which Marx criticized in capitalist system and which communism was supposed to abolish: an identifiable elite class enjoying higher incomes, more perquisites and better life chances than the mass of the population, an *exploited* working class at the bottom of society, persistent material shortages especially of consumer goods, an extensive system of political containment and repression, and a failure—despite rapid development hitherto—to catch up to and surpass advanced capitalist living standards.

These analyses by and large amount to a critique of state bureaucratism and the administrative 'class' that has arisen around the state apparatus. Thus, the Yugoslav politician, Milovan Djilas in the early fifties formulated the concept of an essentially non-productive, repressive and ossified 'New Class'.[19] Djilas, applied Michels's 'Iron Law of Oligarchy' to Marxist analysis. This new class, like its capitalist predecessors, had a vested interest in extracting a surplus—though pre-eminently for development purposes rather than self-aggrandizement—from the workers. The class enjoyed better living standards, much greater disposition over power, more, and more diverse privileges *(pajoks)* and entitlements than the common people; and indeed, the class was beginning to perpetuate itself as a communist 'bureaucratic bourgeoisie' via various forms of patronage, nepotism, special schools for its offspring and the like.[20]

Ota Sik, in a more sustained critique, denied the appellation

[19] See, Milovan Djilas. *The New Class* (New York: Praeger, 1957), *passim*.
[20] Ota Sik, *The Communist Power System* (New York: Praeger, 1981), *passim*.

'socialist' to the Eastern European regimes which he classifies as 'state monopolistic' or 'party-bureaucratic' 'perversions' of the socialist ideal—the former economic theorist of the Dubcek regime in Czechoslovakia explains the pathology of the Communist state in terms of a growing contradiction between the highly socialized means of production and the state-bureaucratic mode of appropriation of the surplus value.[21] Thus the Soviet-style state bureaucracy is at its bottom the structural edifice of a new exploiting class; and where the private capital of the market economy has been replaced by state capital controlled by a party bureaucracy. For Sik, state socialism must be dissolved by a 'Third Way',[22] a state form combining decentralization and central direction, individual initiative and social concern, debureaucratization and socialization of the productive process.[23]

Rudolf Bahro, a former functionary in the GDR cultural bureaucracy, set out to render a critique of 'actually existing socialism' modelled on Marx's Critique of Political Economy. For Bahro, as for Sik, in the beginning stands the Machine, as it were. The Soviet-type regime for him represents a special socio-economic formation generated by the 'non-capitalist road' to development which the Soviet Union, contrary to Marx's intent, was forced to follow. The root problem of the persistent crisis of states—socialism is a series of 'deep socio-economic contradictions, essentially in the relations of production', so that:

The abolition of private property in the means of production has in no way meant their immediate transformation into the property of the people. Rather, the whole society stands property-less against its state machine. The monopoly of disposal over the apparatus of production, over the lion's share of the surplus product, over the proportions of the reproduction process, over distribution and consumption, has led to a bureaucratic mechanism with the tendency to kill off or privatize any subjective initiative.[24]

Thus for Bahro the malaise of Soviet 'socialism' goes much further than the evolution of a 'new class', the 'betrayal of the revolution' or any 'cult of the personality' to include the actual mode of production. Therein lies the 'historical tragedy of the socialist ideal'. Determination of capaitialism in itself cannot create human emancipation, since a new antagonistic order arises 'the other side of capitalism'. And that

[21] Ota Sik, For a Humane Economic Democracy (trans. F. Eidlin and W. Graf), (New York: Praeger, forthcoming).

[22] Ota Sik, The Third Way (New York: Praeger, 1978).

[23] Which he spells out in some detail in Human Economic Democracy, op cit.

[24] Rudolph Bahro, The Alternative in Eastern Europe (London: NLB, 1977), p. 11.

order's principal symptom and harbinger is the state bureaucracy.

Eastern European revisions of Marxism–Leninism—many more could be cited—thus in many ways hark 'back' to the emancipatory, anti-bureaucratic Marx of The Paris Commune. The Soviet experience, and its pre-eminent Marxist critics reveal clearly that, under conditions of scarcity, the abolition of private ownership of the means of production is in itself an inadequate precondition for socialism, let alone some form of 'actually existing socialism'. On the contrary, the substitution of bureaucratic domination for capitalist domination not only results in the formation of a centralized, oppressive Moloch, it is also less efficient, less responsive and hence less suited to meeting the needs—basic and 'non-material'—of the majority of the population.

THIRD WORLD REVOLUTIONS AND ISSUES OF DEVELOPMENT

Marxist contributions to a theory of administration in the Third World include a critique of bourgeois theories of modernization—especially of development administration. The latter is perceived as an antirevolutionary strategy to reform and strengthen peripheral capitalism. For Third World Marxists, social revolution *is* the alternative mode of development administration.

This critique is inserted in an (often implicit) theory of the state in peripheral capitalist societies. Its basic tenets can be summarized as follows:

(1) The peripheral state is inherently unable to organize hegemony. Profound contradictions are instead managed by direct repression.

(2) The state is not a 'neutral' mechanism where conflicting demands can be accommodated and where equity-producing policies can be formulated.

(3) The socio-economic status quo cannot be changed 'from within' without violently altering the role of the state as an enforcer of the status quo.

(4) The peripheral state is a structure to maintain precisely the dependent and underdeveloped nature of those societies.

It follows then, that development administration—as postulated by Western theories of modernization—is little more than a means to administrate underdevelopment: it is the softer side of counter-surgency.'[25]

---

[25] See J. Nef and O.P. Dwivedi, 'Development Theory and Administration: A Fence

In one sense Third World Marxism has re-encountered some of the problems faced by the Leninist experience, namely, the need to combine socialism with economic development. This has entailed an inversion of the orthodox Marxist formulation, so that now the superstructure determines the base: the anti-imperialist, socialist states apparatus is supposed to generate the conditions of economic growth. In another sense, however, the Third World experience presents a diverse situation of social struggle and the construction of socialism. In the South, a constellation of specific conditions—the importance of the peasantry, the nature of wars of national liberation, the policy of alliances, to mention a few—conditions the nature of the socialist state and the role of the bureaucracy. Third World variants of Marxism—Mao, Cabral, Casino, Kim-II-Sung, etc.—in their own way entail critiques of the bourgeois administrative state. But their critiques point beyond this state, to an insurrectionist-revolutionary path for building a new state and administrative cadres through guerrilla warfare.[26] Likewise, the emphasis is more on basic needs and on rural development than on the Leninist effort towards relentless industrialization and the 'creation' of a proletariat as a precondition for building socialism.

Third World socialism, however, exhibits enormous variety and complexity. Some experiences, such as those where the takeover has been either peaceful (as in Allende's Chile) or the result of negotiation after insurrection (such as Zimbabwe), indicate a general tendency towards rapid bureaucratization of the state. Other cases, where guerrilla warfare led to a direct takeover of the state, (Cuba, Vietnam) indicate an early period or what Rene Dumont calls 'creative chaos' followed by increased bureaucratization. This is especially true where the exigencies of national self-preservation enhance the militarization of the state and the emergence of a 'new class' of sorts,

The central feature of all these socialist strategies lies in the pursuit of induced development through revolution and planning. This is an uneasy task since it presents profound built-in contradictions. One is the issue of mobilization versus the need to institutionalize the revolution (advance vs. consolidation). The other issue is the one between centralization (control) and democratization (mobilization). The third

---

Around an Empty Lot?', *Indian Journal of Public Administration*, vol. 27, no. 1, January–March 1981, pp. 42–66.

[26] See O.P. Dwivedi and J. Nef, 'Crisis and Continuities in Development Theory and Administration: First and Third World Perspectives', *Public Administration and Development*, vol. 2, 1982, pp. 59–77.

issue is the contradiction between growth and distribution (consumption, investment). The fourth and most important issue is the extent to which national autonomy can be maintained vis-a-vis a hostile West or the complex dependency offered by external 'protectors' of the revolutionary process. In all of these contradictions, the role of the administrative apparatus is crucial. It may determine the pace and direction of both mobilization and institutionalization. It may also define the degree to which bureaucracy or elitism will prevail. It directly participates in the limits of consumption and rates of intervention. Lastly, it serves either as a vehicle to enhance national self-determination or to create and maintain international subordination.

A large number of these Third World contributions to a theory of administration exhibit a strong antibureaucratic orientation, an emphasis on mass mobilization through armed struggle (guerrilla warfare) and a pre-eminence of basic needs—satisfaction over accumulation. Others, such as Allende's peaceful road to socialism entail an attempt to utilizing existing bureaucratic channels by means of creating opinion through organs of popular mobilization. In all cases, however, the practice of managing the state, has been in sharp contrast with both the theory and reality of the early phases of popular insurrection. The works of Mao Zedong and Amilcar Cabral[27] contain innumerable instances of analysis of administration as well as practical guidelines for the administration of the revolution. These include an emphasis on popular mobilization, as well as on combating bureacratism and authoritarianism. The historical record, which should include the cases of Cuba, Vietnam and Nicaragua, suggests however, that bureaucratism may well be an all-pervasive trend. Neither 'control' over, nor the 'smashing' of the bureaucracy has taken place. Instead, an entrenched cadre of organizers and enforcers of hegemony—a new managerial class—seems to have emerged as the products and beneficiaries of the process.

Concluding Observations

The analysis of state socialism illuminates a central problematic in the application of Marxist theory to the situation of the lesser developed capitalist societies, one which has been suggested by the two

[27] See Ronald Chilcote, 'Theory and Practice of Amilcar Cabral: Revolutionary Implications for the Third World', *Latin American Perspectives*, vol. II, no. 2 (Spring 1984), pp. 3–14.

concepts: the 'primacy of the political' and the 'non-capitalist road'. Both imply a refutation or revision of the Marxian base-superstructure equation. For in both cases *political power is prior and decisive*, and is deployed to 'create', a state apparatus as the means of effecting accumulation and accelerating development (the 'midwife of progress'). In other words, political power is pre-requisite to economic power, rather than vice versa, as in the case of the capitalist state created by and for an economically pre-eminent bourgeoisie. To be sure, neocolonial, capitalist Third World states in general convert state-generated revenues into private appropriation and thus are best comprehended as state-capitalist, while Eastern European states are subject to certain collectivist uses of accumulated capital and hence more appropriately termed state-socialist. Nevertheless, an adequate Marxist analysis of these post-capitalist states forms requires substantial revisions to the Marxist paradigm.

A related problematic is the *internationalization of the class struggle* in the twentieth century. As Bahro's concept of 'the noncapitalist road' suggests, countries no longer move toward socialism (or for that matter, toward any model of development) entirely on the strength of their own internal developments and contradictions. Rather, these are decisively influenced by external interests and forces. Anti-imperialism for instance is a salient explanatory factor in contemporary world politics. Similarly, the conditioning factor of the development imperative is crucial, as summarized in the slogan 'the world countryside against the world town'. Here, the value of Lenin's notion of a class struggle on a global scale is most useful: No longer are class struggles enacted between a national bourgeoisie and a national proletariat, but between imperialist-dominated countries against international imperialism. This, according to Bahro, is the common experience of all communist regimes so far, whether in the Soviet Union and Eastern Europe or in China, Cuba and elsewhere in the Third World.[28]

In retrospect, it appears as if the hopes for socialist democracy as Leninism proved in practice, are inevitably bound to be stalked by the spectre of Pareto and Michels. It is precisely this dialectical 'riddle'— the inevitability of bureaucracy—that a Marxist theory of development and administration has yet to address systematically. This involves the formulation of a 'conception of the relationship between consciousness and structures and between the general development

[28] Bahro, op cit., Chs 3 and 4.

of socialist revolution and its immediate localized realization.'[29] It also entails an explicit critique of elitist centralism and the dictatorship of the proletariat as well as an attempt to link the organic, spontaneous sphere of every life with the universal realm of politics.[30]

Thus, in all three paradigms discussed above, the state as a matrix of social relations generates a complex organizational apparatus, namely the state bureaucracy. In terms of public administration theory, by incorporating Marxist analysis of 'social relations' into a Weberian model of organizational control, it is possible to analyse this control in which state and civil society are fused. 'They are fused in the terms of the development of the organization of the capitalist labour process in relation to the institutional rules governing it.'[31] Marxian analysis is interested in the former (labour process related to surplus-value-production), while the Weberian analysis is oriented towards a 'system of rationality in the organization' with its distinct features of central hierarchy, and authority.

The state in capitalist society must try to fulfil two basic though contradictory obligations: (a) accumulation of profit, and (b) legitimization by maintaining hegemonic domination over all. With respect to the first obligation, the state in capitalist society must try to create and maintain (or defend) those conditions by which some may accumulate profits. But for the second, the state needs to seek legitimization for its existence/role by requiring or creating conditions of apathy, acquiescence and loyalty from the majority in the society who are economically exploited and socially disadvantaged groups (such as women, ethnic minorities, etc.). The state must simultaneously facilitate the exploitation process, yet appear to be protecting the interests of all the people. Bureaucracy is, then, the optional means of achieving these two obligations.

When viewed in Marxian terms as a partisan political agency, the modern administrative state in the West must continue to uphold two central myths. One is that politics and administration are somehow separate, which merely indicates the privileged position of bureaucrats under the guise of political 'neutrality' and 'anonymity'. The myth allows administrators to engage in politics and policy-making

---

[29] Carl Boggs, 'Gramsci's Theory of the Factory Councils: Nucleous of the Socialist State', *Berkeley Journal of Sociology*, XIX, (1974–75), p. 171.

[30] Ibid., p. 178.

[31] Alexander Kouzmin, 'The Politics of Public Sector Administration', in A. Kouzmin (ed.), *Public Sector Administration: New Perspectives* (Melbourne: Longman Cheshire, 1983), p. 3.

without being held accountable for the outcome of their actions. At the same time, the myth helps elected politicians to obscure demands for reform, and to exonerate themselves from policy failures. The second myth is that public servants protect the 'public interest' and contribute to the public weal. But in reality, they are surrounded by special interest groups whom they were supposed to regulate and balance out. Interest groups have direct links with administrators and government officers, offer pre-planning consulative reports, provide data (based on their own sources), thus gaining privileged access. This 'cooperative venture' between the regulators (administrators) and the 'regulated bunch', excludes broader social interests. Departments generally consult with 'soon-to-be-affected' organizations and pressure groups before an item of legislation is introduced. In such a situation, collaboration turns into the colonization of public bureaucracy by powerful interest groups. Viewed in that perspective, then the theory of the modern administrative state conjures up an image of a Leviathan 'by which state institutions influence many aspects of the lives of citizens'.[32] In such a situation, the administrative machinery and the governing process itself become the principal instruments in the formulation and implementation of all state policies and programmes, affecting almost all aspects of an individual's life. As the state bureaucracy evolves into an organized interest representing mainly itself—as underlined by experience so far in the First, Second, and Third Worlds—it is progressively alienated from the population whose 'servant' it was ostensibly intended to be. George Orwell's *1984* and Franz Kafka's *The Castle* are perhaps two good depictions of this situation. Marx, we have seen, was aware of these alienating and subjugating tendencies of the state and the concentration of power in the hands of a few. His comment on this aspect is worth reproducing to conclude our analysis:

The bureaucracy is a circle from which no one can escape. Its hierarchy is a hierarchy of knowledge. The top entrusts the understanding of detail to the lower levels, whilst the lower levels credit the top with understanding of the general, and so, all are mutually deceived.[33]

---

[32] V. Wilson and O.P. Dwivedi, 'Introduction', in O.P. Dwivedi (ed.), *The Administrative State in Canada* (Toronto: Toronto University Press, 1982), p. 5.

[34] Karl Marx quoted in A. Hegedus, *Socialism and Bureaucracy* (London: Allsion and Busby, 1976), p. 160.

PART II

PUBLIC ADMINISTRATION AND GLOBALIZATION

CHAPTER FIVE

Administration in the Eighties
Major Trends and Challenges

V. Subramaniam

There is much disagreement about the crucial problems of this planet but considerable agreement, if not consensus has emerged about the potentiality of efficient management and administration in tackling each problem. The pessimists of the Club of Rome and their supporters claim that the world's resources of energy, minerals and even plant food resources are so severely limited in comparison with the increasing demands from a growing population that the only way to avoid total disaster is to plan for zero or even negative economic growth—a polite euphemism for accepting a lower standard of living.[1] The environmentalists assert that the continuous stream of dangerous waste pouring into the environment would, if unchecked as at present, swallow us all ingloriously.[2] Defence and foreign policy experts and political scientists have been warning us for much longer than environmentalists and negative growth apostles, about the dangerous possibility of a nuclear holocaust happening through human miscalculation or accident. The leaders of the Third World or the poor South, have claimed more recently that their continued

---

[1] For some details regarding the Club of Rome and Zero growth see: Donella H. Meadows et al., *Limits to Growth*, Universe Books, New York, 1972; Rudolph Klein, 'Growth and its Enemies', *Commentary*, June 1972. For further comments see: Martin Greenberger, *Models in the Policy Process*, Russel Sage Foundation, New York, 1976, Chapter 1.

[2] Environmentalists have put forward their view propagandistically in their journals and thousands of articles. For a more academic study, by a Nobel Laureate, see: Wassily Leontief, 'Environmental Repercussions and the Economic Structure: An Input-Output Approach', *Review of Economics and Statistics*, vol. 52, no. 3.

impoverishment constitutes a problem not only for the South but the North as well.[3] Even on the optimistic side, futurologists such as Alvin Toffler declare with propagandist assurance in *Future Shock* that the fast rate of technological and social change will leave behind the uncomprehending majority puzzled and giddy.[4]

But, regardless of the nature of the universal problem or disaster they predict as impending, several leading intellectuals imply or declare that any of these can be tackled hopefully with better management and administration. Macro-economists such as Galbraith, management professors such as Peter Drucker and several think-tankers, all of them have placed some faith on better management or administration.[5] We may admit that this term is used by many in a rather, wide sense to cover all cooperative human endeavour, more loosely organized than administration/management and we may again admit that doubts have been cast from more than one viewpoint about the limits of organization.[6] On balance, there is still much faith placed in their efficacy to tackle the major challenges of this planet.

That takes the question to the next level: what are the crucial challenges and trends in administration/management on which so much depends in facing these problems. The Niagara of journal articles in public administration and management is too often concerned with very narrow specific problems such as urban development, hospital administration, university administration, training methods, inter-governmental relations, marketing techniques or case studies.[7] We may, however, look behind these for general themes and trace some more enduring concerns in some path breaking books and

[3] For a general idea of the North-South dialogue, see the regular feature, 'North-South Dialogue' in *Third World Quarterly*, London, 1979 and 1980.

[4] We must add that Alvin Toffler's, *Future Shock*, has been severely criticized for selective use of facts to present a sensational picture. In fact, some of the trends he anticipated have not materialized at all.

[5] A famous think-tanker of the Rand Corporation, New York, Herimann Kahn, during his visit to Australia in July 1980, said that most of the difficult problems of the future could be dealt with by good 'management' but there was not enough of it now.

[6] Authors like Chris Argyris (*Personality and Organization*) and Ralph Hummel (*Bureaucratic Experience*) deal with the dehumanizing effects of bureaucracy, while Robert Merton deals with its dysfunction. More recently, Kenneth Arrow, in his *Limits of Organization*, Norton & Co., New York, 1974, deals with the inbuilt structural limits of all organizations, in communication as well as goal achievement.

[7] An examination of the issues of *Public Administration Review*, Washington and *Administrative Science Quarterly*, Ithaca, reveals that the majority of articles deal with very specific administrative problems.

conference sessions. In addition, as a third world social scientist, I can rely on my own observation—from a non-western point of view—not only to identify the major trends in the industrialized management-oriented West but also in the Afro-Asian countries, seeking to modernize, largely through management and administration.[8] While my identification of such major trends is bound to be coloured by my interests and experiences, I would like to believe that the following items are of sufficient general interest for a brief discussion.

My short list includes :

(a) the inadequacies of public policy making as well as private business policy making in comparison with the needs of the situation;

(b) the problems arising from the rapid universal spread of organization and bureaucracy on the one hand and the emerging debureaucratization phenomena on the other;

.(c) the enormous importance attached to management, particularly the American techniques of management and the active emulation and importation of it into Europe and Soviet Russia;

(d) the rather exaggerated reliance on public or government administration and on public enterprises in developing countries as the key to economic growth; and

(e) the shortcomings and imbalances in the development of our knowledge of organizations.

All these five trends are interrelated as they are part of a self-exciting socio–economic world system with several self-reinforcing aspects. We will, however, deal with them in the above order, pointing out interrelations as and when they arise.

PUBLIC POLICY MAKING

The rapidly increasing concern with government or public policy making can be traced back to Harold Lasswell's path breaking book if not earlier to Paul Appleby and similar authors of the New Deal era.[9] The reason for the new interest was some frustration with earlier studies of institutional structures of government and law—on the

[8] As a university teacher for about a quarter of a century, I have spent two-thirds of it in Western universities and a third of it in Africa and India and can hope to obtain a more comparative view than pure Western academics.

[9] David Lerner and Harold Lasswell, *The Policy Sciences: Recent Developments in Scope and Method*, Stanford University Press, 1951.

negative side—and deep interest in actual 'big government' as its policies were changing all aspects of society. This stream was joined and broadened by the more precisely formulated decision theory stream into a mighty river from the nineteen fifties onwards—drawing a high proportion of top academics and administrators into researching and writing on it. While it is impossible to summarize the variety, sophistication and depth of this literature as well as actual developments in a few paragraphs, the following items may be identified as the major concerns of those involved.

In the first place, there is a deep concern about the topmost importance of public policy-making in contrast to the poor quality of it as of now. Yehezkel Dror perhaps brings out this contrast most effectively in the introductory chapters of his *Public Policy Making Reexamined*.[10] His main argument is that only a small fraction of the available knowledge is used in policy making. Lasswell and several other political scientists rate public policy as important, more in terms of the enormous opportunity available to improve individual and social life through public policy, the study of which should form the centre of political science.[11] Geoffrey Vickers uses the more subtle argument—of how the socio-political developments following the industrial revolution and capitalism have made all Western society so highly complex and interdependent that any public activity affects many more sectors than it did in the centuries earlier with many more unanticipated consequences and hence public policy has to be made with far greater care, knowledge and forethought.[12] In a sense the argument of great opportunity for policy making (Dror and Lasswell) and the argument of necessity for careful policy making based on complex interdependence, are complementary and apply as much to the rich North as to the poor South.

But there is far less agreement on how to improve present public policy making between the 'incrementalists' and the 'optimalists'. Lindblom and Braybrooke advocate 'incrementalism' essentially in the context of a pluralist democracy in a developed industrial society

---

[10] Yehezkel Dror, *Public Policy Making Re-examined*, Chandler Publishing Company, Scranton, Penn., 1968. Part I is entitled appropriately, 'The Mission'.

[11] Lerner and Lasswell (ed.), op cit.

[12] Geoffrey Vickers, *Value Systems and Social Process* and *Freedom in a Rocking Boat* (both Penguin) discuss in some detail how developments in the last century and a half have made every Western society self-exciting, full of mutually dependent subsystems and highly complex. See in particular his chapter 'The End of Free Fall', in *Value Systems and Social Process*.

like the USA though they do not themselves see this connection.[13] Gradual changes in existing policy are most widely accepted by rival interest groups—and they seem also defensible in the context of a level of widening affluence. Their argument about the difficulties in thinking derivatively from absolute values and the contextual nature of all policy is true up to a point. But incrementalists overdo their case in several ways. In the first place, they spend too much energy jousting against a caricature of a rational-comprehensive model. Secondly, they under emphasize radical policy changes that have been pushed through during and after the Second World War in Britain and western Europe, or the massive changes in American defence policy—and they also treat cumulative radical changes wrought by a few increments as quite similar to incremental changes which simply make the *status quo* more widely acceptable. In short, an incremental change has to be defined quantitatively to make sense and, even so, one must distinguish between radically-oriented and maintenance-oriented 'increments'.[14] Thus incrementalism is at best a warning against recklessness on the one hand and fantasizing on the other. Some of Aaron Wildavsky's criticisms are directed against this fantasizing; the so-called zero-based budgeting in Georgia he shows to be just the old procedure with the usual results but with frills; the US budgetary process is all politics with a little bit of economics and the grandiose plan fantasies of poor Third World countries are paper exercises they could do without. Wildavsky is not so much a direct incrementalist but an indirect one asserting the primacy of the non-rational political element in policy making in the West and of international constraints on poor countries.[15]

The optimalists in policy making such as Dror pin their hopes on better models and techniques of policy making, on the one hand, and the structured use of social science researches as policy sciences, on the other. In regard to the former, several models may be experimented

[13] David Braybrooke and Charles E. Lindblom, *A Strategy of Decision*, Free Press, 1970. Both authors argue their 'strategy, in a North American context, e.g. chapters 4 and 8. The assumption is that there is something to 'distribute' and that there is peaceful competition for this by organized groups.

[14] A radically oriented incremental policy is one in which the increment is small enough to cool down opposition temporarily, but large enough to attract further support from those who benefit by it—to make further and larger increments in the same direction.

[15] Aaron Wildavsky, *The Politics of the Budgetary Process*, Little Brown & Co., Boston, 1964; Aaron Wildavsky, *The Revolt Against the Masses*, Basic Books, New York, 1971; Naomi Caiden & Aaron Wildavsky, *Planning and Budgeting in Poor Countries*, Wiley, New York, 1974.

with but the greatest problem is how to sense a problem before it stares one in the face. Progress in this area has been slow and meagre for several reasons. Vickers' formulation of a continuous process of 'appreciation'—with 'reality judgment' and 'value judgment' interacting—is perhaps the most perceptive, while Eric Jantsch's *Design for Evolution* is boldly speculative but wanders too far out into esoteric realms.[16] For socio-economic decisions Marxists have asserted that the nature of the modern capitalist state excludes certain problems automatically from recognition.[17] Much more attention needs to be devoted to this pre-problem recognition stage, at the individual and social level.

The concept of policy sciences has caught on fast, with about half a dozen periodicals exploring it and a large number of policy study institutes springing up everywhere, but the gains are rather limited.[18] Elaborate descriptions and definitions of the attributes of policy science by Dror and others have not given it any special identity—and this may be after all not a bad thing. The majority of articles appearing in these journals and the majority of studies put out by policy study institutes may be characterized simply as applied social science investigations on specific substantive issues. As such they could have appeared in academic journals of sociology, economics or political science with further processing and compression. It is good that such applied research can be published in reasonable time in policy science journals or monographs without a long wait to appear in the few academic journals pressed for space. In a sense they are doing what the Mills, Macaulay, Trevelyan and Sir James Stephen did with Bentham's ideas in putting them across to the powers that be. But to

---

[16] Geoffrey Vickers, *Value Systems and Social Process*, Penguin, See, Chapter, 'Appreciative Behaviour', For further discussion of the pre-problem recognition stage, see V. Subramaniam, 'Reflections on Trends in Organization Theory', *Australian Journal of Public Administration*, Sydney, Sept–Dec., 1980.

As it is not easily definable, the pre-problem recognition stage may be extended to cover *all* mental activity and this is what Eric Jantsch slips *into*.

[17] E.g., Claus Offe, 'The Theory of the Capitalist State and the Problem of Policy Formation', in Leond Lindbergh et al., *Stress and Contradiction in Modern Capitalism*, Lexington Books, D.C. Heath & Co., New York, 1975.

[18] The number of policy study institutes and their ramifications in North America alone is so large that they have to be listed in several directories: Stuart Nagel & Marian Neef, *Policy Research Centres Directory*, 1978; *Policy Grants Directory*, 1977; *Policy Studies Directory* (2nd ed.), 1976; all published by the Policy Studies Organization, University of Illinois., Urbana.

The better known policy journals are: *Policy Analysis, Policy Sciences, Policy Review, Policy Studies Review, Annual, Public Choice* and *Futures*.

claim any special identity for policy science other than being applied and more immediate, is misleading. Policy journals and institutes have done much less to promote techniques for policy makers to do this homework by themselves.[19] Most of the well-known tools of decision-making such as operations research or linear programming are mathematical tools which help to evaluate different alternatives rather than formulate them and decision analysis with the use of the decision-tree and utility-probability measures goes only one step further. These are aids to be used after the administrator has squarely formulated the problem and even alternatives. Tools such as the Delphi method and its variations go a little further but they call for a considerable amount of sophistication and specialization.

There is, of course, the moral problem of rendering advice and help to the powers that be who make policy, though this has not figured prominently in the literature. In a western democracy it is assumed that both the advice and policy process are open as well as reversible. Hence right and left wing experts are equally free, useful and blameless, in working on policy problems and indeed Dror's accusation was that academics indulge in a self-perpetuating isolation from actual policy matters for several flimsy reasons, a situation which was changing fast even as he wrote.[20] The moral position is more ambivalent in regard to policy advice to the poorer African one-party states; serious advice about how to make the best of a bad situation can be interpreted as perpetuating the elite minority, while advice not to plan at all in view of their poor resources in a competitive world can be treated as cruel cynicism.[21]

[19] In regard to (a) information sifting or information generating and (b) problem recognizing, which are crucial for policy makers, leading institutes, such as the Rand Corporation and Defence Research establishments, do not publicize their techniques for quite some time. What gets published is the final product. Academics, of course, discuss their methodology with their findings together, but here again it is the 'findings' that evoke the interest of policy makers.

[20] Yehezkel Dror, *Public Policy Making Reexamined*, Chandler, 1968, Chapter 17 titled, 'Changes Needed in Knowledge'.

[21] For example, Curry and Rothchild's *Scarcity, Choice and Planning in Middle Africa*, has been criticized for offering suggestions to the elite in Power about how to make policy. This is obviously meant to entrench them in power—according to critics. Caiden and Wildavsky's advice to live from day to day, in view of world market forces, while realistic, is also 'cruel'. President Nyerere's approach to the North-South dialogue, particularly in his lecture at the Austrian Institute for International Affairs (for summary see Julius Nyerere. 'How the North can help the South—Now', *Asia Week*, Hong Kong, Aug. 29, 1980) seems to make the realistic case for selfish generosity.

To sum up, public policy making occupies the centre of attention in academe as well as in practice—as evidenced by the many policy institutes and journals devoted to it, the proliferation of courses on it in most universities and large new sections in every government administration assigned to formulate policy rationally with tools ranging from PPBS to a variety of economic tools.[22] As an index of attention this is good, but not good enough as an index of achievement. There is much frittering of attention on quantification, much cosmetic repetition of old wisdom and much hair-splitting with courses repeating old material on constitutions and institutions as policy resources,[23] with journals and institutes replicating the work of old enquiry commissions or finding justification for current policy. All this needs to be ruthlessly and relentlessly criticized even as we acknowledge good public policy as the best hope of our collective future.

UNIVERSAL BUREAUCRATIZATION AND DEBUREAUCRATIZATION[24]

The rapid tentacular expansion in the number, size, and ambit of control of public and private organizations has been the subject of active comment and analysis for nearly half-a-century. Well before World War II, there were complaints from *laissez faire* liberals about the increasing invasion of government administration into business and industry and demands from welfare liberals and labour parties for more intervention—into employment and health—while the Depression, New Deal and Keynesian economics legitimized

[22] Various management tools have been introduced by Western governments and their introduction and usefulness has been studied in several journal articles in *Public Administration Review*, Washington and *Public Administration*, London, e.g., Aaron Wildavsky, 'The Political Economy of Efficiency Cost-Benefit Analysis, Systems Analysis and Program Budgeting', *Public Administration Review*, vol. 26, no. 4.

[23] This observation about courses on Public Policy replicating much old material is based on ten years of observation of such courses in North America and, in particular, on a more recent examination of several such courses leading to an M.A. in Public Policy in prestigious U.S. universities by a committee of the Public Administration group at Carleton University, Ottawa in 1978–9.

[24] For an account of the debureaucratization thesis, see Warren G. Bennis, *Beyond Bureaucracy: Essays on the Development and Evolution of Human Organization*, McGraw-Hill, New York, 1966. For a challenge to this thesis and a debate, see G. Shariff 'Persistence of Bureaucracy' and Bennis' reply in *Social Science Quarterly*, vol. 60, no. 1 (1979). See also the special issue of the *American Behavioural Scientist*, vol. 22, no. 5 on bureaucracy.

government intervention for reasons of economic system mainte-nance. The total character of World War II promoted and justified further expansion of government administration for tentacular social economic control while super power rivalry and the arms build-up after the war continued this trend. In western Europe, the period of reconstruction and economic 'miracles' was underpinned by expan-sion of government administration, while the final acceptance of all the elements of the modern welfare state all over Western Europe—following the British and Scandinavian leftwing governments rein-forced this expansion.

In the private sector too, the post-war period witnessed an explo-sion of economic and organizational expansion, first through the increasing internal demands and purchasing power of expanding western economies and increased advertising and, secondly, through the establishment and expansion of multinational firms in oil, ship-ping, minerals and several manufacturing industries. Indeed the rate of expansion of business administration during the fifties was per-haps greater than that of public administration.

The decoloniziation of Asia, Africa and the Caribbean by the colo-nial powers from (India's independence in) 1947 onwards set the newly independent countries on the path of administrative expan-sion. Filling up positions vacated by colonial administrators was only a small part of it as the colonial powers had restricted their administrative responsibilities considerably. The major part of the expansion was occasioned by taking on the task of economic devel-opment through multifarious public enterprises which we will deal with in some detail later in the paper. We may add that in addition to these three areas of organizational expansion in Western public ad-ministration, Western business and industry through multinationals and in many newly independent countries, there was a correspond-ing degree of expansion in the communist world and in various international organizations.

There is general agreement about this spread of organization to all human activity from machines to meditation and from sport to sex in every part of the world, particularly in the post-war decades, about this relentless bureaucratization of the world but attitudes to this phenomenon differ. There are those who see this as the crucial reason for making the study of bureaucracy the centre of all social science.[25]

[25] The references are to Henry Jacoby, *The Bureaucratization of the World*, University of California, Berkeley, 1973.

There are pessimists like Presthus (*Organizational Society*) or Whyte (*Organization Man*) who bemoan the loss of human inventiveness and human personality by total socialization in one or other bureaucracy[26] and some of them feel that this phenomenon will produce its own remedy, as Elliott Jacques in *A General Theory of Bureaucracy* (Wiley 1976). There are others who just accept the spread of bureaucracy as inevitable.

In contrast, a small group of social scientists such as W.G. Bennis notice the opposing tendency of debureaucratization as emerging and gaining ground.[27] While there are some indications in this direction in the USA, it seems to me that they have been exaggerated—and on balance I agree with those like Sharif who dispute the debureaucratization thesis and recognize bureaucratization as the dominant tendency, more significantly so in the developing countries and communist countries.

There are, of course, some compensating tendencies against bureaucratization. As it spreads to all social action, stressing the task-oriented 'instrumental' human activities, human nature reasserts itself by bringing in its 'expressive' side into organization itself—as there is no other way out—through informal groups, through politicization of 'instrumental' activity and through sheer sabotage and withdrawal. Secondly, what is often seen as bureaucratic organization is not purely formal but a mixture of the elective and appointive offices. What is spreading is more the increasing 'gesellschaftization' of societies rather than bureaucratization. Debureaucratization is still weak and embryonic and the real problem of developing Afro-Asian countries (which we discuss later) is the polarization between a gemeinschaft society and a highly formal bureaucracy that makes interaction difficult.

BORROWING AMERICAN MANAGEMENT

Even while the shortcomings of formal organization are discussed in America, western Europe and Soviet Russia, both fear the efficiency of American management and seek to emulate it actively. West European journals in the 1970s published a few articles about how American management, not American capital, would swallow European

[26] One may add to this Ralph Hammel's *Bureaucratic Experience*, which argues that the whole human personality is impossibly twisted by bureaucracy.

[27] The evidence is scrappy. The present tendency in USA and Canada to contract out government work to private agencies, only shifts the burden to private organizations.

industry and business. While such exaggerated fears have subsided, American management education and consultancy have established themselves in Europe. More interestingly, Soviet Russia has, over the last two decades, adopted almost all the major elements of American management with a few mild explanations and apologies, and has now produced its own literature on organization and management.[28] This massive drive towards (Western) management is well documented. We will highlight three of its main features.

In the first place this process is based on the initiative and blessing of the highest office holders and organs in the land and embraces all aspects of Western capitalist management. Thus Brezhnev declared in Kharkov in 1970 April 14 that 'I think there is no special need to prove that without good management and perfection of organization, neither capital-investment, nor new technology, nor the selfless labour of workers and Kolkhoz workers will give the desired effect'. This position was made more formally an official programme by a directive of the 24th Congress of the CPSU. The special section on 'Perfection of Planning and Management' contains the following declaration :

Without continued and endless perfection of management, progress in increasing the productivity of labour—increasing the quality of production and growth in the efficiency of production is impossible. An increase in the scientific nature of administration is an important factor in raising its efficiency.

This concern for better and more scientific management covers all aspects of Western management, some of which are capitalistic.

Thus management consultancy is warmly recommended by the Dean of the Moscow Institute of National Economy—in an article in *Literaturanaya Gazetta* (24 June 1970). Its immense contribution to the development of private and public enterprises in the West is summarized in the article in some detail and the editorial supports the article by saying that MCS are of decided interest even to a planned socialist economy. Some time after this in 1976, the Chicago consulting firm of Arthur Anderson & Co. was given a consultancy contract. More interestingly, even Western advertisement techniques are being carefully studied.

[28] The brief account in this section is based upon the joint research of my student John Jaworsky and myself which we propose to publish as a book shortly.

For some more details, see Richard F. Vidmer 'Administrative Science in the USSR: Doctrinal Constraints on Inquiry' and Michael E Urban, 'Theory and Ideology in Soviet Administration: A rejoinder to Vidmer' both in *Administration and Society*, Beverly Hills, vol. 12, no. 1.

The quality and popularity of Russian publications on management and administration is another indication of the strength of this pro-management movement. Books by authors like Popov and Gvishiani cover practically all aspects of organization and management, as any good American text, and sell anything from 25,000 to half a million copies.

The second main feature of this movement is its fairly obvious and acknowledged American inspiration. Indeed Lenin's example of taking over scientific management was revived and there was a small distinct group of 'Communist Americanizers' who started this movement in the early sixties, such as D.M. Gvishiani whose *Sociology of Business* borrowed considerably from American theorists and V.I. Tereshchenko who emigrated to the USSR in the sixties from the USA. Over 110 American periodicals are monitored and studied. Of course, the leading Russian theorists adapt American ideas to their own needs.

Thirdly, the justification for this process is broadly the same as Lenin's. Thus the *Literaturanaya Gazeta* of 10 January 1968 virtually echoed Lenin:

The Science of management is on the order of the day. The Science of management of men in a Socialist Society and the Science of managing men in a Capitalist Society are two opposing phenomena in their ends and substance. But it would be totally unreasonable to ignore the experience of Capitalism in this sphere: it would be irrational from the economic point of view not to utilize this experience.

The passage weaves together two strands of justification which are found in Russian defence of adopting American management. It is value-free instrumental knowledge and hence it will serve a socialist society as well as a capitalist society. Secondly, it can be 'purified' and made more productive in a socialist society.

We should, however, add that Western Marxists look askance at Soviet borrowings of American management which they regard as part of Western capitalist ideology.[29] We cannot deal with this controversy in detail here, but we refer to the total problem of transplanting administration and management towards the conclusion of this paper. Let us, however, take note of the fact that regardless of some ideological or cultural differences, 'American' management

---

[29] See Claus Offe, 'The Theory of the Capitalist State and the Problem of Policy Formation', in Leon N. Lindberg et al., *Stress and Contradiction in Modern Capitalism*, Lexington Books, D.C. Health & Co., New York. 1975.

(transplanted or rediscovered) has done well in western Europe and Soviet Russia, whereas 'Development Administration' failed to justify the high hopes raised by its proponents in Afro-Asia. We must search for some explanation as that constitutes the major challenge for the Third World and is the essence of the North-South dialogue.

The Failure of Development Administration and Public Enterprise

The loud laments by Third World statesmen in the early 1970s about the failure of the development decade in Afro-Asian 'developing' countries more or less coincided with the ruthless criticisms by several academics of (i) the political and administrative elite of these countries for this failure, (ii) of Western colonial capitalism for creating conditions of economic dependency earlier, and (iii) of international capitalism and neo-colonialism for perpetuating and making worse such dependency. This outpouring was followed in the late nineteen seventies by a demand from several Third World leaders and economists for a 'New International Economic Order' and the reluctant initiation of a North-South dialogue. According to some, this evolution from frustration to analysis to demand for action is the most significant international one of the post-war decades, even more significant than super-power rivalries. We cannot, however, deal with it as a whole in this brief article but we must take note of its administrative aspects. Briefly put in a somewhat over-simplified form, we have to explain the inordinate importance attached to administration as *the* tool of development by the newly independent countries of Asia and Africa, the reasons for its failure and the continued reliance on public enterprises regardless of that. This is the most crucial problem and challenge for the Third World administrators—with or without reference to the success of management in the West as well as Soviet Russia. The explanations of this by right and left wing academics have been useful up to a point but they are too doctrinaire to encompass the failures. I am adding my own brief explanation without much ideological underpinning to elicit more thought and discussion.

The inordinate reliance on public administration as the key to development which started in India was the result of a concatenation of factors, namely, the availability of administrative and professional manpower from a sizeable educated middle class and Prime Minister Nehru's commitment to government-planned development in a mixed economy together with his nausea for the Indian capitalist class more for aesthetic rather than ideological reasons. It was a combination of the objective fact of the availability of administrators and a clear value preference on the part of the major architect of modern India. This combination was legitimized theoretically in bits and pieces by New Dealer Paul Appleby, F. W. Riggs an avid theory-seeker using system concepts, and several others. These ideas of development administration found some favour with British colonial administrators in Africa who were planning and executing some development schemes in a hurry partly out of guilt feelings—and more with American governmental aid agencies, who would rather deal with their compeers in another country rather than private agencies. Very soon development administration, this chance child of a context and concatenation, became an article of faith with many administrators and a growth industry in academe.

The relative failure of developmental efforts was not, however, due to its theoretical hollowness entirely but rather due to other circumstances beyond its control. The freedom fighters of India claimed in the 1930s and 40s that, with independence, economic growth would occur automatically, assuming that the rest of the world would stand still while India was catching up with the industrial revolution. The actual situation was the exact opposite; the first two post-war decades when India and some other countries tried to 'catch up' was also the period of the most aggressive self-exciting, self-sustaining spurt of capitalist expansion switched on by Marshall aid in western Europe, the post-occupation economic recovery in Japan and in USA itself, by the new breed of multinational companies. It was a losing game for 'developing countries' if only for this reason, apart from several other reasons.

Let us return to the objective basis for the faith in development through administration, namely, the availability of administrators from a large educated middle class. It was this class that used that faith to initiate a number of development projects and which clings to that faith despite proven failure. Unfortunately, this 'class' has been more misinterpreted than any other class, group, stratum or social formation, whichever category we choose to put it into. My own limited interpretation of colonial socio-economic history puts it in better perspective.[30]

[30] I have dealt with the derivative middle class in much greater detail in two conference papers listed below: 'The Derivative Middle Class: A Colonial Residue', East African Universities Social Science Conference at Dar-es-Salaam, December 1970—

European colonialism of the late 18th and 19th centuries was different from earlier imperialisms in that the ruling British and French and the ruled Asians and Africans were basically different in terms of race, religion and technology, but even more in terms of social organization. West-European society was increasingly organized in terms of gesellschaft or artificial voluntary associations for specific purposes (such as firms or departments) whereas Asian and African societies were still organized in terms of gemeinschaft natural groups (such as family, caste or tribe) with membership by birth and comprehensive functions. Communication between the rulers and the ruled was therefore possible only through a mediating class or group, but such a group had to satisfy the demands of the rulers and the context of 19th century colonialism. This class which I christen 'Derivative Middle Class' (DMC) arose in good time first in India and later in Africa and the Caribbean. It also developed very early its four crucial characteristics, namely, of being derivative, imitative, lopsided and frustrated. Unlike the European middle class which evolved naturally without external conquest or occupation, this DMC was derived from colonial conquest and confrontation and, unlike its European counterpart, which was balanced between its economic–commercial middle men and its professional wing of the salaried and self-employed lawyers, accountants, engineers, architects and civil servants, the DMC was made up almost solely of the latter. The colonial government needed them for various mediatory functions, e.g., lawyers to interpret the ruler's criminal law to the ruled and customary law to the ruler; civil servants for communication between the two and tax collection and teachers to produce this class; but it did not need commercial intermediaries (except in the early stages of the East India Company) nor did they want to encourage local industry. Hence the Indian middle class was made up mostly of the salaried and self-employed, while Indian capital kept aloof for long in traditionalist isolation.[31] The DMC imitated the rulers functionally in regard to

---

reprinted as Appendix II in my *Transplanted Indo-British Administration*, Ashish, New Delhi, 1977, and 'Ideology and Reality of Social Stratification in Zambia', Canadian Association of African Studies Conference, February, 1975, Toronto.

[31] For the composition of India's managerial class drawn from non-commercial groups, see V. Subramaniam. *The Managerial Class of India*, All India Management Association, New Delhi, 1971.

Professor B.B. Misra in his, *The Indian Middle Classes*, was the earliest to identify the predominance of the salaried and self-employed in it—in contrast to the western middle class. What he failed to note was: (a) the sociological reasons for this in colonial

punctuality and keeping official affairs separate from domestic, and unfunctionally in dress and drink. When its demands for social equality, political control and economic opportunity were rebuffed by the rulers, it faced frustration which drove it in due course to organize the nationalist freedom movement, finally winning independence from colonial occupation.

This general story of the DMC which started in India was replicated with variations in all colonies British or French. Thus it was that an exogenous mediatory class of the salaried and self-employed took over political and administrative power in all newly independent countries. Its limited experience and background disposed it to accept public administration, the only tool it knew, as the means of development, and when it was buttressed by legitimation both from the left as 'Planning', and right as 'Development Administration', the tool was virtually entrenched.

Another equally obvious reason was that private capital was poorly developed in all these countries, partly by colonialist discouragement, and could not have contributed much to development in a short time. In India, where capital was most developed, it had bogged itself down for a century and a half in money-lending and in ultrasafe ventures, and had also kept aloof from modern management practices partly because of its suspicion of the professional educated middle class.[32] In Africa, there was little capital in African hands, some financial middle level capital in the hands of the Lebanese and Indians, and most industrial capital was available only from the metropolitan country. To sum up, capital for economic development in most newly independent countries was more easily available either from: (i) government investment or (ii) aid or loans from metropolitan governments or international aid agencies or (iii) multinational companies. Sources in (i) and (ii) meant the extensive use of government bureaucracy for development while source (iii) meant, apart from dependence on the MNCs; the creation of a parallel government bureaucracy to interact with and control them.

The reasons for the reliance on government administration are thus clear. The reasons for the failure of developmental efforts have been detailed by dependency theorists and Marxian political economists which we may note in passing. In the first place, comes the

---

confrontation, and (b) the universal nature of the phenomenon in the colonial context in Africa as well as Asia.

[32] V. Subramaniam, *The Managerial Class of India*, AIMA, New Delhi, 1971. Chapter 5.

colonial exploitation process itself which creates and entrenches a secondary dependency relationship for the colonies—as explained by Walter Rodney in *How Europe Underdeveloped Africa*. After independence, capital from outside the country through MNCs and other means controls local production, while the combined power of international macro-capital controls the world market and export prices, thus effectively dictating both ways to a post-colonial economy, as explained by Samir Amin and others in their theories of neo-colonialism.[33] These theorists also suggest that the local middle-class in power—variously called national bourgeoisie, or national elite, or bureaucratic bourgeoisie—cooperates with this neo-colonial exploitation as 'compradors' or agents.

These blanket theories contain some truth, some gaps and some exaggeration, though we do not discuss these here. The main question is not just why government administration as a tool of development has failed, but why it persists in the form of public enterprises, centralized planning and various controls and subsidies. I would suggest that failure is not totally due to deliberate colonial underdevelopment and neo-colonial exploitation, but other reasons as well and persistence in the older path is not simply 'compradorism' but rather persistence in an established internal power relationship. Recognition of this aspect takes us to our last topic about the deficiencies in our organizational knowledge.

CULTURE AND ORGANIZATION

Organization and management, of course, in alliance with other material, capital and technological resources are credited with having worked miracles of development in the West and are also expected to solve the problems of a self-exciting, resource-wasting society in the future, while the same pair seems to have failed partly or wholly in developing countries. The answer to this paradox is not, however, simple. In the first place, their failure in developing countries is relative and has been partly exaggerated. Thus public enterprises have been only moderately successful at best anywhere, and India, Malaysia, African countries and the Caribbean would do well to note that their failures are similar and are within the same broad limits.

[33] Samir Amin, *Neo-colonialism in Africa*, Penguin edition. For a brief statement see Julius Nyerere, *Asia Week*. August 29, 1980.

There is a growing literature of dependency theory and the best source for references is *Review of African Political Economy*, London.

Some of this failure is due to the unduly high hopes of development they have raised for themselves in a madly competitive situation. Perhaps their economies might have been even worse off without such essays in public enterprise, perhaps with MNCs running them. We have evolved no realistic standards of comparison except profit. The hopes about public enterprises, as well as the lament on their failures, are both exaggerated.

A good part of the explanation based on neo-colonialism also seems to be valid in that public administration and public enterprises in developing countries have to battle against a far more competitive, even hostile international environment in terms of investment capital, import of capital equipment and technology, and exports into a highly controlled market.

But, in addition to these factors, there is an equally important third major factor in the discrepancy between the gesellschaft administrative organization and its gemeinschaft environment. The professional and salaried administrators of these countries run government and even private organizations on broadly the western principles of administration and management and are largely drawn from an urban educated middle class, very much inbred, but the clients on whom they have to act successfully to trigger off a positive response belong mainly to a rural gemeinschaft society.[34] The gap varies somewhat from one country to another and from one region to another but is substantial in contrast to the much narrower gap in understanding between administrators and the public in western societies, including Soviet Russia, in this century. This gap in communication is a more significant factor than emerging class conflicts, and is a product of the exogenous evolution of a middle class unable to carry the rest of society with it fast enough. To this Japan's social evolution offers an important contrast where the ruling elite, by keeping out the colonizing West, controlled the development of social factors in their own way, making use of even feudal loyalties for modern ends. That exercise is now beyond the capacities of any country in an open world.

SOME REFLECTIONS

The position of administration and management in a world perspective presents interesting paradoxes both in the West and the East. As

---

[34] See V. Subramaniam, *Social Background of India's Administrators*. Publications Division, 1971, for the highly urban middle class origins.

public policy and as management it is expected to be the saviour of a complex self-exciting Western society, but as bureaucracy its spread is dreaded as causing equally complex human problems. In developing countries, the problem is reversed; public administration has been far less productive of economic development for several reasons including a discrepancy between a formalized administration recruited from a limited urban middle class and a large gemeinschaftish rural society. An obvious observation is that administration and management have their limitations depending on the total culture and economy of a society. They produce better results in a gesellschaft society, regardless of ideology, but also make worse its human problems while they are less effective in a gemeinschaft society. Our organizational knowledge is thus reasonably sound and useful in terms of intra-organizational matters of structure and goal achievement, but is highly defective in terms of inter-organizational and the societal-organizational relations. There is much room here for humility, hesitation and further investigation.

CHAPTER SIX

The Consolidation of Adjustment
Implications for Public Administration

Richard Batley

The governments of most developing countries have been
subject to pressures, especially through structural adjustment
programmes, to reduce the direct role of the state in the supply
of services. New forms of service supply are emerging, in
which government has only an indirect role as enabler and
regulator of other actors: but there has been little practical
guidance on how these 'new' roles are to be performed in the
specific context of developing countries. The danger is then of
the adoption of inappropriate practices from more advanced
countries. The argument of this article is that governments
face several difficulties in managing the 'post-adjusted state':
the inheritance of social and political strains, and of reforms
made abruptly under pressure; the complexity of identifying
the appropriate role of the state for particular services under
particular circumstances; the technical difficulty of managing
new administrative roles; and the contradiction, particularly
in respect of systems of accountability, between the new and
the old requirements on public administration.

INTRODUCTION

Structural adjustment programmes for developing countries have
promoted the 'new conventional view' that the state should
directly supply services only where necessary. It has increasingly to

* *Public Administration and Development*, vol. 14, 1994.

act in what we will describe as a 'provider role', ensuring that essential goods and services are delivered but not aiming to be the sole deliverer or producer.

Although this requires less direct action by government agencies, the argument of this article is that state withdrawal often implies the paradoxical need for public administration to perform new tasks which are more complex than the old ones. It has now to regulate and support private, community and arms-length agencies; these tasks are technically difficult, politically sensitive and difficult to accommodate together with established styles of administration. However, little attention has been given to the practical performance of these new tasks in developing countries. Development agencies, governments and researchers have focused more on the process of withdrawal than on how governments are to perform regulatory and enabling roles after they have withdrawn.

The article indicates the difficult circumstances under which governments are being urged to change their roles, the complex analytic issues which have to be considered in deciding the respective roles of the public and private sectors, and the question of the capacity of public administration to undertake its new roles. All this is occurring in a context where governments are under multiple pressures to make different and often contradictory reforms in their established administrative arrangements.

The issues raised in the article emerged from research on the management of urban services in several countries of Latin America, Africa, South and South East Asia (Batley 1992). This brought to light the problem of regulation in the context of state withdrawal in countries subject to structural adjustment programmes. Further research is planned, focusing on the question of the state's role in regulating and enabling other actors.

Issues for Government in Adjustment

Stabilization and adjustment programmes have been applied to the economies of developing countries with the support (or insistence) of the International Monetary Fund and the World Bank. In many respects they have provided a framework within which other donor agencies also operate. Among the main elements of these programmes have been (i) the liberalization of external trade and exchange rate policies, (ii) the elimination of governmental control of internal prices, and (iii) the reduction of the scale of the public sector and its role as a producer of goods and services. It is the last of these which concerns this article, particularly with regard to public services.

The redefinition of the 'boundaries of the state' has frequently taken place under difficult circumstances, partly caused by the structural adjustment programmes themselves. These have a powerful impact on the capacity of governments to make and sustain reforms. The difficulties may be outlined as follows:

Delayed and Imposed Reform

Adjustment in the 1970s was delayed and therefore ultimately more traumatic than it might have been. Oil crisis, falling commodity prices and recession in the West led to increasing balance of payments difficulties. African and Latin American governments generally lacked strategic vision to engage voluntarily in adjustment; instead they tried to maintain the scale of government employment and public subsidies by borrowing in the late 1970s and early 1980s to cover tax shortfalls and debt. In Africa as in Latin America, but not in South Asia, government expenditure became a growing proportion of shrinking GDPs (Cornia et al., 1987, Sandbrook, 1993; Bulmer-Thomas, 1992): employment and public subsidies were maintained for political reasons while expenditure on investment and the maintenance of public services and infrastructure were allowed to slip. International shocks thus helped to enhance the visibility of public sector inefficiency and ineffectiveness.

Involuntary, though in many respects necessary, adjustment was most likely to be imposed by the IMF and the World Bank with the greatest force on the weakest governments, with the greatest dependence and the least capacity to negotiate (Mosley et al., 1991, ch. 5). However, it is in these countries that many elements of the neo-liberal package, may be least appropriate (United Nations Economic Commission for Africa, 1989, p. 20).

Different Levels of Appropriateness of the Adjustment Package

It is at least questionable whether stabilization and adjustment policies have been universally appropriate to South Asian and Sub-Saharan African countries (Mosley et al., 1991). The Indian state is a classic case of the sort of bureaucratic, controlling, regulatory and protectionist regime at which neo-liberal structural adjustment lending (SAL) is addressed (Lal, 1983, Toye, 1987); even from a left perspective (Bardhan 1984) it can be seen as a rent-seeking arrangement for vested interests. However, the liberal agenda may have been less relevant to many African countries where the lack of the legal-bureaucratic state rather than its over-emphasis could be said to underlie the failure of entrepreneurial development (Sandbrook, 1993, p. 30). Although there are some countries with a stronger tradition of effective bureaucracies with some accountability—Zimbabwe, Botswana, Côte d'Ivoire, Cameroon—in general these are 'weak states' (Azarya and Chazan, 1984; Charlton and May, 1986) whose problems are their incapacity to offer real services and maintain popular legitimacy.

Stress Arising from the Redistribution of Poverty

Cornia et al. (1987) demonstrated a somewhat undifferentiated increase in poverty in most countries of Africa and Latin America. The World Bank (1990a) has questioned the evidence, and its World Development Report for 1992 revealed a stabilization in the percentage incidence of poverty (Moser et al., 1993). Moser et al. distinguish the effects of SAL on different groups (particularly the urban poor) of changes in prices, employment structure and wages. The poor and 'borderline poor' are particularly affected by the removal of subsidies and controls on food prices but also on government services. A 'newly poor' category has been created in Africa and Latin America by the shift of employment out of public administration, urban commercial services and protected industries into tradeable export goods, generating underemployment and drastically lower wages. However, the experience of South Asia (or at least India and Sri Lanka) has been dramatically different with accelerating growth and a declining incidence of poverty.

Rapidly Declining Public Services

The rate of growth of social expenditure declined everywhere in the 1980s, particularly in 'intensely adjusting' countries, but actual reductions per head were more common in Latin America than in Asia or Africa; however, Ghana undertook one of the most severe cuts as, in Asia, did Sri Lanka. India is notable for its extraordinarily low, though stable, per capita social expenditure (Moser et al., 1993, Table 34). Where cuts have taken place, they have mostly affected basic services (preventive and primary health care, and primary education) and capital over recurrent expenditure (Moser et al., 1993). There is widespread evidence of decline in investment and in maintenance of infrastructure with consequential adverse affects not only on households but also on enterprises, particularly small firms (Stren and White, 1989; Moser et al., 1993, pp. 65–6; Sandbrook, 1993, p. 45).

Cuts and Demoralization in Public Administration

Programmes for the reduction of employment in public administration have been the most tangible aspects of adjustment programmes of institutional reform. Overstaffing after a long period of growth (Abernethy, 1988) has been one of the World Bank's main criticisms of public administration, and reductions seen as the best way of reducing public expenditure (World Bank 1983, 1989). However, cutting employment represents a considerable political challenge, undermining government's role as employer of last resort and threatening its constituency of support (Sandbrook, 1993, p. 44). This is a particular problem in democratic regimes such as India, whose public sector unions represent a considerable block of support, and also in countries with strong ethnic differences (Malaysia, Sri Lanka, Kenya) where public sector employment offers the possibility of balancing dominance in the private sector (Norris, 1992). Effectiveness in restraining civil service expansion seems to have been greater in the more ideologically committed countries of Latin America and in the more dependent countries of Africa (Moser et al., 1993, p. 40; Sandbrook, 1993, p. 61; World Bank, 1989 and 1991).

It is easier to allow real wages to erode than cut staff. In many cases urban wages as a whole halved during the 1980s (Amis, 1989) and public sector wages fell below subsistence levels in Sudan, Ghana, Uganda, Guinea (World Bank, 1988; Sandbrook, 1993, p. 49). Wage freezes have been part of many adjustment programmes (Moser et al. 1993 p. 41) . The result is a process of institutional collapse with increased demoralization, corruption and moonlighting (Sandbrook, 1993, p. 48; Amis, 1992).

POST-ADJUSTMENT OR THE CONSOLIDATION PHASE

While the 'transition' has been well researched, as outlined above, there are major and under-considered questions of the long-term management of the post or continually adjusting state. Given the liberalizing nature of adjustment, the longer term questions are to do with how government manages its relationships with other actors.

However, the problems pre-dating adjustment and the problems of transition are influential on the performance of government in the longer term. The generation of adjustment out of crisis and donor pressure means that changes in the role and performance of government have to be managed under difficult circumstances wrought with political tensions, resistance from the losers in the population, demoralization in the public sector and multiple changes occurring at the same time. The particular package of adjustment may be more a product of pressure and capacity of negotiation than of studied response to particular circumstances. Moreover, change is likely to be abrupt and ill-prepared with inadequate consideration of the sustainability of reforms (Bulmer-Thomas, 1992, p. 15; Birch and Primo Braga, 1992, p. 9; Edwards and Baer, 1992, p. 9.; Adam et al., 1993, p. 66).

In addition to these difficult underlying conditions, governments face technical, political and administrative difficulties in developing or supporting the wide variety of newly emerging forms of service delivery in which they have now only an indirect stake. These forms include:

- the spontaneous survival strategies of the poor and newly poor who, particularly in Africa, must increasingly rely on household and community resources for access to essential goods and services
- the development of compensatory and relief packages (nutrition, employment, health, education, housing, water) often under the direction of international aid agencies and involving international and local NGOs. Government has a role but as one among other actors. (Moser et al., 1993)
- programmed privatization in which governments make policy decisions to sell assets, to franchise or to contract operations. This has been concentrated in certain sectors: commerce, industry, agricultural marketing, urban services and public utilities. 'Progress' in formal privatization has been modest except in some specific more advanced countries: Chile, Mexico, Argentina, Malaysia, Thailand and to some extent in French West Africa. It has often been imposed by fiscal crisis, debt, donor pressure and political last resort (Adam et al., 1993; Edwards and Baer, 1992; Cook and Kirkpatrick, 1988)
- incremental 'privatization' in response to the failure of public services, where enterprises and households find their own market solutions especially in the spheres of essential personal services (transport, education, health) and infrastructure (water, power)
- changes in public sector management to replicate some of the

claimed efficiencies of the private sector. This has included measures to create quasi-market conditions through the introduction of user charges, the exposure of public operators to private competition, the introduction of performance measurement and reward into the public sector and the devolution of management responsibility to budget centres or semi-autonomous agencies.

In the context of a state in which the public sector has retreated and government now has to work with other actors, the following three sorts of roles for the public sector seem to be particularly important in the 'consolidation phase':

i) Core Administration and Direct Service Supply

The national context and the characteristics of certain goods and services will mean that in many spheres government continues to act as a direct supplier. However, the way it performs this role has been subject to changes which need research and support. There are changes in internal administration and the increasing emergence of 'half-way house' arrangements where government collaborates with communities or non-governmental organizations, for example in the delivery of compensatory programmes or in joint ventures with the private sector.

ii) Regulating and Enabling Other Service Operators

The incremental decay of public services and haste under pressure to pass responsibility for direct supply to other actors are both widely held to have led to inadequate consideration of government's controlling and supporting roles. As the state withdraws from direct supply or fails to accompany growing demand, leaving more to market operators, arms-length public agencies, communities and households, it may nevertheless retain a concern with ensuring that provision of essential goods and services takes place to certain standards. There has been little research on the performance of government's emerging roles of enabling and regulation in the service sectors of less developed countries (Adam et al., 1993; Sandbrook, 1993: Edwards and Baer, 1992; Bennett, 1991; Bennett and Tangcharoensathien, 1994; Birch and Primo Braga, 1992).

iii) Policy Analysis and Srategy

Working with and through other actors implies a range of new analytic roles and skills. Governments will have to be able to analyse the performance of markets so as to decide the need for intervention and the capacity of public and private actors to undertake their respective roles. They will have to be able to establish economic and social sector strategies respected by the main private actors and supported by public sector institutions, resources and investment. For weaker governments, it will be necessary to develop the capacity of negotiation with donors on the subsequent assistance programmes (Sandbrook, 1993; Rodrik, 1992; World Bank, 1990b).

INSTITUTIONAL ARRANGEMENTS FOR SERVICE SUPPLY

Governments will have to be able to assess the case for intervention and, depending on the case, intervene appropriately. This implies the development of capacities of analysis of existing distribution systems (including markets), of formulation of policies involving the public and private sectors, and of management of a range of different sorts of relationships with private and community actors. Below are indicated the bare bones of the considerations which need to be taken into account in making these judgements about how any particular service could be supplied, given a basic commitment to reducing the direct role of the state.

Neo-classical economic theory accepts three main sorts of argument for government intervention:

i) The Public Goods Argument

Some goods and services are described as by their nature 'public' in the sense that private firms on their own would simply not provide them because there is no means of charging consumers. This would occur, for example, in the case of police services where the benefits are collective and it is impossible to measure how much any individual has consumed.

ii) The Market Failure Argument

In a wide variety of circumstances, even where private enterprise could operate, it may, fail to do so efficiently or at all if

a)   there is a tendency to monopoly, that is the nature of a service or the scale of the necessary investment required prohibit competition;

b)   the necessary investments are so large scale or the returns so uncertain that private firms are not prepared to undertake them;

c)   the wider society would benefit from extension of a service even though the direct consumers may be unwilling or unable to pay for it: an example of such 'positive externalities' would be vaccination;

d) producers can pass on costs to the wider society, allowing them to keep their costs to the direct consumers artificially low: an example of these 'negative externalities' would be pollution;

e) consumers or producers have too little knowledge to make informed choices: this sort of situation may arise in the case of professional services (such as medical services) where clients may not reasonably be able to assess the value of options.

iii) The Equity or 'Merit Good' Argument

There are in practice basic commitments in any society such as everybody should have access to certain goods and services, regardless of their ability and willingness to pay the market price. Education and health typically fall into this category.

These concepts provide a set of considerations against which to consider the case for government intervention, but they should be treated with caution. There are few goods or services which fall neatly and wholly into any category, and where they do belong depends on local circumstances. It also depends on judgement: the value of costs and benefits to wider society, the level of risks and the importance of access to services are all matters of interpretation. Moreover, governments have a variable capacity to correct market failure; they may often fail in the same places and for the same reasons as markets (Adam et al., 1992, pp. 79–82).

The theoretical approach does, however, have the virtue of bringing these considerations into the open, forcing us to identify the reasons for intervention. These may be, for example, to control the abuse of monopoly, to inform or to subsidize consumers, to ensure that the polluter pays the costs imposed on others, or to manage the supply of 'public goods'. For different services in differing national contexts there will be different *reasons* for government to be involved, and these imply diverse *levels* and *forms* of involvement. Intervention may clearly stop short of full state ownership and responsibility for supply; equally, privatization can rarely signify the complete abnegation of the state's interest.

The wide range of possible relationships between the public and private sectors becomes clearer if we distinguish between two components of supply—'provision' and 'production'—which have frequently been artificially collapsed into each other leading to the assumption that the state must do both or neither (Ostrom, et al., 1993; Wunsch, 1991).

Provision is the act of ensuring that a given good is available and might include roles such as establishing policies or plans and ensuring their implementation; ensuring standards of service and the availability of information; financing, advising, enabling, coordinating, regulating and licensing private producers: or maintaining public ownership and contracting producers. *Production* is the business of physically generating, delivering and maintaining the service, and might include the construction of plant or facilities, their maintenance and the management of service delivery.

In most circumstances governments could, in principle, achieve their objectives without getting into the direct production or delivery of services. Monopolies can be left in private hands but regulated by public agencies; consumers can be subsidized to allow them to purchase privately produced services; even the classical 'public goods' can be privatized in the sense that, while retaining responsibility for their provision, government can contract and pay the private sector to deliver them.

According to this argument, there is only really a case for state involvement in the production and delivery of goods and services under extremely severe conditions. These would be when several of the factors justifying public sector involvement exist in combination: for example, where there is no way of charging customers according to their consumption, the production process is large scale and monopolistic, and the service has wide positive and negative effects on society as a whole.

There are many possible permutations of provision and delivery activities in different institutional arrangements for supply; furthermore these institutional arrangements may involve not only government and the formal private sector but also informal enterprises, self-help, community organizations and large non-governmental organizations.

Table 1 describes nine possible systems of supply (combining public and private actors in alternative aspects of provision and delivery), showing how each might be more or less appropriate to the supply of goods or services with different features. For example, the strongest case for pure state supply would be for public goods with a high tendency to monopoly, large scale and high externalities—this would apply to sewerage or mass health education. Lease or franchise arrangements could only apply where a return can be earned by

Table 1: Supply Arrangements and their Appropriatenness to Services

Supply Arrangements	Factors Favouring the supply arrangement	Examples of appropriate services
Pure State Supply		
– government assumes full responsibility for all aspects of supply (although sub-contracting is possible)	In the case of public goods and services with a tendency to monopoly, large scale and high externalities	Water, sewerage, solid waste treatment, mass health education
Community Supply		
Community/neighbourhood takes full responsibility for supply	In the case of public goods and services of small scale and limited externalities beyond the community	Neighbourhood improvement, community level water and drainage, local roads
Licensed private supply		
Government takes minimal role in licensing private suppliers	In the case of private goods and service with low externalities	Taxis, markets, public transport, food retail
Government responsibility and property with private production		
Government pays private – works contractor – service or management contractor for up to 5 years to undertake specific operations and maintenance	Appropriate to public goods and services. Contracting presupposes divisibility of the production process and capacity of government to control contractors	Public works, maintenance of works and equipment, aspects of administration (computing, legal or accounting services etc)

(contd)

184

Table 1 (contd)

Supply Arrangements	Factors Favouring the supply arrangement	Examples of appropriate services
Government ultimately responsible but operative responsibility transferred to private producers	Presupposes excludability; the capacity of firms to finance investment and to tolerate risks; the capacity of government to supervize contract compliance	Water supply, gas, electricity, markets, public transport
– lease contracts for around 10 years. The leaseholder assumes responsibility for the financing of maintenance		
– concessions or franchises for around 20 years, Contractor finances investment and maintenance		
Partnership between public and private suppliers.	Where there is mutual interest in projects which offer the possibility of return on investment: the private sector needs government to cover risks or make basic investment. The public sector hopes for public benefits from private investment	Acquisition and development of land for residential and business development
– joint ownership		
– joint investment		
– joint ventures in which the distinct roles of public and private sectors are combined		

(contd)

Table 1 (contd)

Supply Arrangements	Factors Favouring the supply arrangement	Examples of appropriate services
Public subsidy for private consumption		
Government subsidizes the consumer to enable purchase of private goods and services eg: vouchers allowing beneficiaries to choose between deliverers; tax waivers	Where increases in consumption of private goods external benefits and private production is more efficient	Food, housing, education, curative health services
User control of public supply		
The users participate in the management of goods and services	In the case of public goods and services of small scale and without strong divisions of interest between users	Neighbourhood improvement, community water and drainage, local roads and schools
Public supply with market processes		
– charging for services received	In the case or goods and services which have private characteristics, where consumption can be related to capacity to pay and there are important redistributive considerations	Land, housing, public transport, metered water and energy

charging for the service and non-payers are excludable; at the same time, given that responsibility is substantially transferred to the private sector, government has to have the capacity to make cast-iron contracts and to effectively police them.

Each supply arrangement is appropriate under particular circumstances, and each implies a different role for the public sector, whether as direct deliverer or as a licensor, contract-maker, regulator, subcontractor, enabler, financier, partner, subsidizer or as arbitrator between users. In principle, governments should have the capacity to assess where each arrangement is appropriate, taking into account their own politico-administrative ability to fulfil their role. This requires sophisticated assessment skills and autonomous technical judgement, free from immediate political and donor pressures.

Administrative Capacity

Public administration requires the capacity not only to make these initial assessments about how to supply public services but also, of course, to administer the state's roles once they are established. The problem is that different and even conflicting capacities are required to perform the 'post-adjustment' roles of public administration, defined earlier as i) core administration and direct service delivery, ii) regulation and enablement of service delivery by other actors, and iii) policy analysis and strategic decision.

These roles or aspects of the 'new' public administration diverge in their premises about, firstly, the relationship of accountability between officials and political leaders, and, secondly, the relationship between public administration and society, whether as neutral regulator or developmental advocate. Structural adjustment, neo-liberalism and in Africa, the collapse of public administration have re-opened these Weberian questions. Governments of developing countries are subject to conflicting messages about the way forward; it may be necessary to proceed on all fronts but this is not easy, especially for states whose administrations are already weak.

The following outline will distil some of the key issues from the reform debate about the three aspects of public administration, in order to illustrate the divergence.

Core Public Administration

This debate centres on the core administration of central and local government, rather than on the field agencies of development. The key points of reference are the Weberian principles of bureaucracy as a mechanism to manage the relations between politicians and the public, to disinterestedly execute policy and to manage and regulate routine tasks. The virtues of bureaucratic administration are widely recognized as those of neutrality, fairness, accountability and (though not in the popular view) efficiency. Even those who criticize its functioning in some respects usually recognize its appropriateness to the routine tasks of government (World Bank, 1991b; Chambers, 1993). Sandbrook (1993, pp. 46, 82) argues that the absence of effective Weberian bureaucracy is a key aspect of government failure in Africa.

Bureaucratic public administration has been held to question for the following reasons: its difficulty under any circumstances given the 'tense balance' between politics and bureaucracy, its particular precariousness in the political climate of development, doubts about its appropriateness to the tasks of development, and its (possibly) declining relevance in the modern, liberalized world (Brett, 1988).

Four broad ways forward, within the framework of 'top down' (central or local) administration, have been pursued since the 1970s. All are concerned with the improvement of the productive efficiency and responsiveness of administration but they have contradictory implications for accountability and bureaucratic performance.

i) Civil Service Reform and Accountability

Most developing countries ... have persevered in their conviction ... that public administration, mainly through bureaucratic structures, should be the main—but not the only—instrument by which development activities are implemented' (Esman, 1988, p. 132). Civil service reform programmes, supported by donors, have emphasized questions of organizational structure, financial and human resource needs, and basic administrative competence appropriate to the development function (United Nations, 1992; ODA, 1989; Wunsch, 1991; Dwivedi, 1989). Such programmes increasingly occur in the context of structural adjustment together with the down-sizing of government. What has been newly emphasized is the other half of the Weberian equation: the development of the *legal and political* conditions which can hold politicians and officials to account for just and effective administration, for example in ODA's good governance programme (ODA, 1993; Paul, 1992).

ii) Back to Public Administration

The logic of the neo-liberal approach is to retreat from development to public administration, with the limited ambition of maintaining the minimal enabling conditions for the private sector and for the freedom of citizens (Glentworth, 1989; Sandbrook, 1993, p. 59). Economic activity is, so far as possible, privatized and deregulated; the state reverts to its core regulatory duties: policing, upholding the law, private property and contract.

iii) The Project Approach

Escape from the deficiencies of public administration by the setting up of special agencies, linked to donor projects, has been a widespread practice—and one which may even be accelerating as development aid becomes increasingly re-oriented to relief. The key criticisms are that projectization may achieve isolated successes while, by-passing and even weakening conventional administration (Rondinelli, 1983a; Honadle and Rosengard, 1983; Bremer, 1984; Hirschmann, 1994). The defence is that projects have permitted experimentation and the injection of learning into public administration (Rondinelli, 1983b).

iv) The Injection of Private Sector Motives of Efficiency and Value for Money

Israel (1987) describes ways in which the tasks of government can be given specific objectives and thrown into a competitive environment so as to inject incentives to performance. This has clearly been a major theme in American and British reforms. Richards (1992) describes a shift from the 'public administration paradigm' to the 'efficiency paradigm', in which market disciplines are applied within the public service to act as a counterpressure to the 'producer interest'. Particular functions may be contracted out or 'market-tested'; even where there is no real market, management may be devolved and put on a contractual basis.

This agenda raises conflicting pressures and yet reforming countries are frequently exposed to all at the same time. Points i and ii put a premium on the classical Weberian requirements for capacity to make and support rules, and assume hierarchic lines of accountability upwards towards political leaders; probity rather than efficiency is required. Points iii and iv sidetrack this sort of accountability, orienting it instead to the donor or directing it to efficiency criteria or to the client; the principal concern is not with the probity of process but with efficiency of outcome.

Regulation and Enablement of Other Actors

The question of 'over-development' of the state and bureaucracy has been a concern since the early days of aid and its academic study. Behind development administration's 'big government' orientation there was always a background of concern with community development and small business development. The liberalism of the 1980s enhanced this strand of policy, focusing on non-government organizations not only as objects of development by government but as themselves, autonomous agents of development. There is a re-orientation of the public sector from directly delivering development to enabling and regulating other bodies.

Esman (1988, pp. 129–31) attributes to the 'new development administration' the 'more mature and realistic orientation' that government administration must admit its limitations, accept uncertainty and work with private and community agencies. Chambers (1988 and 1993) describes the need for 'bureaucratic reversals' in the many situations where officials know less than their clients: professionals should move from being experts transferring information to become consultants and collaborators of the poor. Korten (1989) admits that this is effectively to overthrow Weberian bureaucracy in the sense that development agencies cease to be accountable to 'policy direction from above' and become accountable to 'the people'. The political feasibility of public officials engaging in such activities, particularly in the politically vulnerable conditions of developing countries, is at least dubious (Batley, 1993, p. 179). 'People centred development' therefore effectively means that the agents of development must be non-governmental organizations (Korten, 1990). If government administration does have a role it is to create an enabling environment. The objective is to develop self-provisioning by communities and user groups and, in so doing, to strengthen 'civil society'—and hence, ultimately, the conditions for a more responsive state.

Working with community based organizations, user groups and NGOs is one aspect of government's growing need to work with and through other bodies. Another is its changing relationships with the private business sector and with governmental arms-length agencies, which are often a product of structural adjustment. Here government administration cedes the responsibility for the direct production and delivery of public goods and services to other bodies through the variety of supply arrangements described earlier. There is now a wide literature on the privatization process and its impact (Adam et al., 1992), but little on how arms-length producers are to be regulated and supported in developing countries (Collins and Wallis, 1990).

The new managerial tasks have general relevance: analysing and maintaining market conditions, setting broad frameworks of policy and standards, managing contracts, regulating contractors and monopolists, coordinating, financing and supporting producers, enabling community self-provision, supporting consumers with information, quality control and finance. However, there are particular difficulties in performing these roles in less developed countries where skills and information are lacking, governmental enforcement capacity is weak, producers often more powerful, and the dangers of regulatory capture are great (Batley, 1992; Bennett, 1991; Bennett and Tangcharoensathien, 1994; Adam et al., 1992). There is an irony 'that the need for regulation is greatest in economies which have the most limited capacity to manage it' (Adam et al., 1992, p. 77). But the design of regulatory and enabling arrangements, where it exists, is frequently imported from Western countries without regard for its appropriateness to the national context (Birch and Braga, 1992, p. 14).

This agenda also raises conflicting pressures. Internally, it is not easy to combine the regulatory style and skills with the enabling, supporting requirements; there are difficult boundaries between laissez-faire and intervention. There are also conflicts with the traditional public administration mode: whereas the old forms of regulation were bureaucratic and accountable through long hierarchies to politicians, the new regulation is a form of enabling, oriented to maintaining market conditions. It demands interaction with community and private producers, raising new questions of accountability and probity.

Policy Analysis and Strategic Capacity

While blueprint national planning is now discarded, the definition of the new roles of public administration in the neo-liberal era commonly includes a concern with the capacity of governments to undertake policy analysis and formulate policy (World Bank, 1990b). The enabling and regulating roles assume that government has the capacity of oversight, analysing the operation of markets, identifying the need for intervention and setting the policy framework for other actors.

Such administrative capacities are widely called for (United Nations, 1992, p. 31; Baldwin, 1989; Dotse, 1991; Collins and Wallis, 1990) but there is scarce evidence of their existence. They require not only highly developed professional skills but also political conditions which would allow officials to negotiate and plan with market agents and donors. Sandbrook (1993, p. 59) doubts that the conditions yet exist for the emergence of such 'developmental states' in Africa. Grindle (1980) and Grindle and Thomas (1991) have described policy-making in developing countries as occurring in practice during the process of policy implementation rather than through processes of policy analysis and formation.

The wide literature on the East Asian 'developmental states' provides one point of reference, though not because it indicates easy opportunities for replication (Hamilton, 1987; Ranis, 1989; Morris and Adelman, 1989; Jenkins, 1991; Naya and Imada, 1990). Wade (1990) provides one of the few studies of the administrative culture, skills, personnel systems and structures of authority associated with the development of strategic capacity in South Korea and Taiwan. In several respects the factors he identifies—corporatism and delayed democratization—contradict some Western views of what composes good government'.

This agenda again raises the possibility of conflicting pressures for government administration. Unlike the traditional public administration formulation, it draws officials into the policy-making process challenging their hierarchic relations with politicians and promoting interactive policy-making with the private sector. A more corporatist relationship with leading actors in the private sector may conflict with the demands for political pluralism and democratic accountability.

Conclusion

Considerable attention has been given by governments, donors and researchers to the process of structural adjustment. Much less attention has been given to the question how governments are to manage their relationships with other actors in the liberalized environment. We have emphasized the need for governments to adjust to performing the role of provider, enabling and regulating other service operators. This role is frequently urged on governments but little practical advice is given relevant to the difficult circumstances of developing countries.

Changes in public and private roles often occur under ideological pressure or through force of circumstance as public services fail to accompany demand. Economic theory provides a framework for considering more objectively what are the justifications or requirements for government involvement and what institutional arrangements might be appropriate to the supply of particular services. However these have to be considered case by case and in particular national contexts: there are no standard, easily transferable solutions. There is a major question about the capacity of governments to administer the new roles assigned to them. Public administration has become more difficult with structural adjustment. There are continuing requirements for bureaucratic administration as well as growing needs to manage other service operators and to develop overall strategy. These different forms of administration are all necessary but they may impose conflicting pressure on politicians and officials.

REFERENCES

Abernethy, D. (1988) 'Bureaucratic Growth and Economic Stagnation in Sub-Saharan Africa' in S. K. Commins (ed.) (1988), *Africa's Development Challenges and The World Bank*, Lynne Rienner, Boulder, pp. 179-214.

Adam C., Cavendish. W., and Mistry, P. (1992). *Adjusting Privatization: Case Studies from Developing Countries*, James Currey Ltd; London.

Amis, P. (1989). 'African Development and Urban Change: What Policy-Makers Need to Know', *Development Policy Review*, 7, 375-391.

Amis, P. (1992). 'Urban Management in Uganda', Institutional Framework of Urban Management, DAG. University of Birmingham.

Azarya. V., and Chazan, N. (1984). '*Disengagement from the State in Africa: Reflections on the Experience of Ghana and Guinea'*. Presented to 27th Annual Meeting of the African Studies Association, Los Angeles, 25–28 October.

Baldwin, A. (1992). '*An Approach to Appraisal Methodology for Civil Service Institutional Reform in Africa'*, Overseas Development Administration (1989).

Bardhan, P. K. (1984). *The Political Economy of Development in India*, Blackwell, Oxford.

Batley. R. A. (1992). 'Cooperation with Private and Community Organisations', *Working Paper 6*, DAG. University of Birmingham.

Batley. R. A. (1993). 'Political Control of Urban Planning and Management' in Devas, N. and Rakodi, C. (1993), *Managing Fast Growing Cities*, Longman

Bennett, S. (1991). *The Mystique of Markets; Public and Private Health Care in Developing Countries*, Department of Public Health and Policy, Departmental Publication No 4, London School of Hygiene and Tropical Medicine, London.

Bennett, S. and Tangcharoensathien, V. (1994). 'A Shrinking State? Politics, Economics and Private Health Care in Thailand', *Public Administration and Development*, 14(1) 1–17.

Birch, M. and Primo Braga, C. (1992). 'Regulation in Latin America: Prospects for the 1990s', Texas Papers on Latin America, University of Texas, Houston.

Bremer, A. (1984). 'Building Institutional Capacity for Policy Analysis: An alternative Approach to Sustainability', Public Administration and Development, 4(1) 1–13.

Brett, E. A. (1988). 'Adjustment and the State: The Problem of Administrative Reform', Bulletin of the Institute of Development Studies, 14(4) 4–11.

Bulmer-Thomas, V. (1992). 'Life After Debt: The New Economic Trajectory in Latin America', ILAS.

Chambers, R. (1988). 'Bureaucratic Reversals and Local Identity', Bulletin of the Institute of Development Studies, 19(4) 50–6.

Chambers, R. (1993). Challenging the Professions, IT Publications.

Charlton, R. and May R. (1986). 'State Weakness in Africa: A Critique', Politics, 6(2) 25–32.

Collins. P. and Wallis. M. (1990). 'Privatization, Regulation and Training', Public Administration and Development, 10(4) 375–87.

Cook, P. and Kirkpatrick, C. (eds). (1988). Privatisation in Less Developed Countries, Wheatsheaf, Brighton.

Cornia, G., Jolly, R., and Stewart, F. (eds). (1987). Adjustment with a Human Face, Vol. I, Clarendon Press, Oxford,

Dotse, F. M. (1991) 'The State of Training in Public Policy Management in Ghana', Public Administration and Development, 11(6) 525–40.

Dwivedi. O. P. (1989). 'Editor's Introduction: Administrative Heritage, Morality and Challenges in the Sub-Continent since the British Raj', Public Administration and Development, 9(3).

Edward, S J. and Baer W. (1992). 'The State and Private Sector in Latin America: Reflections on the Past, the Present and the Future', Texas papers on Latin America, University of Texas, Houston.

Esman, M. J. (1988). 'The Maturing of Development Administration', Public Administration and Development, 8(2) 125–34.

Glentworth, G. (1989). 'Strategic Issues in Civil Service Reform', in ODA (1989).

Grindle, M. S. (ed) (1980). The Politics of Policy Implementation, Princeton University Press, New Jersey.

Grindle, M. S. and Thomas, J. W. (1991). Public Choices and Policy Change: The Political Economy of Reform in Developing Countries, Johns Hopkins University Press, Baltimore.

Hamilton, C. (1987). 'Can the Rest of Asia Emulate the NICs?' Third World Quarterly, 9(4) 1225–56.

Helm, D. (ed.) (1989). The Economic Borders of the State, Oxford.

Hirschmann, D. (1993). 'Institutional Development in the Era of Economic Policy Reform: Concerns, Contradictions and Illustrations From Malawi', Public Administration and Development, 13(2) 113–28.

Honadle, G. and Rosengard, J. (1983). 'Putting Projectized Development in Perspective', *Public Administration and Development*, 3(4) 299–305.

Israel, A. (1987). *Institutional Development: Incentives to Performance*, Johns Hopkins University Press, Baltimore.

Jena, P. K. (1994). 'Stabilization and Structural Adjustment: Two Years of India Experience and Export Vulnerability', *Papers in the Administration of Development 56*, Development Administration Group, University of Birmingham.

Jenkins, R. (1991). 'Learning from the Gang: Are there Lessons for Latin America from East Asia?'. *Bulletin of Latin American Research* 10/11, 37–54.

Korten, D. (1989). 'The Community: Master or Client? A reply', *Public Administration and Development*, 9(5) 569–75.

Korten, D. (1990). *Getting to the 21st Century*, Kumarian Press.

Lal, D. (1983). *The Poverty of Development Economics*, Institute of Economic Affairs, London.

Morris, C. and Adelman, I. (1989). 'Nineteenth Century Development Experience and Lessons for Today', *World Development*, 17(9) 1417–32.

Moser, C., Herbert, A., and Makonnen, R. (1993). *Urban Poverty in the Context of Structural Adjustment: Recent Evidence and Policy Responses*, Discussion paper, Urban Development Division, World Bank, Washington, D.C..

Mosley, P. (1990). 'Structural Adjustment: A General Overview 1980–89', Paper presented to conference on New Directions in Trade Policy at University of Paris I, 18-20 January.

Mosley, P., Harrigan, J., and Toye, J. (1991). *Aid and Power: The World Bank and Policy-Based Lending*, Vols 1 and 2, Routledge, London.

Mosley, P. (1994). 'Indian Macro-Economic Policy Before and After Liberalization—Impact on the Poor', ODA Workshop on Poverty Reduction and Aid Policy. Institute of Development Studies, Brighton.

Naya, S. and Imada, P. (1990). 'Development Strategies and Economic Performance of the Dynamic Asian Economies: Some Comparison with Latin America', *Pacific Review*, 3(4) 296–313.

Ostrom, E., Schroeder, L. and Wynne, S. (1993). *Institutional Incentives and Sustainable Development: Infrastructure Policies in Perspective*, Westview Press, Boulder, San Francisco, Oxford.

Overseas Development Administration (1993). *Taking Account of Good Government*, Government and Institutions Department, Technical Note No 10.

Overseas Development Institute (1992). 'Aid and Political Reform, Briefing Paper', London, January.

Paul, S. (1992). 'Accountability in Public Services: Exit, Voice and Control', *World Development*, 20(7) 1047–60.

Paul, S. (1988). 'Emerging Issues of Privatization and the Public Sector', The World Bank, Washington, D.C..

Ranis, G. (1989). 'The Role of Institutions in Transition Growth ...' *World Development*, 17(9) 1443–53.

Richards, S. (1992). 'Who Defines the Public Good? The Consumer Paradigm in Public Management', Public Management Foundation.

Rodrik, D. (1992). in Goldin, I., and Winters, L. A. (1992). *Open Economics: Structure Adjustment and Agriculture*, Cambridge University Press.

Rondinelli, D. (1983a). 'Projects as Instruments of Development Administration: A Qualified Defence and Suggestion for Improvement', *Public Administration and Development*, 3(4) 307–27.

Rondinelli, D. (1983b). *Development Projects as Policy Experiments: An Adaptive Approach to Development Administration*, Methuen

Sandbrook, R. (1993). *The Politics of Africa's Economic Recovery*, Cambridge University Press, Cambridge.

Toye, J. (1987). *Dilemmas of Development*, Blackwell, London.

Triche, T. A. (1990). 'Private Participation in the Delivery of Water Supply Services, the Case of Guinea', World Bank, March.

United Nations (1992). *Size and Cost of the Civil Service: Reform Programmes in Africa*, UN Dept of Economic and Social Development, DESD/SEM92/1, INT-90-R 78.

United Nations Economic Commission for Africa (1989). 'African Alternative Framework for Structural Adjustment Programmes for Socio-Economic Recovery and Transformation', Addis Ababa.

Wade, R. (1990). *Governing the Market*, Princeton University Press, New Jersey.

World Bank (1983). *World Development Report 1983*, Oxford University Press; New York.

World Bank (1989). *Sub-Saharan Africa: From Crisis to Sustainable Growth*, World Bank, Washington, D.C..

World Bank (1990a) 'Adjustment Lending Policies for Sustainable Growth', Policy and Research Series No 14, World Bank, Washington, D.C..

World Bank (1990b), *A Framework for Capacity Building in Policy Analysis and Economic Management in Sub-Saharan Africa*, World Bank, Washington, D.C..

World Bank (1991a). 'The Reform of Public Sector Management, Lessons from Experience', *Policy and Research Series*, No. 18, World Bank, Washington, D.C..

World Bank (1991b). *World Development Report, 1991*, Oxford University Press, New York.

Wunsch, J. S. (1991). 'Institutional Analysis and Decentralization; Developing an Analytical Framework for Effective Third World Administrative Reform', *Public Administration and Development*, 11(5) 431–52.

CHAPTER SEVEN

The Governance Agenda
Making Democratic Development Dispensable[*]

Niraja Gopal Jayal

Democracy and development must be seen as intimately related functioning under similar constraints, and equally subject
to political negotiation. Thus for instance, social inequality in
India both retards balanced development and distorts the logic
of democracy. It is precisely this distorting logic of democracy
in an unequal society that necessitates state welfare for the
protection of the vulnerable, for the concerns of distributive
justice cannot be fulfilled by governance alone. The answer
therefore is not to look towards the state but at different ways
of approaching and defining democracy and development.

I

This article seeks to examine the ideology and politics of the
project of 'good governance' that has, in recent years, quite in-
sidiously infiltrated into the discourse and practice of development
assistance. As part of the project of globalizing democracy, this agenda
also has an important bearing on the ways in which questions of
development and democracy are currently being understood and
conceptualized. In the post-cold war era, the imperative to subsidize,
for geopolitical reasons, the development of markedly undemocratic
Third World states has receded. The thawing of the ideological frost
between East and West has, however, been replaced by the logic of
another cold reason—wearing the mantle of virtue—which now

[*] *Economic and Political Weekly*, 22 February 1997.

dictates that development aid be tied to political reform in order to effectuate the project of the 'new international order'. If the suspension or withdrawal of such aid was once used punitively, it is now sought to be deployed proactively through the instrument of 'political conditionality' (Landell-Mills and Serageldin, 1992, p. 308).

Though the IMF has for long used political conditionality as a lever of control over debtor governments, the World Bank's Articles of Agreement formally rule out interference in the affairs of recipient nations.[1] This explains why the project of 'good governance' appears, on the Bank's definition of it, to be a chiefly technical instrument. The more political definition of it is to be found in the aid and foreign policies of the OECD countries. Very much a creature of its times, the European Bank of Reconstruction and Development, established in 1991, is the first multilateral financial institution which is statutorily obliged to take governance criteria into account. Not merely the European Community, but even the Commonwealth, the OECD and the OAU have sent out the clarion call of governance. There is thus little doubt but that development assistance today is increasingly suffused with the discourse of governance.

It becomes necessary, at this point, to examine the rationale offered for the project of governance in recent years, and the definitions—both managerial/technical as well as political—of the term, preliminary to unpacking its contents.[2] Governance was first problematized in a World Bank document of 1989 on Sub-Saharan Africa, which suggested that the Bank's programmes of adjustment and investment in that area were being rendered ineffective by a 'crisis of governance'.

---

[1] Currie (1996) suggests that there is some ambiguity about the extent to which the World Bank's articles of agreement actually disallow interference in the internal politics of a country, as the Bank generally justifies its exercise of the right to advise borrower countries on policy in terms of 'good economics' rather than political principles, to ensure the success of the projects it finances.

[2] Crook and Manor have argued that the emphasis on 'good government' was initially associated chiefly with the bilateral aid policies of particular western countries, which insisted on multi-party democracies replacing the corrupt and inefficient regimes which were seen as obstacles to the emergence of free-market capitalist economies in the third world. The shift to the term 'governance', adopted by multilateral agencies such as the World Bank, was intended to be a more apolitical, technical term descriptive of the institutional factors involved in managing development (1995, p. 310). The term 'good government', however, continues to be in active use. Thus, a recent statement of British policy on overseas development states that, among the four key aims of the Overseas Development Administration, is 'encouraging sound development policies, efficient markets and good government' (Foreign and Commonwealth Office, 1996).

Good governance, on this account, came to be equated with 'sound development management', and was defined as 'the manner in which power is exercised in the management of a country's economic and social resources for development' (World Bank, 1992, p. 3). Its four key dimensions were, further, specified as follows:
- public sector management (capacity and efficiency)
- accountability
- the legal framework for development
- information and transparency

In its discussion of the symptoms of 'poor governance', this document identified the following: the failure to make a separation between public and private, thereby facilitating the appropriation of public resources for private gain; the failure to establish a predictable framework of law and government conducive to development; excessively regulatory rules which impede the functioning of market misallocation of resources following from priorities not consistent with development; and non-transparent decision-making (ibid., p. 9).

While an evaluation of the governance capacities of individual countries form a part of the confidential Country Assistance Strategy documents, the World Bank has compiled data from 455 projects across three regions during the fiscal period 1991–93, to show the extent to which governance is a component in its lending operations (see Table 1).

Table 1

Category	Proportion of lending operations with governance content (per cent)
Legal framework	6
Participation	30
State-owned enterprises reform	33
Economic management	49
Capacity building	68
Democratization	68

Source: World Bank (1994) xv.

The specifically political meaning of governance came to be elaborated in the policy pronouncements of leaders of OECD countries, and there is enough evidence to show that the US, France and Japan have explicitly built political conditionality into their policies of bilateral assistance (Uvin, 1993, pp. 65–7). The documents of the

OECD Development Assistance Committee draw upon the World Bank's definition of governance and proceed to link it with the participatory development, human rights and democratization. This conception of governance enjoins legitimacy of government; accountability of political and official elements of government; competence of governments to make policy and deliver services; and respect for human rights and the rule of law. The last category includes individual and group rights and security, a framework for economic and social activity, and participation (World Bank, 1994 p. xiv). Within this framework, good governance refers to a liberal-democratic state, with a pluralist polity, in which representatives to the legislature are chosen by regular, free and fair elections. Further, such a system should protect and guarantee human rights, and exemplify the doctrine of the separation of powers, with legislators having the capacity to check executive excesses. These political requirements are, of course, assumed to subsist within economic structures that are essentially capitalist, and the 'democratic capitalist regime, presided over by a minimal state is also part of the wider governance of the New World Order' (Leftwich, 1993, p. 611).

It is no surprise that the governance agenda should express, and be perfectly consistent with, neo-liberal principles of politics and economics. At the heart of these lies a strong case for the 'rolling back of the state', and its withdrawal from redistributive commitments which are seen to be morally unacceptable. It is not a coincidence that the 1980s were also the years when the neo-liberal agenda in politics and economics—as expressed in the writings of political philosophers like Robert Nozick and economists like Milton Friedman, and Murray Rothbard—was the regnant influence on public policy in more than one advanced capitalist society of the Western world. Richard Falk has appropriately described, as a powerful type of contemporary fundamentalism, the tendency of 'market-driven interpretations ... to reduce democratization to empty forms of state/society constitutionalism in contexts of enthusiasm by prevailing elites for the unbridled logic of capitalism' (Falk, 1995, p. 112).

On the neo-liberal account, the withdrawal of the state should make way for the voluntary sector (viz, non-governmental organizations), on the one hand, and free market forces, on the other. The shift to NGOs has frequently been justified as an expression of the emphasis on 'popular participation' or 'participatory development', and has been much favoured by multilateral agencies. The parallel emphasis on the market has, of course, tended to satisfy the demands of global capital and transnational corporations, even as it has been consistent with the demand for the retreat of the state within western societies. This two-pronged strategy of the state making way, simultaneously, for NGOs and market forces, is noticeably coherent with the argument in the Approach Paper to the Eighth Five-Year Plan in India, which makes a strong, though apparently contradictory, plea for a greater role for the voluntary sector—through strategies of decentralization and people's participation— as well as for market forces (Government of India, 1990).

The widespread recognition of India as a democracy, with regular elections, high voter participation and a multi-party representative system, has meant that India has enjoyed relative immunity from political conditionality. The programme of economic reforms has also entailed changes in the regulatory regime, better known as the licence-permit raj. On the question of human rights, however, it has come to be regularly pilloried, especially in the annual reports of Amnesty International, and even the European Community has entered a human rights-based caveat in its commercial negotiations with India (Pedersen, 1993, p. 102).

II

In what follows, we shall attempt an evaluation of the ideology and politics of the project of good governance, in terms of its implications for the role of the state; the understanding of politics; democracy and development; and issues of participation and citizenship. These themes will be explored through the resources of political theory, which suggest that the agenda of 'good governance' is inescapably burdened by four internal contradictions, the first of which is methodological, while the remaining three are emphatically political in nature.

Universal Goals, Particular Constraints

The first, essentially methodological, contradiction is that between the universalizing and particularizing elements of the governance discourse. Good governance, as a condition of development, is recognized as a universally valid project, rather like modernization was in the development theory of the 1960s. This follows from the conviction that failures in development efforts have largely been the result of poor governance i.e., political factors that are uncontrollable and democratic processes that induce inefficiency.

In one rather more enlightened account, the idea of cultural relativism is invoked to argue that the modern state has undergone processes of both universalization and indigenization in non-European societies, processes that have been significantly influenced by cultural factors, and ethics of values, which account for the differing state forms to be found in Africa, India and Japan. It follows that good governance cannot be introduced from the outside, but must address itself to questions such as: What do people consider good? Does the law embody the idea of good? What are the most trusted and effective types of social organization? What is the basis of local ideas of accountability? How should those seeking good governance deal with the pervasive distrust of power and the state? (Martin, 1992, pp. 336–9).

This argument, even as it recognizes cultural diversity and specificity, does not radically interrogate the project of good governance, or its relationship with development (viewed as synonymous with and equivalent to economic performance). By reducing the question of political constraints on development to differences of culture, it needs to address itself merely to the task of working out the content of good governance in a culture-specific way. That culture (a shared ensemble of ethical values) is sought to be related to political culture, but culture itself is treated as a static given, rather than one that changes in its dynamic interaction with modern political processes. In attempting to make the project of governance more sensitive to particularities in the form of cultural differences, it fails to question whether cultural specificity also demands different ways of conceptualizing development.

There is a striking continuity between this discourse of the aid regime, and the construction of 'otherness' that feeds into commonsense western understandings of Third World and its 'problems'. In a penetrating analysis of some such cultural processes, John Gabriel has shown how, underlying the western media's coverage of the Bhopal disaster (or indeed of famine in several African countries) is a pervasive myth about the Third World, viz, that 'it is peopled by victims, rather than by active participants in struggle' (Gabriel, 1994, p. 134). Further, such victims are inevitably constructed in 'mass' terms, rather than as individuals. This is in sharp contrast to media coverage of disasters in the West, where viewers are encouraged to individualize suffering. It is hardly surprising then that redress should take the form of charity, rooted neither in rights-claims nor in a sensitivity to potential rights-claims, but rather in a neocolonial sense of philanthropy. If these popular western images of the Third World can be said to constitute a form of orientalism, the recent discourse of development aid—with the project of 'good governance' at its core—may be seen as constituting an attempt to institutionalize orientalism.

Putting the State Out Again

The second contradiction this paper seeks to identify relates to the conception of the state in the project of 'good governance'. Even as it favours market-oriented societies, the World Bank endorses the role of governments in providing two sorts of public goods: (i) the creation and enforcement of rules to make markets work efficiently, in the absence of which production and investment would be deterred and development consequently hindered; and (ii) compensating market failures through corrective interventions which includes, where necessary, a key role in providing education, health and essential infrastructure. The rationale offered is that a well-educated labour force and good infrastructure are crucial to the quality of private investment. In order to provide these public goods, the state needs to raise revenues and deliver services, and it is these that necessitate accountability, transparency, clarity about rules, and adequate information (World Bank, 1992, p. 6).

The argument for governance introduced an element of messiness in the otherwise neat fit between the advocacy of neo-liberal principles of politics and economics for the countries of the developed as well as developing world. The source of this messiness was the simultaneous insistence on the minimal state and on good governance. Of course, good governance was not treated as being important in its own right, but only instrumentally, as a means to the achievement of better economic performance. Thus, the reforms entailed by structural adjustment programmes included a retreat of the state, to be effectuated—ironically and paradoxically—by the state personnel. It also implied that while a scaling down in the size and scope of the state was required, an expansion in state capacity was necessary to give effect to the reforms process. This in turn required a measure of state autonomy from powerful interest groups in society, to preclude the possibility of its 'capture'.

The governance agenda's account of the state thus recommends a model found in classical liberal political theory,[3] with a strong

---

[3] It has been argued that the World Bank constructs governance at least partly from liberal theory, and in doing so reproduces the ambiguities and tensions inherent in that

Weberian overlay in the emphasis on rules, institutions, and an efficient bureaucracy, all characterized by impersonality, motivated by considerations of efficiency, and divorced from any normative concerns. Such an exercise of political model-building was faced, however, with the embarrassing challenge of the 'developmental states' of east Asia which had sustained efficient and productive economies in combination with essentially authoritarian governments, some of which have enjoyed the requisite autonomy from social interests.

In sum, the conception of state-society relations advanced with the package of governance is, in one authentic version, as follows:

positive governance in developing countries depends on the state's capacity to provide a meta goal or meta idea that serves as the organizing principle of a changed society and endows the state with the power to withstand capture from private interests. This conception of governance suggests that the capacity to enforce law and order and promote effective policy is contingent on state autonomy, which in turn is contingent on sources of state power distinct from those of the major economic players in society, which, finally, is contingent on the state's ability to project a culturally bound vision of a reorganized society (Frischtak, 1994, p. 25).

This conception is manifestly governed by the efficiency criterion. It demands a lean state, with expanded governance capacity, though without expanded government. Even as it recognizes society as the only latent source of power, and recognizes also the embeddedness of the state in society, it suggests that governance is premised on the state's capacity to deploy power from society, and therefore ultimately on its autonomy. Only transcending societal constraints can, on this account, create state capacity and render governance possible.

There are, thus, two contradictions here, one internal and the other external. The internal contradiction is the paradox between a reduced state, in terms of size as well as scope of intervention, and greater state capacity. The external contradiction expresses itself in the consequences of this formula for the project of democracy. At one level, the good governance package explicitly includes democratization, respect for human rights, a plural polity, a multiparty system, and accountability and transparency. But how does autonomy relate to the minimal requirements of accountability and transparency?

---

theory, e.g., the problematic distinction between the right and the good which is echoed in the supposed neutrality of the reforms process, or the assumption of the universal liberal self that is necessary for the kind of civil society that is sought to be fostered [Williams and Young 1994: 92ff].

Indeed, the east Asian example provides a good illustration of this. Abstracting core elements from the developmental states of east Asia— a high degree of state autonomy, an effective ruling bureaucracy, control of labour, non-interference by popular groups in the setting of development priorities, and the outlawing of political pluralism—it has been argued that these states exemplify a non-democratic bias. On this basis, then, it may even be possible to conclude that ' "soft authoritarianism" is the optimum political form for the developmental state' (Sorensen, 1993, pp. 13–14)]. For those to whom such a political solution is anathema, good governance carries with it the suspicion of providing the shell of democracy, without its substance.

A final aspect of the conception of state contained in the project of good governance is the role envisaged for non-state players, chiefly non-governmental organizations. Though NGOs are more central to World Bank policies on poverty and the environment, than to its governance agenda, it is appropriate to point out that, between 1988 and 1991, NGOs were involved in 27.6 per cent of all new approved projects. This contrasts sharply with the corresponding figure of five to six per cent for the earlier period between 1973 and 1988 (Gibbon, 1993, pp. 57–8). Using and idealizing NGOs as having state-substitutive capacities, has a certain ideological and practical value for multilateral agencies that cannot be underestimated.[4]

Politics Outlawed

The flaws in the account of the state offered by the governance agenda are anchored in, and premised on, its definition of politics, and our third contradiction therefore is that between governance and politics, which are implicitly posited as mutually exclusive. Even as cultural specificities are recognized as playing a role in giving effect to the project of governance, perhaps even allowing for indigenous definitions of governance (Martin, 1992, p. 326), it appears to preclude the possibility that the demand for good governance be seen to emerge from the political process, its form and definition politically articulated by the citizens of a particular society.

While some accounts of political conditionality do enumerate the practical constraints on the effectiveness of such conditionality, there is relatively little normative and political interrogation of the governance agenda. Arguments against external interferences have taken a

[4] On the limited usefulness of developmental NGOs financed by donor agencies, and on the relationship between NGOs, on the one hand, and the state and local society on the other, see Hadenius and Uggla (1995).

variety of forms. Recipient nations have mostly defended their case by invoking arguments of national sovereignty, economic and political. In India, this argument of the moral unjustifiability of political conditionality has been appropriated equally by political parties of the right and left. Some other developing countries have either followed the strategy of finding alternative donors, or have evaded conditionality by enacting some policies that appear to fulfil it even as they take other measures to subvert it. On the donors' side, the principle of interdependence of members of the community of nations, with mutual and legally binding obligations, is sometimes invoked to argue that constraints on sovereignty, as embodied in international conventions, do not constitute infringements of sovereignty, and that governance may be seen to belong to this category of constraints (Landell-Mills and Serageldin, 1992, p. 308). Hence, it is said, the development community can and should persuade and assist countries in improving governance without intruding on their sovereignty.[5] An additional argument, ostensibly couched in moral terms, is that if the citizens of a country are poor but badly or undemocratically governed, holding back assistance on account of the poor governance record of their rulers, unjustly punishes them.

It is being argued here that the project of good governance is simultaneously a project for the elimination of politics, for its banishment from the nation–state. It is guilty not only of seeking to universalize a particular set of choices of regime form, but also of ruling out the generation of a governance agenda that is a product of democratic politics, rather than a condition of it. The question of whether governance can be effectively imposed from the outside has been asked (Leftwich, 1993; Uvin, 1993). But the question of whether demands for governance—good or efficient or equitable—should emanate from the citizens of a polity, and exclusively from them, is not generally raised. This paper is concerned to argue that governance criteria are both culturally and politically specific; that the definition of good governance in a particular society must be the product of consensus—or perhaps even the outcome of effectuating a project of

[5] One attempt to address this question has taken the rather peculiar form of suggesting a contractarian basis for governance as a conditionality, such that donors and recipients are equally seen to be parties to a contract intended to enhance the benefits of social co-operation between their citizens. On this account, 'each party may reasonably ask the other to consider conditions it believes to be conducive to this end, and some of these conditions may be political' (Hawthorn and Seabright, 1995, p. 81). This argument does not, however, take cognizance of the obvious inequalities of status and power between the so-called contracting parties.

good governance and sustaining it requires a certain kind of political negotiation, which can only be the product of democratic politics. In the absence of such a view, an emphasis on governance will provide nothing more than 'an analysis of a dysfunctioning elite system' (Kothari, 1995, p. 627). As such, it will ignore the mismatch between the institutions of governance and genuine social demands.

Democracy, Development and Good Governance

A restrictive definition of democracy—in terms of formal institutions and procedures alone—necessarily follows from the outlawing of politics. Governance without politics forces us to question the centrality accorded to audit and accountability. Does, that is, good governance entail accountability to the citizens of a democratic policy, or are the lending institutions its chief auditors? Conversely, if the formal conditions of democracy are fulfilled—as say, in India—does good governance logically follow?

It is outside the scope of this paper to consider the question of the extent to which good governance is—factually or empirically—*the* or even *a* critical variable impacting economic performance in developing countries. There are, however, two important challenges to the assumptions that link this triad of concepts: democracy, development and good governance. The first challenge relates to the relationship between democracy and development, while the second pertains to the value—instrumental or intrinsic—of governance as a goal.

It is apparently no longer assumed, as it was perhaps in the 1960s, that democracy is an inevitable consequence of processes of modernization and development. In fact, as already noted, the east Asian experience has presented an embarrassing challenge to the proponents of good governance, showing that there is no necessary or inevitable relationship between democracy and development. If the weak patrimonial and undemocratic states of Africa were developmentally ineffective, the equally undemocratic, 'soft authoritarian' states of east Asia were highly effective in bringing about economic development (the notion of development that lay at the heart of these debates being, of course, an uncomplicatedly derivative one).

The obvious counter-example to this is that of states like India which enjoy the conditions of formal democracy—a pluralist polity with an elected legislature, regular elections, a free press, and so on—but without realizing a spectacular record of economic growth. Indeed, the uniquely democratic mechanisms of accommodation and compromise have been effectively deployed by political elites to prevent demands for radical economic change from acquiring greater political charge. Sarwar Lateef, one of the chief authors of the World Bank publication *Government and Development*, has elsewhere commented on Indian democracy as follows:

The experience of India illustrates the difficulties facing even flourishing democracies. It also illustrates that no clear relationship exists between the form of government and the attributes or dimensions of good government: accountability, predictability and the rule of law. Accountability exists in the formal sense in India. We have the option to 'throw the rascals out', and frequently do. But accountability is eroded by the lack of true choice for voters; the high cost of elections, which makes elected representatives dependent on the corporate sector and is at the heart of much of the corruption in government; the cynicism of the elite; the nexus between criminals and politicians; a vast bureaucracy pursuing its own agenda; and over centralized political structures that put a distance between the rulers and the ruled (Lateef, 1992, p. 297).

To assume, further, that economic liberalization is the key to democratization is also problematic. As Atul Kohli has argued, this may result in the creation of 'two-track polities', which restrict democratic practices to the political (i.e., electoral) arena, even as they insulate governmental decision-making from popular pressures. This cannot but render economic policy devoid of social content, an exercise in technical efficiency, conducted behind closed doors (Kohli, 1993, p. 683). The unimpeded logic of democracy, on the other hand, and surely its very rationale, should be to undermine class and other forms of social inequality, and nudge or even push policy in a redistributive direction.

Secondly, if the value of good governance is seen to lie exclusively in its instrumental purpose—of facilitating a better economic performance—then the east Asian states meet the requirement more than adequately, and the task of governance is reduced to its technical component (as per the World Bank's definition of it). If, on the other hand, good governance is inherently valuable, it is a political value which must be negotiated by the political community in question, and speak to the relations between citizen and state. To accomplish this independently of democratic political processes is impossible. The maintenance and consolidation of democracy, moreover, requires not external assistance or pressure, but indigenous initiatives for democracy. Such a conception of democracy will, of course, be less than meaningful unless it is part of an egalitarian strategy, in both economic and political terms.

An allied concept which frequently makes its appearance in World Bank discourse is that of participation. Participation, in this literature, is to be treated both as a means and as an end. Its inherent desirability is seen to lie in the fact that it enlarges human talents and potential which is the goal of development (Uphoff, 1992, p. 135). But its more practical advantage, for project effectiveness and sustainability, is the fact that it gives people a stake in the project, makes them willing to support it, and thereby reduces waste in resources. There are, however, certain costs entailed by participation, viz, it is time-consuming, difficult, allows for free riders to take more than their share, and so forth (Dichter, 1992, p. 89).

In this perspective, then, participation in development is a component of project design, and as such confined to the details of project implementation. By implication, it is outlawed from democratic discussion about the model of development, the determination of development priorities (local or national), the acceptability or otherwise of particular development initiatives, and so on. It is also, as a component of externally-assisted development projects, definitionally insulated from political processes and political concerns. In this sense, it is entirely coherent with the agenda of 'good governance' which, as we have seen, is also concerned to marginalize politics.

Despite its apparent affinities with the western liberal-democratic model of government, therefore, the governance agenda appears to espouse definitions of politics, of democracy and of participation that are quite distinct from those that have historically evolved in western societies. Thus, the citizen is transformed into a subject: a passive recipient of rights, enjoyer of governance, beneficiary of development. At best, s/he is a citizen-in-the-making of a well-governed society, equally in the process of becoming.

III

The arguments thus far suggest not only that governance is objectionable as a component of aid conditionality, but also that its content is contradictory, and deserves interrogation from both the methodological and the political standpoints. Implicit in this paper is the idea that an alternative conception of governance is possible, but that such a conception can only be the product of political contestation and negotiation within a society. A well-ordered society, in which (a) the political framework is determined and sustained by popular consent, with adequate avenues for the free expression of rational disagreement and dissent on particular issues; (b) economic organization provides for the creation and equitable distribution of wealth; (c) the individual and group rights of citizens—regardless of religion, region, caste, and gender differences are respected, with these differences not forming the basis of discrimination in either society or public policy. The role of the state (in the sphere of welfare for instance) and the nature and extent of citizens' participation must also be coherently integrated into such a conception.

In a third world context, the idea of governance as a more or less technical facilitator of development, delinked from conceptions of democracy and welfare, is a highly impoverished notion. The western recognition that the simple equation between governance and democracy, and of both these with economic prosperity, is belied in the experience of many countries of the third world, has led to the application of a different set of standards for the latter, whereby democracy and development are seen as possibly incompatible, and democracy is sought to be substituted by governance. This notion of governance partakes of some of the elements of classical liberal-democracy, incorporated into a minimalist institutional design. In fact, development appears to require more governance, and less democracy. This assumption suggests not only a restrictive view of democracy, but also an uncritical acceptance of the priority of developmental goals, defined in a universalistic manner. In this perspective, then, development is not open to political contestation. Both development and democracy (in the minimalist sense, encapsulated in the idea of good governance) are implicitly defined in ways that ensure conformity with an essentially Western ethos.

Even those scholars who are critical of the World Bank's project of good governance on the grounds that it purges development of its political content, tend to fall into a similar trap. Possibly the most significant critique of this kind has been developed by Adrian Leftwich, over several important essays (1993, 1995a, 1995b). Leftwich argues that what matters for development is not the system of government, but the type of state, irrespective of whether it is democratic or not (1995a: 5). It is in this sense that development is political, rather than administrative or managerial, as the World Bank and IMF assume it to be. This is why even the success or failure of structural adjustment programmes has varied across different countries.

... good governance and democracy are not mere components which can be inserted into any society at any point in its development like a sprocket or valve. On the contrary, both good governance and democracy depend crucially on the character and capacity of a state which, alone, can institute and insist on it. And the capacity of a state to deliver good governance and protect democracy is in turn a function of its politics and its developmental determination ... The only social process that can both institute and sustain both good governance and democracy is the process we know as politics which I defined earlier as consisting of all the processes of conflict, cooperation and negotiation involved in the use, production and distribution of resources (Leftwich, 1995a, p. 17).

The capacity of the state is here highly parasitical on a particular definition of politics, which in turn has a purely descriptive character, completely isolated from any normative conception of its substance. It is precisely this profound absence of normativity that sustains the emphasis on the facticity of politics, allowing for it to be democratic or non-democratic, as the case may be. Politics is a given, a factor that will determine the character of the state, and together with it the capacity of the state to effect development as well as provide governance.

Leftwich clearly privileges development above any other goal, such as democracy or welfare. He isolates developmental states from the non-developmental states of the third world, explicates their features, then examines more closely such of these as are democratic, in howsoever limited a fashion. His most preferred option is for democratic developmentalist states (even with limited democracy, such as Botswana and Malaysia); his second preference is for non-democratic developmental states, such as Korea, Taiwan, China and Indonesia; and his third and final preference is for democratic but non-developmental states, such as Jamaica and Costa Rica (Leftwich, 1995b, p. 282). The decisive, and normatively preferred, variable for which explanation is being sought is thus development, rather than democracy. In the search for factors which optimize developmental outcomes and possibilities, democracy becomes a purely instrumental criterion. What is important is the factors that make development happen, and the presence of even some elements of formal democracy are sufficient to approve the model. Thus, Leftwich argues, democratic developmental states may be thought of as 'authoritarian democracies', because they fall short in some respects of the full requirements of liberal democracy (ibid., p. 290). Such states are led by determined developmental elites, and these elites and the state institutions they command enjoy a relative autonomy from special interests. Consequently, these states have powerful and competent bureaucracies who can shape development policy. Civil society is often weak or controlled by the state and human rights records may therefore be very poor (ibid., pp. 285ff).

Even as Leftwich argues passionately for putting politics into development, for recognizing the importance of politics as a factor determining development, he shies away from any explicit reference to the need to *democratize* development. He seems to take as given the politics of a society, as it impacts the nature of the state which in turn influences the success of the developmental project. He fails to consider the possibility that there are multiple ways of conceiving development, not merely through measurable indicators like the GDP. It is precisely because the costs of development are different in different societies, that it becomes both necessary and desirable that the nature and substance of development be subject to political contestation, and determined by it. Any delinking of politics and democracy is artificial. Thus, while Leftwich's critique of Fukuyama for suggesting that liberal-democracy is the ideological terminus of history is entirely apposite, the same searchlight needs to be turned on Leftwich's notion of development, which conforms to the Western industrial model, and suggests an economic (but not for that reason any the less ideological) terminus of human history.

Privileging development—whether as explanation or as policy prescription—may, as we have seen, result in having to accept non-democratic outcomes. On the other hand, the cost of exclusively privileging democracy may arguably be development (as conventionally defined). If democracy cannot be made to order, nor can development. The literature on governance had at least realized this much. They must be seen as intimately related, functioning under the same or at least similar constraints and equally subject to political negotiation. Thus, for instance, social inequality in India both retards balanced development and distorts the logic of democracy. It is precisely this distorting logic of democracy in an unequal society that necessitates state welfare for the protection of the vulnerable, for the concerns of distributive justice cannot be fulfilled by governance alone. The answer therefore is not to look towards the state, but at different ways of approaching and defining both democracy and development: a view of democracy, for instance, that goes beyond the procedural to seek the substantive democratization of not only the state, but also society and social relations; and a view of development that possibly departs from the conventional ways of measuring this goal by focusing not on GDP and GNP, but on the enlargement of human capabilities and the enhancement of the quality of life for all citizens. The multiple meanings these concepts have acquired in particular societies have emerged out of rich histories of political practice and discourse. Concerns of governance must necessarily be deeply imbricated in these meanings and definitions.

REFERENCES

Crook, Richard and James Manor (1995). 'Democratic Decentralization and Institutional Performance: Four Asian and African Experiences Compared', *Journal of Commonwealth and Comparative Politics*, vol. 33, no. 3, November.

Currie, Bob (1996). 'Governance, Democracy and Economic Adjustment in India: Conceptual and Empirical Problems' in *Third World Quarterly* (forthcoming).

Dichter Thomas (1992). 'Demystifying Popular Participation: Institutional Mechanisms for Popular Participation' in Bhuvan Bhatnagar and Aubrey C. Williams (eds), *Participatory Development and the World Bank*, World Bank Discussion Paper 183, World Bank, Washington, D.C..

Falk, Richard (1995). *On Humane Governance: Towards a New Global Politics*, (Report to the World Order Models Project), Polity Press, Oxford.

Foreign and Commonwealth Office, UK (1996). 'British Policy on Overseas Development: Change and Continuity', Background Brief, London.

Frischtak, Leila L. (1994). *Governance Capacity and Economic Reform in Developing Countries*, World Bank Technical Paper 254, World Bank, Washington, D.C..

Gabriel, John (1994). *Racism, Culture, Markets*, Routledge, London.

Gibbon, Peter (1993). 'The World Bank and the New Politics of Aid', *The European Journal of Development Research*, vol. 5, no. 1.

Government of India (1990). *Towards Social Transformation: Approach to the Eighth Five-Year Plan 1990–95*.

Hadenius, Axel and Fredrik Uggla (1995). *Making Civil Society Work*. Uppsala Studies in Democracy No 9, Uppsala University.

Hawthorn, Geoffrey and Paul Seabright (1995). 'Governance, Democracy and Development: A Contractualist View' in Leftwich (ed), *Democracy and Development*, Polity Press, Cambridge.

Kohli, Atul (1993). 'Democracy Amid Economic Orthodoxy: Trends in Developing Countries', *Third World Quarterly*, vol. 14, no. 4.

Kothari, Rajni (1995). 'Globalization and Revival of Tradition', *Economic and Political Weekly*, March 25.

Landell-Mills, Pierre and Ismail Serageldin (1992). 'Governance and the External Factor', *Proceedings of the World Bank Annual Conference on Development Economics 1991*, Washington, D.C..

Lateef, Sarwar K. (1992). 'Comment on Governance and Development' by

Boeninger, *Proceedings of the World Bank Annual Conference on Development Economics* 1991, World Bank, Washington, D.C..

Leftwich, Adrian (1993). 'Governance, Democracy and Development in the Third World', *Third World Quarterly*, vol. 14, no. 3.

—— (1995a). 'On the Primacy of Politics in Development' in Leftwich (ed), *Democracy and Development*, Polity Press, Cambridge.

—— (1995b). 'Two Cheers for Democracy'? Democracy and the Developmental State' in Leftwich (ed), *Democracy and Development*, Polity Press, Cambridge.

Martin, Denis-Constant (1992). 'The Cultural Dimensions of Governance', *Proceedings of the World Bank Annual Conference on Development Economics 1991*, World Bank, Washington, D.C..

Pedersen, Jorgen Dige (1993). 'The Complexities of Conditionality: The Case of India', *The European Journal of Development Research*, vol. 5, no. 1.

Sorensen, Georg (1993). 'Democracy, Authoritarianism and State Strength', *The European Journal of Development Research*, vol. 5, no. 1.

Uphoff, Norman (1992). 'Monitoring and Evaluating Popular Participation in World-Bank Assisted Projects' in Bhuvan Bhatnagar and Aubrey C. Williams (eds), *Participatory Development and the World Bank*, World Bank Discussion paper 183, Washington, D.C..

Uvin, Peter (1993). 'Do as I Say, Not as I Do': The Limits of Political Conditionality', *The European Journal of Development Research*, vol. 5, no. 1.

Williams, David and Tom Young (1994). 'Governance, the World Bank and Liberal theory', *Political Studies*, vol. XLII.

World Bank (1992). *Governance and Development*, Washington, D.C..

—— (1994). *Governance: The World Bank's Experience*, Washington, D.C..

CHAPTER EIGHT

Governance as Theory
Five Propositions*

Gerry Stoker

Anglo-American political theory uses the term 'government' to refer to the formal institutions of the state and their monopoly of legitimate coercive power. Government is characterized by its ability to make decisions and its capacity to enforce them. In particular, government is understood to refer to the formal and institutional processes which operate at the level of the nation state to maintain public order and facilitate collective action.

Theoretical work on governance reflects the interest of the social science community in a shifting pattern in styles of governing. The traditional use of 'governance' and its dictionary entry define it as a synonym for government. Yet in the growing work on governance there is a redirection in its use and import. Rather governance signifies 'a change in the meaning of government referring to a new process of governing; or a changed condition of ordered rule: or the new method by which society is governed' (Rhodes, 1996, pp. 652–3).

The process of governance lead to outcomes that parallel those of the traditional institutions of government. As Rosenau (1992, p. 3) comments:

To presume the presence of governance without government is to conceive of functions that have to be performed in any viable human system ... Among the many necessary functions, for example, are the needs wherein any system has to cope with external challenges to prevent conflicts among its members ... to procure resources ... and to frame goals and policies designed to achieve them.

* *International Social Science Journal* (on Governance) March 1998, 155.

Governance is ultimately concerned with creating the conditions for ordered rule and collective action. The outputs of governance are not therefore different from those of government. It is rather a matter of a difference in processes.

Reviews of the literature generally conclude that the term—governance—is used in a variety of ways and has a variety of meanings (Rhodes, 1996; Stoker, 1997). There is, however, a baseline agreement that governance refers to the development of governing styles in which boundaries between and within public and private sectors have become blurred. The essence of governance is its focus on governing mechanisms which do not rest on recourse to the authority and sanctions of government. 'The governance concept points to the creation of a structure or an order which cannot be externally imposed but is the result of the interaction of a multiplicity of governing and each other influencing actors' (Kooiman and Van Vliet, 1993, p. 64).

What is interesting is how governance is used in a range of practitioner and academic settings in an attempt to capture a shift in thinking and ways of working. In Britain and the United States the word governance has undoubtedly entered the vocabulary of elected and unelected officials. Governance also has a resonance in the policy debates of other western democracies. In developing countries, too, governance has entered the policy arena. For the World Bank it is at times reduced to a commitment to efficient and accountable government. Others use it more broadly, and in tune with the tenor of this article, to recognize the interdependence of public, private and voluntary sectors in developing countries.

Of course governance is sometimes used for rhetorical rather than substantive reasons. At times in Osborne and Gaebler (1992) governance appears to be used in place of government as if 'government' was a difficult word to sell in a privatized, market-oriented society. Governance is about a 'reinvented' form of government which is better managed. The Osborne and Gaebler work is about how a government might make sensible and effective use of a wider range of tools beyond the direct provision of services. Governance for them is about the potential for contracting, franchising and new forms of regulation. In short, it is about what others refer to as the new public management (Hood, 1991). However governance as used in this paper is about more than a new set of managerial tools. It is also about more than achieving greater efficiency in the production of public services.

Governance is on occasions used to provide the acceptable face of spending cuts. It is a code for less government. The rise of governance undoubtedly reflects to a degree a search for reductions in the resource commitment and spending of government. It involves a recognition of the limits of government. Yet its rise reflects a range of broader forces. Governance is not the narrow product of fiscal crisis.

The academic literature on governance is eclectic and relatively disjointed (Jessop, 1995). Its theoretical roots are various: institutional economics, international relations, organizational studies, development studies, political science, public administration and Foucauldian-inspired theorists. Its precursors would include work on corporatism, policy communities and a range of economic analysis concerned with the evolution of economic systems. Insights can be drawn from this literature but its very diversity requires the development of a governance perspective.

The contribution of the governance perspective to theory is not at the level of causal analysis. Nor does it offer a new normative theory. Its value is as an organizing framework. The value of the governance perspective rests in its capacity to provide a framework for understanding changing processes of governing. As Judge et al. (1995, p. 3) comment, such conceptual frameworks 'provide a language and frame of reference through which reality can be examined and lead theorists to ask questions that might not otherwise occur. The result, if successful, is new and fresh insights that other frameworks or perspectives might not have yielded. Conceptual frameworks can constitute an attempt to establish a paradigm shift'. The value of such frameworks can be found in their identification of what is worthy of study.

The governance perspective works if it helps us identify important questions, although it does claim to identify a number of useful answers as well. It provides a reference point which challenges many of the assumptions of traditional public administration.

The discussion of governance in this paper is structured around five propositions. The aim is to present a number of aspects of governance for consideration rather than make a series of statements that can be shown to be either true or false. The five propositions are:

1. Governance refers to a set of institutions and actors that are drawn from but also beyond government.
2. Governance identifies the blurring of boundaries and responsibilities for tackling social and economic issues.

3. Governance identifies the power dependence involved in the relationships between institutions involved in collective action.
4. Governance is about autonomous self-governing networks of actors.
5. Governance recognizes the capacity to get things done which does not rest on the power of government to command or use its authority. It sees government as able to use new tools and techniques to steer and guide.

These propositions are considered to be complementary rather than contradictory or in competition. Each proposition has associated with it a certain dilemma or critical issue:

*   There is a divorce between the complex reality of decision-making associated with governance and the normative codes used to explain and justify government.
*   The blurring of responsibilities can lead to blame avoidance or scapegoating.
*   Power dependence exacerbates the problem of unintended consequences for government.
*   The emergence of self-governing networks raises difficulties over accountability.
*   Even where governments operate in a flexible way to steer collective action governance failure may occur.

Governance refers to a complex set of institutions and actors that are drawn from but also beyond government

The first message of governance is to challenge constitutional/formal understandings of systems of government. In the British case it provides a challenge to the 'Westminster model' (Gamble, 1990). From the perspective of this model the British political system was characterized by parliamentary sovereignty, strong cabinet government and accountability through elections. The dominant image was of a unitary state directed and legitimated by the doctrine of ministerial responsibility. Governance suggests that institutional/constitutional perspectives, such as the Westminster model are limited and misleading. The structure of government is fragmented with a maze of institutions and organizations. The Westminster model in particular fails to capture the complex reality of the British system. It implies that in a unitary of the state there is only one centre of power. In practice there are many centres and diverse links between many agencies of government at local, regional, national and supranational levels. There is a complex architecture to systems of government which governance seeks to emphasize and focus attention on.

Complexity is in part ensured by the scale of the modern government which in Britain has created a highly functionally differentiated system. The phenomenon of complexity has been compounded by the trend towards establishing principal-agent relations throughout much of the machinery of government. In Britain the establishment of agencies, direct service organizations, opted-out hospitals and schools are visible expressions of the widespread use of a purchaser-provider paradigm. In addition, there has been a 'hollowing-out' of the national state as it has lost powers to the inter-governmental and local/regional level.

The governance perspective also draws attention to the increased involvement of the private and voluntary sectors in service delivery and strategic decision-making. Responsibilities that were previously the near exclusive responsibility of government have been shared. Contracting-out and public-private partnerships are now part of the reality of public services and decision-making in many countries.

The governance perspective in part builds on the challenge to the legal/constitutional tradition that up to the 1950s dominated the study of politics. It argues for a shift of focus away from formalities and a concern with what should be, to a focus on behaviour and what is. In the modern world of government 'what is' is complex, messy, resistant to central direction and in many respects difficult for key policy-makers let alone members of the public to understand. Broadly the governance perspective challenges conventional assumptions which focus on government as if it were a 'stand alone' institution divorced from wider societal forces.

It is the confusion and uncertainty created by a system that is now so far divorced from our formal constitutional understanding that reveals the first dilemma of governance. Research conducted for the ESRC Local Governance Programme shows that the emerging system in which responsibilities are shared between local authorities and a range of other public and private providers lacks strong normative underpinning in public opinion (Miller and Dickson, 1996). The public demonstrated a strong preference for organization and control of local services to be in the hands of an elected council as against appointed bodies or private sector providers. The model which was seen as the most appropriate and which attracted in the abstract the highest levels of support was the traditional model of the local authority as the dominant agent for providing community services. Models of provision run by appointed bodies, private-sector providers or even those run directly by service users were not seen as legitimate. Overall appointed bodies and private-sector providers received a modest negative rating from the public.

The divorce between the normative codes used to explain and justify government and the reality of the decision-making in the system creates tensions. As Peters (1993, p. 55) comments: 'We must be concerned with the extent to which complex structures linking the public and private sectors ... actually mask responsibility and add to the problems of citizens in understanding and influencing the actions of their governments.

The issue is more than there being a 'cultural lag' while public attitudes catch up with the new reality of public services. The public and more specifically, the media lack a legitimation framework in which to place the emerging system of governance. In the British case, tensions have surfaced beyond local governance in concern about unaccountable quangos, the difficulty of separating policy and operational matters, the influence of faceless bureaucrats and the nature of ministerial accountability.

The exercise of power needs to be legitimate. This argument is more than a normative assertion. It rests also on the pragmatic grounds that to be effective in the long run power-holders must be seen to be legitimate. A legitimation deficit undermines public support and commitment to programmes of change and ultimately undermines the ability of power-holders to mobilize resources and promote co-operation and partnership.

Beetham (1991, p. 19) suggests that there are three dimensions to the legitimacy of a political system. Beetham's criteria come not from abstract philosophical reflection but from empirical observation of the workings of political systems.

For power to be fully legitimate ... three conditions are required: its conformity to established rules: the justifiability of the rules by reference to shared beliefs: and the express consent of the subordinate, or the most significant among them, to the particular relations of power.

Legitimacy according to this approach is not an all-or-nothing affair. Within any political system there will be some ambiguity about rules and some who do not accept their validity and who will not give their consent to the power-holders. The point is that it is possible to make the rules of power more or less legitimate. In short a system can be designed and operated in a way that either decreases or

increase its legitimacy. Governance lacks the simplifying legitimizing 'myths' of traditional perspectives, such as the British Westminster
model. The issue to be considered is whether or how governance can
obtain enhanced legitimacy.

Governance recognizes the blurring of boundaries and
responsibilities for tackling social and economic issues

The governance perspective not only recognizes increased complexity in our systems of government, it also draws to our attention a shift
in responsibility, a stepping back of the state and a concern to push
responsibilities onto the private and voluntary sectors and, more
broadly the citizen.

At its most abstract, governance is about a change in the long-
standing balance between the state and civil society. A welfare system
that stimulates dependence is no longer acceptable to either Right or
Left of the political spectrum. A citizenship that emphasizes rights
and responsibilities is also part of an emerging consensus. A right to
welfare support needs to be complemented by a duty on those who
are offered help to take it and respond. A concern with 'active' citizenship links governance to wider debates about communitarianism and
'family' values. Governance is connected to the concern about social
capital and the social underpinnings necessary to effective economic
and political performance (Putnam, 1993).

The shift in responsibility finds institutional expression in a blurring of boundaries between the public and private, which in turn
finds substance in the rise of a range of voluntary or third-sector
agencies variously labelled voluntary groups, non-profits, non-
governmental organizations, community enterprises, co-ops, mutuals
and community-based organizations. These organizations range over
a wide variety of social and economic issues and operate in the
context of what has been termed a 'social economy' that has emerged
between the market economy and the public sector.

The governance perspective demands that these voluntary sector
third-force organizations be recognized for the scale and scope of
their contribution to tackling collective concerns without reliance on
the formal resources of government. One estimate suggests that in
Britain alone the social economy contributes about £12.3 billion to the
Gross National Product, employs about 400,000 full-time equivalent
workers and involves about four million in some form of voluntary
activity. It is claimed that needs are met and problems are managed
through such organizations without recourse to an over-arching

authority or a formal system of control. Such a claim takes us beyond a simple recognition of the plurality of groups that seek to influence government to a recognition of a range of groups that have taken over some of the traditional tasks of government.

Responsibilities have also been taken up by the private sector as well as not-for-profit organizations. There are here the well-known examples of former public enterprises sold off by governments: airlines, utilities, and so on. There have also been extensive changes in the urban services sector with entire areas becoming dominated by private enterprise and a few company names—Générale des eaux, Rentokil—gaining wide recognition and significance (Lorrain and Stoker, 1997). In other areas such as government information systems there has been a rise in government outsourcing with again certain key private suppliers becoming dominant actors in the market.

The dilemma suggested by the blurring of responsibilities is that it creates an ambiguity and uncertainty in the minds of policy-makers and public about who is responsible and can lead to government actors passing off responsibility to privatized providers when things go wrong. Worse still is the enhanced possibility of scapegoating raised by more complex governance systems. Those in a position to interpret and lead public debate can, often with considerable effectiveness, blame others for failures and difficulties. Blame avoidance and scapegoating are not new political phenomena but governance structures do extend the capacity for such activity.

Governance identifies the power dependence involved in the relationships between institutions involved in collective action

Power dependence implies that:

(a) Organizations committed to collective action are dependent on other organizations;
(b) In order to achieve goals organizations have to exchange resources and negotiate common purposes;
(b) The outcome of exchange is determined not only by the resources of the participants but also by the rules of the game and the context of the exchange.

In a governance relationship no one organization can easily command, although one organization may dominate a particular process of exchange. National-level government or another institution may seek to impose control, but there is a persistent tension between the wish for authoritative action and dependence on the compliance and action of others (Rhodes, 1996). Governing from the governance perspective is always an interactive process because no single actor, public or private, has the knowledge and resource capacity to tackle problems unilaterally (Kooiman, 1993).

In the case of the United Kingdom over the last two decades it is quite common in the context of relations between central and local government for the charge of centralization to go hand-in-hand with a concern about lack of co-ordiantion. Attempts to dominate various policy fields by central government have brought a whole host of unintended consequences.

The other side of the coin of power-dependence is that to argue for local autonomy in the context of an emerging system of governance is increasingly meaningless. To tackle the social and economic issues confronting their communities local councils inevitably need to draw on the resources of other actors in the private and voluntary sectors. They are also likely to require partnerships with higher levels of government. Local councils could demand the resources to become a significant player, an attractive partner, but they cannot demand autonomy.

Governance as an interactive process involves various forms of partnership. It is possible to distinguish between: principle-agent relations, inter-organizational negotiation and systemic co-ordination. The principal-agent form rests on one party (the principal) hiring or contracting another (the agent) to undertake a particular task (Broadbent et al., 1996). The inter-organizational form involves organizations in negotiating joint projects in which by blending their capacities they are better able to meet their own organization's objectives (Jessop, 1996). The systemic co-ordination form of partnership goes a step further by establishing a level of mutual understanding and embeddedness that organizations develop a shared vision and joint-working capacity that leads to the establishment of a self-governing network.

The systemic co-ordinated form of partnership differs from the others in that it involves 'games *about* rules' rather than 'games *under* rules'. Systemic co-ordination results in designed, intentionally chosen and adopted governance orders or structures. 'Games under rules' are, in contrast, characterized by unintended and unanticipated consequences as the game unfolds.

Recognizing the power dependence in collective action means accepting intentions do not always match outcomes. In principal-agent relations the principal does not have complete control over the agent and has only partial information about the agent's behaviour. In negotiated relationships seeking the best 'deal' for your organization provides the defining characteristic of the process which in turn can lead to ambiguous outcomes which can be interpreted appropriately by the various partners. Game-playing, subversion, creaming and opportunism in a range of forms are observed in both principal-agent and negotiated relationships.

Opportunistic behaviour may add to the complexity and uncertainty of outcomes. However, as Hirschman (1991) argues, not all unintended effects are necessarily perverse. Unintended is not necessarily undesirable. Governance implies a greater willingness to cope with uncertainty and open-endedness on the part of policy-framers.

Governance is about autonomous self-governing networks of actors

Under governance the ultimate partnership activity is the formation of self-governing networks. Such networks are related to the policy communities and other forms of function or issue based groupings much discussed in the policy studies literature (Atkinson and Coleman, 1992; Marsh and Rhodes, 1992). Governance networks, however, involve not just influencing government policy but taking over the business of government.

In urban politics the focus has been on the formation of regimes usually composed of elite actors drawn from public and private sectors (Stoker, 1995). Thus, following Stone (1989, p. 4), a regime can be defined as 'an informal yet relatively stable group with access to institutional resources that enable it to have a sustained role in making governing decisions'. Participants are likely to have an institutional base, that is, they are likely to have a domain of command power. The regime, however, is formed as an informal basis for co-ordination and without an all encompassing structure of command.

Actors and institutions gain a capacity to act by blending their resources, skills and purposes into a long-term coalition: a regime. If they succeed they pre-empt the leadership role in their community and establish for themselves a near decision-making monopoly over the cutting-edge choices facing their locality. The establishment of a viable regime is the ultimate act of power in the context of an emerging system of governance.

Regime-building is easier in relation to some policy goals than others. Feasibility favours linking with resource-rich actors. It also favours some goals over others whose achievement may be more intractable and problematic. The difficulties and challenges of collective action become more intense as regimes propose more radical and socially inclusive change.

The international relations literature also uses the term 'regime' to capture the formation of self-governing networks which enable partners to meet shared concerns. International regimes are systems of norms and roles agreed upon by states to govern their behaviour in specific political contexts or issue areas (Rittberger, 1995). Regimes are formed to provide regulation and order without resort to the over-arching authority of a supranational government. In short, regimes are a response to the challenge of governing without government (see Mayer et al., 1995). The analysis of international regimes has largely concentrated on the coming together of state actors, although the involvement of non-state actors is not entirely neglected (see Haufler, 1995).

A related concern with self-governing networks is found in Ostrom's work on the management of common-pool resources in poor rural communities (Ostrom, 1990; Keohane and Ostrom, 1995). The focus of this work is one the various institutional arrangements that can be created to enable people to co-operate over resources which are finite to which they have open access. Incentives and sanctions are identified assuming that rational and self-interested actors will respond appropriately. Increasing the availability of information and reducing transaction costs are seen as essential to designing effective systems. Self-organized systems of control among the key participants are seen as more effective than government-imposed regulation.

The dilemma created by the emergence of such self-governing networks is that of accountability. If governance requires the blending together of the resources and purposes of different institutions, an accountability deficit can be experienced at two levels: with the individual constituent elements of the network and by those excluded from any particular network. Members of particular groups may be dissatisfied with the network arrangements agreed by their leaders and yet find it difficult to express, or more particularly act on, the dissatisfaction because of the powerful nature of the glue provided by the network of which their group is part. Even if all constituents of member groups are satisfied a problem of accountability can still arise since all networks are to a degree exclusive. They are driven by the self-interest of their members rather than a wider concern with the public interest or more particularly those excluded from the network.

The solution would appear to rest in bringing government back in some form. The networks have a significant degree of autonomy (and indeed need that autonomy to achieve their purposes), yet government, while not occupying a sovereign position, can indirectly and imperfectly steer networks, so the argument goes of those who believe that governance can be managed.

Governance recognizes the capacity to get things done which does not rest on the power of government to command or use its authority. It sees government as able to use new tools and techniques to steer and guide

The Anglo-American literature is striving hard to find adjectives to describe the new 'light touch' form of government appropriate to the circumstances of governance. 'Enabler', 'catalytic agent', 'commissioner', have all been offered to capture the new form of governing. A recent 'mission statement' for local government in the United Kingdom gives an indication of what might be involved (Hill, 1996). It refers to the need for local government to give leadership, build partnership, protect and regulate its environment and promote opportunity. In a more general way Kooiman and Van Vliet (1993, p. 66) classify 'the tasks of government in a governance' in the following way:

- decomposition and co-ordination;
- collaboration and steering;
- integration and regulation.

The first task involves defining a situation, identifying key stakeholders and then developing effective linkages between the relevant parties. The second is concerned with influencing and steering relationships in order to achieve desired outcomes. The third is about what others call 'system management' (Stewart, 1996). It involves thinking and acting beyond the individual sub-systems, avoiding unwanted side effects and establishing mechanisms for effective co-ordination.

It is far from clear that most of those involved in government have the capacity or indeed even the desire to behave in tune with such a 'mission statement' and governing style. Faced with the complexity and autonomy of a system of multi-level governance there is a strong tendency for political leaderships to seek to impose order and issue directives. Government in these circumstances becomes a vast and unresolvable principal-agent problem. Another option would appear to be to concentrate on media image and symbolic politics, leaving the more substantive elements of government to one side.

Government in the context of governance has to learn an appropriate operating code which challenges past hierarchical modes of thinking. There is evidence of some success as well as failure in meeting the challenge.

The paradox of the governance perspective is that even where government develops an appropriate operating code governance failure may still occur. Tensions and difficulties with the institutions of civil society, as well as inadequacies in the organizations that bridge the gaps between public, private and voluntary sectors may lead to governance failure. Failures of leadership, differences in time scale and horizons among key partners, and the depth of social conflict can all provide the seeds for governance failure (see, for example, Orr and Stoker's analysis (1994) of the difficulties of Detroit). The concept of governance failure is crucial to understanding the new world of governing.

The concept of governance failure suggests the need to think beyond the retooling of government to a broader concern with the institutions and social and economic fabric beyond government. The design challenge with respect to our 'public' institutions becomes complex and demanding. Goodin (1996, pp. 39–43) suggests some desirable design principles revisability, robustness, sensitivity to multinational complexity, public defendability and variability to encourage experimentation.

Goodin's list suggests a concern with designing institutions that have a sustainable life but that are capable of evolution, learning and adaptation. It is also necessary for institutions to be capable of being publicly and openly defended. Finally, institutions need to recognize that both self-regarding and other-regarding elements are likely to play a part in human behaviour within any institution.

Of course identifying a set of appropriate principles is only the starting point. The ultimate challenge is to turn them into proactive ones. Even then some humility is called for in recognizing that institutions can shape policy outcomes but cannot determine them. Governance means living with uncertainty and designing our institutions in a way that recognizes both the potential and the limitations of human knowledge and understanding.

CONCLUSIONS

The article has argued that a governance perspective provides an organizing framework for students and practitioners of a broadly defined public administration. Its contribution to theory is that it helps providing a map or guide to the changing world of government. It identifies key trends and developments. The governance perspective offered here also brings into focus a number of key dilemmas or concerns about the way in which systems of government are changing.

Like all maps the governance perspective applies a simplifying lens to a complex reality. The issue is not that it has simplified matters but whether that simplification has illuminated our understanding and enabled us to find an appropriate path or direction (Rhodes, 1996; Gamble, 1990). If the governance perspective is to be rejected it has to be on the basis that there is a better map or guide rather than on the basis that it fails to provide a comprehensive or definitive account. The governance perspective deliberately selects various trends and developments for our attention. Its valued is to be judged by how good or bad the selection has been.

The governance perspective, again like a map, is date and place specific. One of the difficulties of identifying an organizing perspective that is devoted to understanding a changing system of governance is that no sooner is the perspective outlined than the object of study changes. It is to be hoped, therefore, that the governance perspective can develop in an evolutionary way to capture the processes of adaptation, learning and experiments that are characteristic of governance. It is also to be hoped that although the governance perspective outlined here draws on British and more broadly western democratic experience, it has been framed and argued in a manner that achieves an appropriate resonance with those from other backgrounds and experiences. Undoubtedly there is a sense in which the map that has been provided reflects the origins and realities of where the person who draws the map is based.

An organizing perspective makes its theoretical contribution at a general level in providing a set of assumptions and research questions. It provides a language in which to identify key features of a complex reality and also to pose significant questions about that reality. Such is the claim of the governance perspective offered in this article. It does not advocate governance. Nor does it explain the multiple and various relationships that exists within governance. How governance works in different countries and how governance dilemmas are addressed are the issues it identifies for study but it does not provide all-embracing explanations and answers to these issues. For the governance perspective the questions it poses are as important as the answers it offers. It is saying: the world of governing is changing in ways which mark a substantial break from the past and that that changing world is worthy of study.

REFERENCES

Atkinson M., Coleman W. (1992). 'Policy Networks, Policy Communities and the Problems of Governance', *Governance*, 5 no. 2, pp. 154–80.

Beetham D. (1991). *Legitimation*, London: Macmillan.

Broadbent J., Dieirich M., Laughlin R. (1996), 'The Development of Principal-Agent, Contracting and Accountability Relationships in the Public Sector: Conceptual and Cultural Problem', *Critical Perspectives on Accounting*, 17, pp. 259–84.

Gamble A. (1990). 'Theories of British Politics', *Political Studies*, 30, pp. 404–20.

Goodin R. (1996). 'Institutions and Their Design', in R. Goodin (ed.), *The Theory of Institutional Design*, Cambridge: Cambridge University Press.

Haufler V. (1995). 'Crossing the Boundary between Public and Private: International Regimes and Non-State Actors', in Rittberger 1995, pp. 94–112.

Hill R. (1996). 'Mission Possible: A New Role for the Local State', *Renewal*, 4: 2, pp. 11–21.

Hirschman A., 1991. *The Rhetoric of Reaction*, Cambridge, Mass.: Harvard University Press.

Hood C. (1991). 'A Public Management for All Seasons', *Public Administration*, 69, pp. 3–19.

Jessop B. (1995). 'The Regulation Approach and Governance Theory: Alternative Perspectives on Economic and Political Change', *Economy and Society*, 24: 3, pp. 307–33.

Jessop, B. (1996). *Partnership in Greater Manchester and the Thames Gateway*, Paper for DoE Seminar.

Judge D., Stoker G., and Wolman H. (1995). 'Urban Politics and Theory: An Introduction', in D. Judge, G. Stoker and H. Wolman, *Theories of Urban Politics*, London: Sage, pp. 1–13.

Keohane R., Ostrom E. (eds) (1995). *Local Commons and Global Interdependence*, London: Sage.

Kooiman J. (1993). 'Social-Political Governance: Introduction', in J. Kooiman (ed.), *Modern Governance*, London: Sage, pp. 1–9.

Kooiman J., Van Vliet M. (1993). 'Governance and Public Management', in K. Ehassen and J. Kooiman (eds), *Managing Public Organisations* (2nd edn), London: Sage.

Lorrain D., Stoker G. (1997). *The Privatization of Urban Services in Europe*, London: Pinter.

Marsh D., Rhodes R. (eds) (1992). *Policy Networks in British Government*, Oxford: Oxford University Press.

Mayer P., Rittberger V., Zern M. (1995). 'Regime Theory: State of the Art and Perspectives', in Rittberger, 1995, pp. 391–431.

Miller W., Dickson M. (1996). *Local Governance and Citizenship*, University of Strathclyde: ESRC.

Orr M., Stoker G. (1994). 'Urban Regimes and Leadership in Detroit', *Urban Affairs Quarterly*, 30: 1, pp. 48–73.

Osborne D., Gaebler T. (1992). *Reinventing Government*, Reading Mass.: Addison Wesley.

Ostrom E. (1990). *Governing the Commons: The Evolution of Institutions for Collective Actions*, Cambridge: Cambridge University Press.

Peters G. (1993). 'Managing the Hollow State', in K. Ehassen and J. Kooiman (eds), *Managing Public Organizations* (2nd edn), London: Sage.

Putnam R. (1993). *Making Democracy Work*, Princeton: Princeton University Press.

Rhodes R. (1996). 'The New Governance: Governing without Government', *Political Studies*, 44, pp. 652–67.

Rittberger V. (1995). *Regime Theory and International Relations*, Oxford: Clarendon Press.

Rosenau J. (1992). 'Governance: Order and Change in World Politics', in J. Rosenau and E. O. Czempiel (eds), *Governance without Government: Order and Change in World Politics*, Cambridge: Cambridge University Press, pp. 1–30.

Stewart J. (1996). 'A Dogma of Our Times—The Separation of Policy-Making and Implementation', *Public Policy and Management*, July–September, pp. 1–8.

Stoker G. (1995). 'Regime Theory and Urban Politics', in D. Judge et al., *Theories of Urban Politics*.

—— (1997). 'Public-Private Partnerships and Urban Governance', in J. Pierre (ed.), *Public-Private Partnerships in Europe and the United States*, London: Macmillan.

Stone C. (1989). *Regime Politics*, Lawrence University Press, Kansas.

CHAPTER NINE

Running Government
Like a Business
Implications for Public Administration
Theory and Practice*

Richard C. Box

The public sector faces increasing demands to run government like a business, importing private-sector concepts such
as entrepreneurism, privatization, treating the citizen like a
'customer,' and management techniques derived from the production process. The idea that government should mimic the
market is not new in American public administration, but the
current situation is particularly intense. The new public management seeks to emphasize efficient, instrumental implementation of policies, removing substantive policy questions
from the administrative realm. This revival of the politics–
administration dichotomy threatens core public-sector values
of citizen self-governance and the administrator as a servant
of the public interest. The article examines the political culture
that encourages expansion of market-like practices in the
American public sector, explores the issues of the purpose and
scope of government and the role of the public-service practitioner, and offers a framework for the study and practice of
public administration based on citizenship and public service.

Increasingly, public administration practitioners and academicians
are faced with demands from politicians and citizens that

* *American Review of Public Administration*, vol. 29, no. 1, March 1999

government should be operated like a business. By this, they mean that it should be cost efficient, as small as possible in relation to its tasks, competitive, entrepreneurial, and dedicated to 'pleasing the customer.' But, despite the considerable success of market-like reforms in increasing the efficiency of governmental bureaucracies, there remains a sense that something is wrong. For people who are concerned about the quality of public service and attention to issues of social injustice, fairness in governmental action, environmental protection, and so on, something about running government like a business does not feel right. It seems to degrade the commitment to public service, reducing it to technical—instrumental market functions not unlike the manufacture and marketing of a consumer product. Gone is the image of citizens determining public policy and its implementation to shape a better future because customers do not actively participate in governance but wait passively to respond to an 'agenda set by others' (Schachter, 1997, p. 65).

The idea that the public sector should conduct its affairs in a businesslike way is not new in the United States. Though there are enduring classical republican elements in American political thought that emphasize citizens working together for the good of the community, the American public sector exists within a context of market capitalism and classical liberalism. The values of this context include limited and efficient government in combination with individual liberty and political competition. Relatively little attention is given to problems associated with the workings of the market, such as economic inequality or reduced opportunities for collective citizen decision making through discourse.

A strong governmental apparatus can operate to set the parameters of market activity and its impact on the lives of citizens, but in the United States big government must exert control without seeming to be like a centralized European-style state. Although they wanted a stronger government than that provided by the Articles of Confederation, the founders of the United States intended to avoid forming a state apparatus with a purpose and values of its own and a mandate to shape the broader society. This initial 'statelessness' (Stillman, 1991) is manifest in contemporary public administration debates over the issue of legitimacy (*Public Administration Review*, 1993). The concept of statelessness can be overdrawn, as Americans built an extensive government to meet the challenges of the years 1877–1920, including 'the emergence of a nationality based market' and 'the growth of trusts and oligopolies with national orientations and national economic power' (Skowronek, 1982, p. 11). Due to this institution-building effort, contemporary American government has a significant interactive relationship with the private economy, but it retains from the founding era the cultural expectation of minimal interference in the private sector. This expectation forms a political-cultural context in which the values of the private sector are primary and the values of collective citizen deliberation and the public interest are secondary. Even in this setting, there historically has been recognition of a unique and different role for the public sector, however difficult to define. This was true in the founding era, in the era of Jacksonian democracy, in the reform era, and through several decades of the post World War II era.

Today, even those elusive public–private differences are fading as the public sector is increasingly penetrated by the metaphor of the market, of 'running government like a business.' The expansion of such thinking in the public sector has important implications for theory and practice. This article examines the nature of the political culture that encourages market-based practices in the American public sector, explores the issues of the size and scope of government and the role of the public service practitioner, and offers a framework for the study and practice of public administration in this economistic environment that is based on citizenship and public service. The article is not about the specifics of any particular reform effort, and the intent is not to bemoan the condition of the public sector. Rather, the article suggests constructive ways in which public-service practitioners and academicians can approach these issues in their work, seeking to preserve and enhance the essence of public service within the market context.

PUBLIC ADMINISTRATION'S RESPONSE TO MARKET PRESSURES

Expansion of market concepts in the public sector is taking place at the end of the 20th century thrust to build administrative systems that address the problems of a growing urban–industrial nation. That thrust produces a public sector that appears today to be large, cumbersome, wasteful, and beyond citizen control (King & Stivers, 1998b, p. 11), isolated from and out of touch with the rest of society (Peters & Pierre, 1998, pp. 228–9). Large government requires that a few elected people represent the wishes of the masses, and representative democracy has grown so remote from the everyday lives of people that it no longer bears a clear relationship to common experience (Hummel &

Stivers, 1998). Many citizens are so alienated from the concept of self-governance that they think of government as something separate, not a reflection of their own will, though some others would like to participate directly in re-creating the machinery of government to allow for genuine self-governance. As a potential remedy, many politicians and citizens believe that government should be run more like businesses, becoming trim and lean, exhibiting competitive behaviours and giving greater attention to the needs of 'customers'.

Evidence of the expansion of market concepts in the public sector may be found in the literature and practice of public administration in an emphasis on a constellation of cost-cutting and production management concepts taken from the private sector, currently drawn together as new public management. These concepts include, among others, privatization, downsizing, rightsizing, entrepreneurism, re-invention, enterprise operations, quality management, and customer service. New public management seeks to separate politics (in the sense of decision making by the people or their representatives) from administration, allowing (or making) managers to manage according to cost–benefit economic rationality, largely free from 'day-to-day democratic oversight' (Cohn, 1977). Such a separation resembles the old politics–administration dichotomy and Herbert Simon's (1945–1997) description of administrative decisions that are largely 'factual.' In this reformed management setting, the public–private distinction is 'essentially obsolete' and management is generic across sectors (Peters & Pierre, 1998, p.229).

This desire to separate the activities of politics (deciding about public policies) and administration (implementing them) is part of a redefinition of the function of government based on 'a new elite consensus on the role of the state in society. A substantial public sector is to be maintained, but its purposes and operating values are considerably different from that which was characteristic of the social welfare state. The goal is no longer to protect society from the market's demands but to protect the market from society's demands' (Cohn, 1997, p. 586). This is both an American and international phenomenon (Cheung, 1997; Cohn, 1997; Hood, 1996; Kettl, 1997; Lan & Rosenbloom, 1992), and it may be seen as evidence of a new equilibrium in relations between economic classes. We may no longer find useful the 'stale discourse of class warfare' (Barber, 1998, p. 8), but expansion of economistic concepts in the public sector could reflect the reality that' big government has always been an ally of the little guy, and downsizing it has generally been a recipe for upgrading the power of private-sector monopolies. Schoolroom bullies are forever questioning the legitimacy of hallway monitors' (Barber, 1998, p. 5).

At the level of governmental operation, the question is the extent to which the functions of government should be modeled after the private sector. This gets to the heart of the matter for public-service practitioners, who want to know what is expected from public agencies, how they should relate to citizen (their customers, to use the language of the market), and what is the proper source of policy direction—professional interpretation of the public interest, decisions by elected officials, or the desires of citizens. For over a century, public administration practitioners and academicians have debated the normative role of practitioners, with opinions ranging from neutral implementers of policies determined by others to practitioners as active participants in the policy-making process (Kass & Catron, 1990; McSwite, 1997). Despite the intent of new public management, market concepts are not likely to remove the practitioner from policy making because government is so complex that citizens and elected representatives cannot govern alone.

Instead, running government like a business means that public managers increasingly regard the public as customers to be served rather than as citizens who govern themselves through collective discourse processes. They keep the public at a distance by conducting surveys and focus groups to identify existing opinions rather than engaging citizens face-to-face in exchange of information, ideas, and values that result in informed governance. As elected officials withdraw from direct and frequent involvement in administration, the balance of control shifts toward professionals (Cope, 1997). With citizens excluded from collective governance and elected officials withdrawn from the daily world of policy implementation, the question becomes, 'Who then is accountable?' (Peters & Pierre, 1998, p. 228).

An important task before public administration theorists is to describe the impact of governing and managing by market theory and practice on public service at all levels of government and to explore how theorists and practitioners can respond. Is a complete transformation of the public sector, mimicking the private sector, the answer in the face of pervasive public preference for use of market-like management practices and the apparent reduction of many processes and interactions to cost–benefit calculations? Is this really a problem, or are we approaching the old ideals of pure businesslike efficiency by walling off 'unrelated' matters of politics and preferences from public management, squeezing out of professional practice substantive consideration of whether what we do efficiently, instrumentally, is the right thing to do?

Furthermore, in this market-like environment, is it possible to identify aspects of public service that are in some way fundamental to our notions of a good political culture, aspects that can coexist with market concepts of structure and function? At some point, theorists, and more so practitioners, may find it makes sense to worry less about the apparently unstoppable expansion of the market in the public sector and search for constructive ways to respond to it. For practitioners, one way to do this is to simply comply, mastering the expected economic techniques and carrying out policies as given without taking part in their formulation or questioning them. This response fits well with the traditional split between politics and administration, emulating the model of the neutral bureaucrat. For the academician, this approach means confining research to technical matters of management, such as pay-for-performance plans, budgeting systems, or information technology, thus avoiding critical analysis of the effects of market concepts on the public sphere.

A second way to respond to the expansion of market concepts in the public sector would be to protest vigorously in the hope that someone, someday, will listen, or at least that if the pendulum swings in the other direction in the future, we will be well positioned to say 'we told you so.' This could be a risky strategy for practitioners in the work world and it could position academicians as useful critics of current practice or place them so far outside the mainstream as to be ignored. A third path in responding to the current situation would be to hope for moderation of the impacts of market concepts in the future, but for today, to seek reasonable ways to adapt public service values to the dominant economic paradigm. This is the path outlined in the final section of the article.

THE SOCIAL AND POLITICAL CONTEXT

We can gain a broader perspective by considering the nature of the society that surrounds public administration, the society that creates, supports, and demands services from the public–governmental sector. A description of the nature of society may seem somewhat removed from daily administrative affairs, but of necessity public administration is a reflection of societal values. It is impractical, maybe irresponsible, to operate inside public organizations as if the demands of society do not matter. If we do, sooner or later the external environment will catch up with us, making painful demands for accountability and change that might have been foreseen and dealt with in less traumatic ways.

We have known for some time that the modern market economy would have serious impacts on society and in particular on democracy. In 1906, Max Weber asserted:

... it is utterly ridiculous to see any connection between the high capitalism of today—as it is now being imported into Russia and as it exists in America—with democracy or freedom in any sense of these words ... The question is: how are freedom and democracy in the long run at all possible under the domination of highly developed capitalism? (in Gerth & Mills, 1958, p. 71)

In 1931, John Dewey expressed concern for the future of democratic governance:

The dominant issue is whether the people of the United States are to control our government, federal, state, and municipal, and to use it on behalf of the peace and welfare of society or whether control is to go on passing into the hands of small powerful economic groups who use all the machinery of administration and legislation to serve their own ends. (in Campbell, 1996, pp. 178–9)

Ramos (1981–1984) took for granted the 'intrusion of the market system upon human existence' with its accompanying emphasis on instrumental rationality that advances the goals of the market, rather than substantive rationality that offers the individual an opportunity to achieve 'truly self-gratifying interpersonal relationships' through reason, the activity of the human psyche (p. 23).

Scott and Hart (1979) documented the transition from a society based on the value of the individual in the preindustrial era to one of organizational values in the 20th century. Now, in an age in which we are replaceable parts of large systems, we think with nostalgic fondness of a time when each person was an integral part of a local community. We spend part of our leisure time watching movies or television shows that glorify the heroic loner, but most of us in real life fulfill our destiny as small productive parts of larger systems.

In the United States, the nation's founders created a governmental structure that allowed limited popular participation in national political life while emphasizing order and stability. In so doing, they established a semidemocratic form in which 'the people was no longer being defined, like the Athenian demos, as an active citizen community but as a disaggregated collection of private individuals whose public aspect was represented by a distant central state' (Wood, 1996, p. 219). The focus was on individual rights and protection from the power of government, as contrasted with the classical republican ideal of citizen self-governance.

With the rise of capitalism in the 19th century, it became possible to combine democracy and capitalism by clearly separating the economic and political spheres. Thus, citizens maintained their formal public-sector liberal equality in relation to rights, voting and the law, whereas private-sector inequalities of wealth and power generated by capitalism were largely off-limits to collective, public action. These were the conditions of creation of modern liberal democracy (Adams, Bowerman, Dolbeare, & Stivers, 1990; Wood, 1996, p. 234), a 'Lockean accommodation' that 'reconciled representative government with capitalism by disenfranchising the group most likely to contest the hegemony of wealth—the working class itself' (Bowles & Gintis, 1986, p. 42). It is semidemocratic in that the mass of people participate in a limited and marginal way in collective decision making. In the balance between the public and economic spheres, the public sector is allowed to trim off the rough edges of economic excess in relation to treatment of workers, consumers, and the physical environment, in exchange for keeping public-sector interference with the inequalities of the economic sector to a minimum. Thus, as the market has 'insinuated itself into the domains of sentiment, life-style and psyche,' it has 'bound the state with subtle threads of economic dependency' (Bowles & Gintis, 1986, p. 34).

There do not at present seem to be any viable alternatives to this semidemocratic capitalist model (Dryzek, 1996). On a global level, there were competing models for much of the 20th century, but now those models have largely vanished. There are a few socialist enclaves remaining, and a number of relatively undeveloped countries with authoritarian regimes, are now being pressured by the public and private institutions of developed nations to change their economic systems to conform with the semidemocratic capitalist model. Over time, it may be discovered that this model is not optimal for all nations, that it works best for mature, stable societies with institutions that can support it. It may not work well for a range of nations with cultural and political histories very different from those of developed Western societies, nations in which the semidemocratic capitalist model can lead to hardship and social unrest (Kaplan, 1997).

Today, even the possibility of alternative systems seems to be disappearing, and the market metaphor is dominant. We are apparently in the midst of post-modern conditions characterized by *thick* interpretations of reality at the micro, local level where people can interact directly and form coherent mutual interpretations of values and identity, and *thin* reality at the macro level of broad classes of people, regions, and nations. This results in a profusion of difference, an 'assertion of the random nonpattern and the unassimilable anomaly' (Fox & Miller, 1995, p. 45) that shifts and changes constantly. In such an environment, post-modernists believe it is difficult if not impossible to identify grand themes of common belief or interest across large groups of people or geographic areas.

In the midst of this apparent fragmentation of meaning, the daily mechanics and values of the market permeate social, political, and economic life. Families are pressed by economic circumstances to alter their expectations about work, retirement, child rearing, and care of the elderly. Workers are forced to abandon the certainties of lifetime employment, instead constantly keeping an eye on the job market and the best opportunities to increase earning power. Private, public, and nonprofit organizations must constantly adapt to their rapidly changing environments. In the public sphere, it becomes harder and harder to generate large-scale communities of shared interest through direct discourse and personal action, even at a time when people yearn for a return to a sense of community and personal efficacy (Bellah, Madsen, Sullivan, Swidler, & Tipton, 1985; Box, 1998; Eberly, 1994). So, we live in post-modern times characterized by large-scale fragmentation of values and intensification of interest in local action, yet we are surrounded by the seemingly universal, global phenomenon of market mechanisms. Within this universal phenomenon, there appears to be general agreement that people are competitive self-maximizers out to lobby legislatures for their benefit at the expense of others, get the largest quantity of consumer goods their resources will command, climb over the backs of colleagues for career advancement, compete at the community level to draw the best companies to their town at the expense of other towns, and so on. Furthermore, this view seems to reflect not only a description of what we are but also a normative vision of what we should be in a 'celebration of wealth that now threatens to drown all competing values' (Lasch, 1996, p. 22). Times change, and if this competitive, consumerist life pattern affects the world's physical environment and social stratification in ways that clearly threaten individuals, the pendulum of public opinion and political action may shift, as it did during parts of the 1960s and 1970s. But for now, 'more is more' instead of 'less is more' and the market is our guide.

In such circumstances, it is hardly surprising that the language and methods of the market have made significant inroads into public-sector thought and practice over the past two decades. However, American public administration has not been a pure entity removed from the influence of the market during any period in its development. At all levels of government throughout the nation's history, there has been evidence of market-like behaviour, such as 19th-century spoils politics that affected policy implementation at the national level and the local-level graft and machine politics that inspired urban reformers to take action. The progressive-era reaction to these perceived abuses was to separate politics and administration at least to the extent that administration would be more businesslike and scientific. Ironically, this meant that reformers wanted to use the management methods of the market to reduce the extent of market-like behaviour in the public sector.

In the 20th century, with the rise of the administrative state, public professionals became more prominent in the formulation as well as implementation of public policy. As the overall scope of government expanded dramatically, the internal management of government retained an expectation of efficiency in the midst of a sense of broader public purpose. There were repeated examinations of management of the national government that advocated application of scientific, businesslike methods to improve efficiency (Arnold, 1995). At the local level, the council–manager plan was built on a corporate structural model with the expectation that it would produce efficiency and effectiveness.

Beginning in the 1950s, some economists turned their attention to the public sector, applying their assumptions about individual and collective behaviour to the public sphere. By focusing on the individual as the unit of analysis, assuming that individuals seek to maximize their personal preferences in the 'political market' as they do in the private sector, and treating the behaviour of citizens, elected officials, political appointees, and public professionals as examples of self-seeking regard for their own interests, the public choice scholars discovered a public world very different from that of public administration scholars (Johnson, 1991). Where traditional theorists found people searching for a better society and public interest, economic theorists found the public sector operating like an alternative form of market. In this view, traditional bureaucratic, hierarchical government is not a means to social betterment, but a mechanism that distorts private economic behaviour, reduces individual freedom, and makes the economy less efficient. The way to reduce these negative effects, according to economists, is to decentralize government, make it smaller, and introduce market-like concepts such as fees and user charges, vouchers, and systems to monitor employee performance, such as merit pay plans (Jennings, 1991, pp. 115–16; Ostrom, 1973–1991).

At the conceptual level of the size and scope of government, the economic view is that, when it will be to their benefit, individuals, groups, politicians, and bureaucrats seek to maximize their gains by competing with others for the benefits offered by collective action (Downs, 1957; Niskanen, 1971; Olson, 1965). Corporations seek to make it harder for potential competitors to enter the market, associations seek tax breaks others cannot have, politicians fight for the power and money of office, and public-sector bureaucrats want their agencies to grow so that their status and freedom to act are increased. Governmental action coerces individuals in society into behaving in a manner consistent with majority will, whether or not they agree with it, and those who stand to benefit the most from governmental action will spend the time and resources to influence public policy decisions. A basic assumption of economics is that free and uncoerced individual choice should be maximized and that, where a clear need for collective action in the public interest is lacking, citizens should be allowed to act alone or in voluntary cooperation without governmental coercion (Schmidtz, 1991, chap. 7). But government grows larger and more powerful as people use it to gain advantage over one another. This rent-seeking behaviour joins the economic inefficiency of government-as-monopoly-provider-of-services as an argument for smaller and more limited government.

At the conceptual level of public agencies and employees, economic rationality has had a significant impact on scholarly thinking about behaviour in organizations. Niskanen's argument that public bureaucrats will seek to increase the size of their agency's budgets (1971; or as modified in 1991, the size of the discretionary budget) was an effort to reconceptualize the behaviour of public employees, moving away from models of control by legislatures or a sense of duty to the public interest, to a model of the public professional as a self-interested maximizer of competitive position in the bureaucratic world. Niskanen's ultimate purpose was to shift attention from the attributes of bureaucrats to the characteristics of public agencies, especially the structural features that provide incentives for people to behave in certain ways (Niskanen, 1991, p. 28).

In the past few decades, economically oriented examination of public organizations has been a growth industry, adopting a variety of complex and interesting approaches. Summarizing this work in 1984 in an article on 'The New Economics of Organization,' Moe noted that it is 'perhaps best characterized by three elements: a contractual perspective on organizational relationships, a focus on hierarchical control, and formal analysis via principal–agent models' (p. 739). Among approaches to organizations that fall within the new economics rubric, principal–agent theory is especially applicable in the public sector, where the relationships between citizens (principals) and politicians (their agents) and between politicians (principals in this case) and bureaucrats (their agents) are a constant source of fascination. Agency theory deals with questions that arise because 'the desires or goals of the principal and agent conflict and it is difficult or expensive for the principal to verify what the agent is actually doing' (Eisenhardt, 1989, p. 58). It is assumed that agents will naturally do less work than principals want done or fail to do work in the way principals want it done. This is the problem of shirking, and principals meet it by seeking information on the activities of agents; this monitoring is time-consuming and costly. Thus, it behooves the principal (e.g., boss, superior, capitalist, or politician) to seek a wage rate that will motivate agents (employees, subordinates) and a level of monitoring that is not too costly but convinces agents that the risk of being caught shirking is substantial (Bowles & Gintis, 1986, pp. 77–8).

There are important implications of this line of though for behaviour in public organizations. The economics-based management tools being applied in the public sector are grounded in the economist's assumptions that employees will shirk and that monitoring is essential (though the assumption of economically rational behaviour has been under attack for some time; see Anderson & Crawford, 1998). The focus is on explicitly specifying performance, through mechanisms such as clearly articulated contracts and/or pay-for-performance systems. In New Zealand, for example, many public agencies have been changed so that 'top managers are hired by contract, rewarded according to their performance, and can be sacked if their work does not measure up' (Kettl, 1997, p. 448). Although this is more extreme than typical implementation of principal–agent concepts in the United States, such thinking can be found in the emphasis on various techniques to measure and reward performance and outcomes, as well as movement away from rigid civil-service systems. Although the elegantly simple structure of principal–agent theory is becoming more cumbersome and problematic with the accumulation of empirical data on its application (Waterman & Meier, 1998), it remains a powerful tool in the hands of contemporary governmental reformers.

It was in the 1980s amid the antigovernment ideology of the Reagan administration and a wave of public sentiment for shrinking the public sector, that market-like concepts broke through the weak wall of separation between the values of the market and the values of public management. Trickle-down, supply-side economics and public choice economics pointed the way to prosperity through smaller government, and it was thought that bureaucratic waste could be eliminated through contracting out and becoming entrepreneurial, and soon the entire public sector would, supposedly, be as efficient as the private sector was assumed to be. The negative aspects of treating public purposes as if they were private became apparent through events such as the savings-and-loan crisis at the national level and reevaluation of the tenets of 'reinvention' at the local level (Gurwitt, 1994), but the transformational impact of this period cannot be denied. This is reflected in the writing of a deputy project director for the Clinton administration's new-public management-inspired National Performance Review. Although noting that 'there is no single intellectual source for the reinventing government movement,' he says that it 'evolved during the past 10 to 15 years based, in part, on the pioneering intellectual work of public choice theoreticians such as Mancur Olson, E.S. Savas, Gordon Tullock, and William Niskanen' (Kamensky, 1996, p. 248).

THE SIZE AND SCOPE OF GOVERNMENT

As Weintraub (1997) has pointed out, there are several meanings of the distinction between *public* and *private*, including the following: the liberal-economistic model, based on neoclassical economics, which regards the public–private distinctions the same as that between state administration and the market economy; the civic perspective, which views the public realm as separate from both the market and the administrative state; and other perspectives, including feminism, that examine distinctions between public and private as involving the spheres of sociability and family and household (pp. 16–17).

Here, we take a viewpoint looking outward from inside the administrative state to examine penetration of the market metaphor into public administration, so we are concerned with the liberal-economistic model that is 'dominant in most "public policy" analysis' (p. 16).

Given the development of the political environment described above, it is not surprising that Americans have always been searching for an acceptable balance between what is private and what is public. In the early to mid-19th century, there were debates over the national government's role in banking and funding internal improvements such as telegraph transmission and canals for water transportation. For the most part, the trend was toward resisting expansion of the national role amid prevailing public opinion hostile to action by the national government (White, 1954, pp. 437–81). Efforts to expand the role of government were more successful in the late 19th century and into the 20th century, as the regulatory and welfare state was built in response to the changing character of national economic life. Then, beginning with the Reagan administration in the 1980s, the growth of the national government was again brought into question. At the local level, the scope of governmental activity grew steadily, accelerating after World War II as the population expanded and suburbia was built.

Along with questioning the size and scope of government in the 1980s, there was a revival of interest in localism and limited government. If it seems to the individual that the national or state government is too distant, too big, and so dominated by enterenched interest groups that he or she cannot have much effect on public policy, it is natural to turn attention toward a locus of action small enough to offer the possibility of quick and satisfying results. As president, Ronald Reagan encouraged this sentiment as he sought to dismantle the welfare state and return its functions to states, localities, and private and nonprofit sector organizations. The communitarian movement emphasized nongovernmental action and citizen duties as well as rights. These ideas were given additional thrust by the withdrawal of the national government from many domestic initiatives and the phenomenon of tight resources at all levels of government.

In the midst of the 1980s milieu of negativity toward government, with its bureaucrat bashing and belief that government is the problem rather than the solution, economic thinking about the role of government in society blossomed and became part of the ordinary vocabulary of normative debate. By the 1990s, the idea that government needed to be smaller and more efficient had become accepted as common wisdom (though the reality was different at the state and local levels, as government continued to expand; see Walters, 1998). Of those people who spend time thinking about the size and scope of government and its role in society, many have come to hold the view that government at all levels is too big and it would be wise to spin off functions from the national government to the states and localities, or from government to the private and nonprofit sectors.

The economist's conceptual scheme for determining what is public and what is private has become standard fare for students of public affairs and underlies much of the public discourse about the role of government (Mikesell, 1995, pp. 1–6). Thus, we distinguish between public goods, such as national defense, and private goods, such as household appliances or a hamburger. Public goods would not ordinarily be offered by the private sector acting on the incentive of making a profit because people cannot be excluded from using it and so have no incentive to pay for it (the market failure to provide a good). If it is provided at all, it is available to everyone, and one person's use of a public good does not exhaust its usefulness to others (because I experience the benefits of being defended from foreign aggression does not mean that you cannot experience them, too). Since people could experience the benefits of public goods without paying for them (the free rider problem), government coercively forces members of the public to pay taxes or face financial penalties or imprisonment.

In the real world, things are not so simple, so there are modifications and exceptions to the concept of pure public goods and pure private goods. Toll goods are services that many people use but from which people may be excluded (such as swimming pools open for public use or expressways that charges fees), and common-pool resources are goods that can be exhausted as many people use them but for which exclusion is difficult (notably natural resources such as fisheries). The distinctions between types of goods are often fuzzy, and public sector decision makers use criteria of public demand and political action to choose which services to offer rather than ideal conceptualizations of types of goods. Thus, government becomes involved in providing a variety of services that might appear to belong in the private or nonprofit sector. In addition, government regulates the activities of private actors as they work with toll, common-pool, or private goods, attempting to control negative effects (externalities) of private economic activity on people or the environment.

To add to the complexity, a distinction is made between the provision of public services and their production. Provision is the fundamental question of whether or not government will cause a service, or good, to be offered. It is a policy question to be decided by the people or their representatives. If the answer is negative ('No, we don't want to provide garbage pickup service'), then either private or nonprofit organizations will provide the service or no one will. If, using the example of garbage pickup, no one provides the service (a market failure), there will likely be a discussion on the public health implications and a revisiting of the negative provision decision. Production is a separate issue. If the provision decision is positive, then the question remains how to actually deliver the service, how to produce it. Osborne and Gaebler argued in their book *Reinventing Government* (1993) that government often does a better job of governance, or *steering* (making policy decisions) than of delivering services, or *rowing* (see chap. 1). Osborne and Gaebler included in the steering–rowing distinction between governmental decision making about contracting out services and a governmental role in serving as catalyst for private and nonprofit initiatives such as downtown renewal or building sports facilities.

In an appendix to their book, Osborne and Gaebler built on the work of Savas (1987) to offer decision-making criteria for choosing public, private, or non profit action, such as stability, regulation, and enforcement of equity (public-sector strong points), expertise and willingness to take risks (private-sector attributes), and compassion and promotion of community (nonprofit-sector attributes). Vincent Ostrom (1973–1991; 1977; 1991–1994) has written extensively about institutional structures, intergovernmental arrangements, and building institutional capacity that helps to govern themselves. Using a combination of public choice theory and a historical analysis of American government, Ostrom emphasizes the benefits of a multifaceted, polycentric system of governmental organizations and their private and nonprofit partners, organized to fit the services they offer so that the result is best possible blend of efficiency with responsiveness to the public (e.g., community police patrol may be more efficiently and effectively organized on a small local scale, whereas police communication systems, detention facilities, and crime laboratories may be handled better through large-scale organization [1977, pp. 1518–1520]). These ideas appear to be helpful, although the circumstances surrounding specific decisions are often complex and uncertain, making application of decision-making criteria difficult.

In the end, it appears that determinations about which goods are to be distributed free to the public and which they need to pay for,' and production arrangements are a matter of trial and error according to political preferences. At the national level, our attitudes about the scope and size of government change periodically as we face new challenges and social and economic conditions. In response to evidence of widespread poverty, hunger, and injustice, we mount a campaign to redistribute incomes, taxing the middle class and wealthy to help the poor. In good economic times, politicians find ways to give tax breaks and programmatic 'goodies' to the middle class to secure their votes in the next election.

At the local level, the choices made about which services to offer vary significantly from community to community. Some places confine themselves to providing the basics of public safety, streets, and sewer and water. Others provide a wide variety of services, for example, public pools, bicycle trails, recreation programmes, public hospitals, downtown redevelopment programmes, public–private partnerships to encourage economic development, and so on. In a community in which the author of this article lived for eight years, the city utilities department discussed offering repair of home appliances to residential customers to make the city more competitive when private-sector firms enter the deregulating market for electric service. As one might imagine, people in the appliance repair business were not pleased with this potential entrepreneurial endeavour, viewing it as public expansion into an area thought of by most as a private-sector activity.

The complexities of intergovernmental relations, deciding whether services should be offered by small local units of government, larger ones, or regional agencies, which services will be provided by government and which will be produced by government or by the non-profit or private sectors, and so on, are matters often resolved incrementally. To some extent the theory of public goods may influence such decisions, but its likely it serves in large part to describe and critique what has taken place after the fact. For some time, there has been disagreement in the public administration community about the size and scope of government and the application of market thinking, with its elements of maximum individual choice, decentralization, and privatization. These issues are unlikely to be resolved anytime soon, if ever (see, e.g., Golembiewski, 1997; Kettl, 1997; Lyons & Lowery, 1989; Phares, 1989; Ross & Levine, 1996, chap. 11; Stillman, 1991, pp.176–85; Waldo, 1981, p. 97).

MARKET VALUES AND THE NATRUE OF PUBLIC SERVICE

Given the importation of private-sector management techniques into the public sector in the past two decades, many public administrators are expected to be entrepreneurial, offer great customer service, and practice the latest management techniques inside the agency (total quality management, pay for performance, and so on). On the surface, it appears that such techniques would make the public service much more efficient, with results that would please citizens (they get better service), elected officials (they get credit for public agency efficiency), and career public-service practitioners (they get more approval and respect from citizens and elected people). And indeed, anecdotal evidence as well as scholarly research indicate that market-based reforms have produced some desired changes in the way government operates in the United States, as well as significant changes in several other nations (Kettl, 1997).

There are, however, potential problems with making the public service more businesslike because there is a difference in the operating norms of private and public-sector organizations. Terry (1993) described entrepreneurial values as including 'autonomy, a personal vision of the future, secrecy, and risk-taking' (p. 393), along with 'domination and coercion, a preference for revolutionary change (regardless of the circumstances), and a disrespect for tradition' (p. 394). According to Terry these values are at odds with values of 'democratic politics and administration,' such as 'accountability, citizen participation, open policy making processes, and "stewardship" behaviour' (p. 393). In a response to Terry, Bellone and Goerl (1993) espoused 'civic-regarding entrepreneurship' which offers a community-minded model of administration that is accountable to the public. Terry, however, is not sure entrepreneurship can easily be combined with public service. His overriding concern is that 'public entrepreneurs of the neo-managerialist persuasion are oblivious to other values highly prized in the U.S. constitutional democracy. Values such as fairness, justice, representation, or participation are not on the radar screen' (Terry, 1998, p. 198).

The contemporary emphasis on entrepreneurship makes this debate appear new. However, it is to some extent a repackaging of the old politics–administration question that has been in play since the late 19th century and was highlighted by the Friedrich–Finer argument in the early 1940s over the role of the administrator as relatively independent, expert actor, or tightly constrained agent of political officials (for a description of this argument, see McSwite, 1997, pp. 29–52). The repackaging is occasioned by renewed pressure to manage like a business as economic concepts permeate the thinking of policy makers and implementers. Although administrators are pushed to use entrepreneurial and scientific techniques to please the 'customer's' assumed desire for businesslike government, they paradoxically become less accountable to the public, whose member lose some control over administration. For example, administrators may use expenditure-control budgets, which allow flexibility to spend as the professional sees fit, and to save money to carry over for discretionary spending later to avoid direct budgetary control by politicians. The assumptions are that this flexibility will make for more nimble response to changing conditions, give managers an incentive to be frugal, and remove political motivations from what ought to be expert decisions. Using Bellone and Goerl's reasoning, the good public administrator will, in exercising this greater degree of discretionary space, take into account the wishes of citizens in making choices. This logic reopens the question of representative democracy and agency; that is, do public administrators answer to the public, or to their elected representatives (Box, 1998; Fox & Miller, 1995; Kelly, 1998)?

The argument against such flexibility in budgeting is that clear and detailed line-item budgets were created to avoid problems of financial abuse and to ensure that money is spent as citizens or their elected representatives decide it should be spent. Saving up money means that it has not been spent as intended by representatives but instead will be spent as nonelected administrators decide—thus, a question of accountability. Supposedly scientific techniques administered by experts, such as cost–benefit analysis, reengineering, and quality control, may lead to more precise and economically efficient service delivery, but they may also crowd out competing citizen preferences for public policy and service delivery, preferences that can be shown by experts to be inefficient or impractical. This sort of result is often seen in disputes over such relatively minor issues as whether to preserve a historic building or remove esthetically pleasing landscaped medians in major streets to make traffic flow smoothly.

In these and similar instances, there is a conflict between the idea of public management as efficient, businesslike, and scientific, and public management as responsive to these and to other public values as well. Jennings (1991) offered three approaches to public administration that capture the essence of this conflict. The bureaucratic approach 'takes efficiency and equal treatment of citizens as its primary values,' the pluralism approach 'emphasizes responsiveness to multiple interests,' and the market approach 'takes efficiency as its prime value,' differing from the bureaucratic approach in emphasizing diversity of product and maximum consumer choice (p. 122). It may be argued that public administration theorists have in the past tended to prefer one of the first two approaches. Those who favour greater status and discretion for public administrators lean toward the bureaucratic approach, and those who favour greater citizen discourse and self-governance lean toward the pluralist approach. But today, most agree that some measure of market-like matching of public services to consumer preferences, along with efficient and technically competent management, is inevitable if not desirable. The question is how much, in what ways, and whether there are aspects of public service that should not be governed or managed from a market perspective.

The problem in seeking a reasonable balance between approaches in the face of demands to run government like a business is that operating with private-sector entrepreneurial techniques in the public sphere can subvert values of openness, fairness, and public propriety. In such cases, the public-service practitioner may take on the appearance of an independent actor separated from the public, concerned less about the public interest (however defined) and more about making money and maximizing individual power and freedom to act without review. This decreased accountability carries the possibility of unexpected programme outcomes, uneven treatment of citizens, and behaviours that have not generally been thought of as consistent with public service. Again, using the example of city utilities in a community in which the author lived, this time in relation to the question of openness, the utilities department attempted to deny public access to many of its documents on the premise that it must operate secretly to level the playing field with its private-sector counterparts. In relation to fairness and a sense of public propriety, the local publicly owned hospital in the same community is semiautonomous, competes aggressively and successfully for market share with the other hospital in town, advertises its high-tech services widely, makes a sizable surplus, and pays its top executive approximately $300,000 per year, including bonuses based on how much the hospital makes. To some people these may not seem like appropriate behaviours for the public sector.

Movement toward a market model thus may result in loss of citizen self-determination in the creation of public policy and the operation of public organizations. Today, most people recognize that a general return to the participatory democracy of an earlier time and simpler society is impossible. However, in this post-progressive era, many are working to rebuild citizen capacity for self-governance through discourse and active citizenship (Barber, 1984; Box, 1998; Eberly, 1994; King & Stivers, 1998a). Not everyone will take part in such efforts, but, as Fox and Miller (1995) put it, having 'some-talk' is better than having 'few-talk' (pp. 129–59). The goal is to move beyond the typical model of citizen participation that is 'not designed primarily for citizens but for agencies' (Timney 1998, p. 98), in which administrators use citizen involvement processes for 'informing, consultation, and placation' (Timney, 1998, p. 97) rather than enabling people to govern themselves.

Market-driven new managerialism can run counter self-governance, as it is structured around the idea of happy consumers rather than involved citizens. This is a problem because government is not a business from which customers can voluntarily decide whether to purchase a product. It is, rather, a collective effort that includes every person within a defined geographic area (city, county, district, state, nation), and membership is involuntary unless a resident moves out of the jurisdiction. Mandatory membership carries with it a sense of the right to be involved if one so wishes in the process of deliberating and deciding on creation and implementation of public policy. As Barrett and Grenee (1998) wrote, 'Governments that buy too heavily into the idea that customers are a higher form of life than citizens risk losing the participation of taxpayers as partners' (p. 62).

Customers, on the other hand, are people to be persuaded and sold an image, a product, or a service rather than people who deliberate and decide. Schachter (1997, pp. 57–8) pointed out that only some public agencies can have customers in the manner of private-sector organizations. Many public agencies cannot easily identify their customers because the public they deal with is divided into a variety of individuals and groups with conflicting goals. Many others are regulatory or stewardship agencies for which the immediate client may not be the true beneficiary of the service. An example of the former would be a school district, for which the customers could be students, parents, or all adults in the community. Examples of the latter could include a restaurant regulated by the local health department (is the department's customer the restaurant owner or the people who eat at the restaurant?), or the forest service (is the customer the wood products industry or current and future generations who would use the forests?). These examples illustrate the fundamental difference between the market and the citizenship models of governance. The model of management formed around the market metaphor may lead to channeling resources into creating an image through public relations, surveying citizen opinion, and responding to perceived individual service preferences, rather than bringing citizens together to make their own decisions. This requires keeping the public at arm's length while operating in an entrepreneurial manner behind a façade that gives the appearance of involving citizens and making decisions in the general public interest.

CONCLUSIONS: PRACTICING PUBLIC SERVICE IN THE MARKET ENVIRONMENT

Few would argue that government should be inefficient on purpose or inattentive to the needs and desires of its clients. In this sense, reinvention, privatization, enterpreneurism, customer service, and other such techniques are good things, bringing a breath of fresh air, challenge, and constructive change to the public sector. But market-like techniques may become problematic when they overwhelm values traditionally associated with the public sector and with public service. The economic assumptions of individual self-maximization, the public interest as the aggregate of private interests, and the public sector as just another form of market are powerful, focused, elegantly simple tools of analysis. Like other powerful and narrow theoretical constructs, they draw appropriate attention to matters of importance, but they also insist on their way of knowing the world while excluding other valuable theoretical orientations.

James March (1992) argued that in the past few decades economic theorists have softened the pure application of their ideas to the public sector, moving from methodological individualism to recognition of the fabric of institutional and structural relationships that make up a community. They now take into account, along with their original assumptions, 'a rich, behavioural interpretation attentive to limited rationality, conflict, ambiguity, history, institutions, and multiple equilibria' (p. 228). He also noted that this softer, more subtle application of economic concepts has not yet penetrated into the world of applied theory because 'the news of the transformation of rational theory spreads rather slowly from the inner temples of microeconomics to the rationalizing missionaries in the rest of an economizing society and social science' (p. 229). As this news spreads, the current reforms will fade and reformers will move on to new ideas, but like earlier reforms, they are likely to leave a legacy. The legacy of economistic theory in the public sector may include greater attention to 'performance-motivated administration' and the integration of economic concepts into the traditional intellectual matrix of public service (Lynn, 1998, p. 232).

Turning toward application of these ideas to the size and scope of government, the historical American attitude toward the public sector has been that it should not compete with the private sector but should provide services that the private sector will not. However, with time, the clarity of the public–private distinction has faded as people ask government to do more and citizens grow accustomed to things as they are. In the past two decades, this combination of a preference for limited governmental scope with incremental accumulation of services in violation of that preference has been complicated by expansion of economics-based theory and practice. The public-choice side of the running government like a business metaphor suggests shrinking government by contracting out services or returning them to the private sector on the premise that the private sector is more efficient (in the case of contracting) or the assertion that the public sector should simply be smaller (in the case of true privatization). Meanwhile, the entrepreneurial side of the metaphor suggests that government may retain its traditional services and operate them like a business, plus operate services ordinarily thought of as private in order to make money. One way government officials are able to accommodate these diverse demands without making government smaller is to make it appear to be morphing into a publicly owned business by charging user fees, contracting parts of its services, or adopting the language and practice of the private sector by, for example, calling certain services companies or businesses and using a variety of private-sector internal management techniques.

In the area of application of market concepts to the conduct of public service, the potential impacts are significant. The prevailing American attitude about the nature of public service has been to expect market-like efficiency and business like operation but in combination with public service values such as accountability, fair and equal treatment, democratic self governance, social justice, protection of the physical environment, and others. Schachter (1997) pointed out that progressive-era reformers, although striving for a more efficient government, also advocated informing citizens so they could be more active in governing. Today's expansion of economic thinking and the potential separation of expert service provider (public service professional) from customer (citizen) may be one of the most serious threats to public service values Americans have experienced.

This leaves contemporary academicians and practitioners with the task of defining preferred normative balances of public and private and of market-like management and public service. We can identify four broad areas in which economic thinking prompts reexamination of substantive assumption about the public–private relationship and public service. As we do so, we recognize that these assumptions about public institutions are unique understandings that incorporate our history, institutional development, interpersonal interactions, and the surrounding political, social, and economic environment. They are unique because they vary and change by place, time, and human action; their 'structural properties' exists as 'practices and memory traces orienting the conduct of knowledgeable human agents' (Giddens, 1984, p. 17) rather than as fixed and fully understood phenomena. Taken together, the narrative of these four areas outlines a framework for discourse about the nature of the American public sector and public service. This framework cannot provide clear normative answers to the challenge of the economistic environment, but it can point toward ways of preserving a public-regarding essence of citizenship and public service while responding constructively to the contemporary economic–political environment.

Services the public sector should provide: In every community, region, state, and at the national level, there are at a given time services that a majority of citizens believe should be provided by the public. This belief may not be based on extensive knowledge and could change if people were to have more information (this is the problem of improving the quality of public judgment; see Yankelovich, 1991), but it is possible to identify attitudes about what services should be public. There are likely a range of reasons that people would give for wanting to have certain services provided by the public sector rather than by the private sector or not at all, but there may be a primary characteristic of public services that most Americans would agree forms a sound decision rule for determining what is public and what is private.

We may hypothesize that, asked to consider a particular service that they think should be publicly provided, people would generally agree that they want certainty that the public has the ability to maintain or change the service in keeping with what the majority thinks to be in the public interest (however defined; in this case, it can be assumed to be the long-term interests of the greatest number, when the public is provided adequate information to make a determination). The standard example of national defense is one on which strong majority agreement can be found and other examples would draw varying responses according to place, time, and the sampled population.

The decision rule of ability to maintain or change a service in accord with a majority view of the public interest is different from the market-driven service rule that uses individual preferences as the basis for governmental response. It focuses not only on efficiency or businesslike operation but also on citizen beliefs about the public interest, the good community, whatever it is that citizens think is best for themselves and others, acting collectively. How to inform and involve citizens in making such decisions may be unclear, but it is clear that this is a decision milieu driven by different values than those of the market. It is also a process that includes collective public deliberation and assistance from public-service professionals.

Services the public section should produce: Within the category of services that people believe should be provided by public, there are services involving discretion and accountability such that the public is uncomfortable with an arm's length contractual relationship and the possibility of the profit motive rather than public interest determining outcomes. Examples could include police patrol and crime investigation, protective services for children, land-use regulation, and some human resources functions.

These services can be contrasted with a range of things that do not involve the same level of discretion and accountability and are good candidates to be contracted out or fully privatized for reasons of cost efficiency, purchase of specialized expertise that would cost too much to maintain on staff, or greater flexibility in staffing levels. Examples could include operating a police impoundment facility for seized vehicles, conducting psychological evaluations of defendants awaiting trial, and constructing valid test instruments for jobs that draw large numbers of applicants.

Democratic governance: There are processes of governance that most

Americans expect will be maintained as purely public, rather than being contracted, privatized, or operated by public employees in a closed, unilateral, market-like manner. Though people like good customer service when they need to pay their water bill or have a street repaired, they want to know that they have the option, whether exercised or not, to take part in determining policy and assessing implementation. This goes beyond Osborne and Gaebler's idea of steering rather than rowing, as the issue is not just what government does (steering, or making decisions, versus rowing, or carrying them out) but who has the right and ability to make policy and implementation decisions. This is at the heart of citizenship and self-governance.

Thus, although most would agree that government should use efficient business methods in technical, operational areas, this does not mean that business principles of efficiency, scientific management, or closed and centralized decision making should dominate the creation or evaluation of public policy, or exclude citizens from self-governance. To accept a broader a view of governance is to assert that government is not ultimately guided by a market model of competition and efficiency but by a citizenship model of governance. This broader view places business like management techniques in an instrumental position subordinate to the larger sphere of governance. It draws citizens, elected officials, and public service professionals together in the joint project of creating and implementing public policy.

The role of the practitioner: It might be assumed, in the manner of the old politics–administration dichotomy or the current policy–management split of the market metaphor, that public-service practitioners should not play an active part in shaping issues, debates, and decisions on the questions of what is public or private or whether public policy and services should be approached using the market or the citizenship models. However, there is little doubt today that practitioners are an important part of policy formulation and implementation, providing information needed by citizens and elected officials to frame policy decisions and generating proposals that often form the basis for public action.

Thus, practitioners fill multiple roles in addition to the traditional bureaucratic role, serving as expert advisers and as facilitators of citizen discourse. The open question is how this is to be done in a society that expects nonelected public servants to maintain a position clearly subordinate to elected officials and citizens. This question involves issues of legitimacy and leadership. Is it possible to be an important actor in the creation and implementation of public policy without straying outside the legislative mandate or becoming dominating, self-serving, and causing restriction of public access and freedom to act?

Public practitioners are, because of proximity and knowledge, deeply involved in the broad issue of the extent to which the market metaphor should guide public governance. They exercise influence in discussions about what services should be public, how they should be operated, and whether the public practitioner serves customers or citizens. Though there will always be concern about the legitimacy of this role, many practitioners are in a position to shape the public sector by offering their knowledge to peers, citizens and elected representatives trying to meet the challenge of governing in an economics-driven political culture. In doing so, they can serve the interests of public service and democratic will formation by keeping in mind the shifting and dynamic nature of the relationship of the market to the public sector and the importance of their actions in shaping the future.

REFERENCES

Adams, G. B., Bowerman, P. V., Dolbeare, K. M., & Stivers, C. (1990). 'Joining Purpose to Practice: A Democratic Identity for the Public Service', In H. D. Kass & B. L. Catron (eds), *Images and Identities in Public Administration* (pp. 219–40). Newbury Park, CA: Sage.

Anderson, T. T., & Crawford, R. G. (1998). 'Unsettling the Metaphysics of Neo-classical Micro-economic and Management Thinking', *International Journal of Public Administration*, 21, 645–90.

Arnold, P. E. (1995). 'Reform's Changing Role', *Public Administration Review*, 55, 407–17.

Barber, B. R. (1984). *Strong Democracy: Participatory Politics for a New Age*, Berkeley: University of California Press.

Barber, B. R. (1998). *A Place for Us: How to Make Society Civil and Democracy Strong*, New York: Farrar, Straus, and Giroux.

Barrett, K., & Greene, R. (1998, March). 'Customer Disorientation', *Governing*, 11, 62.

Bellah, R. N., Madsen, R., Sullivan, W. M., Swidler, A., & Tipton, S. M. (1985). *Habits of the Heart: Individualism and Commitment in American Life*, New York: Harper & Row.

Bellone, C. J., & Goerl, G. F. (1993). 'In Defense of Civic-Regarding Entrepreneurship or Helping Wolves to Promote Good Citizenship', *Public Administration Review*, 53, 396, 398.

Bowles, S. & Gintis, H. (1986). *Democracy and Capitalism: Property, Community, and the Contradictions of Modern Social Thought*, New York: Basic Books.

Box, R. C. (1998). *Citizen Governance: Leading American Communities into the 21st Century*, Thousand Oaks, CA: Sage.

Campbell, J. (1996). *Understanding John Dewey: Nature and Cooperative Intelligence*, Chicago: Open Court Publishing.

Cheung, A. B. L. (1997). 'The rise of Privatization Policies: Similar Faces, Diverse Motives', *International Journal of Public Administration*, 20, 2213–2245.

Cohn, D. (1997). 'Creating Crises and Avoiding Blame: The Politics of Public Service Reform and the New Public Management in Great Britain and the United States', *Administration and Society*, 29, 584–616.

Cope, G. H. (1997). 'Bureaucratic Reform and Issue of Political Responsiveness', *Journal of Public Administration Research and Theory*, 7, 461–71.

Downs, A. (1957). *An Economic Theory of Democracy*, New York: Harper & Row.

Dryzek, J. S. (1996). *Democracy in Capitalist Times: Ideals, Limits, and Struggles*, Oxford, UK: Oxford University Press.

Eberly, D. E.(1994). *Building a Community of Citizens: Civil Society in the 21st Century*, New York: University Press of America.

Eisenhardt, K. M. (1989). 'Agency Theory: An Assessment and Review', *Academy of Management Review*, 14, 57–74.

Fox, C. J. & Miller, H. T. (1995). *Postmodern Public Administration: Toward Discourse*, Thousand Oaks, CA: Sage.

Gerth, H. H., & Mills, C. W. (1958). *From Max Weber: Essays in Sociology*, New York: Oxford University Press.

Giddens, A. (1984). *The Constitution of Society: Outline of the Theory of Structuration*, Berkeley: University of California Press.

Colembiewski, R. T. (1977). 'A Critique of "Democratic Administration" and Its Supporting Ideation', *American Political Science Review*, 71, 1488–1507.

Hood, C. (1996). 'Beyond "Progressivism": A New "Global Paradigm" in Public Management?' *International Journal of Public Administration*, 19, 151–177.

Hummerl, R. & Stivers, C. (1998). 'Government isn't us: The Possibility of Democratic Knowledge in Representative Government', in C. K. King & C. Stivers (eds), *Government is Us: Public Administration in an Anti-government Era* (pp. 28–48), Thousand Oaks, CA: Sage.

Jennings, E. T., Jr. (1991). 'Public Choice and the Privatization of Government: Implications for Public Administration', in J. S. Ott, A. C. Hyde, & J. M. Shafritz (eds), *Public Management: The Essential Readings* (pp. 113–29), Chicago: Nelson-Hall.

Johnson, D. B. (1991). *Public Choice: An Introduction to the New Political Economy*, Mountain View, CA: Mayfield.

Kamensky, J. M. (1996). 'Role of the "Reinventing Government" Movement in Federal Management Reform', *Public Administration Review*, 56, 247–55.

Kaplan, R. D. (1997, December). 'Was Democracy Just a Moment?' *Atlantic Monthly*, 280, 55–80.

Kass, H. D. & Catron, B. L. (1990). *Images and Identities in Public Aministration*. Newbury Park, CA: Sage.

Kelly, R. M. (1998). 'An Inclusive Democratic Polity, Representative Bureaucracies, and the New Public Management', *Public Administrtion Review*, 58, 201–8.

Kettl, D. F. (1997). 'The Global Revolution in Public Management: Driving Themes, Missing Links', *Journal of Policy Analysis and Management*, 16, 446–62.

King C. S., & Stivers, C. (1998a). *Government is Us: Public Administration in an Anti-government Era*, Thousand Oaks, CA: Sage.

King C. S., & Stivers, C. (1998b). 'Introduction: The Anti-government Era', in C. S. King & C. Stivers (eds). *Government is Us: Public Administration in an Anti-government Era* (pp. 3–18), Thousand Oaks, CA: Sage.

Lan, Z., & Rosenbloom, D. H. (1992). 'Public Administration in Transition?' *Public Administration Review*, 52, 535–7.

Lasch, C. (1996). *The Revolt of the Elites and the Betrayal of Democracy*, New York: Norton.

Lynn, L. E., Jr. (1998). 'The New Public Management: How to Transform a Theme into a Legacy', *Public Administration Review*, 58, 231–7.

Lyons, W. E. & Lowery, D. (1989). 'Governmental Fragmentation versus Consolidation: Five Public Choice Myths about How to Create Informed, Involved, and Happy Citizens', *Public Administration Review*, 49, 533–43.

March, J. G. (1992). 'The War is Over: The Victors have Lost', *Journal of Public Administration Research and Theory*, 2, 225–31.

McSwite, O. C. (1997). *Legitimacy in Public Administration: A Discourse Analysis*, Thousand Oaks, CA: Sage.

Mikesell, J. A. (1995). *Fiscal Administration: Analysis and Applications for the Public Sector* (4th ed.), Belmont, CA: Wadsworth.

Moe, T. M. (1984). 'The New Economics of Organization', *American Journal of Political Science*, 28, 739–77.

Niskanen, W. A. (1971). *Bureaucracy and Representative Government*, Chicago: Aldine Atherton.

Niskanen, W. A. (1991). 'A Reflection on Bureaucracy and Representative Government', in A. Blais & S. Dion (eds), *The Budget-Maximizing Bureaucrat: Appraisals and Evidence* (pp. 13–31), Pittsburgh, PA: University of Pittsburgh Press.

Olson, M. (1965). *The Logic of Collective Action*, Cambridge, MA: Harvard University Press.

Osborne, D., & Gaebler, T. (1993). *Reinventing Government: How the Entrepreneurial Spirit is Transforming the Public Sector*, New York: Penguin.

Ostrom, V. (1977). 'Some Problems in Doing Political Theory: A Response to

Golembiewski's "Critique"', *American Political Science Review*, 71, 1508–25.

Ostrom, V. (1991). *The Intellectual Crisis in American Public Administration*, Tuscaloosa: University of Alabama Press. (Original work published 1973)

Ostrom, V. (1994). *The Meaning of American Federalism: Constituting a Self-governing Society*, San Francisco: ICS. (Original work published 1991).

Peters, B. G., & Pierre, J. (1998). `Governance Without Government? Rethinking Public Administration', *Journal of Public Administration Research and Theory*, 8, 223–43.

Phares, D. (1989). 'Bigger is Better, or is it Smaller?' *Urban Affairs Quarterly*, 25, 5–17.

Public Administration Review. (1993). Forum on public administration and the Constitution. *Public Administration Review*, 53, 237–67.

Ramos, A. G. (1984). *The New Science of Organizations: A Reconceptualization Of The Wealth of Nations*, Toronto, Canada: University of Toronto Press. (Original work published (1981).

Ross, B. H., & Levine, M. A. (1996). *Urban Politics: Power in Metropolitan America* (5th ed.), Itasca, IL: F. E. Peacock.

Savas, E. S. (1987). *Privatization: The Key to Better Government*, Chatham, NJ: Chatham House.

Schachter, H. L. (1997). *Reinventing Government or Reinventing Ourselves: The Role of Citizen Owners in Making a Better Government*, Albany: State University of New York Press.

Schmidtz, D. (1991). *The Limits of Government: An Essay on the Public Goods Argument*, Bolder, CO: Westview.

Scott, W. G., & Hart, D. K. (1979). *Organizational America*, Boston: Houghton Mifflin.

Simon, H. A. (1997). *Administrative Behaviour: A Study of Decision-making Processes in Administrative Organizations* (4th ed.), New York: Free Press. (Original work published 1945).

Skowronek, S. (1982). *Building a New American State: The Expansion of National Administrative Capacities, 1877–1920*, Cambridge, UK: Cambridge University Press.

Stillman, R. J. II (1991). *Preface to Public Administration: A Search for Themes And Direction*, New York: St. Martin's.

Terry, L. D. (1993). 'Why we Should Abandon the Misconceived Quest to Reconcile Public Entrepreneurship with Democracy', *Public Administration Review*, 53, 393–5.

Terry, L. D. (1998). 'Administrative Leadership, Neo-managerialism, and the Public Management Movement', *Public Administration Review*, 58, 194–200.

Timney, M. M. (1998). Overcoming Administrative Barriers to Citizen Participation: Citizens as Partners, Not Adversaries', in C. S. King & C. Stivers (eds), *Government is Us: Public Administration in an Anti-government Era* (pp. 88–101), Thousand Oaks, CA: Sage.

Waldo. D. (1981). *The Enterprise of Public Administration: A Summary View*, Novato CA: Chandler & Sharp.

Walters, J. (1998, February). 'Did Somebody Say Downsizing?' *Governing*, 11, 17–20.

Waterman, R. W., & Meier, K. J. (1998). 'Principal-agent Models: An Expansion?' *Journal of Public Administration Research and Theory*, 8, 173–202.

Weintraub, J. (1997). 'Public–Private: The Limitations of a Grand Dichotomy', *Responsive Community*, 7, 13–24.

White, L. D. (1954). *The Jacksonians: A Study in Administrative History, 1829–1861*, New York: Macmillan.

Wood, E. M. (1996). *Democracy Against Capitalism: Renewing Historical Materialism*, Cambridge, UK: Cambridge University Press.

Yankelovich, D. (1991). *Coming to Public Judgement: Making Democracy Work in a Complex World*, Syracuse, NY: Syracuse University Press.

PART III

PUBLIC ADMINISTRATION IN INDIA

CHAPTER TEN

The State and Its Permanent Government*

L.I. and S.H. Rudolph

A leading state issue during the founding period that reappeared in the 1970s and will affect the course of events in the 1980s is the kind of policy-level bureaucracy India requires. India became a republic, casting aside the autocratic monarchical doctrines and administrative state of king-emperor and viceroy; a democracy, where for the first time the political masters, those who would represent and govern, were chosen on the basis of universal suffrage; and a welfare and socialist state, committed not only to economic growth and self-reliance but also social justice and national power. The ICS, which had governed and administered the British raj, was available. Acting within the imperial and viceregal tradition, British civil servants under the raj had not only represented state interests but had governed directly; they constituted a colonial version of bureaucratic absolutism. A distant king-emperor and his secretary of state and a viceroy close at hand were political masters of a sort, but the British raj approximated bureaucratic more than monarchical absolutism. The steel frame and the guardians needed and took little political or policy direction. Was such a service suitable for the new state and nation? If it was, what changes in orientation were required of its successor service, the IAS, and could they be realized?[1]

---

* L.I. Rudolph and Susanne Hoeber Rudolph, *In pursuit of Lakshmi: The Political Economy of the Indian State*, University of Chicago Press, Chicago, 1987.

[1] For autobiographical accounts that provide insights into the problematics of this transition, see that of an ICS officer whose experience spanned the British and Indian period, E. N. Mangat Rai (*Commitment My Style* [New Delhi: Vikas, 1973]) and of a civil

At a time when many Third World states were struggling to build qualified and effective career services, the standing of India's senior bureaucracy was exceptional. It gave the state after independence an autonomy and continuity that has persisted in times of uncertainty and unsteady political control at the national and state levels. In the era of Patel and Nehru and, after 1950, in the Nehru era of Congress party dominance, the services were relatively sheltered from challenge and attack. The policy-level bureaucracy returned to the centre of controversy and political debate with the onset of party alternation, a new development for the Indian political system. It began with the election of 1967 and its aftermath, when opposition coalitions governed half of India's sixteen large states, and it became more pronounced with the elections of 1977 and 1980, when the central government changed hands. States issues focusing on the senior civil service were brought to the top of India's political agenda by the temporary sharpening of socialist objectives after the Congress split of 1969 and the ensuing demands for commitment, the strain on the constitutional and legal obligations of civil servants created by the emergency, and the penetration of IAS state cadres by state politics and regional nationalism.

A variety of issues were debated but unresolved. The doctrine of 'neutrality' was challenged by the doctrine of commitment; the meaning and operational consequences of commitment were disputed. The rise of personal loyalty as the test of commitment threatened the viability of career services and a government of law.

The doctrine of neutrality was the product of an era of partisan party competition. In England, such an era followed the coming of political stability in the early eighteenth century and of the concept of loyal opposition in the early nineteenth.[2] The doctrine was exported to India when, at the provincial level in the 1920s, Indian party politicians took charge of a limited range of ministerial portfolios, and it became a central doctrine of state theory at independence when India embarked on its experiments with parliamentary democracy. It was a convenient doctrine. Of the approximately 1,000 ICS officers serving at independence, 453 were Indian and became the policy bureaucracy of the successor states.[3] Neutrality served not

---

servant who joined in the special recruitment just after independence, Mohan Mukerji (*Ham in the Sandwich* [New Delhi: Vikas, 1979]).

[2] See, for example, Ernest Barker, *The Development of the Public Services in Europe* (New York: Oxford University Press, 1944).

[3] For the shift from the ICS to the IAS, see B. B. Misra, *The Bureaucracy in India: An*

only to explain and legitimize their role in the context of party government but also to provide a cover for their translation from political masters and jailers of Congress leaders to loyal servants of the new state.

Congress members of the Constituent Assembly were not easily convinced that the ICS should continue. As yesterday's nationalists, democrats, and reformers, they preferred to rid the state of an imperial legacy known for its elitism and conservatism. But more statist counsel prevailed. Patel, referring to the interim government that took office in November 1946 and the Government of India that came into being on August 15, 1947, warned the Constituent Assembly in 1949: 'I have worked with them during this difficult period ... Remove them and I see nothing but a picture of chaos all over the country.'[4] Nehru, who had been unconvinced, changed his stance as he had done with respect to the INA and the Indian Army: 'The old distinctions and differences are gone. ... In the difficult days ahead our Service and experts have a vital role to play and we invite them to do so as comrades in the service of India.'[5]

Nehru's remarks were premature. 'Distinctions and differences' from the colonial era were not so easily forgotten. The most powerful metaphor for the services, the 'steel frame,' lingered on. The ICS was the vehicle of colonial administration, which featured law and order and the collection of revenue. For nationalists, law and order meant repression; for nationalists and socialists, revenue collection meant a

---

Historical Analysis of Development up to 1947 (New Delhi: Oxford University Press, 1977), pp. 299–308. Misra, citing Home Department file no. 30/28/47-ESB(S), reports that there were 980 ICS officers on January 1, 1947. Of these, 468 were Europeans, 352 were Hindus other than 'depressed classes,' and 101 were Muslims. The balance were from other religious and social communities (p. 306 n. 163).

[4] As quoted in W. H. Morris-Jones, *The Government and Politics of India*, 3d. rev. ed. (London: Hutchinson, 1971), p. 26. Patel insisted, on pain of his own and the entire ICS's resignation, that the Drafting Committee of the Constituent Assembly include constitutional guarantees protecting conditions of service for the ICS comparable to those enjoyed under the raj. Patel told Constituent Assembly members opposed to guarantees for the ICS, 'If you decide that we should not have the service at all, in spite of my pledged word, I will take the service with me and I will go. I will tell the servicemen, "Let us go. The nation has changed." They are capable of earning their living' (T. V. Kunhi Krishna, *Chavan and the Troubled Decade*, [Bombay: Somaiya Publications, 1971], p. 273, as quoted in Francine R. Frankel, *India's Political Economy, 1947–1977* [New Delhi: Oxford University Press, 1978], pp. 80–81 n. 24).

[5] Jawaharlal Nehru, *Independence and After* (New York: John Day, 1950), p. 9, as quoted in Robert L. Hardgrave, Jr., *India: Government and Politics in a Developing Nation*, 3rd ed. (New York: Harcourt Brace Jovanovich, 1980), p. 71.

failure to promote economic growth and social justice.[6] The steel frame was a negative metaphor until, in the face of the difficulties of governing the country, it lost its pejorative meaning. A new question emerged: was the steel frame strong enough and neutral enough? It became apparent in the late seventies, even as the position of the services was subject to buffeting from all sides, that a steel frame was useful for maintaining continuity and stability and sustaining national integration. In the face of their dramatic deterioration, maintaining law and order acquired new standing as an administrative virtue rather than a colonial vice.

'The guardians' was another image from the colonial era that lingered on after independence to provide a target for nationalists, democrats, and socialists. Philip Mason, a leading scholar of the ICS and himself a member of it, used the phrase to characterize it. He explicitly compared its self-image and outlook to those of the rulers in Plato's *Republic*, whose special knowledge of the good made them superior to ordinary men and justified their rule over them.[7] Translated into vulgar imperial relations, the guardians were the bearers of the white man's burden, the `heaven-born' superior beings whose duty it was to civilize the lesser breeds without the law and to enlighten the benighted. The guardian and heaven-born mentality lingered on, providing that special sense of calling that fortified IAS officers against the often philistine and populist onslaughts of democratic politicians, the elected representatives and ministers who were their newly installed masters. It lingered on too in the mistaken belief that amateur generalists were equipped to perform the technical and expert tasks involved in managing a vast and complex industrial and

---

[6] Stanley Heginbotham has disaggregated four organizational ideologies of civil servants, among which the 'colonial' is one. See his *Cultures in conflict; The Four Faces of Indian Bureaucracy* (New York: Columbia University Press, 1975).

[7] Philip Woodruff, *The Men Who Ruled India*, 2 vols (New York: Schocken, 1967). Mason used Woodruff as a pseudonym when he published his remarkable if apologetic biographical and historical study of raj administrators. Also useful are B. B. Misra, *The Administrative History of India, 1834–1947* (Oxford: Oxford University Press, 1970); and David C. Potter, 'Bureaucratic Change in India,' and Bernard S. Cohn, 'Recruitment and Training of British Civil Servants in India, 1600–1860,' in Ralph Braibanti, ed., *Asian Bureaucratic Systems Emergent from the Imperial Tradition* (Durham, N. C.: Duke University Press, 1966). W. H. Morris-Jones's chapter on governance in *Government and Politics of India* (chap. 4) still provides the best short account of the services. Henry Hart has provided a thoughtful recent assessment of governance: 'Political Leadership in India: Dimensions and Limits' (Paper presented at the Conference on India's Democracy, Princeton University, March 14–16, 1985).

financial public sector, and in an ideology that state servants were uniquely equipped to speak for the public interest.

The guardian mentality also provided ample ammunition to those who demanded that the civil service shed its superior airs and become more socially representative, on the mistaken premise that those who were of the people would ipso facto be for the people. It is doubtful whether a more socially representative IAS composed of the children of middle and small cultivators or of urban petty traders would be more socialist, secular, or democratic than the children of the English-educated professionals who have been disproportionately represented in the senior and central services.[8] In much of the furor about representativeness, class style and more equal opportunities for social mobility were as often the issue as ideological orientation. In any case, as ministers and elected representatives became more rural and less professional, educated, and anglicized, they found their role as political masters threatened and compromised by state servants cut from the very different cloth of elite colleges and high-income urban and professional families.[9] Noting that 80 to 95 per cent of India's higher civil service, as in most other countries, was drawn from the professional middle classes, they called for a more socially representative bureaucracy.[10]

[8] V. Subramaniam reports that 89,81,77,80, and 79 per cent, respectively, of entrants to the Indian Foreign Service, IAS, Indian Police Service, Audit and Accounts Service, and Customs and Postal Services between 1957 and 1963 were from families whose father's occupation was 'professional middle class,' (e.g., higher or lower civil servant, employee of a private firm, school-teacher, professor, doctor, and lawyer). See his *Social Background of India's Administrators* (New Delhi: Government of India, Publications Division, 1971), table 6. See also David C. Potter, 'The Indian Civil Service Tradition within the Bureaucratic Structures of State Power in South Asia: 1919–1978' (Paper presented at the Sixth European Conference on Modern South Asian Studies, 1978; published as a pamphlet by the Centre National de la Recherche Scientifique [Paris], 1978).

[9] For an insightful discussion of the strains between state servants and their political masters in India, see Richard P. Taub, *Bureaucrats under Stress* (Berkeley and Los Angeles: University of California Press, 1969).

[10] For the original use of the term 'representative bureaucracy,' see J. Donald Kingsley, *Representative Bureaucracy*, (Yellow Springs, Ohio: Antioch Press, 1944); for an able critique see V. Subramaniam, 'Representative Bureaucracy.' For a more recent restatement, see Samuel Krislov, *Representative Bureaucracy* (Englewood Cliffs, N. J.: Prentice-Hall, 1974). Subramaniam presents data for six countries for 1957–63, showing the middle-class origins of their higher services (p. 1016). He also notes that such origins make a civil service more representative in a society where the middle classes compose 60 per cent of the work force (e.g., the United States) than in one where they constitute nine per cent (e.g., India) (p. 1015).

At the national level, the disparity in educational levels and cultural styles was less marked and caused less difficulty than at the state level. During the Nehru era, the ICS and the IAS were Nehru's allies as well as state servants. The shared objective of national power through the creation of a modern society and economy overrode whatever differences there may have been with respect to socialist commitment.[11] As Nehru's coauthors and implementors, civil servants were the vanguard of the lobby for an industrial strategy, collaborating in the creation of basic and heavy industry under the second and third five-year plans. They brought into being the third actor in the Indian economy, the state sector, which rivaled and then surpassed private capital and organized labor. As the 'new class' of a semisocialist state, they were among its principal beneficiaries. In Marxist terms, the policy bureaucracy of the permanent government was a leading element of the progressive national bourgeoisie, dominating state policy and being rewarded for it. Its members shared a common life-style; they talked the same languages, not only the king's English but also state capitalism, science and technology, and secularism. And they were 'committed' to the government's policies and programmes.

A distinguished member of the ICS entitled his administrative autobiography *Commitment My Style*. He found that the services were 'infinitely more efficient' following the departure of the British at independence. The reason was the enormous challenge and 'bursting promise' of administration at that time. 'It is policy and direction, integrity and depth, that give [the civil servant] cohesion and knit him, in spite of heterogeneity, to the thrust of effective, massive organization, pursuing and achieving difficult and complex tasks... It is in the failure of policy, direction and integrity' that 'our present [1973] malaise' is to be located.[12]

After Nehru's death (May 1964) and two successions (1964 and 1966), the alliance forged between a prime minister and a policy bureaucracy to build a powerful nation fell on evil days. It was

[11] At the state level, see, for example, Mangat Rai's discussion of the administrative-political collaboration in constructing the Punjab's contributions to economic development, including the Bhakra Dam and the Punjab Agricultural University at Ludhiana. He also provides microdata, of which much more is needed, to support or discredit the unproven proposition that the IAS is not development minded. His instances tend to fall fairly evenly on the pro and con sides of the argument. See, for example, *Commitment My Style*, p.133. For a detailed account of development work at the local level by senior officers, see Stanley Heginbotham, *Cultures in Conflict*.

[12] Rai, *Commitment My Style*, pp. viii, ix.

shaken by the weak direction and confused initiatives of less able and confident national leadership and by the onset, even before Nehru's death, of Congress's decline, followed by the first signs of party alternation (1967).

Neutrality as a doctrine was a suitable rationalization for the transition from imperial rule to party government. It posed few problems so long as one-party dominance put no strain on the loyalty of civil servants.[13] But it began to be questioned when civil servants were asked to serve a variety of party masters in the states after 1967 and at the centre after 1977. Mrs Gandhi successfully challenged the old guard state bosses by backing radical policies such as bank nationalization, split the Congress in November 1969, and then twice led Congress to victory—first early in 1971 with the slogan 'abolish poverty', then in the 1972 'khaki election' that followed the Bangladesh war. It was in this context—of a weak and divided Congress organization and the striking early success of the plebiscitary politics that were to become her hallmark—that Mrs Gandhi called for a committed civil service. Speaking to the Congress parliamentary party, she referred to the administrative machinery as a stumbling block, adding 'the country would be in a rut' if it followed the British system in which civil servants were not supposed to be concerned with which political party was in power. Her then colleagues but future political opponents, the Congress's left leaders Chandra Shekhar and Mohan Dharia, joined her call for the 'creation of an administrative cadre committed to national objectives and responsive to our social needs.' 'The present bureaucracy, under the orthodox and conservative leadership of the ICS with its conservative upper-class prejudices can hardly be expected to meet the requirements of social and economic change along socialist lines.'[14] In 1972, the Gandhi government, in the name of equality, abolished by amendment constitutionally protected perquisites of the ICS. The gesture was not only vindictive but also gratuitous, since only eighty ICS officers remained in service, but it had high symbolic payoffs for a leader professing socialism and egalitarianism.[15]

[13] For an account and explanation of bureaucratic responsiveness in the 1970s, see Dennis J. Encarnation, 'The Indian Central Bureaucracy: Responsive to Whom?' *Asian Survey* 19, no. 11 (November 1979): 1126–45.

[14] Cited in C. P. Bhambhri, *Administrators in a Changing Society* (New Delhi: National Publishing House, 1972), p. 24. For a series of case studies that illuminate the relationships between senior bureaucrats and politicians, see also his *Bureaucracy and Politics in India* (New Delhi: Vikas, 1971).

[15] In September 1972, in a renewed effort, this time successful, to eliminate the

Mrs Gandhi was not satisfied when civil servants and public figures argued that neutrality meant giving one's best to the government of the day, from policy advice to ministers to programme implementation. For her, commitment went beyond active support for Congress programmes to belief in the party leader's mandate from the people. She wanted a style of commitment more suited to a bureaucracy serving a single party and its leader than to one serving alternating-party governments.[16] In the face of party deinstitutionalization and the rise of plebiscitary politics, she attempted to substitute state bureaucracies for party based organizational support.

Mrs Gandhi also wanted commitment of the sort patrimonial rulers command: personal loyalty to herself and, from 1975, to her son Sanjay. This view of commitment fed and grew first on prudence, then on opportunism and, under the emergency, on fear. Better to show loyalty even to the extent of bending or breaking the law than to risk disfavour or punishment by too principled conduct.

When the Janata party swept the Congress emergency regime from office in 1977, it further muddied the doctrinal waters, complicating and compounding the issue of appropriate behaviour for civil servants. It meant to restore the doctrine and practice of neutrality. In fact, it began to discipline or put on trial the civil service loyalists of the emergency era who had engaged in excesses. The Janata government favoured not just upright professionals but also those committed to its own people and measures. Some of its ministers confused good ends with partisan advantage and correct procedure with victimization. When Mrs Gandhi returned to power in 1980, her party government, often invoking Janata examples and precedents, restored to office and favor those whom Janata had found most culpable.[17] As

---

guarantees Sardar Patel had insisted on putting in the 1950 Constitution, Parliament passed the Former Secretary of State Service Officer (Conditions of Service) Bill. It became the Twentieth Amendment Act, 1972, revoking article 314 of the constitution, which had committed the Indian state to maintain the same conditions of service and rights as those enjoyed by ICS officers under the British raj. As a result, ICS officers served under the less favourable terms applicable to IAS officers.

[16] D. P. Dhar, planning minister and a Gandhi loyalist 'pleaded for a civil service which is committed not only to the policies and ideas enshrined in the Constitution but also the policies and programmes of the ruling party which was backed by a majority of the people in the country' (quoted in Vishnu Sahay, 'What Does it Mean,' *Seminar*, cited by K. K. Tummala, *The Ambiguity of Ideology and Administrative Reform* [Bombay: Allied, 1977], p. 177).

[17] The roster of national-level reassignments in 1975, 1977, and 1980 is long and complex, and they were by no means all mala fide. Illustrations of some widely

India entered the 1980s and victims became heroes and heroes victims, all three doctrines—neutrality, commitment, and loyalty—had to be reargued in the light of a transformed historical context.

With the rise of alternating-party or coalition governments, the need for a politically 'neutral' but *professionally* committed policy bureaucracy that can shift masters has become more pressing. India's interventionist, managerial state can no longer pretend that its policy bureaucracy is neutral in the sense or being anonymous and voiceless.[18] At the cabinet level, effective policy coordination and guidance requires officials who are loyal to the responsible minister and

---

considered to be so are the following: the abrupt removal of N. K. Mukherjee, ICS, as Home Secretary when the emergency was declared; Mukherjee was posted to the Department of Tourism. T. C. A. Srinivasavardhan, due to retire, was replaced as home secretary by M. H. Burney when Congress returned to power in 1980. Burney had been secretary, Ministry of Information and Broadcasting, a critical emergency department and was considered an emergency stalwart. Burney was sent back to Orissa, to whose cadre he belonged, when Janata came to power. His next in line at the Ministry of Information and Broadcasting, M. K. N. Prasad, who handled press censorship under the emergency, was transferred by Janata to the relatively harmless Police Research Bureau. The director of the Central Bureau of Investigation under Janata was transferred by Congress in 1980 to his home state of Tamil Nadu. The 1980 Congress appointments most widely criticized were the promotion, over the seniority claims of many others, of P. S. Bhinder to police commissioner of Delhi and the promotion of Jag Mohan, Delhi development commissioner under the emergency, to lieutenant governor of Delhi (a union territory). Both were close to Sanjay Gandhi and figured centrally in the Shah Commission's examination of emergency excesses. They were associated with Sanjay's beautification programs that led inter alia to the highly controversial clearance of Muslim quarters around the Jama Masjid and Turkman Gate. Bhinder, in particular, was responsible for police arrangements when many poor Muslims who rioted at Turkman Gate against slum clearance and vasectomy camps died as a result of police firing (*Statesman*, April 13, 1980 and Government of India, Ministry of Home Affairs, *Shah Commission of Inquiry: Interim Report II* [Delhi, 1978], chaps, 8, 9, particularly pp, 96–101, 120–46). For an up-close account by a craftsmanly administrator in the: emergency, see Mohan Mukerji, *Non-story of a Chief Secretary During Emergency, Etcetera* (New Delhi: Associated Publishing House, 1982).

[18] Rajni Kothari believed that the cure for a rule-bound and routinized bureaucracy characterized by lack of trust, confidence, and spontaneity was a radical restructuring of the relationship between bureaucracy and party: 'The point of all this is to politicize the administration' (*Democratic Polity and Social Change in India* [Bombay: Allied, 1976], pp. 67–9). In the perspective of the 1980s, such a critique and cure need to address the balance between the legal obligations and programmatic obligations of civil servants on the one hand and demands for purely partisan resource and patronage allocation on the other. In 'Where Are We Heading,' *Express Magazine*, November 29, 1981, Kothari wrote a powerful polemic along lines similar to those advanced here. He argued for 'an institutional framework that protects the country from both the cult of personality and the politics of survival.'

committed to the minister's policies. But it also requires that ministers are themselves professional. In France, prime ministers and cabinet ministers have for some time drawn directors and chiefs of ministerial 'cabinets' from senior civil servants who seemed loyal to them personally as well as committed to their policy objectives. It is assumed that if senior officials are to help a minister make and coordinate policy they must loyally share the minister's interests, a mix of policy and politics distinct from and often in conflict with both the interests of the permanent bureaus and the organized interests in relevant policy arenas.[19] In America, at least since the creation of the executive office of the president in 1939, loyal as well as committed president's men have been a legitimate feature of policy bureaucracies at the cabinet and subcabinet as well as the presidential level. Often drawn from outside the ranks of the senior civil service, policy intellectuals and professionals are chosen for personal loyalty as well as for their special knowledge and policy commitment. They become members of a responsible political official's team and are vital to that official's ability to make and control policy.[20] In Britain, the Fulton Commission recommended that civil servants publicly explain and defend government policy. India's Administrative Reforms Commission of 1966 failed to deal with the issue, recommending only that the present arrangements be properly adhered to.[21]

Policy innovation and coordination require an Indian version of French and American institutional arrangements that will mitigate if not eliminate the struggle over neutrality, commitment, and loyalty. However, in the early 1980s, commitment and loyalty were not being interpreted in policy and professional terms. Instead many ministers,

[19] See Ezra N. Suleiman, *Politics, Power and Bureaucracy in France: The Administrative Elite* (Princeton: Princeton University Press, 1974), chaps. 8, 9, pp. 181–238.

[20] For an extended discussion of loyalty and team spirit in bureaucracies, see our 'Authority and Power in Bureaucratic and Patrimonial Administration: A Revisionist Interpretation of Weber on Bureaucracy,' *World Politics* 31 (January 1979).

[21] The Administrative Reforms Commission found that the principal weakness of India's higher civil service (IAS) was the supremacy of the generalist and 'generalism.' Its solution was to recommend that specialists and experts be given more senior posts and to call for more professionalism in the outlook and training of the senior bureaucracy (Government of India, Ministry of Home Affairs, Administrative Reforms Commission, *Report of the Study Team on the Machinery of the Government of India and Its Procedures at Work* [New Delhi, 1968]), pt. 2, vol. 1, pp. 106–7. See also Shriman Maheshwari, *The Administrative Reforms Commission* (Agra, India: Lakshmi Narain Agarwal, 1972). For an account that argues that professionalization leads to rigidity, and that criticizes insulation of bureaucracies, see Encarnation, 'Indian Central Bureaucracy.'

behind a facade of policy concerns, were more interested in patronage that served partisan and personal interests. Loyalty and commitment became willingness on part of civil servants to accommodate themselves to ministerial manipulations of this kind. Rajiv Gandhi's managerial orientation toward government; his reluctance to use the services for political and personal ends to the extent his mother did, and the resuscitation in 1985 and 1986 of the Administrative Reforms Commission's recommendations favouring professionalization and specialization of the services; provided a more favourable climate for dealing with this issue.

The demand that the IAS shed its superior airs and become more 'socially representative' has been fulfilled in ways not anticipated by its proponents. The real salaries of senior officials both in the public services (IAS, Indian Foreign Service, Indian Police Service) and in public-sector enterprises declined significantly in the 1970s. The highly differential levels of 'dearness allowance'—the inflation equalizer in government salaries—had the effect of eroding the emoluments of lower level clerks by two per cent while those of higher officers and public-sector executives eroded by as much as 37 per cent. The ratio between the highest and lowest paid in government shrank from 15: 1 in 1973 to 10: 1 in 1978.[22] Only in 1986 was this erosion halted and reversed by the report of the pay commission.

The more socially representative political milieu of state governments also weakened the IAS's national orientation and professional ethos.[23] The ways in which civil servants are posted have enabled local politicians to appropriate administration to partisan and personal ends. Frequent transfers, which render the life of a civil servant more difficult by disrupting the schooling of his or her children and the routines of life, have long been used by influential politicians to bring to heel or oust inflexible officers that resist inappropriate requests for resource allocation.

The 1984 crisis in the Punjab made it clear that civil and police services were incapable of maintaining public order. One cause was the capture of the services by local factions and communities. The formula for allocating officers of the centrally recruited but state-assigned IAS required that persons from the state not make up more than 50 per cent of the state cadre. The rationale for the formula was

---

[22] Government of India, Ministry of Finance, *Study Group on Wages, Incomes and Prices: Report* (Delhi, 1978), tables 14, 15. (This is generally referred to as the Boothalingam Report.

[23] For an early intimation of this problem, see Taub, *Bureaucrats under Stress.*

'to insure that officials were not subject to local pressures and took a more objective and national view.'[24] When Prime Minister Gandhi addressed an extraordinary meeting of secretaries to the Government of India soon after the Indian army had battled its way into the Golden Temple in June 1984, she 'voiced concern over the growing tendency on the part of state government to dilute the original formula by not only reducing the proportion of officers hailing from other states but also making a systematic effort to remove them from key administrative positions.'[25] She revealed that the fifty-fifty rule had been breached to the extent that 70 rather than 50 per cent of IAS officers were serving in their state of origin.

The public services have not always strengthened the state as entrepreneur. The inability of the IAS to manage undertakings in the enormous public sector efficiently and profitably has contributed to the erosion of the Indian state. But for a few exceptional years, India's public sector has been in the red. Over the thirty-year period between 1950 and 1980, the incremental capital-output ratio for India as a whole has deteriorated, but in the public sector the position is considerably worse. For the economy as a whole, the ratio has roughly doubled (from 2.79 to 6.22), while in the public sector it has more than tripled (from 3.12 to 10.58).[26] We have discussed in chapter one the disputes over the meaning of these figures. Many critics have attributed some portion of this failure to the role of generalist IAS officers in public-sector undertakings. This role is played at two levels, policy guidance and the management of firms. Public-sector firms, instead of being allowed to operate autonomously, have been brought de facto under the close supervision of government ministries, whose IAS officer secretaries to government not only guide long-term policy—which is appropriate—but also intervene in day-to-day decisions. As a former chairman of the Food Corporation of India, one of the largest public-sector undertakings has observed, 'Generally the ministries adopt a superior fatherly attitude, trying to run the whole show. The autonomy of [public-sector undertakings] is reduced to a myth, since all decisions of importance and magnitude are taken by them.'[27]

[24] *Hindu,* June 23,1984.

[25] Ibid.

[26] P. R. Brahmananda, *Productivity in the Indian Economy* (Bombay: Himalaya Publishing House, 1982), table 19.02.

[27] R. N. Chopra, *Public Sector in India* (New Delhi, Intellectual Publishing House, [c. 1983]), p. 85. For an account of conflict between the IAS and technical officers in the

The management of public-sector firms needs career professionals who combine technical knowledge with long-term experience in particular technologies and industries, such as steel, oil, transportation, and mining. The IAS officers do not possess such knowledge and skills, and their career experience fails to develop it. The insulation of IAS generalists from an understanding of their relevant specialties is illustrated by the career patterns of the officers in the Ministry of Information and Broadcasting, charged with overseeing Doordarshan, India's state-run television. In 1983, all three of the ministry's senior officers left before completing two years of service in that post. One had come from the chairmanship of the State Electricity Board of Madhya Pradesh and gone on to become secretary in the Coal Department; one had come from being commissioner of a division in Maharashtra and returned to manage that state's State Finance Corporation; and one had come from district administration and left for a training course abroad. 'It is hardly to be expected', wrote the Joshi Working Group on Doordarshan, 'that the problems of Doordarshan ... can be appreciated and resolved by such birds of passage.'[28]

The generalist traditions of IAS officers and the frequency with which they are transferred militate against their performance as managers of the still-expanding public sector. At the level of the states, IAS officers occupy 75 per cent of the posts of chief executive officers of public-sector firms and their average tenure in such posts is fifteen months.[29] Occasionally, a good IAS officer is exempted from the rapid turnover characteristic of the service and can develop expertise via extended incumbency, but such experiences are the exception.

In 1986, the Rajiv Gandhi government introduced measures to address the professional quality of the services and insulate them from inappropriate political pressures. Many of these measures were based on recommendations of the Administrative Reforms Commission of 1966. The government proposed to prevent frequent transfers of officers, to protect them against appropriation by local interests, to

---

public sector, see Howard Erdman, 'Politics and Industrial Management: The IAS in Joint Sector Fertilizer Companies,' *Journal of the Institute of Public Enterprises*, January–March 1986.

[28] 'An Indian Personality for Television: Report of the Working Group on Software for Doordarshan,' pt. 2, published unofficially in *Mainstream*, April 14, 21, and 28, 1984 and May 1984 (Nehru no.).

[29] K. S. Bhat, 'Tenure of the Chief Executives and Composition of the Board: Two Issues in SLPE Corporate Management' (Hyderabad, 1984, mimeograph). The author is on the faculty of the Institute of Public Enterprise, Osmania University Campus.

encourage specialization, and to break the monopoly of the IAS on the highest positions by opening alternative recruitment channels to high-quality candidates from technical services and the nongovernment sector. Only time can tell whether these measures will survive opposition and achieve their goal.[30]

India was endowed at independence with a permanent government that surpassed that of other Third World countries and rivaled those of many industrial democracies. The forces that have challenged the services since independence, such as the call for partisan and personal commitment and regional loyalty are powerful and long term. They have taken their toll, but they have not as yet prevailed.

---

[30] In January of 1986, the Ministry of Personnel and Administrative Reforms proposed a scheme by which newly appointed IAS officers would have no more than three appointments in their first eleven years, including the two probationary years; new entrants would be encouraged to specialize; senior officers in their seventeenth year would be subject to 'data based performance assessment' before further promotion; officers would be selected into an 'integrated management pool' from the three all-India services (Indian Police Service, IAS, Indian Forest Service) and other central services on the basis of proven administrative ability to fill senior positions in the administration; and entrants to the all-India services would be assigned to one of five zonal cadres instead of the present practice of assignment to a state, to break up the locality-based cliques and factions into which officers are now frequently drawn (*Times of India*, January 29, 1986; *Statesman*, January 18 and January 29, 1986).

CHAPTER ELEVEN

Civil Service
Continuity and Change*

P.C. Alexander

The administrative framework which India inherited at the time of independence was one which had continued for nearly a century under British rule. The founding fathers of the republic had wisely decided to adopt all the institutions of the parliamentary system of democracy in the United Kingdom which they considered useful for India. The most important among these were an independent judiciary, a free press, legislatures elected on universal adult franchise, an executive responsible and accountable to the legislature and a permanent civil service which was selected on competitive merit and working on the principle of political neutrality and impartiality. Even though the civil service which independent India inherited had been designed to serve the interests of the colonial power, the leaders of the new nation were convinced that with a suitable orientation and redefinition of the role of the civil service the old administrative system could effectively be used to serve the requirements of the *sovereign democratic republic* which was being established.[1]

The new role of the civil service was that it should serve the basic objectives laid down in the preamble of the Constitution, namely to secure for all citizens: 'justice, social, economic and political, liberty

---

* Hiranmoy Kalekar (ed.), *Independent India: The First Fifty Years*, Oxford University Press, Delhi, 1998.

[1] A Constitutional amendment later made it into a 'sovereign, socialist, secular, democratic republic'.

of thought, expression, belief, faith and worship, equality of status and opportunity and to promote among them all, fraternity assuring the dignity of the individual and the unity and integrity of the nation.' Article 38 of the Constitution had proclaimed as a directive principle of state policy that the state 'shall strive to promote the welfare of the people by securing and protecting as effectively as it may a social order in which justice, social, economic and political, shall inform all the institutions of national life.'

When the East India Company established its first organized cadre of civil servants in India in 1765, it was with the sole objective of assisting it to collect revenues from the people of Bengal, Bihar and Orissa where the Company had been granted the Diwani or the right to collect revenues by the Mughal emperor. The dual role of the East India Company as trader and ruler continued till 1833 by which time the Company had acquired control over extensive territories all over India. The Company in its new role as ruler recognized the need for establishing a bureaucracy exclusively devoted to administration unburdened by any responsibility for trading operations and started creating one. In 1853, the Company accepted the most distinctive feature of the Covenanted Civil Service of India which became the Indian Civil Service (ICS) after India came under the direct rule of the British Crown in 1858—selection through competitive examinations.[2] In the early years the service was open only to university graduates in Britain in the age group of 18–23. The selection of civil servants at a young age on merit, and training them before assigning them to the tasks of administration thus became the recognized principles of the new bureaucracy from the middle of the nineteenth century. Efficiency and honesty were the hallmarks of the service which everyone was expected to live up to.

It was an exclusive service of white men when it was first established. In due course Indians came to be admitted to the service, but the role of the civil service remained essentially one of preserving and strengthening British power in India. During the period of the freedom struggle under the leadership of Mahatma Gandhi, civil servants, particularly those serving in executive positions in the districts, had become the visible symbols of British domination over India and thus an attitude of distrust and confrontation had developed between the people of India and members of the civil service. In the eyes

---

[2] The nomenclature 'Indian Civil Service' was given statutory recognition by the Indian Civil Service Act of 1861.

of the common people bureaucrats, including the Indian members of the civil service, were instruments of repressing the peoples' movement and the main pillars of foreign rule. However, the senior leaders of the freedom movement had little doubt about the patriotism of Indian members of the civil service. They understood that when these bureaucrats jailed freedom fighters and tried to suppress the movement, they were only carrying out the law which they were bound to enforce. The national leaders were confident that they could effectively use the administrative machinery which they inherited from the British to achieve the goals of the new republic. Therefore, when independence came, they were willing to extend to civil servants all the safeguards and guarantees necessary for functioning with impartiality and without fear.

At the time of framing the Constitution there was a debate on whether the guarantee of permanency of tenure for civil servants should be constitutional or statutory. Sardar Patel, who was Home Minister in Jawaharlal Nehru's cabinet, wrote to Nehru strongly supporting constitutional guarantees for civil servants. In his letter of 27 April 1948 he stated: 'Constitutional guarantees and safeguards are the best medium of protection for these services and are likely to prove more lasting. On the other hand if we leave matters to be regulated by central or by provincial legislature the chances of interference with the services and seriously prejudicing their efficiency on account of the interaction of central and provincial politics are closer.' Sardar Patel's strong views on this subject were eventually reflected in Article 311 of the Constitution which stated that no civil servant shall be dismissed or removed or reduced in rank except after an enquiry in which he has been informed of the charges against him and given a reasonable opportunity of being heard in respect of those charges. With this guarantee civil servants felt assured that they could discharge their duties without fear of oppression or discrimination.

The new civil service for all practical purposes was the continuation of the old one with the difference that it was now to function in a parliamentary system of government, accepting the undoubted primacy of the political executive which in turn was responsible to the people through their elected representatives in the legislature. The change-over for civil servants belonging to the old colonial administration, to the new culture of democracy with accountability to elected representatives of the people, was remarkably smooth.

Bureaucrats of the pre-Independence Indian Civil Service occupied almost all senior positions in the administrative hierarchy during the first two-and-a-half decades of independence. Gradually the old civil servants started fading out through retirement and by the 1970s almost all senior positions in the bureaucracy, both at the centre and the states, had come to be occupied by members of the post-Independence service. Even though the last member of the Indian Civil Service (ICS) retired only in March 1980, the Indian bureaucracy at all senior levels during the last two-and-a-half decades consisted mainly of those recruited after Independence.

HAVE STANDARDS OF EFFICIENCY DECLINED?

A widely held perception in the country about the bureaucracy is that the standards of efficiency have deteriorated seriously since the pre-Independence days. The assumption behind this assessment is that a decline in standards was inevitable because of the vast increase in the numbers recruited every year after Independence. But is it correct to assume that an increase in the number of recruits to the ivil service would necessarily lead to dilution of quality? A fact ten forgotten in such an assumption is that recruitment to the all-ndia civil services is now from a much larger base compared with the base in pre-independence days. It is not that more people are now loing the same work done in the past. The need for larger numbers of cruits arose because of the vast expansion in the activities of the government consequent on it taking on responsibilities for various development programmes.

In the early years of the ICS, candidates who appeared for the selection examinations were mainly the products of British public schools and of half-a-dozen well-known universities of the United Kingdom such as Oxford, Cambridge and London. Most of the Indians selected through the examinations held in Britain were from families which could afford the expenses involved in sending their boys to the United Kingdom for their education and for competing in the selection examinations. Higher education in India was then largely the privilege of the affluent classes and the number of people who could compete in the selection examinations was relatively very small. Compared with the old system of selection from a very limited base, the selection now is through a process in which a very large number of young men and women from all social backgrounds get an equal chance. In spite of a very large base of selection, the numbers ultimately selected are very small, making the selection process a very strict one. Let us take as an example from the statistics of selection to the 1995 batch of the civil service:

1. Number of applicants for the preliminary examinations.   2,57,651
2. Number of candidates who appeared for the preliminary   1,30,088
   examinations.
3. Number who qualified for the main examination.   11,847
4. Number selected for the interview.   1,456
5. Number selected for all the central services including   705
   the IAS[3] & IPS[4]
6. Number finally selected for the IAS out of the five above   80

It will be seen from these figures that only 705 candidates, i.e. 0.54 per cent of the 1,30,088 who took the preliminary examination made the grade in the final list. Out of these only 80, that is, 0.06 per cent of those who took the examination were selected for the IAS. It is doubtful whether there is a stricter selection for civil services in any other country in the world than the one followed in India now.

It is also important to state in this connection that the candidates who take the examination for the civil service now come from all disciplines of higher education—engineering, technology, management, medicine—besides arts and sciences. We can find in the final list of the selected candidates some of the best products of the Indian universities including Indian institutes of technology, Indian institutes of management and so on. With this system of very stringent screening and selection, it will be unfair to say that standards of recruitment to the civil services have deteriorated in the post-Independence years.

The question then is whether after recruitment and training standards of efficiency tend to deteriorate. We have to understand correctly the concept of standards of efficiency. If civil servants in the past did not attract public criticism or adverse comment from legislators, this by itself cannot be a criterion for concluding that their

---

[3] After Independence, the Indian Civil Service (ICS) was redesignated the Indian Administrative Service (IAS). The principles and pattern of recruitment, however, remained basically the same.

[4] IPS stands for Indian Police Service, the superior all-India Police Service. The other all-India services include the Indian Foreign Service, Indian Audit and Accounts Service, Indian Revenue Service (Income Tax), Indian Revenue Service (Customs), the Indian Railway Service (Traffic), Indian Railway Accounts Service, Indian Posts and Telegraph Service, Indian Postal Accounts Service, Indian Information Service, and so on.

standards of performance were higher than those of civil servants today. Here one should take into account the vastly different nature of the responsibilities and the work environment of civil servants now and before Independence. The civil servant in pre-Independence days had the relatively easy tasks of revenue collection and maintenance of law and order. Today civil servants have, in addition, to cope with the whole range of development administration. They have also to acquire knowledge and skills in many areas of work rarely needed under the colonial regime. Negotiations for bilateral trade agreements, participation in discussions in international fora such as the International Monetary Fund, the World Bank, the World Trade Organization, and so on; responsibilities for export promotion, industrial development, family planning and a variety of other such tasks which today's civil servants have to perform demand much greater versatility and competence compared with the duties of those in pre-Independence years.

The civil servant today works within the parameters of a full-fledged democracy, which means a vigilant press, an alert public and a watchful legislature, while those in pre-Independence days worked in a relatively protected atmosphere. They were responsible to executives who in most cases were themselves senior civil servants and with whom they shared a common work culture. On the other hand today's civil servants work under politicians who are accountable to the people who elect them.

The civil servant today is really a servant of the people while his predecessors in service represented the authority of the colonial power. The people who were *subjects* of the British rulers of the past are *masters* today and any comparison between the working of civil servants in pre-Independence days and now will not be fair if basic differences in the environment and nature of work are overlooked.

The perception of a deterioration in standards of efficiency in the civil service should also be seen in the context of the widely-held belief in our country that standards in every profession have deteriorated compared to those in the old days. The trend in our country is to decry the standards of all professions today and to think of the old days as something of a 'golden age'. Any discerning observer would know that 'old' was not necessarily 'gold' in all cases. To state this is certainly not to offer an excuse for the decline in standards of efficiency in individual cases; it is only a plea that generalizations about the deterioration in standards are not fair.

Bureaucrats and Politicians

The crucial area where bureaucrats have to face most of the challenges and problems today is their relations with politicians. The most difficult among the problems are those related to decision-making.

In a parliamentary democracy there can be no doubt as to who is the final authority in decision-making; it is always the political executive because he has the mandate of the people through the electoral process to take decisions. This does not mean that every decision has to be taken at the level of the minister. In day-to-day administration a vast range of decisions is taken by bureaucrats without having to seek the approval of ministers. Among the bureaucrats themselves all cases do not move up to the top levels for decisions; many are disposed of by officers at the intermediate levels without the officers at the top having to see them.

There are no hard-and-fast rules about the type of cases which should move up to a secretary for decision or which should move from the bureaucratic level to the minister. There are some well-established practices which serve as guidelines to officers in this matter. In some offices there may also be written orders laying down clearly the levels at which particular decisions are to be taken. But even where such instructions exist, there is considerable scope for discretion with the bureaucracy. Some bureaucrats who wish to play safe may push up every case to the minister for orders. There may also be some ministers who want every case to be put up to them for their orders. Rigid rules about division of responsibilities between bureaucrats and ministers therefore become difficult.

A distinction is often made between policy-making and, policy implementation. It is often said that all matters involving policy-making or policy interpretation are the responsibility of ministers and those relating to policy implementation are the responsibility of bureaucrats. But bureaucrats are also very actively involved in the formulation of policies and their interpretation and, therefore, cannot be excluded from such responsibilities. Framing policies in a ministry or department is not an isolated exercise. It often involves inter-ministerial consultations and in most cases approval by the cabinet committee or the full cabinet. A wise minister should be only too glad to get the advice of his experienced bureaucrats in the making of policies or changes in existing policies.

If a line is to be drawn between the responsibilities of the minister and the civil servant, it may be said that all 'important' matters whether they are concerned with policies or administration should have the approval of the minister. Here again difficulties may arise in deciding whether a matter is important enough to justify being put up to the minister for his orders.

A more difficult problem concerns the manner in which orders of the minister are to be obtained in a specific case. Here again a general proposition can be that orders in all important cases should be obtained *in writing* on the file from the minister. However, sometimes decisions even in important matters may have to be taken by a secretary without getting the orders of the minister in writing. There may be situations where it may be possible only to take oral orders from the minister. Sometimes, situations may arise when decisions will have to be taken by the secretary without an opportunity to get even the oral approval of the minister. Such cases should invariably be put up for ex-post-facto approval by the minister. Ultimately bureaucrat–minister relations will depend on the degree of trust between the two rather than on office orders or written guidelines on the subject.

Justice M. C. Chagla in his report (1958) on the enquiry into the Mundhra case had made some important observations about norms that should be followed in the relationship between bureaucrats and ministers in taking decisions. The issue inquired into by Justice Chagla was whether H. M. Patel, principal secretary in the ministry of finance, had acted correctly and with the proper approval of his minister T. T. Krishnamachari when he advised the Life Insurance Corporation to invest in certain companies of H. D. Mundhra, an industrialist from Kanpur. Mundhra was in serious financial troubles and the LIC investments were intended to help him out of his problems. While discussing how the decision in this matter was taken by H. M. Patel, Justice Chagla agreed that in certain situations secretaries may have to act on their own. He said: 'Administration would become impossible if a secretary had to hold his hands until he received the formal consent or approval of his minister. In day-to-day administration, in cases of emergency, the secretary must take the responsibility and must act in a manner which according to him would ultimately meet with the approval of his minister.' However, Justice Chagla did not accept that the decision in the Mundhra case was one of 'day-to-day administration' or 'emergency'.

The most important verdict of Justice Chagla was that constitutionally the minister was responsible for the actions taken by his secretary. T. T. Krishnamachari maintained in his statement before parliament that he did not know all facts about the deal until the deal was concluded and that H. M. Patel was not following his directions or policy in concluding the deal. Nevertheless he resigned as minister and his resignation was accepted by the prime minister.

Two important principles were established through the report of Justice Chagla in the Mundhra case. First, the minister must 'fully and squarely' accept responsibility for the decisions of the civil servant. Second, the civil servant while taking a decision on his own should act in a manner which according to him would ultimately meet the approval of his minister .

When it is said that the minister has the final responsibility for decision-making in his ministry it does not mean that he can take decisions ignoring the laws and regulations relevant to the subject. If a minister feels strongly that the existing laws or regulations are not consistent with the requirement of good administration as he sees it, he can try to get them changed through the legislature. But so long as a law stands, the minister is bound by it. If a minister proposes to take a decision in violation of the law, it is the duty of the civil servant to advise him about the illegality of his proposed action. No reasonable person would like to violate the law knowing that he is doing so.

Some ministers expect bureaucrats to be 'co-operative' and 'helpful' in preparing notes on files to suit their wishes in particular cases even when such action may not be consistent with rules and regulations. It is here that conflicts often occur between ministers and their civil servants. Civil servants who point out the rules and regulations which may not suit the minister's wishes are often dubbed 'obstructionists' or 'rigid'. Some civil servants are only too willing to please the minister and become pliable instruments in the minister's hands. The only option for an honest bureaucrat in dealing with a minister who has scant respect for rules and regulations is that he should express his views firmly and clearly on the file and submit them to the minister. He should never allow himself to be pushed to do anything violative of law and regulations and be always prepared to face the 'punishment', if any, for taking such a stand.

While ministers have the right to overrule the advice of bureaucrats and insist on their decisions being carried out, certain elected members of the legislature seem to think that they too have the right to demand such compliance from bureaucrats in cases in which they are interested. Bureaucrats in the districts are sometimes subjected to such pressures from Members of Parliament and Members of the Legislative Assembly from the district. Pressures become intolerable when bureaucrats are asked to bend or break the rules to favour a particular person's interests supported by the legislator. Transfers of subordinate officers in the districts are a subject where some legislators try to apply pressures on bureaucrats. A remedy open to the bureaucrat in these circumstances is to report such pressures to his senior officer, who in turn may be able to get the intervention of the appropriate political authority in favour of the bureaucrat's correct stand.

In a democracy elected representatives of the people have the right to bring to the attention of bureaucrats the grievances of people or the needs of the constituencies they represent. Some officers unfortunately are unduly sensitive to receiving representations from MLAs or MPs and are apt to interpret them as attempts to 'pressure' them. They may claim that the people have the right to approach them directly and therefore there is no need for MLAs and MPs to assume the role of intermediaries. But it is also the democratic right of the people to decide how and through whom they should make representations and bureaucrats should not resent this practice so long as the representatives of the people act in the public interest. However, it would be a healthy practice if legislators take up issues of public interest as far as possible at level of ministers instead of at the level of officers. By and large this has been the tradition at the central government level and this tradition is worth emulating at the state and district levels too.

Another matter which causes strain in the relations between bureaucrats and legislators is the practice of some legislators using the forum of the legislature to criticize the actions of individual civil servants. Legislators are well within their rights to criticize the actions of the minister in the legislature but it is not fair on their part to use the privileged forum of the legislature to criticize individual officers. In a parliamentary democracy the minister is responsible to the legislature for the acts of omission or commission of the officers who work under him and therefore criticism when necessary should be directed at the minister and not the officer. At any rate it is not fair for a legislator to criticize an officer in the legislature when the latter has no opportunity to defend himself in that forum.

DISTURBING TRENDS

Having discussed the role of bureaucrats before and after Independence and some problems which arise in the relations between bureaucrats and political executives, I now proceed to focus attention on a few disturbing trends which have appeared in recent years in the functioning of the bureaucracy.

The basic requirement for the efficient working of the bureaucracy in a democracy is that it should be able to operate in an atmosphere of fairness and with the confidence that honest and efficient performance of duty will get its recognition without individual officers having to worry whether their rights and legitimate claims for career advancement may get overlooked or denied. While Article 311 of the Constitution gives the bureaucrat permanency of tenure and the assurance of due process of law, this by itself will not be adequate for creating the confidence in him that he will always get justice from the system in matters which affect him most, namely postings, transfers, promotions, and so on. He will be able to perform his duties at optimum levels of efficiency and commitment only when he feels confident that what is his due will never be denied to him because of favouritism shown by the powers that be to someone else.

The cases where ministerial interference and favouritism are seen in their worst form are in postings and transfers. Fortunately at the central level the system has retained its credibility fairly well all these years as civil service boards consisting of senior members of the service have been given the right to make recommendations on postings and transfers based on certain recognized principles and procedures. However, in some of the state governments postings and transfers take place with a great deal of arbitrariness, resulting in denial of justice to some and the showing of favouritism to others.

Frequent transfers from one post to another or one place to another cause considerable inconvenience to the officers concerned. The arbitrary exercise of such powers and interference with the decisions of bureaucrats responsible for the transfers of junior officers have become common in many states. Transfers are sometimes made to show the displeasure of the minister concerned against a particular officer. Sometimes an officer gets needlessly inconvenienced because the minister wants to favour someone else. Every state government has certain norms and procedures regarding postings and transfers, such as the number of years an officer should stay on a particular post or the time of year when transfers should take place, but often such norms are violated by political executives.

Some civil servants try to win the favour of their political bosses to get the positions or places of posting they prefer. This has encouraged cronyism and caused considerable demoralization in the ranks of honest bureaucrats. Needless to say, this has led to the erosion of the concept of bureaucratic impartiality and independence. Unfortunately, there is a widespread feeling now among bureaucrats in many states that cultivating political patronage is necessary to survive in the present system.

Mass transfers of officers every time there is a change of government is another trend that has come about in recent years. In these days of frequent changes in the office of the chief minister, such mass transfers of officers which routinely follow changes in government affect the morale of the service and its independent functioning. The obvious implication of these mass transfers is that the chief minister can have trust only in some bureaucrats and he or she expects from bureaucrats not commitment to duty but personal loyalty to him or her. After a few such postings and transfers, bureaucrats get identified with particular political parties or leaders and people lose faith in their impartiality and objectivity.

Some senior politicians have set a very bad example by carrying with them their own trusted bureaucrats to whatever ministerial posts they get assigned. Of course it is the privilege of a minister to choose his personal staff or to carry such staff with him to a new place whenever there is a change in his portfolio. The members of his personal staff, such as private secretaries and personal assistants, do not belong to the permanent bureaucratic establishment. They come and go with the minister, but the case of an officer like the secretary or a joint secretary in a ministry is different. They are expected to serve any minister assigned to the ministry with loyalty and commitment. A prime minister or a chief minister is expected to treat all civil servants impartially without giving the impression that he can trust only certain people known to him. This type of political favouritism strikes at the very root of fairness and impartiality in the civil service and weakens the trust of the public in the bureaucratic system.

The only remedy to the maladies mentioned above is to leave postings and transfers to service boards consisting of senior officers themselves. Of course recommendations regarding postings and transfers of senior officers have to be approved by the chief minister/ prime minister, but if these boards function according to well-established norms and principles, senior political executives will not be inclined to disagree with their recommendations.

SUPERFLUOUS LEVELS

Almost all committees or commissions which have gone into the problems of administrative reforms in post-Independence years have emphasized the need for eliminating superfluous levels in the bureaucratic hierarchy. However, far from abolishing such levels in the hierarchy, the trend appears to be for perpetuating existing levels and adding new ones. Today there is a Director between the Deputy Secretary and the Joint Secretary, an Additional Secretary between the Joint Secretary and Secretary, and a Special Secretary between Additional Secretary and Secretary. Then there is a convenient designation of 'OSD' or Officer on Special Duty which can be fitted into any level depending upon who is to be appointed. Some of these posts are created merely to ensure avenues of promotion for officers without any relevance to work efficiency. 'Level jumping' has often been suggested to ensure the speedy movement of files but this is more talked about than practised. Files in the secretariat continue to travel through every level in the hierarchy, causing unnecessary delay and adding little to efficiency. The remedy is not 'level jumping' but 'level abolition'. If avenues of promotion to higher steps in the pay scale are to be provided for, it should be done without creating new levels of authority in the hierarchy.

Inter-departmental or inter-ministerial consultations on files and through meetings have become the routine practice in government secretariats these days. Often officers refer files to other ministries in order to dilute responsibility in decision-making. They try to involve as many persons and departments as possible in decision-making as an insurance against possible criticism from future parliamentary committees or audit. Seeking the concurrence of the finance department in every case is still a must in spite of considerable devolution of financial powers to the ministries. Routine reference to the Planning Commission has also become a regular part of decision-making. Again, even the much advertised 'single window clearance system' has often turned out to be something different from what it was intended to be. Sub-windows seem to be sprouting fast in 'single windows', thus perpetuating the dilatory procedures of the past.

While promotions to senior posts in the central government are done on the basis of seniority-cum-merit, it has become a regular practice in the state to base such promotions only on seniority. At the central level the service boards carefully assess the merits of officers based on records of their performance in their confidential reports and prepare panels of officers eligible for promotion. Selection to senior-level posts at the centre is made strictly from the approved panels but at the state level very little importance is given to the confidential reports on performance. Very often an officer found unsuitable for inclusion in the panel of additional secretary at the centre may be appointed as chief secretary in the state. This practice of ignoring merit in promotions to higher level posts in the states affects the efficiency of administration and creates the feeling of complacency among officers that they will get their promotions with seniority irrespective of their performance.

A golden rule for bureaucrats in the past was that they should remain anonymous and restrain their tongues. When one opts to become a member of the civil service, one agrees to be bound by the discipline and code of conduct prescribed for the service. An equally important rule is that an officer should never take credit for himself in speeches or writings for the contributions he would have made for the evolution of a policy or a decision. Nor should he criticize the decisions or policies of the government once they have been announced, whatever might have been the reservations he would have expressed at the time of their formulation.

A reprehensible trend seen of late is for some bureaucrats to assume for themselves the role of 'crusaders' for certain causes. There have been instances when bureaucrats have come out with statements publicly supporting or opposing a particular policy or action of the government or championing causes which they consider to be in the public interest. Some have even participated in protest meetings, processions, and so on, in support of or in condemnation of a cause. It is obvious that the right to free expression guaranteed in the constitution cannot be invoked as defence for indisciplined conduct by a bureaucrat. If a civil servant has very strong views against certain policies and decisions of the government and feels compelled to express such views, the proper course open to him is to resign from the service and become a social activist and champion the causes close to his heart. Discipline may prove irksome to some bureaucrats, but in the civil service discipline is integral to work. One cannot remain in government service and at the same time flout its discipline.

EROSION OF INTEGRITY

In the earlier part of this paper I had stated that efficiency and integrity are the basic foundations on which the civil service rests and had refuted the charge that there has been a deterioration in standards of efficiency. I wish I could take the same stand about the charge of deterioration in standards of integrity. Unfortunately, some developments in recent years do not justify such a stand. There has been corruption in the bureaucracy in the past, but what is new is that corruption has now crept into the senior levels of the bureaucracy as well. Instances of corruption among senior bureaucrats may be only on a very small scale at present, but what is disturbing is that the trend has already appeared and, whatever may be its scale at present, it has all the potential for destroying the credibility and usefulness of the service.

Till a few years ago absolute integrity in the all-India services was taken for granted and departures from the normal rules of rectitude and integrity were very rare aberrations. Unfortunately, what was very rare is no longer so and one is shocked to find regular reports in the newspapers about the arrests and prosecutions of senior officials like secretaries and even chief secretaries to state governments and heads of departments on charges of bribery, unaccounted wealth, defalcation and so on.

It may be said that the permissive attitude of our society to corruption in general has been the main reason for the spread of this evil even to the top levels of the bureaucracy. While it may be true that our society is becoming increasingly tolerant of corruption, it can never be a defence for corruption among top bureaucrats who enjoy the benefits of high salaries and perquisites which should normally place them above such needs. Greed is the only reason for their turning to corruption and whatever may be the fall in standards of integrity in other professions, there can be no justification whatsoever for such deterioration in the ranks of top civil servants who are expected to function as watchdogs of integrity in the bureaucracy.

I am of the view that our indulgent attitude to what is called 'petty corruption' in the lower levels of the administration has been one of the important causes for the emergence of the phenomenon of corruption at top levels. Our society has been very tolerant of corruption among lower-level employees and had even termed them as *mamool* or payments traditionally due to them. It is here that we have made the fundamental mistake. If we tolerate petty corruption at lower levels, we will eventually have to reckon with big corruption at top levels and this is what has actually happened now. A bribe is a bribe whether it is of a petty amount or taken by a petty officer. The fight against corruption in the bureaucracy has to cover all acts of corruption at all levels without trying to condone so-called petty corruption by lower-level employees. Perhaps most of them indulge in petty corruption only because they have no opportunities for big corruption in their present jobs. Another important reason for the wide prevalence of corruption in our country is the ease with which the corrupt officials can get away without punishment. The complicated nature of laws and procedures are ideally suited to the crooked and the wicked in the system, and this encourages many more to follow the tempting route of corruption.

The most dangerous trend of late has been *joint ventures* between corrupt bureaucrats and corrupt politicians. The combination of corrupt bureaucrats and corrupt politicians has assumed such dangerous proportions in some states that the time-honoured system of checks and counter checks and scrutiny by senior officials, parliamentary committees, audit and so on have been reduced to a farce. Those who have the responsibility for counter-checking are themselves perpetrating frauds which they are expected to prevent.

The whole rationale of an all-India civil service recruited through a competitive selection process and given the highest scales of salary available to any group of government employees is that it should not only be efficient but also clean under all circumstances. The task of keeping the bureaucratic system clean cannot be left to courts and jails; it is essentially the responsibility of bureaucrats themselves. Ultimately the remedy against corruption in bureaucracy lies in the will of the civil servants themselves to remain clean.

CHAPTER TWELVE

Voluntary Associations and Development Imperatives
The Indian Experience

Bidyut Chakrabarty

India is a planned economy in which the state is pre-eminent. The Planning Commission plays a crucial role in charting out the course of development in the country. Given its obvious link with the state, the commission usually, if not always, reflects the socio-economic priorities of the state. In other words, the Planning Commission generally represents the state-directed formula of development. The centralized planning provides an answer to India's economic ills. By resorting to planning, the nationalist leadership strove to strengthen the future Indian state, which was to emerge after the British withdrawal. Planning was perhaps an outcome of the Congress endeavour to transform India from 'a civilization of classical antiquity' into a modern nation state.[1] The euphoria for planning continued till the early 1970s when the idea itself was challenged as simply 'inadequate' to ensure an all-round development in a country with a long colonial past. It was argued that planning was an instrument that, in order to be effective, needed to be supplemented by both 'organized'

[1] Jawaharlal Nehru was perhaps most categorical in defend.ng planning as the most effective instrument for alleviating poverty of the Indian masses. In a memorandum in February, 1940, Nehru thus states, 'it is important to bear in mind that the outlook governing a planned scheme is different from the outlook of an unplanned private economy. It is this outlook which must be kept in view in drawing up the plan, so that all the different sections of the plan must be integral and coordinated parts of the full programme. Such control as may be necessary to bring this about will have to be taken by the State'. Jawaharlal Nehru, 'Objectives of Planning', *Indian Annual Register*, vol. II, p.238.

and 'unorganized' voluntary efforts. It was a watershed in India's developmental planning. Articulated by the 1978 Ashok Mehta Committee, voluntary agencies were accorded significance in developmental activities especially in rural areas. The aim of the paper is to trace the growing importance of voluntary organizations in India's socio-economic development focusing on the report of the Planning Commission and other relevant committees. Furthermore, in the backdrop of the emerging literature on voluntary organizations which are primarily 'civil society' organizations, there will be attempts to identify its theoretical roots. This is, however, not to suggest that these 'non-state' agencies are post Cold War phenomena, as is generally assumed;[2] instead, the paper seeks to argue that their roots can be found in various endeavours, undertaken in India long before the Cold War seeking to provide a different, if not an alternative, path of development. In order to pursue that argument, the expression voluntary associations is preferred to non-governmental organization (NGO) since the latter is relatively new in the contemporary lexicon on development. While grasping voluntarism as a specific effort, an attempt will also be made to identify the distinctive features of the development paradigm that itself is the offshoot of contestations both at the level of activities and also at the level of theoretical configurations. The principal aim of the paper is to understand the role of voluntarism in development in contrast with the state-led development in India.

SETTING THE PERSPECTIVE

In the contemporary discourses on development,[3] the voluntary sector provides a significant input. Voluntarism in development is

[2] For a nuanced treatment of this argument, see Sangeeta Kamat, *Development Hegemony: NGOs and the State in India*, Oxford University Press, New Delhi, 2001. As Kamat argues that a cursory review of the literature reveals that NGOs are the new patrons of public interest, posing a serious challenge to the legitimate function of the state. That is, among the range of organized forces and institutions of civil society, NGOs are regarded as representing the interests of the people, to the greatest extent possible. In other words, NGOs have come to replace other well-established civil organizations such as trade unions, welfare associations, religious associations and trade associations that traditionally represent the interests of various constituencies of society. Compared to these organizations, it is argued that NGOs represent the interest of the broadest swath of people, the poor and underprivileged of society, who tend to have no forum of representation in public affairs, except perhaps the right to vote during election.

[3] Amartya Sen in his *Development as Freedom* has provided a refreshing insight on

characterized by the participation in the process of economic production, exchange or distribution of non-state agencies, individual groups or association, imbued with a certain purpose.[4] Although its impact on the development process varies from one society to another, its role can never be completely ignored simply because the state-directed development has largely failed in the 'Third World' context. The growing importance of the voluntary sector is but an aspect of the decline of the development state that drew significantly on the model the colonial power had bequeathed. It is true that the post-colonial state expanded its activities to reach out to those in the periphery. But what was undertaken as development of the people was, in most cases, appropriated by a powerful minority and those who were underprivileged continued to remain so. One of the reasons for distortion in development has to be located in the failures of the state-driven programmes for the people which were, by definition, formulated by those at the top of state bureaucracy. The hiatus between the aim of development and its actual manifestation clearly identifies three interesting features of Third World Development, engineered by western capitalism: (a) the rise of inequality reflects the inability of the capitalist developed economies to transfer the mechanism of capitalist growth to the non-capitalist world of Asia, Africa and Latin America; (b) decolonization was not really a break with the past since the post-colonial state failed to allocate resources into those production lines which were essential for the transition to self-sustained growth largely because there was a clear continuity in

---

the conceptualization of development. According to him, development is a process of expanding real freedoms that people enjoy. Development requires, he further argues, 'the removal of major sources of unfreedom: poverty as well as tyranny, poor economic opportunities as well as systematic social deprivation, neglect of public facilities as well as intolerance or over-activity of repressive states. Despite unprecedented increases in overall opulence, the contemporary world denies elementary freedoms to vast numbers—perhaps even the majority—of people'. Freedoms are not only the primary ends of development, they are also among its principal means. Political freedom (in the form of free speech and elections), for instance, help to 'promote economic security'. Social opportunities (in the form of education and health facilities) 'facilitate economic participation'. Economic facilities (in the form of opportunities for participation in trade and production) can help to 'generate personal abundance as well as public resources for social facilities'. Amartya Sen, *Development as Freedom*, Oxford University Press, New Delhi, 1999, pp. 3–4, 11.

[4] Some of the well-known examples are Gandhi's *Harijan Sevak Sangh, Gramodyog Sangh* (promotion of village industries), *Hindustan Talem Sangh* (for educating people). Vinoba Bhabe's *Bhoodan Movement* is another illustration of the success of voluntarism in recent years.

the basic economic agenda; and (c) by believing in statism and statist view of development, the process that unfolded actually undermined what was already there in terms of voluntaristic base of the Third World societies as well as the new voluntaristic thrust that came up in the wake of the struggle against the alien power.

Voluntarism is a significant input in development especially in the context of foreign rule that invariably pushed a particular process of development in consonance with its own ideological agenda. Given its long colonial past, India is probably the best example to illustrate the role of voluntary organizations[5] in development both as an instrument as well as a conceptual framework to understand the development process where the role of the state is pre-eminent. As regards voluntary organizations, one comes across two types of roles. On the one hand, voluntary organizations complement the activities of the state that come under their purview. In other words, there are activities, initiated and funded by the state, in which voluntary organizations participate to complete the task. In such a situation, since their role is virtually conditioned and governed by the state they merely act as agents of the state. Apart from their involvement in the state-directed development, the voluntary organizations, on the other hand, undertake activities where the state is either absent or its role is negligible presumably because they are not complementary to the goal of the state. This is an area where the part, the voluntary organizations play, is most crucial for two specific reasons: *first*, they bring forward those areas of developmental activities which may not have interested the state for obvious ideological bias, but are decisive for development; *secondly*, by suggesting new areas of activities which are both necessary and significant for the over-all development, voluntary organizations contribute to a process in which an alternative to the state-engineered development is always sought. As they are

---

[5] Voluntary Organizations have been generally defined as voluntary, autonomous, non-profit organizations or groups of citizens established to address various problems and disadvantages in the society. What differentiates the voluntary organizations from the rest is that they are, whether their workers are paid or unpaid, initiated and governed by the members without external control. Voluntary denotes 'of one's own free choice'. Since voluntary and autonomous also connote 'non-govermental' they are also characterized as 'non-governmental organizations' (NGO). It is very difficult to define the NGOs in a precise way because the term, as John Mencher argues, 'is a catchword for an enormous variety of structures, pursuing diverse strategies, of widely differing sizes, aims or missions, and defies definition because of this diversity'. See, John Mencher, 'NGOs: Are They a Force for Change', *Economic and Political Weekly*, 24 July, 1999, p. 2081.

not dependent on the government, not only do they select their agenda they also decide their *modus operandi* to attain the goal. What it invariably results in is the involvement of the people in the developmental activities that are structured around the agenda, which the participants articulate as the most appropriate to their needs.

In view of the gradual withdrawal of state from social sector, voluntary organizations have grown in importance not only as an alternative to what is being pursued as development but also as a relatively new experiment in which the role of the conventional agencies is largely being eclipsed. Voluntary agencies are therefore those civil society organizations working on different issues for different interest groups separately or in combination. They play the role of activists, executing programmes and delivering services and also as 'the mobilisers of opinions, awareness and support of the people concerned with and affected by social and economic and political problems'.[6] The growing importance of voluntary organizations[7] is therefore both an outcome of and a challenge to what is construed as development in today's parlance. The 1994 World Bank Report on structural adjustment in Sub-Saharan Africa is a clear articulation of future developmental plans for the 'Third World' countries in which the role of the state is minimal. Underlining the importance of 'rolling back of the state', the report also seeks to minimize

[6] According to Arjun Sengupta, the voluntary associations are agencies 'of executing public action [articulated through a process of] converting public sentiment into programmes of change'. See Arjun Sengupta, 'delivering the right to development: ESCR [Economic, Social and Cultural Rights] and NGOs, *Economic and Political Weekly*, 9 October, 1999, p. 2921. For a refreshing thematic exposition of civil society, see Sudipta Kaviraj and Sunil Khilnani (ed.), *Civil Society: History and Possibilities*, Cambridge University Press, Cambridge, 2001; and also Neera Chandhoke, *State and Civil Society: Explorations in Political Theory*, Sage, New Delhi, 1995

[7] A distinction, that is absolutely analytical, is usually made between voluntary organizations and people's organizations. People's organizations can, for instance, be defined as democratic organizations that represent the interest of their members and are accountable to them. They are formed by people who know each other or who share a common interest or activity and their continuity does not depend on outside initiatives or funding. Panchayats, Cooperatives, Trade Unions and various formal or informal organizations based on locality, interest gender, age etc. at the level of community or village or their networks at higher levels are examples.

On the other hand, voluntary organizations are those working with and very often on behalf of people, focusing their work and activities on issues and people beyond their own staff and membership which may be local or from outside. However voluntary organizations have close links generally with people's organizations and render enabling, promotional, professional and financial assistance to them.

restrictions on the free play of market forces. Its significance lies in projecting an alternative in opposition to those many economies that remain organized around a state-led model. The report is an intervention in those economies in the form of promoting specific models of development that incorporated a 'pro-market' and 'anti-state' emphasis. So, what is sought to be pursued in India in the name of developmental plans is the outcome of indigenous efforts, undertaken over a historical period and also the external inputs, articulated through the intervention of the 'transcendental' agencies including the World Bank and the International Monetary Fund.[8] An in-depth study of the role of voluntary organizations in India's socio-economic development both in the context of the nationalist movement and in the aftermath of freedom clearly brings out the gradual importance of these efforts which are ordinarily dismissed as 'futile' in the state-driven development schemes and programmes.

VOLUNTARISM DURING THE FREEDOM STRUGGLE

An assessment the Gandhi-led freedom movement clearly demonstrates that overarching importance of voluntarism in consolidating anti-British struggle. The formation of national schools and colleges in the wake of the 1920–1 Non-Cooperation Movement is illustrative of a trend that had its roots in opposition to the British rule. Although these schools and colleges never posed a serious threat to the English education, they were nonetheless well-designed efforts to construct an alternative system of learning based on ideas, opposed to British imperialism. Suggesting a parallel way, the nationalist leadership also articulated a different system of education that sought to indigenise the process of learning even during the alien rule. As an effort, it was not as successful as anticipated because it did not strike roots in the British-Indian provinces other than Bengal. Its symbolic importance can never be denied simply because national schools and colleges were probably one of those first attempts where voluntarism led people to participate in projects with a clear political undertone.

Similarly, Gandhi's constructive programme is another illustration of an alternative to the state-driven development. Seeking to involve those for whom the programme is directed, Gandhi therefore

---

[8] For a detailed exposition of this argument see, John Pender, 'From "Structural Adjustment" to "Comprehensive Development Framework": Conditionally Transformed?', *Third World Quarterly*, vol. 22, no. 3, 2001, pp. 397–411.

argues, '[r]eaders whether workers and volunteers or not, should definitely realize that the constructive programme is the truthful and non-violent way of winning *purna swaraj*. Its wholesale fulfillment is complete independence. Imagine all the forty crores of people busying themselves with the whole of constructive programme which is designed to build the nation from the very bottom upwards'.[9] Based on his faith on voluntarism, Gandhi had formulated a comprehensive package of constructive work and built-up organizations for implementing different parts of the programme.[10] One of the important segments of the constructive programme was *khadi* that was also 'the cementing force which can bind those whom the three colours of the [Indian] flag represent. [T]he whole fabric of swaraj hangs', as Gandhi argued, 'on the thread of the handspun yarn'.[11]

It is evident that by drawing on voluntarism Gandhi organized probably the most gigantic nationalist movement of the twentieth century. The freedom struggle had both economic and political manifestations. On the one hand, the political battle that he waged against the British inspired people to participate voluntarily in movements despite adverse consequences. Based on non-violence, the Gandhian method was unique in history. Projecting *charkha* as the symbol of unity and also a weapon, Gandhi, on the other hand, invested political contents in an essentially economic programme. So, his economic and political strategies resulted in a unique situation where voluntarism constituted probably the most significant dimensions. Gandhi's achievement lies in articulating *satyagraha* as a political instrument of organizing people in the anti-British campaign. It is equally striking that the constructive programme, initiated and pursued by the people voluntarily, provided an alternative scheme for development under colonialism. It had worked at two different levels. While at one level these programmes popularized the Congress and more particularly Gandhi in areas where the freedom struggle meant little; they, at another level, created specific areas of activities within the broad parameters of the constructive programme, the success of which depended on the people's participation; they were a people-centred process of development with mobilization and

[9] M.K. Gandhi, 'Constructive Programme' (a booklet), Navjivan Press, Ahmedabad, 1941, p. 2.

[10] The notable examples among them were *Harijan Sevak Sangh*, *the Bhil Sewa Mandal*, the All India Spinners and Weavers Associations.

[11] Gandhi's press statement, 20 June, 1947, in Rudrangshu Mukherjee, *The Penguin Gandhi Reader*, Penguin, New Delhi, 1993, p. 89.

organization of community forces. Given the broad scope of these programmes, they were not merely economic strategies, they were also powerful instruments in galvanizing people for action in adverse circumstances. Apart from its basic political content, the constructive programme, as Gandhi conceptualized, was therefore both an alternative strategy for socio-economic improvement in which the state was peripheral or absent as well as a mechanism to ensure and sustain people's participation in development.

VOLUNTARY AGENCIES AND THE PLANNING PROCESS IN INDIA

The role of voluntary agencies in development was recognized when a planning commission was first constituted at the behest of the Indian National Congress in 1938. As its first chairman, Subhas Bose realized the importance of voluntary agencies in India's growth as a stable economy despite having been favourably disposed towards a planned-economy following the Soviet-type.[12] The idea was carried forward in the aftermath of Independence, though it did not receive as much attention in the first Five Year Plans as it did from the Sixth Five Year Plan onwards. Underlining the significance of voluntary agencies in the welfare of a young nation like India, the First Five Year Plan clearly stated that

[a] major responsibility for organizing activities in different fields of social welfare like the welfare of women and children, social education, community organization etc., falls naturally on private voluntary agencies. These private agencies have long been working in their own humble way and without adequate aid for the achievement of their objectives with their own leadership, organization and resources. Any plan for social and economic regeneration should take into account the services rendered by these agencies and the State should give them maximum cooperation in strengthening their effort. Public cooperation through voluntary social service organizations is capable of yielding valuable results in channelizing private efforts for the promotion of social welfare.[13]

A careful reading of the objective of the First Plan clearly shows overarching importance of voluntary agencies in those areas where

---

[12] For details of what finally led to the rise of the planning commission in India in 1938, see my 'Jawaharlal Nehru and Planning', 1938–41, *Modern Asian Studies*, 26, 2, 1992.

[13] First Five Year Plan, Planning Commission, Government of India, p.607—cited in N.V. Lalitha and Madhu Kohli, *Status of Voluntary Effort in Social Welfare*, National Institute of Public Cooperation and Child Development, New Delhi, 1982, pp. 15–16.

they had already made an impact with almost no support from the State. Furthermore, the State was urged to extend all possible support to these efforts since they were result-oriented and therefore useful in development. What was stated in the objective is very significant in another respect. Despite being swayed by the planning as the most effective instrument to radically alter India's economic future, the nationalist leaders who took over after the British left, were also convinced of the possible contribution of voluntary agencies in development. Following the adoption of various welfare schemes for the rural poor immediately after Independence, the importance of voluntary agencies was felt more than before. While some of them were directly involved 'in working with the poor [and] helping them to get the benefits of many anti-poverty schemes, some trained workers for organizations engaged in rural transformation'.[14] Whatever the manifestation of their activities, the role of voluntary agencies is immensely important in development and the Third Plan clearly articulated this by underlining that

properly organized voluntary efforts may go a long way towards augmenting the facilities available to the community for helping the weakest and the most needy to a somewhat better life. The wherewithal for this has to come from the time, energy and other sources of millions of people for whom voluntary organizations can find constructive channels suited through varying conditions in the country.[15]

What is unique in this argument is the shift in the policy direction. Not only is the importance of the voluntary 'organizations' highlighted but that it is most crucial in helping those in the periphery has also been emphasized. Although voluntary agencies did not receive as much attention as it had in the successive plans, the Third Plan was a watershed since for the first time their significance was sought to be assessed for policy purposes. In fact, from the Third Plan onwards, the idea gained ground that the state-driven development was not adequate for India's socio-economic growth and hence voluntary agencies had a supplementary role to play.

The activities in which voluntary agencies have traditionally been engaged[16] may not have been structured around the way development

---

[14] Udaya Bhaskara Reddy, 'Role of Voluntary Agencies in Rural Development', *Indian Journal of Public Administration*, July–September, 1987, p. 548.

[15] *Report of the Third Five Year Plan*, Planning Commission, Government of India, pp. 292–3.

[16] The activities can be broadly classified as: (a) charity: giving food, clothing,

was conceptualized in the planning. Given the philanthropic goal, the activities of these agencies revolve around service to the humanity. With the growing importance of planning in independent India, the inputs provided by the voluntary agencies, become crucial in areas where the role of the state is neither clear nor pronounced. The successive Planning Commission reports have, therefore, clearly laid emphasis on the need for involvement of voluntary agencies as a significant aspect of participation of people in various developmental efforts. Not only do they suggest an alternative path of development involving people they also assist the state in realizing its socio-economic objectives in the following manner[17]: (1) by making the state aware of the difficulties, people confront in availing the benefit of various government programmes to which they are entitled; (2) reporting the irregularities, if any, in the implementation of programmes and (3) motivating the local communities to generate resources from within the community to meet all their needs which fall outside the government programmes.

Various committees dealing with development duly acknowledged the role of voluntary agencies. The 1957 Balvantray Mehta Committee that recommended the three-tier panchayati raj upheld the importance of voluntary agencies by underlining that '[t]oday in the implementation of the various schemes of community development, more and more emphasis is laid on non-governmental [voluntary] agencies and workers and on the principle that ultimately people's

---

medicine, land, buildings etc., and alms in cash and kind; (b) welfare: providing facilities for education, health, drinking water, roads, communications, etc., (c) relief: responding to call of duties during natural calamities, like floods, drought, earthquakes and man-made calamities, like refugee influx, ravage of war etc., (d) rehabilitation: continuing and follow-up of the work in areas, hard-hit by calamities and starting activities that are durable in nature; (e) services: building-up infrastructure in depressed backward areas such as tractor hiring services, providing or facilitating credit supply of seeds, fertilizers, technical know-how etc., (f) development of socio-economic environment around human beings: socio-economic transformation on the area-basis, covering all the people in a given area or concentrating only on a particular group of neglected people in need of help; and (g) development of human beings: conscious raising, awakening, conscientising, organizing, recording of priorities to realize social justice, redeeming the past and opening doors of opportunities to the oppressed and exploited. For details of this classification, see J. B. Singh, 'Testing Voluntary Agencies—Let's First Understand Them', *Yojana*, vol. 28 (nos. 20 & 21, November, 1984, pp. 45–7.

[17] Udaya Bhaskara Reddy, 'Role of Voluntary Agencies in Rural Development', *Indian Journal of Public Administration*, July–September, 1987, p. 550.

own local organizations should take over the entire work'.[18] Seeking to provide an alternative to the state-led development, the 1957 committee is a break with the past. Not only was this committee in favour of rejuvenating the panchayati raj institutions, it also insisted on people's participation for their success in entire process of development. This was further reiterated in the 1966 Rural-Urban Relationship Committee that laid emphasis on the role of voluntary agencies in mobilizing community support for local development activities. As its report unequivocally suggests,

[l]ocal voluntary organizations can be very helpful in mobilizing popular support and assistance of the people in the activities of local body. It is possible to maintain constant and close contact with the people through these organizations. The formation of a network of local organizations, like neighborhood and *Mohalla* committees and citizens' forums, would be useful in mobilizing public participation.[19]

It is evident that by the late 1960s, voluntary agencies became a significant influence in the development process in which the Indian state continued to play a decisive role. It has also been recognized that their role was most important in rural development—an area where the state had failed to make inroads due to peculiar socio-economic constraints in which it had to function.[20] So far, voluntary agencies were identified as inputs to the state-led development. The 1978 Ashok Mehta Committee Report is a break with the past in the sense that not only did it accord importance to the voluntary agencies it also appreciated their contribution in rural development. Identifying them as 'nodal' in micro-planning, the report runs as follows:

[18] Report of the team for the study of community projects and national extension service, vol. 1, Government of India, New Delhi, 1957, p. 107—quoted in Mohit Bhattacharya, 'Voluntary Associations, Development and the State', *Indian Journal of Public Administration*, July–September, 1987, p. 385.

[19] Report of the Rural–Urban Relationship Committee, Government of India, Ministry of Health, New Delhi, 1966, p.113 – quoted in Mohit Bhattacharya, 'Voluntary Associations, Development and the State', *Indian Journal of Public Administration*, July–September, 1987, p. 386.

[20] In his in-depth study of the panchayati raj institutions in a comparative perspective, Atul Kohli has shown how they were neutralized and mostly appropriated by the vested interests in the absence of people's mevements. See Atul Kohli, *The State and Poverty in India*, Cambridge University Press, Cambridge, 1987. Similarly, Marcus Franda has also drawn our attention to the difficulties confronting the voluntary agencies in India largely due to well-entrenched vested interests in rural India. See Marcus Franda, *Voluntary Associations and Local Development India*, Young Asia Publications, New Delhi, 1983.

Of the several voluntary organizations engaged in rural welfare, a few have helped the Panchayati Raj institutions in micro-planning. They prepare comprehensive area development plans, conduct feasibility studies and cost-benefit analysis, explore ways and means to induce local participation in planning and implementation. Association of Voluntary Agencies for Rural Development (AVARD) also provides consultancy services in project formulation and assists its member agencies with technical support. Voluntary agencies, if they have requisite expertise, proven standing and well-equipped organizations, can assist Panchayati Raj institutions in the planning process. They can be particularly involved in formulation of projects and schemes. They can also help to create strong public opinion in support of measures aimed at social change'.[21]

Given their growing importance within a span of twenty-one years (1957–78), voluntary agencies are not merely philanthropic, they are equally crucial in articulating the priorities in the overall development process. The Ashok Mehta Committee is, therefore, a watershed in the history of voluntary agency in India that, so far, was equated only with welfare activities and charity works. What was initiated in this report was supported further in the Sixth Five Year Plan (1980–85) that emphasized the importance of voluntary agencies, formal and informal in nature, as 'new actors' motivating and mobilizing people in specific or general developmental task and also meeting 'the new demands of the growing sphere of developmental activities'.[22] The Sixth Plan is probably the beginning of a process in which the voluntary agencies became an integral part of the development agenda of the Indian state and the following areas where they played a determining role, were thus earmarked:

(a) optimal utilization and development of renewable source of energy, including forestry through the formation of renewable energy associations at the block level; (b) family welfare, health and nutrition, education and relevant community programmes in this field; (c) 'health for all' programmes; (d) water management and soil conservation; (e) social welfare programmes for weaker sections; (f) implementation of minimum needs programme; (g) disaster preparedness and management (floods, cyclones etc.); (h) promotion of ecology and tribal development; (i) environmental protection and education.

[21] *Report of the Committee on Panchayati Raj Institutions*, Government of India, New Delhi, 1978, p. 144.

[22] R. B. Jain, 'NGOs in India: Their Role, Influence and Problems', in Noorjahan Bava (ed.), *Non-Governmental Organizations in Development: Theory and Practice*, Kanishka Publishers, New Delhi, 1997, p. 128.

By recognizing the importance of voluntary agencies in the above areas, the Sixth Plan also registered the shrinking role of the state in development. Although the state was given a peripheral role, it was nonetheless significant given the basic characteristics of planning in India where the state held the key to what was undertaken as development. So, the Sixth Plan is the articulation of a wave clearly indicating, if not fully describing, a new trend where voluntary agencies were not at all an appendage but an active partner in development. The Approach paper on the Seventh Plan (1985–90) characterized the voluntary agencies as 'the eyes and ears of the beneficiaries', the weaker sections of the society who have been left out of 'the mainstream of development benefits'. In conformity with the spirit, expressed in the Third Plan, it was further reiterated in the Seventh Plan that voluntary 'associations' constituted one of the most important sources of inputs for development planning in India. This itself is a radical improvement on the perception of the state in the previous six Five Year Plans. It took three decades 'to legitimize this role of voluntary agencies regarding facilitating the process of making people aware of alternatives—other than the monopolistic delivery system of the government—that legal, democratic and non-violent with a view to bringing about socio-economic change[s]'.[23]

The Seventh Plan is, therefore, a significant benchmark in the growth of voluntary agencies in India for two specific reasons: (a) by formally recognizing their role in the development process, the Seventh Plan upheld the view that there were alternative ways of development, hitherto untapped, in which people's participation was crucial and (b) the emphasis would be more on 'professionalising voluntarism' which meant the introduction of simple, professional and managerial expertise in keeping with resources and capabilities of the voluntary agencies in question. There are two serious implications of this change that undoubtedly strengthened the role of these agencies in development. First, the state, though a determining influence, formally accepted the importance of many village-level groups in the non-governmental sector in the planning for development. The second implication is more significant in the sense that the formal recognition of their role resulted in a radical shift in the approach of the state to development. The state was just an actor, the success of which depended on its cooperation with various other actors, involved in

---

[23] Sanjit (Bunker) Roy, 'Voluntary Agencies in Development—Their Role, Policy and Programmes', *Indian Journal of Public Administration*, July–September, 1987, p. 457.

the process of development. Furthermore, one of the primary aims of village-based voluntary agencies was to make the villagers 'self-dependent' and to evolve those schemes drawing upon their capabilities and resources.

Not only did the Seventh Plan include a chapter on involvement of voluntary agencies in rural development it had also identified specific areas where their role would be crucial. This is a clear indication of the shift in the development paradigm, hitherto dominant in India's socio-economic growth. Voluntary agencies became a significant input in development. This was not a mere coincidence. The growing importance of voluntary agencies was largely due to rising importance of the rural sector in India's economic development. What it resulted in was a new paradigm of development in which the voluntary agencies also have a substantial contribution to make. Articulating the new thrust of development, the Seventh Plan, therefore, identified the following areas[24] in the rural sector as most significant for India's overall development:

i) integrated rural development/rural landless employment guarantee programme/TRYSEM; ii) implementation of land ceiling and distribution of surplus land; iii) enforcement of minimum wages to agricultural labourers; iv) identification and rehabilitation of bonded labourers; v) supply of safe drinking water including repair and maintenance of water supply system with community support; vi) afforestation, social forestry, development of bio-gas and alternative energy sources (solar, wind energy, smokeless *chulas*); vii) promotion of family planning; viii) primary health care; control of leprosy; TB, blindness and preventive health programmes utilizing village resources; ix) programmes for women and children in rural areas; x) innovative methods and low cost alternatives in elementary education and middle school education for children, adult education and non-formal and formal education; xi) consumer protection and promotion of cooperatives; xii) promotion of handicraft and village and cottage industries; xiii) promotion of science and technology; xiv) legal education; xv) rural housing, improvement of rural slums; xvi) environmental ecological improvement and xvii) promotion and encouragement of traditional media for dissemination of information.

Apart from earmarking the areas where the contribution of the voluntary agencies was recognized, for the first time in the history of

---

[24] Sanjit (Bunker) Roy, 'Voluntary Agencies in Development—Their Role, Policy and Programmes', *Indian Journal of Public Administration*, July–September, 1987, p. 462.

planning in India, the state during the Seventh Plan period had also spent a substantial amount through voluntary agencies for anti-poverty and minimum needs programme. A process began whereby the role of the village-based voluntary agencies in development was formally recognized. The Seventh Plan is, therefore, both a culmination of an initiative and a beginning of a new era in which the voluntary agencies became integral to development in India.

The Seventh Plan is remarkable in another respect. There was hardly any serious effort in any of the Five Year Plans till the Seventh Plan to define the role of voluntary agencies. Their role was primarily confined to welfare activities and charity works mostly during disasters, like flood, famine, droughts etc. While planning for development the state usually took into account the inputs, provided by them, the voluntary agencies never became an active partner in the entire exercise probably because they were neither institutionalized nor was their role formally recognized. For the first time, the Seventh Plan codified the following criteria[25] for identifying 'rural' voluntary agencies:

a) The organization should have a legal entity. b) It should be based in a rural area, and be working there for a minimum of three years. c) It should have broad-based objectives serving the social and economic needs of the community as a whole, and mainly the weaker sections. It must not work for profits. d) Its activities should be open to all citizens of India irrespective of religion, caste, creed, sex or race. e) It should have the necessary flexibility, professional competence and organizational skills to implement programmes. f) Its office bearers should not be elected members of any political party. g) It declares that it will adopt constitutional and non-violent means for rural development purposes. h) It is committed to secular and democratic concepts and methods of functioning.

Besides seeking to define voluntary agencies, the Seventh Plan is also serious endeavour to officially recognize the role of voluntary agencies in development. What was codified in the Plan was the outcome of a long-drawn process in which these agencies had significant roles to supplement the government efforts. The state had finally come to terms with voluntary agencies simply because their contribution was too significant to wish away. While the Seventh Plan is appreciated for having upheld the importance of voluntary agencies

---

[25] Sanjit (Bunker) Roy, 'Voluntary Agencies in Development—Their Role, Policy and Programmes', *Indian Journal of Public Administration*, July–September, 1987, p. 461.

in India's socio-economic development, it has also been blamed for having provided the state with a scheme of structuring their role in accordance with a fixed agenda. Voluntary agencies therefore cease to become voluntary since their activities shall be governed by the state in various ways which are detrimental to their existence and continuity. This is clear distortion of the principles to which voluntary agencies owe their emergence. The state, with an alliance with the voluntary agencies, becomes what Rajni Kothari calls 'the new Zamindar [transmitting] a new phase of capitalist growth initiated from the North, based on internal colonization and privatization of community resources that were hitherto left alone (including by the British)'.[26] So the Seventh Plan is also an articulation of the changing perception of the state drawing upon the capitalist path by invoking 'the rhetoric of environment, people's participation and voluntarism for legitimizing actions that in fact destroy resources and exclude people'.[27] What is necessary, under these circumstances, is to conceive of voluntary action as something that is *sui generis* that develops from among the people, performing roles of a different kind than what the government-inspired agencies did, following a development model that had, in fact failed to deliver the goods. According to Kothari, it is, in the parlance of the national movement, 'a shift back to what is known as *rachna* (constructive work) from *vikas* (progress) which is also [commonly] known as development'.[28]

DEMOCRATIC PROCESS AND VOLUNTARY AGENCIES

Voluntary agencies are both an outcome and a facilitator of democratic process. A distinction is usually made between Government Organized NGO (GONGO) and non-Government Organized NGO (non-GONGO). While the former is wholly government-created and largely state-sponsored agency, the latter has its origin in people's effort.[29] Despite their controversial origin, both the GONGOs and

[26] Rajni Kothari, '*State Against Democracy: In Search of Humane Governance*', Ajanta Publications, New Delhi, 1988, p. 83.
[27] Rajni Kothari, '*State Against Democracy: In Search of Humane Governance*', Ajanta Publications, New Delhi, 1988, p. 83.
[28] Rajni Kothari, 'Voluntary Organizations in a Plural Society', *Indian Journal of Public Administration*, July–September, 1987, p. 440.
[29] Separating the merely construction and development-oriented bureaucratic voluntary agencies from those that are relatively small and working at the grassroots, led by dedicated young men and women who have given up their professional careers and gone for working with the people, Rajni Kothari insists that this distinction is necessary

non-GONGOs are involved in activities which are not always strictly within the purview of the state. Operating in a variety of areas, particularly on the periphery of society, the non-GONGOs take on issues and problems affecting the mass of people at the grassroots. The inability of the government to 'deliver goods' to all irrespective of class, caste, creed or region is undoubtedly an important factor for the growth of a large number of non-GONGOs. Their growing importance in development in those areas where they are active clearly suggests a failure of the state-sponsored democratic process to strike roots. Kothari, therefore, argues that '[i]t is this convergence of despair with the system of governance (largely apolitical) and faith in the democratic process (fundamentally political) that is increasingly making the poor draw upon their own resources (both psychic and environmental) and their traditional institutional/organizational and socio-economic wherewithal'.[30]

There are two types of responses which we must take into account while assessing the role of voluntary agencies in development. One type of response, as shown above, is articulated in different forms of opposition *vis-à-vis* the state-directed development. Hence, the centre of gravity has shifted from the government-nurtured institutions to various socio-political institutions which are located and flourish outside the arena of formal structure of governance. The other equally significant response is structured around concerns for reviving panchayat units that have gradually declined due to indifference of those in power for obvious political consequences. In fact, the Eighth Plan set-out the policy directions by proclaiming that

[i]t is necessary to make development a people's movement. People's initiative and participation must become the key element in the whole process of development. A lot in the area of education (especially literacy), health, family planning, land improvement, efficient land use, minor irrigation, watershed management, recovery of wastelands, afforestation, animal

---

'to understand the situation in which the voluntary organizations are increasingly being placed and are being increasingly forced to take cudgels against the state and its agencies'. Characterizing the former as GONGOS (using an NGO profile but wholly government created), he further argues that the GONGOS have been created to devise 'new tools of control on the freedom of genuine voluntary expressions of social movements and democratic struggles of civil society'. See Rajni Kothari, 'Voluntary Organizations in a Plural Society', *Indian Journal of Public Administration*, July–September, 1987, p. 441. For details of GONGOS, see Rajni Kothari, *State Against Democracy: In Search of Humane Governance*, Ajanta Publications, New Delhi, 1988, pp. 84–5.

[30] Rajni Kothari, 'Towards a People's Democracy', *Biblio*, July–August, 1997, p. 10.

husbandry, dairies, fisheries and sericulture etc., can be achieved by creating people's institutions accountable to the community.[31]

In consonance with the above objective, the Seventy-Third Constitutional Amendment Act, 1992 is probably the most dramatic intervention in the political process to extend and strengthen the traditional Panchayati Raj system of village self-government. Signalling the most fundamental shift of power since Independence, the Panchayati Raj institutions are intended to take charge of future development planning and its implementation. It is 'a change that cannot succeed without major capacitations of the development stakeholders now in charge'.[32] The aim is to reduce the margin of political and administrative discretion and 'to allow the decentralized institutions to gather strength on the basis of people's involvement'.[33] Revamping the panchayat system of self-government requires 'credible community-based institutions' that command local trust and local presence. This is where the role of voluntary agencies assumes tremendous significance. The change in policy directions will remain on paper without the capacitation by voluntary agencies of those at the grassroots. So voluntary agencies, especially the non-GONGO type perform two types of functions: on the one hand, they play significant roles in translating the demands of the people at the grassroots into specific policy directions for the state to consider; with their involvement in activities at the grassroots, they also sustain, on the other, the momentum, gained as a result of a continuous interaction with the people. What is evident is that the voluntary agencies have now become a significant influence in development planning and its realization due to both radical changes at the grassroots and also the failure of the state to reach out to those for whom the welfare schemes are recommended.

CONCLUDING OBSERVATIONS

The discussion clearly reveals the growing importance of voluntary agencies in India's socio-economic development. Their contribution

[31] Quoted from Ashok Chatterjee, 'NGOs: An Alternative Democracy' in Hiranmoy Karlekar (ed.), *Independent India: The First Fifty Years*, Oxford University Press, New Delhi, 1998, pp. 285–6.

[32] Ashok Chatterjee, 'NGOs: An Alternative Democracy' in Hiranmoy Karlekar (ed.), *Independent India: The First Fifty Years*, Oxford University Press, New Delhi, 1998, p. 285.

[33] Kuldeep Mathur, 'Strengthening Bureaucracy: State and Development in India', *Indian Social Science Review*, vol. 1 (1), January–June, 1999, p. 22.

is significant in identifying the limitations of state-centred development that tends to ignore India's diversity as a socio-economic unit
due probably to uncritical faith in the Soviet-type centralized planning. Not only do the voluntary agencies assist the state in realizing
its developmental goals, they also contribute to planning and its
implementation by devising new ways which are meaningful and
appropriate to those at the receiving end. Their role is increasingly
being recognized because the voluntary agencies have the special
advantage of the knowledge of local conditions, not only to design
the programmes better but also monitor them effectively. Even their
contribution in making people aware of various developmental
schemes, adopted by the state is now highly appreciated.[34] This
suggests a clear shift in the government attitude towards the voluntary agencies and vice-versa. That both the state and the voluntary
agencies draw upon each other while discharging their respective
responsibilities is a break with the past. The relationship was, in the
past, structured around the patron-client network where the state as
the provider of funds always set the parameters not only for performance requirements but also for structural and spending patterns to
achieve the goal. It is now evident that a large number of voluntary
agencies declined the state assistance primarily because of the imposed conditionalities. Many of the projects—both state-led and those,
devised by the voluntary agencies—did not take-off because neither
the state nor those involved in the voluntary sector came forward
presumably due to mutual distrust.

The attitude that governed the state perception of the voluntary
sector began to change from the Seventh Plan onwards. For the first
time in the history of planning in India since Independence, an attempt was made in this Plan to conceptualize the role of voluntary
agencies as complementary to that of the state in realizing development. What was remarkable was the recognition of the contribution
of the voluntary sector in areas where the state was absolutely peripheral or appropriated by vested interests. As suggested in the

---

[34] Voluntary agencies are always useful in realizing most developmental schemes
which are meant for the people at the grassroots, admits Arjun Sengupta who has
contributed to planning in India in various capacities. According to him, '[t]he leak-
ages in the employment generation schemes, or public works programmes, or special
schemes of mid-day meals for children and nourishment of lactating mothers or
deprived women members of the families can be effectively plugged only with the
help of the [voluntary agencies]' . See Arjun Sengupta, 'Delivering the Right to the
Development: ESCR [Economic, Social and Cultural Rights] and NGOs', *Economic and
Political Weekly*, 9 October, 1999, p. 2922.

approach paper, there was, for instance, no dearth of programmes for tribal development though no substantial improvement was evident simply because most of them remained on paper and the allocated funds were siphoned off conveniently by those involved in both making and implementing the state policies. While the Seventh Plan laid the foundation, the Eighth Plan was a clear policy statement on the importance of voluntary sector in development.[35] Seeking to reorient the national development policies towards social transformation, the approach paper of the Eighth Plan underlined that the meaningful development consists in mobilizing the skills, strength and creative capabilities of the masses of the people and securing their active participation. Given the inadequacies of the state-led development in attaining the goal, the founding fathers stood for, the Eighth Plan is an improvement even on the Seventh Plan because of (a) its emphasis on people-centred development where voluntary agencies (not the GONGOs) had a significant role to play and (b) its suggestion regarding the areas of creative interaction/cooperation between the state and voluntary sector. What was suggested in this Plan received a boost in the Fifth Pay Commission that supported the voluntary agencies in areas where the government was to withdraw following the Commission's directions. By recommending that '[t]he reduction of Government will have to be achieved through privatization and contracting out of many services that are presently being performed directly by Government',[36] the Commission actually sought to broaden the arena of the activities of voluntary agencies in the social sector.

As most of the voluntary agencies depend even for their survival on financial assistance from outside, they simply cannot ignore the conditionalities that follow. Immediately after Independence, the Khadi and Village Industries Board was constituted to channel government resources to the social sector. There are a large number of funding institutions, created specifically to financially support the activities of voluntary agencies.[37] In most cases, the funding institutions dictate terms and the voluntary agencies by deciding to

[35] *Towards Social Transformation: Approach to Eighth Five Year Plan, 1990–95*, Planning Commission, Government of India, New Delhi, 1990

[36] *The Report of the Fifth Pay Commission*, Government of India, New Delhi, 1997, p. 93.

[37] Of the specialized funding institutions of the Government of India, the Central Social Welfare Board (CSWB), the Council for Advancement of People's Action and Rural Technology (CAPART) and the Society for Promotion of Wasteland Development (SPWD) significant.

accept their financial support have no alternative but to follow them. It is also a common practice that since the ministries and departments generally co-opt the voluntary agencies in project implementation, even these institutions have hardly a free hand in this regard. So, ultimately what determines the decision of those in charge of these institutions are factors other than competence of the voluntary agencies. And those who succeed in getting funds are likely to devote more time to pleasing the bureaucrats or politicians for their favour. This is a situation in which the basic thrust of voluntarism is sure to disappear.

Foreign funding has been an even more sensitive issue though it has provided significant opportunities for innovative and participative action. Voluntary agencies receiving foreign assistance are always viewed with suspicion. This is quite common though there are occasions when 'the bogey of foreign hand' is blown out of proportion 'whenever powerful vested interests are threatened' by movements, led by voluntary agencies. Suspicion has other roots as well, such as 'distrust of minorities with outside connections'.[38] As regards assistance from the international institutions like the World Bank, UNDP or UNICEF, the state distributes the funds following their own criteria. Voluntary agencies are not, therefore, actually free to decide their priority because the funding agencies—whether they are international institutions or non-official foreign donors—bring the inevitable baggage of agenda set elsewhere. In other words, barring a few fortunate ones, most of the voluntary agencies are therefore involved, directly or indirectly, in processes, which they would have avoided otherwise.

Analysis of the role of voluntary agencies in development in India highlights three points which are of immense theoretical significance, in grasping the development process particularly in a Third World situation. *First*, their growing strength contributes significantly to the importance of civil society—a space that has largely been encroached upon by the state. Drawing on 'a criss-crossing network of various non-state institutions'[39]—like, families, associations of different types

---

[38] Ashok Chatterjee, 'NGOs: An Alternative Democracy' in Hiranmoy Karlekar, *Independent India: The First Fifty Years*, Oxford University Press, New Delhi, 1998, p. 289.

[39] Ralph Dahrendorf, 'Economic Opportunity, Civil Society and Political Liberty', *Development and Change*, vol. 27, 1996, p. 231. What accounts for the decline of these institutions as André Béteille argues, is '[p]opulist demagoguery [that] weakens civil society as surely as reasoned criticism strengthens it'. Andre Beteille, 'Citizenship, State and Civil Society', *Economic and Political Weekly*, 4 September, 1999, p. 2590.

including trade unions and clubs—voluntary associations are also a serious endeavour to create 'a non state autonomous sphere'[40]. Not only do they restore the space that originally belonged to civil society, they are also significant inputs to conceptualizing development in completely different perspective where state is just peripheral. The *second* theoretical point—an extension of the first—relates to a shift in conceptualizing the role of voluntary associations. Since the dominant paradigm in which the role of voluntary agencies is sought to be articulated, is 'both statist and corporatist' their role is structured around the patron-client network where state is hegemonic. This is an inhibiting conceptualization in the sense that it does not provide even a clue to meaningfully explain voluntary efforts, not rooted in the state or its initiatives. What is needed therefore is an alternative discourse of analysis that draws upon not just political rights against the state but rights that 'obtain from social, ethnic, ecological, gender and ethical mainsprings of a diverse and plural society'. So voluntary associations are probably the most important vehicle in radically altering the development paradigm by suggesting a more action-based agenda, based on 'rights of diverse communities and ecologies and moral orders that have been violated and homogenized'[41] in pursuit of an essentially state-oriented development. The *third* important point concerns with the nature of development and its conceptualization. Given the hegemonic role of the state, development invariably means a programme of action, based on the priority of developmental goals, defined in a universalistic manner. The state is a facilitator of development, articulated in ways that ascertain conformity with an essentially western ethos. In this sense, development is political, and not, at all, managerial or administrative, as it is sought to be made because what accounts for a specific type of development is, as Adrian Leftwich argues, not the system of government but the type of state regardless of whether it is democratic or not. In his words,

development is ... inescapably political ... [f]or at any point in any developmental sequence what is crucially at issue is how resources are to be used

[40] S. H. Rudolph, 'Civil Society and the Realm of Freedom', *Economic and Political Weekly*, 13 May, 2000, p. 1762. In India, however, the meaning, if not the terminology of civil society, as Neera Chandhoke argues, 'has been widely used to delineate the upsurge of popular movements against the state'. For details, Neera Chandhoke, *State and Civil Society: Explorations in Political Theory*, Sage, New Delhi, 1995, pp. 108–9.

[41] Rajni Kothari, 'Voluntary Organizations in a Plural Society', *Indian Journal of Public Administration*, July –September, 1987, p. 452.

and distributed in new ways and the inevitable disputes arising from calculations by individuals and groups as to who will win and who will lose as a result'.[42]

Development is not, therefore, axiomatic and its features vary radically from one society to another simply because of the political processes in which it is articulated. What is evident is that there are multiple ways of conceptualizing development and not merely through 'measurable indicators like the GDP'. The role of voluntary agencies is crucial here. Through contestations, voluntary agencies have not only exposed the inherent limitations of the state-driven development paradigm, they have also put forward a view of development that 'departs from the conventional ways of measuring [development] by focusing not on GDP and GNP, but on the enlargement of human capabilities and the enhancement of the quality of life for all'.[43]

[42] Adrian Leftwich (ed.), *Democracy and Development: Theory and Practice*, Polity Press, Cambridge, 1996, p. 6. According to Leftwich, political is a process that includes all the activities of conflict, cooperation and negotiation involved in the use, production and distribution of resources.

[43] Niraja Gopal Jayal, 'The Governance Agenda: Making Democratic Development Dispensable', *Economic and Political Weekly*, 22 February, 1997, p. 412.

CHAPTER THIRTEEN

Bureaucracy and Politics in India*

Mohit Bhattacharya

In an attempt at explaining the state and politics in India, focusing on the operators of the State machinery, the bureaucracy, provides a suitable point of access. Under the Rajiv Gandhi regime, there is a move to purge the Indian bureaucracy of its deadwood; efforts are on to improve the management skills of the bureaucracy through the introduction of the computer and compulsory and systematic training programmes. 'Management' is the key word now and there is interest being evinced in streamlining the top bureaucracy along lines of private management. Sophisticated management practices and a cadre of public system managers seem to be the need of the hour. The purpose of this paper is to examine the politics of the current management upsurge in government against the background of the deepening crisis of the Indian state. This seems to be a turning point in India's political history, much like the momentous decision taken in the Constituent Assembly immediately after Independence to continue with the all-India services under the explicit patronage of Sardar Vallabhbhai Patel.

Indian politics is obviously amenable to a variety of approaches for analytical purposes. But a post-colonial State with a hangover of bureaucratic domination can be profitably understood through the bureaucratic window. Hamza Alavi's study of the nature of the State in Pakistan and Bangladesh ably demonstrates the efficiency of the approach.[1] What role does the bureaucracy play in the Indian polity?

* Zoya Hasan et al., (ed.), *The State, Political Processes and Identity*, Sage, New Delhi, 1989.
[1] Hamza Alavi, 'The State in Post-Colonial Societies: Pakistan and Bangladesh' in Harry Goulbourne (ed.), *Politics and State in the Third World*, Macmillan, London, 1979.

In answering this question, one has to step outside the conventional Weberian view of an instrumental non-political bureaucracy as a rational element, working at the behest of the political boss. One has also to shun the cultural cliché of the policy–administration dichotomy; studies by western scholars have convincingly proved that bureaucratic mandarins play decisive political roles in the liberal–pluralist regimes of the UK and western Europe.[2]

The Weberian notion of instrumental bureaucracy has been the main guiding thought in public administration in India. However, Weber's political writings have generally been overlooked where he moves away from the instrumental notion to a political view of the bureaucracy. Two of the major shifts in Weber's thought in his political writings[3] are: (i) the bureaucracy in practice seeks to appropriate the goal-setting function of the politician, thus turning into a substitute for the politician; and (ii) the bureaucracy tends to become a separate social group, insulating itself from other groups in society, its self-interest tends to become the dominant concern.

Long before Weber, Marx in his earlier writings (1837–44) presented an invasive view of the bureaucracy. To Marx, bureaucracy is State formalism, a web of practical illusions. Bureaucrats are the jesuits and theologians of the State and the bureaucracy is the priests' republic. The bureaucracy is secret, safeguarded within itself by hierarchy and outside by its nature as a closed corporation. Thus public political spirit and the political mentality appear to the bureaucracy as a betrayal of its secret. The principle of its knowledge is authority, and its mentality the idolatry of authority. But within the bureaucracy spiritualism turns into a crass materialism, the materialism of passive behaviour, fixed principles, attitudes, traditions. As far as the individual bureaucrat is concerned, the aim of the State becomes his private aim, in the form of a race for higher posts, of careerism. 'In bureaucracy the identity of the State's interest and particular private purpose is established in such a way that the State's interest becomes a particular private purpose opposed to other private purposes.'[4]

A telling description of the bureaucracy that comes close to the contemporary Indian scene can be found in *The Eighteenth Brumaire of*

[2] See, for instance, J. Armstrong, *The European Administrative Elite*, Princeton University Press, Princeton, 1973.

[3] David Beetham, *Max Weber and the Theory of Modern Politics*, George Allen & Unwin Ltd, London, 1974, Ch. 3.

[4] *Writings of the Young Marx on Philosophy and Society*, translated and edited by Loyd D. Easton and Kurt H. Guddat, Anchor Books, Doubleday, New York, 1967, pp. 184–7.

Louis Bonaparte. Among other things, Marx describes here the process of the bureaucratization of the society after Bonaparte's *coup d'état* of December 1851:

Every common interest was straightaway severed from society, counterposed to it as a higher, *general* interest, snatched from the activity of society's members themselves and made an object of government activity, from a bridge, a school house and the communal property of a village community to the railways, the, national wealth and the national university of France.[5]

Taking the cue from Marx, the political role of the bureaucracy may be seen as revolving around the issue: how are social activities gradually taken over by the bureaucracy, effecting in the process a mammoth expansion of government activities? How do the members of the bureaucracy play the power game behind the facade of neutrality? Studies on the politics of bureaucracy are of particular relevance to the 'Third World' countries, as most of them have emerged from a colonial experience characterized by bureaucratic rule (Alavi's concept of 'overdeveloped' State). The continuation of the old mode of governing with bureaucratic hegemony, even after independence, has been seen in countries like Pakistan, Bangladesh, Ghana and Nigeria.

Against this background, certain questions can be legitimately raised. Are bureaucrats likely to formulate public policies designed to eliminate mass poverty or to reduce inequality in income distribution? Are they prepared to undertake a thorough change in the power structure and in the resource flows of society with a view to facilitating the 'deep involvement' and 'active participation' of the masses?

In the context of African countries too, the role of the bureaucracy has similarly been questioned. It has been argued that politicians in the new states of Africa have not been able to accept the top-level bureaucracy as a reliable instrument and there has been a general lack of trust between the two groups. One African scholar goes to the extent of suggesting that the present-day popular unrest in many African countries can be traced to the underlying contest for power between politicians and bureaucrats, as popular unrest tends to tarnish the image of the former and weaken their popular base and legitimacy.[6]

---

[5] Karl Marx, *The Eighteenth Brumaire of Louis Bonaparte,* Foreign Languages Press Peking, 1978, p. 124.

[6] Kofi Ankomah 'Bureaucracy and Political Unrest in Africa', *The Indian Journal of Public Administration,* April–June 1983.

In India, earlier studies on the bureaucracy[7] focused on the social background of bureaucrats and the relationship between the bureaucracy and politicians. The suggestion was to go in for a more 'representative' bureaucracy.[8] The 'values' of bureaucracy are supposed to be flowing from their class character. Another trend of thought has been to advocate a balancing of interests between bureaucrats and politicians. Some studies have made oblique references to the phenomenon of 'bureaucrats under stress' in a mixed situation of democracy and development.[9]

Most studies, however, seek to legitimize the bureaucracy by ascribing it a special role in development tasks. Despite dysfunctionalities observed in actual field situations, this normative concept of 'development bureaucracy' has haunted our researchers. The assumption is that the underdevelopment of the Third World is primarily due to lack of 'administration'. Therefore, a special type of administration, development administration has been flaunted as the panacea,[10] not taking into account the fact that administration is a dependent variable whose nature and working is conditioned by history and societal forces.

Important dimensions of bureaucratic politics, like organizational expansion, manipulation of transfers and postings, and large-scale resource misappropriation in the guise of development have virtually gone unnoticed and unexplained. The question may be raised: Is the trend towards centralization of power and the growth of the bureaucratic–military State in India explainable by bureaucratic behaviour? Is perpetuation of poverty a matter of mere implementation failure, or is there a design in it? How far can one attribute the rise of destabilizing forces to the role of the bureaucracy in India?

Under Article 356 of the Indian Constitution, the central government

[7] See, for instance, C. P. Bhambhri, *Bureaucracy and Politics in India*, Vikas, Delhi, 1971, and *Administrators in a Changing Society*, National Publishing House, Delhi, 1972. Other studies of importance are: V. Subramaniam, *Social Background of India's Administrators*, Publications Division, Government of India, New Delhi, 1971; Shanthi Kothari and Ramashray Roy, *Relations between Politicians and Administrators at the District Level*, Indian Institute of Public Administration, New Delhi, 1969.

[8] See in this connection, Haridwar Rai and Sakendra Prasad Singh, 'Indian Bureaucracy: A Case for Representatives', *The Indian Journal of Public Administration*, January–March 1973.

[9] Richard Taub, *Bureaucrats Under Stress*, University of California Press, Berkeley, 1969.

[10] In this connection, see S. P. Verma and S. K. Sharma (eds), *Development Administration*, Indian Institute of Public Administration, New Delhi, 1984.

can take over state administration on grounds of failure of the constitutional machinery. Suppression of state governments is also authorized, under Article 365, in situations when the state fails to comply with the directions given in the exercise of the executive power of the Union. There have been many presidential takeovers-seventy till 1984. Central takeover of state administration means complete bureaucratic control of the state administrative machinery. Since the perpetuation of such a crisis benefits the bureaucracy most, its role in India needs to be explored further. Whatever light has been thrown by the Shah Commission on the working of Mrs Gandhi's Emergency regime does prove the towering presence of an extremely pliable bureaucracy during a political crisis at the cost of open legitimate politics.

The Shah Commission described bureaucratic behaviour during the Emergency in the following words:

Tyrants sprouted at all levels overnight—tyrants whose claim to authority was largely based on their proximity to the seats of power. The attitude of the general run of the public functionaries was largely characterized by a paralysis of the will to do the right and proper thing. The ethical considerations inherent in public behaviour became generally dim and in many cases beyond the mental grasp of many of the public functionaries. Desire for self-preservation as admitted by a number of public servants at various levels became the sole motivation for their official actions and behaviour. Anxiety to serve at any cost formed the key-note of approach to the problems that came before many of them. The fear generated by the mere threat and without even the actual use of the weapon of detention under MISA became so pervasive that the general run of public servants acted as willing tools of tyranny. That the primary, and not infrequently the sole motivation in the case of a number of public servants who acted unlawfully to the prejudice of the rights of citizens, was the desire for self protection—desire for survival, may be regarded as some extenuation of their conduct. Yet, if the nation is to preserve the fundamental values of a democratic society, every person, whether a public functionary or private citizen, must display a degree of vigilance and willingness to sacrifice. Without the awareness of what is right and a desire to act according to what is right there may be no realization of what is wrong. During the Emergency, for many a public functionary the dividing line between right and wrong, moral and immoral, ceased to exist.[11]

This is ample proof of the bureaucracy's alignment with reactionary and fascist forces in times of eclipse of democratic processes. Bureaucratic authoritarianism *surfaced* during the Emergency because

---

[11] *Shah Commission of Inquiry Interim Report II*, 26 April 1978.

of favourable environmental conditions. The implication here is that under conditions of political underdevelopment, there is a built-in bias toward bureaucratic ascendancy. Under propitious circumstances the latent tendencies come out into the open.

From all available evidence it appears that the higher-level bureaucracy in India, especially at the Secretariat level, is deeply involved in policy direction. The precise role of the top bureaucracy in situations such as the Punjab crisis or communal riots is shrouded in obscurity. However, it is generally understood that there is some tension between the generalist administrators and the specialists, including the police. The power game that goes on between the different services at the expense of public interest hardly ever gets publicized. At the grassroots level, 'street-corner' bureaucracy in the form of the VLW, *patwari*, BDO, *thanedar* and field-level officials of the irrigation bureaucracy is known to function as gatekeepers of the public services. As studies on anti-poverty programmes point out, any attempt to reach out to the poor is thwarted and deflected by the social power group in collusion with the field bureaucracy. A Planning Commission Report throws light on this phenomenon:

The attitude of the bureaucracy towards the implementation of land reforms is generally lukewarm and often apathetic. This is, of course, inevitable because, as in the case of men who wield political power, those in the higher echelons of administration also are substantial landowners themselves or they have close links with big landowners. The village functionaries like *patwaris, karmcharis, karnams, sambogs, talatis*, etc., are inevitably petty landowners. They are also under the sway of big landowners.[12]

The politics of privatization of public administration at the grassroots level is another vital area for intensive research. The very fact that the national policy for decentralized development through the instrumentality of panchayati raj institutions has remained a policy on paper, and that such institutions have been languishing in most states is an indication of the stubborn anti-decentralist stance of the bureaucracy. On this issue, the Ashok Mehta Committee on Panchayati Raj Institutions (1978) said:

Bureaucracy had probably its own role in dissociating the PRIs from the development process. Several factors seem to have conditioned their perception. The system of line hierarchy would find favour with them as an organizational principle. The officers would feel that they are primarily accountable

[12] Planning Commission, *Report of the Task Force on Agrarian Relations*, New Delhi, 1973, p. 9.

for results and financial proprieties to the state government. The officials knew no better than to trust their own fraternity. They would, on the one hand, therefore, be averse to PRIs being entrusted with additional functions and on the other would not easily get adjusted to working under the supervision of elected representatives.[13]

Macro-concerns about the nature of the State and politics in India need to be linked to micro-studies of empirical situations at different levels of the politico-administrative system. Each level—be it the grassroots level or the block, district and state level—is not an island unto itself. There are distinct inter-level linkages that sustain the present system as a whole.

The current trend toward 'managerialism' in public administration[14] is an indication of the ascendancy of the generalist administrator who would like to see his relative position among the services strengthened further, making out a case for 'depoliticization' of administration. This attempt, if successful, will lead to a substitution of ministerial and party politics by bureaucratic politics. At the Secretariat level, the general administrator has always played the role of surrogate politician. Each case of central takeover of a state, as earlier stated, has meant appropriation of political positions by the generalist administrator. It will be interesting to examine the role of the generalist administrator in instigating central takeover of states and to illuminate the role played by them in the actual takeover period.

The continuation of the chief field administrator—district collector—as the focal point of administration at the sub-state level has been supported as a guarantor against possible administrative failure. But the collector's position is essentially political, as district-level decisions relate to resource mobilization and distribution, disposition of the law and order machinery, conflict resolution and surveillance over grassroots institutions. The political role of the collector is, again, an unresearched area. But the way collectors are shuffled across districts by state governments (as in Bihar, for instance) does indicate a political use of this key field position. The other consequence of the collector's hegemony at the field level is the gradual languishing of panchayati raj and other local institutions that are

[13] *Report of the Committee on Panchayati Raj Institutions*, Government of India, 1977, pp. 5–6.

[14] See, in this context, the report about a letter written by Mufti Mohammad Sayeed (former Union Tourism Minister) to the Prime Minister inquiring about the reported move to devise the American model of administrative management for our senior bureaucrats. *The Statesman*, Calcutta, 1 October 1987.

often bypassed through the creation of special purpose bodies (e.g., SFDA, DPAP) under the overall control of the indispensable collector. The machinery that maintains law and order, which is the basic function of the State, has virtually been privatized. It is well known that the police in rural areas generally aid the big landlords who have considerable political clout. Suppression of movements of the landless or sharecroppers is common in many parts of India.[15] The National Police Commission, expressing concern about 'pressures' and 'political interferences,' observed:

We are also aware that the unhealthy influences and pressures that are brought to bear on the police do not always originate from political sources alone. Capitalists, industrialists, businessmen, landlords and such others who form the richer and more influential sections of society have immense capacity to generate such pressures to operate at different levels in the police, either directly or indirectly through political sources, and influence the course of police action.[16]

In this context of privatization of government machinery, to talk of strengthening the police organization or increasing its managerial competence is tantamount to augmenting the repressive capacity of the private army—the police.

The Indian State thus has a parallel structural configuration: a political structure erected through the periodic electoral process and a bureaucratic structure permanently fixed as a kind of integral piece of State furniture. Pursuit of 'managerialism' in public administration, if extended too far, would obviously reduce the political structure to a secondary position. This point has been clearly brought out by Kothari in his diagnosis of the political malaise:

... hitching the system to the Westminster model of government was a great mistake. In course of time it turned such a remarkable party system into an instrument of centralized power, led to a manipulative style of politics, and paved the way for the ascendancy of a bureaucratic State which is in many ways a negation of democratic politics.[17]

Issues like Centre–State relations or poverty amelioration are basically political issues and only peripherally managerial issues. It is political capacity, rather than managerial capacity, that needs

---

[15] Moin Shakir, *State and Politics in Contemporary India*, Ajanta Publications, Delhi, 1986, Ch. 3

[16] *Second Report of the National Police Commission*, Government of India, 1979, p. 24.

[17] Rajni Kothari, *Democratic Polity and Social Change in India*, Allied Publishers, New Delhi, 1976.

strengthening in contemporary India. But one suspects that the trend is in the other direction, with obvious consequences for political institutions and formal political role-players.

In most parts of India, the people are yet to emerge as actors on the political stage. They are encapsulated in primordial social formations, such as caste, religion and ethnicity. For a breakaway from parochialism to a universal existential situation the intervention of politics is necessary. Bureaucratic politics has generally been directed towards the atrophy of formal political institutions and opposition to popular participation in the process of politics. To the extent that the current emphasis on bureaucratic managerialism will succeed in practice, the unleashing of popular energies and the emergence of the people as aggressive participants and actors in the polity will get delayed, if not wholly foreclosed.

The political role of the bureaucracy in India and in most 'Third World' countries is subsumed in 'modernization theory' and the allied concept of 'development administration'—both developed by American social scientists on the assumption of the need for State-directed socio-economic changes modelled on Western liberal capitalist regimes. These sponsors of modernization and development have been oblivious of the pre-Independence bureaucratic regimes, weakly articulated political infrastructures and highly segmented and iniquitous socio-economic structures of most 'Third World' countries. It is assumed that the bureaucracy would behave like Platonic guardian kings without any interest of their own.

The colonial administrative structure in India was left undisturbed, by and large, even after Independence, which meant a tacit acceptance of the political role of the bureaucracy operating from crucial administrative positions such as departmental secretary, collector and others. Despite occasional calls for modernization, development and poverty amelioration, the basic structure of the Indian polity has never been tampered with in any radical sense. Rather, the so-called 'development' policy, as studies point out, has reinforced the traditional power structure in many instances. The process of socio-economic development, instead of bringing about radical restructuring, seems to have admirably furthered the cause of the bourgeoisie, the landed interests, the bureaucracy and the politicians. A relationship of close interdependence has developed over the years among these groups. There might be occasional conflicts of interests, but these are few and far between, compared to their united stand in monopolizing the State apparatus and enjoying the fruits of development. Viewed from this angle, the bureaucracy is not an autonomous class but a surrogate class; it puts on the mask of Weberian structural formalism and behavioural neutrality. But in reality, far from being neutral and rule-bound, it bends the rules with alacrity to serve the 'vested interests', which is a way of serving its own interests.

So long as the large masses remain 'culturally' *out of politics* (although seasonally and ritually *in politics*) and the basically feudal–capitalist character of the Indian State persists, the bureaucracy will continue to have a dominant behind-the-scenes political role in furthering centralization, sabotaging decentralization and perpetuating the iniquitous socio-economic structure which, in turn, would facilitate the preservation of its own power position.

To sum up, a false notion of Weberian instrumental bureaucracy and the practice of State-directed development administration have stood in the way of a realistic appreciation of the political role of the bureaucracy in India. What the bureaucracy actually does or does not do needs to be tested empirically and not judged *a priori*. The politics of the bureaucracy is not its own politics but the politics of the dominant interests of which it is an integral part. To understand the role of the bureaucracy, what is needed is to shun the conventional bureaucracy-in-administration mode of analysis and replace it by a bureaucracy-in-society mode.

CHAPTER FOURTEEN

Bureaucracy at Crossroads[*]

Madhav Godbole

INTRODUCTION

The last 50 years since Independence are marked by the continuous downhill journey of the Indian bureaucracy.[1] Time and again, questions have been raised about the imperviousness, woodenheadedness, obstructiveness, rigidity, and rule-and procedure-bound attitude of the bureaucracy. Only the context in which these harsh but often well-deserved judgments have been passed has changed. Initially, it was in the context of lack of enthusiasm of the bureaucracy for the implementation of various development schemes and programmes. Jawaharlal Nehru, the first Prime Minister of Independent India, was often despondent about the administration and lamented about the 'bureaucratic jungle'. After his 17-year term as Prime Minister of India, a foreign correspondent asked Nehru what his biggest failure as a Prime Minister was? Without any hesitation, Nehru replied, 'It is that I could not reform the administration'.

It is often alleged that the bureaucracy is opposed to the decentralization of powers and functions as envisaged earlier in the *Panchayat Raj* and, more recently, in the 73rd and 74th amendments of the Constitution. Thus Indian bureaucracy is perceived as incapable of giving its best in any situation in which it is asked to function.

---

[*] This is an expanded and updated version of the article which earlier appeared in *The Indian Journal of Public Administration*. Special Number, Fifty Years Of Indian Administration—Retrospect and Prospects. July–September 1997, pp. 560–66.

[1] See Madhav Godbole, 'Corruption, Political interference and the Civil Service' in S. Guhan and Samuel Paul (eds), *Corruption in India: Agenda for Action*, Public Affairs Centre, Bangalore, Vision Books, New Delhi, 1977, pp. 60–87.

Currently, the onslaught is in the context of the bureaucracy's opposition to the economic liberalization and globalization policies being pursued since 1991. Prime Minister Atal Behari Vajpayee in his address to the Federation of Indian Chambers of Commerce and Industry in December 2000 bemoaned that the bureaucracy 'shows no sense of impatience and urgency' and simply did not have the 'drive to meet the targets and deadlines'.

A recent news item showed that according to A. T. Kearney's Foreign Direct Investment Index, India has slipped steadily from position number five in June 1998 to number seven in December 1998, before recovering to position number six in June 1999, only to fall again to position 11 in January 2000 and thereafter. An obstructionist bureaucracy (or *Babudom* as a leading newspaper insists on calling it), among other factors, is stated to be responsible for this decline. During the last three years, there have been a number of critical observations in the same vein.

In addressing the issues in this sector, the enormity of the task must not be overlooked. This is particularly true of the 'cutting-edge' level of administration. For example, the Inspector General of Registration's (IGR) office in Maharashtra which deals with registration of documents in the state caters to 10 million clients each year. The documents which are pending in the IGR offices for registration prior to 1984 total 1.7 million—many of which have been destroyed or damaged by now due to unscientific storage. The Maharashtra State Electricity Board caters to the requirement of over 10.2 million consumers of electricity in the state. The work efficiency of these offices can thus affect, either favourably or adversely, a large segment of society. It is also important to note that the government, in most cases, is a monopolistic service provider and the people have nowhere to go if they find the service in a government office unsatisfactory.

In spite of the overwhelming importance of the subject of improving governance, successive governments at the Centre and in the states have neglected the subject of administrative reforms. After the late 1960s, no administrative reforms commission has been appointed either at the Centre, or in most of the states. Even when certain recommendations for administrative reforms were placed before the government from time to time, there has been no administrative or political will to take requisite difficult decisions in the matter. This was amply evident in respect to the recommendations of the Fifth Pay Commission. The Centre as also the State Governments implemented only those recommendations of the Fifth Pay Commission which pertained to increase in the pay and allowances and improvement in other service conditions of the employees. All those recommendations which pertained to improving the productivity and efficiency of the government employees and to make the government leaner and thin.ner were unceremoniously shelved. All political parties in the country were party to these decisions in one state or the other or at the Centre. The same was the fate of the recommendations of the committee of the National Development Council appointed under the chairmanship of Biju Patnaik, the then Chief Minister of Orissa, during the regime of Narasimha Rao as Prime Minister, to consider ways for bringing in economy in expenditure on government employees. But, clearly time is running out. The issues in this sector cannot be neglected any longer.

The Depressing Scenario

There is no denying the fact that the public image of the bureaucracy at all levels has reached its nadir. There is a widespread feeling among the people that the bureaucracy is unresponsive, insensitive, lacks integrity and is neither transparent nor accountable. The ploy of 'systemic failure' used so ingeniously during the bank scam to shield those who were guilty of gross dereliction of duty or worse, has come to roost with a vengeance. Since then all scams and failures of the government have been ascribed to systemic failures, eroding the faith of the people in the civil service. It will not be wrong to say that people would have been prepared to suffer in silence if the bureaucracy was to be only inefficient. What is worse is that it has also become highly corrupt. The feeling has grown that not just the lower bureaucracy but even the higher civil servants are in league with their political masters, industrialists and vested interests, and are together plundering the country. Looking around, one cannot but agree with these unpalatable observations. At no time in the past, so many senior civil servants were facing criminal prosecutions and anti-corruption enquiries. The Uttar Pradesh IAS Association took the very unusual step of identifying, by secret ballot, three of its most corrupt members. Similar moves had started in Madhya Pradesh. It is not surprising that, in a number of international surveys and comparisons, India has been categorized as one of the most corrupt countries in the world.

POLITICIZATION OF SERVICES

We have come a long way from the original objectives and ideals which permeated the creation of permanent civil services while framing the Constitution. All pros and cons of the issue were discussed at considerable length and a conscious decision was taken by the Constituent Assembly to provide some safeguards to the two all-India civil services. Vallabhbhai Patel, the then Union Home Minister, wanted the services to be apolitical, independent, fearless and upright in tendering advice to the government. Largely, it was his foresight which led to the acceptance of the institution of All India Services. Unfortunately, reality has turned out to be quite the opposite. Most of the safeguards have remained on paper. Successive governments, both at the Centre and the states, have continued to take actions in total disregard of the Constitutional obligations cast on them.

The watershed in this process was undeniably the regime of Indira Gandhi as Prime Minister. She made no secret of her contempt for the civil services and took every opportunity to run them down. The concept of 'committed' services did permanent damage to the fabric of the services. The ambitious and upwardly mobile civil servants quickly took the hint. A new breed of civil servants was born who were prepared to crawl when asked to bend and were prepared to do the bidding of their political masters, often anticipating their wishes. The Prime minister's 'household' and her private office started exerting considerable influence in the postings and transfers of officers. No doubt, this process was legitimized by its ready acceptance by civil servants themselves.

UNHEALTHY INFLUENCE OF INDUSTRIAL TYCOONS, GODMEN

The politicization of the services was carried forward by the next Prime Minister, Rajiv Gandhi. During his regime, some of the most eminent civil servants of outstanding calibre and integrity were treated most shabbily. Business tycoons came to acquire a decisive voice in the promotions, postings and transfers of civil servants. Civil servants were treated as second-class citizens who were to be at the beck and call of their political masters. The most intemperate and ill-considered comments of a Supreme Court judge, from the bench, in effect, equating the higher civil servants with one's cook and personal servants, were responsible for further erosion of the prestige, position and standing of the civil services.

The interregnum of the short spells of the National Front and the Janata Dal governments carried this process further. The tenure of Chandra Shekhar as Prime Minister saw the tightening of the vicious hold of large business and industrial houses, astrologers and godmen on the promotions, postings and transfers of higher civil servants. Yet again, the civil servants not only accepted these writings on the wall but quickly became adept at manoeuvring the system and had no compunctions in making full use of these extra-Constitutional centres of power.

The regime of Narasimha Rao as Prime Minister saw the intensification of these forces. The power brokers and their influence over the civil services acquired new legitimacy. The Prime Minister's office once again became all-powerful. For the first time since Independence, a policy of giving extensions in service, beyond the age of retirement, was adopted with respect to officers of the rank of secretaries to the government and those manning equivalent posts, leading to considerable demoralization. The state governments were quick to take advantage of this new policy and asked for similar dispensation with respect to officers serving under them. Thus an altogether new ballgame was started. These and other totally short-sighted policies contributed to the further worsening of the *espirit de corps* in the services.

This rapid downhill journey of the services continued in the regime of the United Front governments at the Centre after the general elections in the country in 1996. After the general elections in 1999, the BJP-led coalition government has continued to pursue the same type of mindless policies with respect to the civil services. Transfers of secretaries and other senior officers have been far too frequent severely curtailing the tenure of officers in these posts. Yet another unnerving development is the premature repatriation of All India Service officers to their parent cadres if they do not toe the line of the ministers. This has created a fear psychosis among the senior officers and has totally undermined their independence and freedom.

The situation in the states in this period has gone from bad to worse. There is no moral authority left with the Centre to tender any advice to the states. And, in any case, it is now the regional parties which are calling the shots and the Centre is in no position to guide the states or to prevail upon them to take any particular line of action. Against this background, one question which has to be addressed is where do we go from here? Is this the end of the road? Should the permanent civil services be abolished altogether as is being advocated by some people?

Comparison Between IAS and ICS and IPS and IP Invalid

Often, comparisons are made between the Indian Administrative Service and the Indian Police Service on the one hand, and their predecessor services, namely, the Indian Civil Service and the Indian Police, on the other. It must be admitted that such a comparison is invalid to begin with. By no means, the record of the work and conduct of the ICS or IP officers was uniformly superior to that of their successor services. There were rotten eggs in these services too. But, more importantly, the conditions in which these services worked were qualitatively different from those in which the civil services have to function now. It is a moot question whether these services would have even been as successful as the present civil services. It would, therefore, be inappropriate to draw any facile conclusions and to suggest that the present civil services ought to follow in the footsteps of these services. To do so will mean remaining in a fool's paradise.

The Way Ahead

A number of steps can be considered to deal with the present highly depressing situation. The first set of measures relates to improving the moral and inner fibre of the services, and the second pertains to institutional and other changes to usher in an open government which is transparent, accountable, sensitive and people-friendly. For lack of space, these remedial actions are considered only illustratively in the following paragraphs.

Creation of Civil Service Boards for Service Matters

Let us first deal briefly with the important pre-requisites pertaining to the morale of the services. One of the main suggestions on this behalf pertains to the setting up of a *statutory* civil services board (CSB), both at the Centre and the states. These Boards could advise the government on matters pertaining to promotions, postings, foreign assignments and transfers. Its advice should be binding on the government. Wherever the government decides to overrule the advice, it should be incumbent on the government to record the reasons in writing which should be open to challenge before an appropriate authority. The stand taken by the Centre on this subject at the chief ministers' conference convened on 24 May 1997 is far too weak and fails to address the basic issues. Effectively, the Centre proposed to the states setting up CSBs *on the lines of those in the Centre.*

The experience, however, shows that at the Centre these boards have hardly inspired any confidence among the officers. In fact, the working of such boards is an example of how ineffective, arbitrary and casual they can be. Further, the recommendations of these boards have not received any particular consideration or respect at the level of the Appointments Committee of the Cabinet (ACC). In an appeal filed by the Centre in the Supreme Court in 1988 against the judgement of the Central Administrative Tribunal in the case of Jagdish Chander Jaitli, the Centre pressed for untrammelled powers to the cabinet secretary and the ACC in deciding matters pertaining to promotions, postings and transfers of officers. This is quite the antithesis of the satutory civil service boards envisaged in the reform of the present system. It is another matter that the states were not prepared to accept even this watered-down version of the CSBs. The statement adopted by the conference shows that 'some misgivings were expressed regarding the mechanism of the CSB', though the Centre clarified that the CSB as envisaged in the Action Plan was basically to aid the political executive to 'implement a streamlined and transparent transfer and promotion policy'. This was clearly a case of clash of opposite objectives! It is also necessary to note that the Centre is not prepared either to set an example by amending its present scheme to have an institutional arrangement which will serve the purpose of bringing about some sanity, rationality and transparency in the system. This basic requirement for upholding the morale of the services has thus become a dead letter even at the stage of initiation of the discussion on the subject.

Putting an End to Transfer Mania

The arbitrary and mindless transfers of government servants have become a matter of serious concern. The states are now playing havoc in the exercise of these powers. Neither is the Centre free from blemish on this account. The main question for consideration is when a transfer may be treated as a punishment. Transfers have become a lucrative industry in several states and there is no possibility of it being delicenced even in this era of economic liberalization! The worst example of this 'transfer mania' is to be found in the actions of successive governments in Uttar Pradesh. It may seem odd but this also includes the period when the state was under President's Rule. Unfortunately, the Supreme Court refused to take cognizance of this totally untenable situation in spite of the public interest litigation filed by the Common Cause, an NGO in Delhi. However, with the transfers of over 600 IAS and IPS officers effected by the BJP–BSP coalition government headed by Mayawati in less than two months since assuming office, the Uttar Pradesh High Court took cognizance of this shocking state of affairs. The High Court noted that all governments in the last decade had been responsible for making transfers and postings a lucrative industry, and observed that 'government servants were being treated like shuttle-cocks to be banged and battered around frequently on political, caste, monetary and other extraneous considerations'. The court suggested the setting up of a high level committee to oversee transfers and postings. The state government promptly went in appeal and got a stay order from a division bench of the court. It is abundantly clear that there is no political will to make any change in the present system.

Ombudsman for Grievance Redressal of Civil Servants

The other suggestions in this behalf such as the creation of an ombudsman for looking into the grievances of government servants, prompt action of investigation, prosecution and punishment of officers who are involved in corruption cases and so on are also unlikely to see any expeditious action. The resolution adopted by the chief ministers' conference on 24 May 1997 itself provides for 'making appropriate allowance for variation on local circumstances', a euphemism for stalling action. Otherwise, the remedies for improving the present mess in the bureaucracy in the country should have been accepted as a universally applicable package of measures for time-bound implementation.

New Code of Conduct and Charter of Ethics

Reference may be made to some other facets of civil service reforms which are long overdue. The most important of these pertains to adoption of a new code of conduct and ethics. Historically, the civil service had an image of absolute honesty, integrity, impartiality, objectivity and sterling character. Over a period of time all these characteristics have been diluted. There is now a common perception that civil servants have made a common cause with politicians and criminals and have developed a nexus with these elements to exploit the society. The common person no longer expects a civil servant to do justice or to be above-board. This has shaken the confidence of the common person and has done incalculable harm to the system. This must change if democratic institutions are to flourish.

The new moral code of conduct and ethics must reflect the aspirations of the people and mirror the expectations the society has from the civil services. Some of the ingredients of such a code may be briefly stated as under. The civil servant must make a commitment and undertake a pledge to:

(i) Uphold rule of law: In a democracy, rule of law should reign supreme. A clear message must be conveyed that howsoever high you may be, the law is above you. Everyone must be treated as equal before the law. And this must be evident every day from the way in which the law is implemented in the country. The civil service must make an unequivocal commitment to uphold the rule of law.

(ii) Promote open government: The government must function in as open and transparent a manner as possible. This alone will strengthen the faith of the common person in the institutions of governance A civil servant can do a great deal to promote open and transparent governance. It is only by his personal commitment that these efforts will get strengthened

(iii) Observe political neutrality: The main justification for a permanent civil service on the pattern of the British civil service, as opposed to the American system, is to have a system in which the civil service would be politically neutral and answerable only to the Constitution and not to the political party which may be in power at any given point of time. This would imply that the advice of the bureaucracy should be free, frank, politically unbiased, impartial and objective.

(iv)Provide good governance: Transparency and accountability are the twin planks of good governance. Civil service must undertake to do everything in its powers to promote these objectives. More than half the battle for good governance would be won if civil servants are committed to this cause

(v) Strengthen human rights: Commitment to human rights by civil services will be a major step forward in preventing abuses of human rights. Neglected and weaker sections of society will feel greatly reassured if civil servants undertake to protect their rights. This is all the more important when various political parties are stoking the flames of communal, caste and religion-based animosities and hatred. Civil society can draw a great deal of strength from the commitment of civil servants to uphold human rights and to undertake all necessary steps in this direction.

(vi) Promote secularism: Secularism is apart of the basic structure of the Constitution but has come under increasing threat in recent times because of compulsions of party politics. The demolition of the Babri Masjid on 6 December 1992 has been a watershed and has divided the country on communal lines. The recent incidents of violence against Christians and other minorities are also a pointer to the threat to secularism in this country. Communalism of both minority and majority communities needs to be deprecated. In an atmosphere of mutual suspicion, hatred and ill-feeling, civil service committed to secularism can be a great bulwark. Secularism of the police force in times of communal violence can be a great source of strength to the minority communities.

(vii) Neither accept nor give illegal gratification: Acceptance of zero-tolerance limit for corruption has to be an inviolable part of any programme of good governance. And any such effort will be futile unless civil service is to be an integral part of such an exercise.

(viii) Uphold integrity not only of oneself but of the entire system: It is often noticed that a civil servant may be a person of absolute honesty, integrity and personal rectitude, but the system under him may be corrupt to the core. It is therefore not enough that a civil servant himself is honest. He must do everything within his powers to apply the same standards to the system under him. Only then can he be said to have made a material difference to the system.

(ix) Uphold not just personal integrity but also intellectual integrity: A civil servant may be personally honest but intellectually dishonest. This can make a great deal of difference when he is in a crucial or senior position to advise the government. It is not uncommon to see a civil servant being intellectually dishonest while tendering a politically convenient advice to the government. Every civil servant owes it to himself and the society at large to take a suitable pledge on this behalf.

(x) Undertake not to bring any influence to bear on the government: It is most common to see civil servants infringing the conduct rules and trying to bring pressure on the government for promotions, transfers, foreign postings, government accommodation and so on. Industrialists, large business houses, astrologers, politicians and such other influence-pedalling persons are used extensively for this purpose. All such help does not come without strings attached and suitable quid-pro-quo. This leads to misuse of office, nepotism, favouritism and corrupt practices. It is imperative that, in any improved system of governance, such practices are stopped.

Beware of Dangerous New Ideas

In reinventing the civil service, one would have to be careful about blind imitation of ill-conceived new ideas from developed countries without regard to the situation and ethos in our country. One of these pertains to a suggestion being canvassed that senior government officers may be sent on deputation to private sector companies for a period of 3–5 years. It is being argued that this will bring the government and the private sector closer and create a better understanding between them. It is argued that this will help the bureaucracy to absorb private sector culture.

It should not be surprising if this quickly converts Indian Administrative Service into an Ambani Administrative Service with senior bureaucrats owing their allegiance to these large houses. Such crony capitalism has fallen into disrepute in a number of countries and rather than learning from their experience, we are now trying to replicate what has been jettisoned by them.

Ensure Freedom of Information

The foot-dragging with respect to measures pertaining to bringing in an open government, with emphasis on transparency and right to information, is a matter of serious concern. By now, Tamil Nadu, Goa, Maharashtra, Rajasthan and Karnataka have passed laws on the subject. Except for the Karnataka enactment, the other enactments have hardly anything to commend themselves. The same can be said of the Bill on Freedom of Information introduced by the central government in Parliament.

The chief ministers' conference in May 1997 provided useful pointer to the direction in which the country was poised to move on this subject as well. Endorsing the proposals on this behalf tabled by the Centre for introducing, in consultation with the states, a legislation for Freedom of Information, and amendment of the Official Secrets Act, 1923, and the Indian Evidence Act, *some of the state governments indicated the need to include provisions which would ensure that the misuse of the provisions under this Right do not lead to embarrassment of the governments.* Here again, the recommendations of the Working Group on Freedom of Information will need to be carefully looked into to make sure that the proposed legislation will not defeat the very purpose of the exercise. For example, the draft legislation proposed by the Working Group suggests a number of exemptions from disclosure. Particular attention may be invited in this context to the following, among other, exemptions:

(a) Information, other than exclusively factual information, in the nature of internal working papers such as inter-departmental/intra-departmental notes and correspondence, papers containing advice, opinion, or recommendation for purposes of deliberative processes in a public authority; and

(b) Information, the disclosure of which would not subserve any public interest;

While, similar provisions may obtain in other enactments in some other countries, it is necessary to consider the relevance or appropriateness of such provisions in the context of a series of scams and scandals which have come to notice over the years and have remained unattended in this country. Even the theology of secrecy of cabinet and cabinet sub-committee papers needs to be questioned. This is particularly true with respect to decisions taken on award of contracts, licences, permissions for foreign investment and so on. Even the Parliamentary Standing Committee on Defence has, in its report in 1994, recommended that all papers pertaining to Defence purchases should not be withheld on the grounds of secrecy as large public funds are involved in such purchases. Further, who is to decide the 'public interest'? As seen in a number of instances, the government can hardly be trusted as the sole authority on the subject. This is amply borne out by the stand taken by the government in a number of public interest litigations in the recent past—death of over 3,000 children of a tribal community in Amravati district in Maharashtra, safety of nuclear installations in the country, and withdrawal of cases against Bal Thackrey for his communal writings and speeches. In all these cases, the government, whether at the state or the Centre, took a stand that it will not be in public interest to divulge the information. This is also true of the celebrated case of Enron power generation project in Maharashtra in which the state government refused to place before the legislature the agreement it had entered into for purchase of power from Enron on the ground that it would mean divulging a commercial secret! This inevitably happens when the government is looked upon by the ruling political party as a private limited company meant for making quick profits and not as a government answerable to the people. Any legislation on right to information to be effective has to take into account the ethos in which it has to work, the maturity of the political parties, their commitment to certain values and principles and so on. Otherwise, like several other enactments, the new central law on freedom of information may also become yet another paper tiger.[2]

Downsizing the Government

The world over questions are being raised on the appropriate ambit or charter of the government. Conscious thought is being given by governments to shed such activities which are no longer relevant for the government to undertake. This is primarily due to the increasing awareness of the lower productivity and efficiency of any governmental activity, the crowding out of the private sector investment and initiative and the resultant lowering of the rate of growth of the economy. In India too, the process of economic liberalization, economic reforms and globalization cannot be carried too far without downsizing the government.

There is no reason why the government ought to deal with all aspects of the community's life. It just does not have the resources or the capabilities to handle all these responsibilities. This is amply borne out by the experience of several state governments. That is why one finds that there are dispensaries and hospitals without medicines, there are schools without teachers, there are veterinary hospitals without doctors and medicines, and there is staff but no money for carrying out development works. It is time the state governments concentrate on their primary responsibilities such as those of law and order, administration of justice, welfare of weaker sections of society, and certain subjects pertaining to development such as primary education, primary health, and tribal development. All other activities ought to be left to the private or co-operative sectors to handle. Even water supply, electricity and such other services can be easily privatized or co-operativized.

DECENTRALIZATION OF POWER

Another major change which is necessary pertains to the decentralization of power. Unfortunately, even after the passing of the 73rd and 74th amendments of the Constitution in 1993, there has been very little action in transferring the powers of the state government to the local bodies. It is equally necessary to reduce the powers of the

[2] See Madhav Godbole, 'Right to Information: Unending Struggle', *Economic and Political Weekly*, August 12–18, 2000, pp. 2899–2901

central government and to transfer as many of the powers and functions to the state governments as possible. It is interesting to see that it was way back in 1970 that the then Administrative Reforms Commission (ARC) had recommended that, 'the role of the central ministries and departments in subjects falling within the State List should be confined to only certain matters as listed by the ARC. An analysis should be made in the light of these criteria of the items of work now handled by the Central agencies and such items as do not fulfil the criteria should be transferred to the States'. It is disappointing to see that even after 30 years, central government policies are exactly in the opposite direction. In fact, in recent years, the central government has created new ministries and departments pertaining to almost all subjects handled by the state governments. Decentralization of powers has to begin from Delhi and has to be taken to the *Gram Sabhas* in the villages.

Appointment of Regulatory Commissions

The state governments must appoint regulatory commissions on a number of subjects to hand over the responsibility of price fixation to such bodies. Recently, a number of state governments have set up electricity regulatory commissions. Their experience during the last two years is very encouraging. These commissions have undertaken the task of revision of electricity tariff in a transparent manner. There has been full participation of community groups and consumers in the public hearings held by the commissions. This has led to general acceptance of the awards of the commissions by the consumers, except in Andhra Pradesh. The subsidies to various consumer groups have been rationalized and made more targeted. Cross-subsidization has been kept within reasonable limits. It is time regulatory commissions are appointed for drinking and irrigation water supply, milk supply, education, hospital services and similar other services.

Making Budget Transparent and User-Friendly

Another reform which is long overdue is to make the budget of the state and central government transparent and user-friendly. Government of Maharashtra had taken initiative on this behalf to appoint a one-man committee under this author to suggest a suitable course of action. In a report submitted to the state government at the end of September 2000, a series of recommendations have been made on this behalf. The report has been accepted by the state government and is expected to be published shortly. The Government of India has introduced in Parliament a Fiscal Responsibility and Budget Management Bill which would carry the same process further in the central government.

Zero-Base Budgeting

Reference must be made to an overriding characteristic of the governments in India. This pertains to the tendency to continue the government schemes and programmes forever without any review, even after they have lost their relevance and have become outdated. Compared to the United States, for example, we do not have a 'sunset' provision by which each scheme and programme comes to an end on a pre-determined date. It is high time such an innovation is introduced. One way of doing so is to introduce the concept of zero-base budgeting by which every scheme and programme is examined afresh each year as if it were being taken up for the first time.

A reference must be made in this context to the implementation of zero-base budgeting by Government of Maharashtra for a period of about three years from 1986 during my term as Principal Finance Secretary of the State. This was the first time that such a revolutionary concept was sought to be implemented in all seriousness in the country. Some of the salient features thereof may be briefly stated as under.

First, every scheme and programme was to be reviewed each year before inclusion in the budget with a view to revising or amending the schemes and programmes, wherever necessary. Schemes which were not doing well were to be discontinued. This gave an opportunity to divert expenditure from less productive to more productive avenues. Second, savings effected by administrative departments by discontinuing or revising any schemes were to be given to the same department for augmenting its other programmes. This was meant to be an incentive to the departments to undertake such reviews vigorously and dispassionately. Third, all subsidies were to be reviewed and subsidies which were not effective or well targeted were to be discontinued. Fourth, all new recruitment was frozen. There was to be no new recruitment except in exceptional cases as may be specifically approved by the Cabinet. Fifth, surplus staff which may be identified as a result of the discontinuance or revision of any schemes was to be taken to the surplus cadre cell for redeployment elsewhere. This was meant to ensure that the whole exercise was not opposed by the employees on the ground that it would lead to unemployment and retrenchment. Sixth, all areas of the functioning of the government were to be reviewed so as to promote cost-effective functioning; do away with age-old, outdated and inefficient procedures; and make the government leaner and thinner. Seventh, items of work which could be contracted out were to be identified so that such items of work could be shed by the government. Eighth, all avenues of cost recovery were to be explored vigorously and kept under continuous review. This included drinking water charges, fees in educational institutions, fees to be charged in government hospitals, irrigation charges and so on. Ninth, the zero-base budgeting was to be used as a management tool and not to be permitted to degenerate into a routine form-filling exercise. Tenth, the whole process of review was to be internalized and administrative secretaries were made fully responsible for its implementation. The finance department was to act only as a catalyst.

With such an imaginative and innovative approach substantial results were achieved in terms of reduction in staff, saving in expenditure, stoppage of unproductive schemes, diversion of resources to more productive uses, better targeted subsidies, greater cost recovery and so on. But, as was to be expected, the scheme met with stiff resistance both at the administrative and political levels and was given up in December 1989. This experiment, however, showed the tremendous potential for reinventing the process of governance.

Pronouncement of Zero Tolerance for Corruption

It is time a firm and unequivocal pronouncement is made by the government, at each level, regarding its zero-tolerance limit for corruption. It must be announced as a major policy plan that corruption in any form will not be tolerated by the government and there will be no compromise with this policy under any circumstances. Such a policy can be operationalized by a series of actions such as enactment of a proper law by Parliament to strengthen the office of the chief vigilance commissioner (CVC) and making the central board of investigation answerable to the CVC; setting up of a state vigilance commissioner's (SVC) office in each state and making the state anti-corruption bureau answerable to the SVC; strengthening the Lok Ayuktas by passing a Central law on the lines of the model legislation prepared by the conference of the Lok Ayuktas; setting up of a Lok Pal; making public the property returns filed by officers and ministers each year for public scrutiny; taking prompt decisions in corruption cases and awarding exemplary punishment in suitable cases; enacting a law to enable confiscation of properties acquired by a public servant by corrupt means; and enactment of a law for the protection of 'whistle-blowers'.

Social Audit

At present, there are no reliable and institutionalized mechanisms for getting a feedback as to what the customers of government services feel. The audit of government expenditure by the Comptroller and Auditor General of India (C&AG) is as impersonal and far removed from the people as the government itself. It is, therefore, necessary that the government departments get a report card on their performance from time to time from people themselves.

The benchmarking of services can cover a number of items such as proportion of applicants/customers claiming to have paid a bribe for getting their work done; average payment per transaction; the number of times an applicant had to visit the office for getting requisite approvals; the number of times back-queries were raised on the application and so on. The Public Affairs Centre in Bangalore conducted such benchmarking with respect to a number of urban services in Bangalore and in some other cities and produced valuable reports. Such efforts need to be institutionalized by the government itself asking well known and renowned NGOs and consumer organizations to prepare such report cards and to conduct social audit of its activities.

Citizens Charter

The instrument of citizens charter has been used in some countries to make the government accountable and answerable for a certain set of actions as publicly agreed upon and undertaken from time to time. The underlying idea is that each government department and public organization should set certain benchmarks against which its performance can be evaluated by its customers. This concept has been adopted by a number of organizations in the Centre and the states. Most of these charters, however, suffer from a number of deficiencies. To name just a few:

(i) Most of the charters have been prepared without a throughgoing analysis of the existing practices and weaknesses and as a result have no relation to the situation on the ground. When one reads most of them, one gets a feeling that a moon is being promised when the reality is far worse.

(ii) There is hardly any consultative process with the staff and as a result they have no mental involvement in or commitment to the charter. There is no ownership of the charter.

(iii) Copies of the charter are often not available in the offices themselves, leave aside becoming easily available to the members of the public.

(iv) The charters do not provide for any compensation to the members of the public for not getting the service within the stipulated time or of the promised quality and standard. As a result, the charter consists of hollow promises without any sanctity.

If the citizens charter is to be made a serious instrument of policy, these and several other deficiencies from which the charters suffer will have to be remedied.

E-Governance

Bureaucracy thrives on conformity, uniformity and the culture of secrecy. Expose it to the sunlight of transparency and several ills will vanish like a magic wand. Maximum advantage must be derived in this process from the advances in information technology in areas of information storage, retrieval and processing.

E-governance can increase the speed of decision-making processes considerably. It can enhance efficiency and productivity and go a long way to increase consumer satisfaction. Once the data is put on the computers, it can reduce the tyranny of rent-seeking government employees such as the proverbial hold which a village level revenue officer has over the VII–XII extracts of land records. The same can be true of the notorious system of registration of documents in sub-registrars' offices all over the country. E-governance can do a great deal to streamline the inventory management in large establishments such as the defence forces. The importance of this can be gauged from the severe indictment passed by the C&AG in his report on armed forces submitted to Parliament in December 2000.

To take another example, the advantages of e-governance in the area of tax administration are overwhelming. With the continuous increase in the number of sales tax dealers and their transactions, there are serious limitations to what can be achieved by reliance only on manual processing of data. One of the biggest advantages of computerization would be the ability to cross-check transactions between registered dealers and pinpoint inconsistencies. Its most important gain would be that it would increase the ability of the department to cross-check claimed purchases from and sales to other registered dealers. This would eliminate to a large extent evasion through claims of not being the first or the last dealer. Computerization would also help in monitoring revenue flows and would provide adequate advance warning of likely shortfalls in collections from specific areas as also specific dealers.

Commodity-wise tax collection data would help cross-check such data with production figures of such commodities. It should also be possible to cross-check this data with import and export figures.

A routine check on computer would show whether a dealer is deliberately suppressing his turnover in any year as compared to the figures of the previous years.

Scrutiny of returns of dealers ought to be on a random basis with certain caveats such as: all those dealers whose turnover is above a particular limit will be subjected to detailed scrutiny; of the remaining, a percentage random check will be carried out in such a way that every dealer's return will be scrutinized at least once in five years; and if any under-reporting is noticed for the years not subjected to scrutiny, exemplary penalty will be imposed on the dealer, apart from subjecting him to detailed scrutiny for the three succeeding years.

Improving the database and having an efficient and quick way of retrieving data is a prerequisite for improved tax administration. It is equally important that the database should be carefully collated with supplementary information from other related sources. Juxtapositioning such information would help identify areas of tax evasion as also tax avoidance. It is unfortunate that in spite of these overwhelming advantages of e-governance in tax administration, it has received such scant attention so far.

It is, however, necessary to appreciate that e-governance does not come cheaply. Its capital as also running costs can be quite significant. The government cannot possibly find enough resources within a reasonable period of time to undertake the stupendous tasks in this area on its own. As the experience of Andhra Pradesh has shown, unless the government is prepared to charge reasonable fees to recover the costs, the process of hastening e-governance is bound to be slowed down. In fact, the effort of the government must be to farm out as many of these tasks to the private sector as possible to run them commercially. There is no reason why people should not be prepared to pay reasonable fees for getting prompt services of high standards through the outlets provided by the government and/or the private sector.

Curtail Areas of Discretion

One of the root causes for corruption is the use of totally unguided and untrammelled discretionary powers by the officers and ministers. A number of our laws can be faulted for having given excessive discretion to the executive in the implementation of the laws. One of the most notorious cases of this kind is the Urban Land (Ceiling on Holdings) Act which has become a goldmine for corruption in terms of the totally unguided discretion given to the executive. It is necessary that a case-by-case review is carried out of all enactments to reduce the areas of discretion to the barest minimum. Wherever it is inescapable to provide for discretionary powers, such areas must be identified clearly and detailed guidelines laid down on the use of such powers. Finally, such guidelines need to be published for information of the people on the internet and through other means.

Summing Up

This is only an illustrative list of measures which need to be taken to address the formidable tasks at hand. The answers to the long-standing ills and deficiencies of civil services will have to be basic and sweeping. Mere patchwork of temporary remedies will not serve any purpose. It is often forgotten that good governance is basic to any other reform and change in society. Everything else can be purchased for a price but not people-friendly, socially conscious, transparent, accountable and clean administration deeply committed not to any particular political ideology but to the basic values of rule of law, respect for secularism, human rights and the welfare of the weaker sections of society. This is the charter for the civil services. Looking at the present state of affairs it sounds utopian but, if it is to be translated in reality, it will require both administrative and political will. Unfortunately, both are missing in this quest for good governance. The bureaucracy is therefore at crossroads. The road it takes will make all the difference to where India finds itself in the twenty-first century and the new millennium. It is a travesty that no one has the time to pause and ponder on these vital issues.

CHAPTER FIFTEEN

Changeful Society and Changeless Governance*

Nirmal Mukarji

> With non-Congressism on the rise in the states and the possi-
> bility of a non-Congress alternative even at the centre in the
> air, the civil service will have to learn to be more independent
> in the political sense. The need for such independence will be
> all the more if democratic self-governance is extended to the
> sub-state levels.

Objective circumstances in a country change much faster than the
ability of its system of governance to adapt to them. What are
the major changes that have taken place in India? What modifications do these call for in the country's system of governance? And
what implications do these have for the civil service?

I

Foremost among the changes in objective circumstances are demographic changes. From about 350 million at Independence, India's
population has gone up to over 800 million and is projected to cross
the billion mark at the turn of the century. The age pyramid remains
as flat as ever, which means that in absolute numbers the young
comprise much more than half the total population. People are moving into the cities in larger numbers owing to a combination of
pull and push factors. Urban population was about 60 million at

* *Economic and Political Weekly*, July 15, 1989.

Independence, rose to 160 million in 1981 and is projected to be 360 million in the year 2001. More than a third of all Indians will be living in cities when that 'glorious' twenty-first century dawns, as against a sixth when we became independent. Economists, planners and the intelligentsia generally view these changes with alarm. There is no question that there is genuine cause for concern. Much, though not all, of the alarm stems from a view that large numbers of people, especially when many of them are young and often aggressively demanding, constitute a liability. If people were to be thought of as human resource and therefore potential asset, the alarm bell might be less clangorous. Liability or asset, the sheer magnitude of the numbers places a question mark on whether a largely static system of governance can cope with the rapidly expanding demographic reality.

Next are the changes brought about by political development. The central legislature we started with, which also doubled as the Constituent Assembly, was elected in 1946 on restricted franchise. The size of the electorate then in the whole of undivided India, excluding the princely states, was 35 million. Then came Article 326 which provided for universal adult suffrage, perhaps the most impactful clause of the Constitution. As a result the electorate for the first general election of 1952 jumped five-fold to 173 million. The figure became 364 million in the last general election of 1984. With the voting age lowered to 18, it will exceed 450 million for the next general election. The change from restricted to universal franchise thus meant moving from elite to mass politics in terms of numbers. If the masses had remained politically quiescent this would have made little difference. But frequent and regular elections served as schools of political education, steadily raising the level of political conscious-ness. The successful overthrow of entrenched regimes in several states and even at the centre had the effect of accelerating the process of politicization. While literacy crawled from 16.7 percent in 1951 to 36.2 per cent in 1981, political education leapt ahead. Given India's powerful oral tradition, the written word was not needed for political issues to be discussed at tea shops across the country with earthy wisdom.

Changes wrought by economic development are a mixed bag. On the one hand, the country has become nearly self-sufficient in foodgrains. The threat of widespread famine has gone and in fact the possibility has opened up for food security measures to be under-taken here and there, like the provision of subsidized rice to the poor in Andhra Pradesh. Indian industry now produces a wide range of products. Infrastructural areas like power, transport and irrigation have registered good progress, thanks mainly to the public sector. On the other hand, the overall growth rate of the economy until the end of the 1970s averaged a mere 3.7 per cent per annum, which with regard to population increase meant only 1.5 per cent per capita. In the 1980s, growth is claimed to have gone past this 'Hindu rate', as the late Raj Krishna called it, and touched five per cent. But much of the increase is accounted for by 'drone' items of the service sector like the bureaucracy and defence. More disturbing is the spread of economic benefits. The top 20 per cent take nearly half of the gross national product, against which the bottom 20 per cent are left with only seven per cent. Economic development has created glaring disparity between the rich and the poor. The poor are not only those defined as such for official purposes but in fact all those other than the rich i.e. four-fifths of the population, i.e. 650 million people today.

The picture that emerges from these dimensions of change is one of a vast and growing population advancing rapidly in political consciousness but being made increasingly aware that the fruits of economic growth, meagre as they are, are not for them but for a chosen few. There are numerous signals that the imbalance between expectations and satisfactions, a familiar enough phenomenon in most societies, is driving individuals and groups outside the system of governance into an extra-constitutional polity. We need to think whether and how the system can be given more stretch and flexibility to cope with discontent. But before coming to that two of the major changes in the political arena need to be noted.

The most significant is the decline of the once-great Congress Party. In a sense the decline started when Congress came into office, for power began to corrupt. By the time the Nehru era ended the rot had set in, creating in its wake room for non-Congressism to arise. This was of three types; Left fronts, self-respect movements like the DMK and Lohia-inspired opposition unity moves to ensure one-to-one electoral contests. The result of this emergent non-Congressism was that, in the 1967 general election, Congress was ousted from power in eight states. This became a turning point. On the one hand, democracy received a shot in the arm because alternatives to Congress were seen to be a possibility. On the other, a shocked Congress unleashed a formidable backlash. First, most of the newly formed non-Congress governments were swept aside. Next, since the states had proved to be vulnerable for Congress, extraordinary measures were adopted to centralize power. On the party side, there was a split with the faction in power adopting the 'fuhrer' model, doing away with intra-party elections. On the government side, huge paramilitary forces were created. The reach of the Intelligence Bureau was extended right across the country and especially to states which persisted with non-Congressism. President's rule began to be imposed more frequently. Economic management and planning were so conducted as to make states increasingly dependent on the centre. Captains of industry, czars of science and technology and indeed all those most favoured by the pattern of development went along happily. The political and economic 'haves' thus made common cause to make the government of the country more centralized than Nehru or anyone else had ever visualized. This was a far cry from the federal democracy the country had opted for.

Correspondingly significant is the rise of countervailing forces. If the benefits of economic development went largely to the top 20 per cent, the gains of political development quietly accrued to the rest of the people. Elite groups corrupted the electoral system to keep themselves in and the masses out. However, when centralization reached its apex in the Emergency, the masses voted the offending regime out at the first opportunity. They did the same to the successor regime when that failed them. Congress wrongly interpreted this as a mandate for renewed centralization and paid for this by losing state after state in a series of elections. Non-Congress elements in the states joined hands to demand that the federal structure of the Constitution, overshadowed for long by the command system of the Congress, be restored and strengthened. Federal reform thus came on the national agenda. Meanwhile, the Left Front in West Bengal innovated a bold programme of land reform coupled with vitalization of panchayats. For the first time since Independence, the masses in that state felt the glow of freedom through active participation in panchayat self-governance. What distinguished West Bengal's panchayats from earlier versions was that they were openly political in character. Karnataka and Andhra Pradesh, which too had non-Congress governments, also t: sformed their panchayats into politically elected units of self-government. The concept of panchayat governments pioneered by these states caught the imagination of the country. Decentralization below the state level through devolution of political power to panchayat governments thus became an important adjunct of the movement for federal reform.

II

This analysis of changing circumstances points to the need for federal reform and for decentralization below the state level. Since federal reform in the present context is a euphemism for decentralization from the centre to the states, the single agenda that stands out is decentralization.

The critical element in this is finance, because functions accumulate where there is money regardless of constitutional lists. Therefore, when thinking of decentralization, there will have to be a new financial regime as between the centre, the states and sub-state levels. Obviously the centre must be left with enough for its basic needs. At the same time, the states and sub-state levels, not being in a position to raise on their own the resources for *their* basic needs, must receive assured funds from the centre in sufficient measure and without strings to make purposeful self-government at these levels possible. So far, Finance Commissions have followed a tax-by-tax approach. A new regime which would ensure finality, avoid recriminations and be simple to operate would be for the Constitution to provide for a fixed percentage out of the centre's aggregate resources to go to the states and out of that a fixed sub-percentage to be passed on to the sub-state levels. The prime minister was right when he told parliament that united grants make for local level planning. The opposite is also true, namely that tied grants cripple local initiative, especially if they squeeze out untied grants, for where there are strings there can only be puppets at the other end. Consequently centrally sponsored schemes, the latest in an expanding array being the Jawahar Rozgar Yojana, are essentially antithetical to the idea of decentralized democracy. Constitutionally guaranteed free-of-strings devolutions to state and sub-state levels would lessen the scope for the centre to play centrally sponsored games and correspondingly strengthen democratic governance at these lower levels.

An equally critical element is planning. So far planning has been thought of as inevitably involving centralization. In a federal polity we need to think of planning as 'national' rather than 'central', and find a way to federalise it. The command system by which Congress ruled during the first two decades after Independence could not but infect the Planning Commission. Instead of adopting the democratic route of seeking consensus on major policy issues, it took to imposing its growth models and investment budgets on the states. It was able to do so because it secured control over the distribution of plan

funds. Discretionary plan devolutions have been rising against assured non-plan devolutions via Finance Commissions, the present
ratio between the two being about 40:60. Planning clearly requires a
measure of discipline, but in a democratic context this should come
more from consent than from financial coercion. Over-involvement
in preparing investment plans has resulted in the neglect of policy
planning. Vital matters like the oppression inflicted on the poor and
the decline of mediatory institutions such as the police and the courts
are treated by the commission as outside its purview. Issues like
South Asian regional cooperation or the balance between defence
and development are excluded because foreign policy and defence
are regarded as holy cows. Even in the 'included' area, not enough
thought goes into problems like mass poverty, regional backwardness, environmental decay and the criminal neglect of women and
children. In a new planning regime, the Planning Commission would
need to pay more attention to major policy questions and allow
investment planning to be decentralized within a framework of
nationally accepted policies.

Thirdly, there will have to be a new regime in the districts. We
simply cannot go on flogging the 'district officer' system any longer.
Today's district officer has been saddled with far too much to do and
as a result is unable to do anything effectively enough. Against this,
the political awakening of the people has led them to expect far more
than the system can deliver. The answer surely lies in letting the
people run their own affairs through elected district governments. If
such governments are not to go the way of panchayati raj institutions
(PRIs) they must possess characteristics the lack of which led to the
failure of those bodies. For one, these governments must be recognized as political entities, with political parties openly contesting
elections. For another, they must look after the totality of district
governance, with the district bureaucracy coming squarely under
them. Dividing the task of governance between regulatory and developmental functions is artificial and untenable. Further, the fate of
district governments must not be left to the tender mercies of state
governments. Elections must statutorily be held at regular intervals
under the overall supervision of the Election Commission. Superses-
sions should be barred, for there is no justification for giving state
governments a handle to remove inconvenient district governments.
Lastly, district governments must be nested in the federal ideal, forming a third tier of the polity. The third tier would subsume self-
governing units at sub-district levels right down to *gram sabhas*. The

introduction of a third tier must not, however, squeeze the intermediate second tier or be seen as attempting to do so.

Fourthly, there will have to be a new regime for urban government, with regard to the fact that urban areas will hold a third of the nation in a mere decade or so from now. The governance of these areas can be considered at two levels. The Ashok Mehta Committee drew attention to the fact that small and medium towns had stagnated for decades while the bigger towns had grown steadily bigger. It ascribed the phenomenon to the former not having developed functional linkages with their rural hinterlands. However, with increased commercialization of agriculture an urban-rural continuum was growing. The committee advocated linking rural areas with urban focal points under the umbrella of PRIs. There is good sense in this line of thought. Consequently, at one level, small and medium towns should be integrated with district governments through some form of federal linkage. The term medium town would have to be interpreted flexibly to include most district headquarter towns considering that they are very much a part of the urban-rural continuum. At another level, the metropolitan and really big cities will need to be treated differently. For they present a major problem of governance, not adequately recognized as such till now because of the persisting impression that India is mainly rural. The National Commission on Urbanization classified urban areas into cities and towns, the former having a population of more than one lakh and the latter less. Elsewhere it suggested a two-tier administration for cities with a population over five lakhs. At yet another place it listed 40 cities which would be more than a million strong in 2001. A practical approach might be to make a beginning with, say, half of these 40 in the matter of installing specialized city governance. Possibly, some initial lessons could be learnt from Calcutta and Howrah which have broken out of the pervasive Bombay corporation model and innovated a mayor-in-council system.

New regimes for finance and planning as well as for district and urban governance would constitute a four-pillar minimum needs programme to bring about needed changes in the system of governance. The four must be viewed as an integrated package. Picking out just one of them, such as district governance, would be like trying to lift a *charpai* by a single leg. This, in fact, is the major defect of the Constitution (64th Amendment) Bill for panchayats. A 65th bill for the urban areas would not cure the defect since the first two agenda items, ie., new regimes for finance and planning involving decentralization from the centre downwards, would remain untouched.

III

What implications would such a reform package have for the civil service? For our purpose, the civil service means mainly the all-India services but also all Class I services of the centre and the states. The constituents of the civil service so defined have their differences with each other over career issues but are nevertheless a recognizable category, if only because they occupy the commanding heights of the administrative machinery and are for that reason the most influential group within the bureaucracy. The attitude of members of the civil service has been conditioned by two factors. For one thing, they have throughout functioned in a centralized and centralizing system of governance, New Delhi being the prime focus of centralization as also the state capitals. Secondly, they largely come from urban backgrounds and their educational attainments class them as English-speaking. Somehow the chemistry of this second factor operates to make civil servants generally comfortable with centralism. Thus, exceptions apart, district officers are eager to complete their stints in the field and get to the state secretariats. Those serving in the states, at least a considerable proportion of them, want to get to the centre. The more enterprising of those who succeed in this immediately begin working to get to what for them is the centre of all centres, namely, the World Bank or one of the many UN agencies.

The thrust of the suggested minimum needs reform is in the opposite direction, its essence being downward democratic decentralization—3Ds—towards more 'vernacular' governance. Therefore, the first implication of the package, if it ever comes about, would be that the civil service would need to do an about-turn in its attitude. Would it be able or willing to do so? We can all entertain our respective doubts. Bureaucracies do have inertia built into them and are resistant to change. But the Indian bureaucracy has shown that it is viscous enough to fit into new political moulds. This was proved when power was transferred from British to Indian hands in 1947, though it must be admitted that the newness of the native mould was more on paper than in fact. It was also proved in the states whenever power was transferred from Congress to stable non-Congress parties. But none of these involved structural change for the civil service. The crucial obstacle for a change in attitude is, in fact, the way the civil service is structured, the highest jobs being at the centre or in state capitals and the lowest in the districts. Successive pay commissions have reinforced this structure rather than change it, because preserving 'relativities' has been their guiding principle. This writer once met a German civil servant who, after having done a term as cabinet secretary to the federal government, had chosen to be a city manager of one of the major cities, presumably carrying his emoluments with him. We need a new kind of pay commission which would free itself from the bind of relativities and allow room for structural changes to take place. The civil service must have enough flexibility to reverse direction and flow more easily into new moulds of people-oriented governance.

Quantitatively, the civil service and the bureaucracy generally of which it is part are increasingly viewed as costing the country more than they are worth. Decentralized governance could easily result in the creation of more posts. But should this necessarily mean expansion of an already oversized and largely parasitic bureaucracy? Should genuine decentralization not mean visibly slimmer central and state secretariats and departmental headquarters? Much praise has been deservedly showered on West Bengal and Karnataka for their panchayat governments, but Calcutta and Bangalore remain as populated by bureaucrats as before. If logic favours smaller bureaucracies at decentralizing points, whether at the centre or in the states, could those found surplus to the requirements of New Delhi and the state capitals not be redeployed in the decentralized units of governance?

Qualitatively, at each level of what effectively would be a multi-tiered federation, the civil service would have to subordinate itself to a democratically elected government and yet maintain its independence. Subordinating one's self may present some ego problems here and there but is otherwise easier done than maintaining independence. It sounds trite but is true that an independent civil service is vital for a healthy democracy, especially so in a multi-tiered arrangement. There is a familiar connotation of independence according to which an independent civil servant is one who is fearless in thought, word and deed. Independence in this sense goes with integrity, for the fearless one cannot afford to have anything to hide. Basically independence has to be rooted in values and principles. That being so, there has to be willingness to face consequences, such as not getting plums or, worse, being harassed in sundry ways. The ultimate contingency of leaving government employment if necessary has also to be faced with equanimity. All of which is not to say that an independent civil servant must wage a running war with elected representatives of the people. On the contrary he must learn to work harmoniously with his political masters without fatally compromising his independence. Happily, there are still many such independent civil servants. But the hard fact is that their number is decreasing. Corruption and collusion with dark forces are taking their toll. If decline is not to turn into decay, it is for the civil service as an institution to rise against these forces while there is still time.

There is the other connotation of independence. A BBC interviewer once put the following question to this writer: To what extent has the civil service retained its independence? The reply given was that the independence of the civil service was a concept relevant to democratic systems in which governments came and went but the civil service was expected to serve successor governments as faithfully as it did the predecessors. That it was pointed out, was the British usage of the word 'independence'. In India, since there was no democracy during British rule, there was no question of the civil service having been independent in this sense. Therefore, the issue was not how far the civil service had *retained* its independence, since it never had any, but how far it had been able to *become* independent in the new democratic context of free India. The difficulty we had to contend with was that Congress had remained in power at the centre almost all the time since we became a democracy and the civil service thus had not had opportunities to adjust to changes of government.

We have far to go with regard to this kind of independence. Sadly, starting with the Emergency, the trend has been in a negative direction. The distinction between the government and the ruling party is tending to get blurred, at the centre as well as in most of the states. The responsibility for this lies primarily with political leaders. But the civil service has also been lending a hand. Only the other day a noted journalist, Tavleen Singh, reported her experience at a 'truly high-power dinner' organized by the joint secretary, external publicity, one Aftab Seth. It was attended by a 'dazzling array of senior bureaucrats', including the cabinet secretary, the principal secretary to the prime minister, the finance secretary, the I and B secretary and 'sundry high-powered joint secretaries'. One of the questions that aroused much discussion related to the advent of the political bureaucrat, that is one who openly supports the ruling party and not just the government. Somehow it seemed to the journalist that the older lot were less susceptible to this tendency.

The implication that all were susceptible, the younger lot only more so, is indeed disturbing.

There is a discernible tendency in the civil service to treat the Congress as the natural ruling party. The mischief was done during the early decades when the only rule was Congress rule. A cosy relationship came into being during this period between Congress rulers and the civil service. Congressmen came to think of civil servants as servitors of Congress power and civil servants, by and large, came to regard Congress rule as naturally ordained. Circumstances have changed since then, for there is no state where Congress has not been dislodged from power at some time or the other, and that applies to the centre too. But mindsets tend to ignore facts. Consequently Congressmen, especially those at the centre, continue to find it difficult to accept the idea of an independent civil service. Civil servants on their part find it equally difficult to graduate out of their tilt towards Congress. It has taken three elections to make the West Bengal civil service begin to accept the inevitability of non-Congress rule in that state. The leadership of the Janata in Karnataka and Telugu Desam in Andhra Pradesh were convinced that there were elements in their respective civil services which had Congress proclivities and for that reason could not be trusted. New-to-power political parties are over-sensitive about such issues. But their suspicions about the civil service in these instances-were not entirely without foundation.

With non-Congressism on the rise in the states and the possibility of a non-Congress alternative even at the centre in the air, the civil service will have to learn to be more independent in the political sense. The need for such independence will be all the more if democratic self-governance is extended to sub-state levels.

CHAPTER SIXTEEN

Strengthening Bureaucracy
State and Development in India*

Kuldeep Mathur

What is the agenda of good governance and how can it be
exported to other countries is now a major issue among the
international aid giving agencies. Development administration as a way to improve state capability faded away two
decades ago. Governance is slowly taking its place. This paper
examines the scope and content of these two major
conceptualizations and investigates the potential success of
the new concept, where the old one failed.

Ideas are the moving force of history. When supported by organization and finance, they have considerable impact on the way
academic agendas are formed and reproduced. One such idea has
been that of development which captured the imagination of people
all over the world about half a century ago. It was Truman who, for
the first time, used the term *underdeveloped*, signifying the division of
the world into those who were developed and those who were not.
He also placed on those who were developed the responsibility to
help develop those who were not. This was the end of the Second
World War and a programme of reconstruction was being initiated in
Europe through massive American aid that came to be known as the
Marshall Plan. Its success inspired a model of development that was
also perceived to be appropriate for those countries too that were

* *Indian Social Science Review*, 1, 1 (1999), Sage Publications, New Delhi, Thousand
Oaks, London.

emerging from colonial rule. For these countries, which together with some others came to be known as the Third World, the prospect provided hope. It was now possible for them to aspire to be like the West and also to be optimistic about fulfilling this aspiration. The West emerged as a role model both as an end and as a process by which this goal could be achieved.

The world has not remained static since then. International agencies came up to promote development and public policies in countries rich and poor, which reoriented themselves to respond to the demands of developmental goals and process. Also, the academic world gave birth to two new concerns—development economics and development administration. Although they do not match each other in either rigour of analysis or content, these two concerns are most popularly associated with the issue of development. For a long time in the post-1950 world, these two concerns attracted the best intellectual talent and by far the largest financial support for their aims. One focused on devising economic policies, the other on strengthening state capabilities to implement them. To that extent, one supported the other in its endeavours.

When international assistance for development began on a large scale in the 1950s, it was realized that many of the recipient states did not have the capability to utilize the aid that was being given. Strengthening state capability through improvement of administration became high on the agenda, and a new field of endeavour known as *development administration* took shape, overwhelming the traditional discipline of public administration. But the 'development' decades of the 1960s and 1970s proved frustrating and disappointing for most countries of the world and academic attention began to wane. By the 1980s, a new challenge had appeared on the horizon. Even though most countries of the world failed to respond to Western developmental efforts, some East Asian Countries like Japan, Korea, Taiwan and Singapore attained heights similar to those of the developed nations. The major South Asian nations (India, Pakistan) in very sharp contrast remained mired in poverty. Answers were sought for this contrast. It was argued that the East Asian countries relied on the free market and got rich very quickly, while the South Asian nations fell prey to the temptation of state intervention and got bogged down by economic stagnation. Consequently, for a large number of policy planners and international donor agencies, a free market became the key determinant of development. However, on closer examination the success of East Asian economies also began to be attributed to their strong and autonomous states (Amsden, 1989; Johnson, 1982; Wade, 1990). A new scholarly tradition emphasizing state power in promoting development emerged.

Development administration as a way to improve state capability faded away two decades ago. A new approach to strengthen state capability is rising and promises to take its place. The purpose of this paper is to examine the scope and content of these two conceptualizations and examine the potential of success of this new concept where the old one had failed.

In the early 1950s, development administration demarcated itself as a field of study and practice. One of the earliest users of the term argued that the aim of the term was to specify the focus of administration on the support and management of development as distinguished from law and order. He went on to claim that 'the function of development administration is to assure that an appropriately congenial environment and effective administrative support is provided for delivery of capital, materials and services where needed in the productive process—whether in public, private or mixed economies' (Gant, 1979, p. 20). While the term seems to have been coined in the early 1950s, the prime mover in conceptualizing the field was the Comparative Administration Group (CAG) led by Fred W. Riggs. Financially supported by the Ford Foundation, CAG sponsored research, conducted seminars and published books and monographs. Much of this history has been documented extensively by Riggs himself when reviewing the work of CAG (Riggs, 1976). The point is that during the decades of 1960s and 1970s, which were also known as the development decades, development administration had an unprecedented influence in shaping the academic agendas of universities and in influencing the policies of international donor agencies like UNDP and the Ford Foundation.

Relying on the belief that the administrators in Third World countries were agents of change and nation builders, the development administration movement directed its energies at improving their capacities. The major thrusts were to strengthen bureaucracy by professionalizing it and giving it a management orientation. An additional thrust was to change the attitudes and behaviour of the bureaucrats to make them development oriented. It was assumed that a broad agreement existed about the goals of nation-building and socio-economic development in the country and all that was needed was an effective administration to translate them into reality. The broad perspective was that of a technically-oriented, professionally competent, politically and ideologically neutral bureaucracy. Such a bureaucracy was seen to be a mirror image of the bureaucracies in the Western world. Thus, a related perception was that institutional imitation was bound to produce results similar to those obtained in the developed world: efficiency, increased rationality, and the like, at a very general level. The more developed (i.e. bureaucratic and Westernized) an administrative system became, the greater the likelihood that it would have developmental effects (Dwivedi and Henderson, 1990, p. 13).

The strategy proposed to bring about this kind of reform was to impart extensive training to civil servants. While structural and procedural changes were not ruled out, it was expected that training would create awareness among the bureaucrats so that they themselves would design these changes without external suggestions. In a United Nations (1975, p. 87) document that succinctly summarized the direction its programme on public administration was taking, training found an important place. It argued that a formal training programme often speeds up the learning process and thus brings civil servants, including new recruits, to a satisfactory standard of performance, in a relatively short period of time. The economy of this method is one of the reasons why formal training is important in development administration and should be one of its key features.

After nearly two decades, disillusionment set in about the whole concept of development administration and its intended focus on bringing about reform in the developing countries. The proliferation of scholarly contributions was not sufficient to get ideas of reform implemented. Increased knowledge did not lead to improved practice. Then the nature of this knowledge began to be questioned, as well as the framework used to generate it. The influence of CAG, which had shone as a star on the academic firmament, began to wane in the 1970s and it lost its financial support from the Ford Foundation. In addition, more important questions began to be raised about the intellectual components of development administration and the reasons why the developing countries neither accepted nor adapted to its message.

It became increasingly evident that the task of nation-building and the goals of development were issues of keen contestation in the countries concerned. There were social groups that mobilized power to design development programmes and strategies in such a way that they stood to benefit from them. The actual design of development then emerged from political compromises and bargains. While there was a possibility that these bargains could be in the larger public interest, it was not always so. The way political power was exercised determined whether or not a programme or policy was in the interest of the larger society. Administration could not merely play a neutral role among contending groups and design policies that would benefit all. Neglecting politics deprived an understanding of its important link with administration, which was seen as a stand-alone solution. Paradoxically, this happened in spite of cautious contributions about the relationship of bureaucracy to political development. Riggs and many of his colleagues attempted to point out the imbalance in the power equations of political and administrative systems in developing countries and to argue that for democratic development the political systems needed to be strengthened (see in particular, Riggs, 1965). In many cases, without effective political control, strengthening bureaucracy opened vistas for misuse of its role, particularly where other weak social groups provided little or no countervailing force. In most colonial countries, civil or military bureaucracy was the most powerful instrument of imperial rule and it was naïve to believe that pious intentions would change their behaviour, specially if such change would dislodge them from a position of power.

In such a situation, attempts at strengthening bureaucracy created administrative situations that were imitative, ritualistic and symbolic rather than conducive to real change. The Western myth of a rational bureaucracy, neutral in its decisions, was held as an ideal for which to aspire. With little empirical support for this formulation of leaving value-laden decisions to the politicians and for keeping administrators out of this domain, the emphasis on professionalizing bureaucracy, and making extensive use of training to do so induced public administration to be inward looking and out of touch with social reality. Insulation made it unresponsive to democratic demands and arrogant in offering technical solutions to social problems.

The seriousness of such evaluation of the movement can be gauged from the 1998 introspection by Fred Riggs himself. He says:

The experts returned from the developing countries confused and frustrated. They felt that the advice based on the prescriptions was often unwelcome or unproductive and sometime inappropriate (1998, p. 22).

[He goes on to say] We assumed that all bureaucracies could be essentially non-political instruments of public policy, subservient to the basic political choices made by some kind of representative government. Our myth of a dichotomy between politics and administration permitted us to ignore the growing prevalence in the Third World of bureaucratic politics; regimes in which appointed officials, led by military officers, were politically dominant. We tended to overlook the political role of public bureaucracies ....

We assumed that bad practices were due to ignorance and that knowledge of better practice would lead folks anywhere to adopt them ... we did not question whether what worked in America would also work in other countries; nor did we suppose that people in other countries may have good reasons for doing what they did or that there were people with vested interests in the status quo who would resist changes that might infringe on their privileges (Riggs, 1998, pp. 29, 23).

The purpose of quoting so extensively from Riggs is to emphasize that we need to learn from experience and to realize that reform and change are not value neutral terms. Changes in society are driven by social and political forces, which are history-specific.

Externally induced reform has not been easy anywhere. The ecological aspect of public administration was recognized very early and Riggs himself wrote extensively on the subject. Paradoxically, his concern did not weave itself into the mainstream thinking of development administration. Thus, a grand project that involved many intellectuals, spawned donor agencies, created training institutions and gave a different slant to studies in public administration came to grief. The waning of enthusiasm coincided with despair about development experiences and with the perceived failure of the state when aspiring to be an engine of growth. Development economists of those years had also believed in the key role that the state had to play in promoting economic development. As Bhagwati (1993, p. 7) notes, even India's highly statist strategy was well received by prominent Western economists who were extremely optimistic and well disposed towards India's planning efforts and methods.

Even though there was frustration with Western development efforts, it began to be noticed in the 1980s that some of the Southeast Asian countries which had been on the margins of development in the 1950s had done remarkably well in the following decades. It came to be widely believed that this happened because these countries, in contrast to others, had worked to release market forces and to limit the role of the state in the economic sphere. The invisible hand of the market had worked the magic. Liberal neoclassical economics rose in influence. But another scholarly tradition also emerged which saw the developmental achievements of these countries as a result of the existence of a strong state. There was not only a call for bringing the state back (Evans et al., 1985), but explanations began to be sought for the transformation of these Asian countries into 'Asian tigers', in terms of the role of the state.

It was argued that while emphasis on loosening up of market forces was important, strong states were still necessary to promote industrialization projects. In this formulation, strong states provided good governance and good governance was the key to the transformation of a predatory state into a developmental one. Good governance in this sense is related to the reduction of the role of the state and the entire case is built on how state intervention creates monopoly rents through regulation and control over the economy. Political pressures dominate economic policy making and there is widespread corruption in bureaucratic allocations of investment licences and award of contracts. A consequence of this system is that the state machinery gets used increasingly for private purposes. When this happens, a predatory state is born. The issue is how contradictions can be created to move such states into becoming developmental ones, so that resources are invested for the good of the society as a whole.

The profile of developmental states is based on the experiences of the Asian tigers. Sorenson (1993) contends that the reflection on the possible features of a developmental state have from the very beginning been plagued by the fact that they commenced not with deliberations concerning state theory and the proper definition or content of states in general and developmental states in particular, but with empirical assessment that some East Asian countries are remarkably more successful than other Third World countries in terms of certain economic indicators. Drawing from these experiences, many scholars have suggested that the role of the state should be confined to the creation and support of institutions that help the markets to perform most effectively. The state can perform this task successfully when the bureaucratic and technical elites in charge of policy making are insulated from the pulls and pressures of everyday politics. Among the enabling conditions for this insulation are the Weberian characteristics of bureaucracy (Evans, 1989). Based on Johnson's (1982) account of the golden years of MITI in Japan, Evans argues that Japan's startling post-war economic growth occurred in the presence of a powerful, talented and prestigious economic bureaucracy, which also had the capacity to network with other social instructions, plus sufficient flexibility to deal with changing technical and market conditions. He describes this networked insulation of the top bureaucracy as the embedded autonomy of the state and regards it as the key to the success of Japan. The idea of embedded autonomy or networking bureaucracy is different from autonomy of decision making by itself. Bureaucratic autonomy was located in an unusual degree of cooperation from the private sector in furthering developmental goals. It forged a unity among elites that was reflected in the success of MITI and similar institutions in Korea and Taiwan.

Most contributors to the discussion of the processes of transformation to a developmental state drew inspiration from this so-called state-centric model of development. The question of autonomy, that is, freedom of elected and bureaucratic officials in economic decision making, was seen as a primary characteristic in pursuing goals of development. The capacity of state structures to arrive at this autonomy emerged from a rationalized bureaucratic system. Emphasis on creating conditions of autonomy and rationality have become an integral part of the agenda of good governance and are now part of the advice being offered by multilateral aid-giving agencies. As a matter of fact, there is little doubt the development assistance is increasingly suffused with discourse on governance (Jayal, 1997).

However, doubts about implicating these features of governance in other countries have begun to be raised. It has been pointed out, for example, that Zaire's elite was strikingly unconstrained by any set of organized social interests. In this sense, it was relatively autonomous but it did not work for societal growth and development (Evans, 1989, p. 571). Taiwan began as an oppressive regime but changed into a developmental state in a short time. The puzzle that Sorenson (1993) highlights is: why some states, enjoying a high degree of autonomy, do not exploit it in the service of development and why some states do not choose to promote development in a consistent and efficient manner. Autonomy can be used by the elite for any purpose. By itself it does not work for development alone.

A more significant criticism of this model of governance entails denial of political processes in development. Too much is made of the development impact of bureaucratic and technocratic decision making while other characteristics are ignored. Leftwich (1994) points out that all development states have been *de facto* or *de jure* one-party states for much of the last 30 years. The effect has been to concentrate very considerable and unchallenged political power at the top in these states, thus enhancing political stability and continuity in public policy. Japan, South Korea, Taiwan or Singapore, all leading examples of developmental states, are also marked by a strong degree of cultural homogeneity as well as tendencies towards an authoritarian state. Many scholars view authoritarian rule as an essential part of East Asian development (Deyo, 1989) but the point still needs to be made that such governments can resist pressure from both business and labour. Growing democratization in many of these states will show whether they will continue to be able to resist such pressures in the future.

Keeping democratic politics out also means that somehow the state is perceived as being outside society and that development goals emerge out of its own predilections without reference to those of society. The state is seen as an actor, a force independent of social dynamics. In a book arguing for bringing the state back in, Skocpol (1985, pp. 20–1) says that, '... states may formulate and pursue goals that are simply not reflective of the demands of interests of social groups, classes or society'. If so, can we conclude that the interests of the state, different from those of society, will always be pro-development?

The immediate question that arises is the lesson to be drawn from the East Asian developmental state model experiences. Is the developmental state model transferable? The concepts of development administration and of governance seem to have grown from the experience of specific countries. In one case, the West is the model; in the other it is East Asia. The efforts in both were directed towards increasing state capability to implement developmental projects. Strengthening the state in both versions has also meant focusing attention on the role of the bureaucracy and accepting the assumption that bureaucrats work for developmental goals. In both cases there are powerful institutions that project them. The Ford Foundation, USAID and UNDP are some of the organizations that provide intellectual as well as financial support to the spread of the idea of development administration. The World Bank and other financial agencies have done the same for the concept of good governance.

Perhaps one should not exaggerate this similarity between governance and the role of bureaucracy in transforming a predatory state into a developmental one, nor equate it with the much wider issues of what development administration did. In the discussion of the processes of transformation of a predatory state into a developmental one, the issue of autonomy has to be seen within the circumstances of unity among the elite in the policy perspectives that provided support to the bureaucracy in taking hard decisions. There was a great degree of cooperation between the public and the private sector. The single-minded pursuit of growth and productivity could be undertaken because problems of distribution were largely ignored. East Asian countries had undergone a radical land reform process while the depredations of war had equalized the level of deprivation among industrialists. In most developing countries, such a situation does not exist. Distributional goals are very much part of their developmental agenda and severe inequalities exist. In the Indian context of a plurality of contending heterogeneous groups, a close liaison and harmony of interests between the state and private business would raise an outcry of foul play and strong political resentment among other groups, particularly organized labour and farmers which, unlike East Asian politicians, India's politicians cannot ignore (Bardhan undated). The tightly integrated relationship of government with private business, which is the concept of embedded autonomy identified by Evans, is very difficult to envisage in the Indian case.

Clearly, the effectiveness of bureaucracy is linked with other features of society and politics in these countries. To that extent, any attempt to implement the model extracted from the experience of East Asian countries will prove counterproductive. As Onis (1991) emphasizes, the transfer of specific policies and strategies to new environments will be self-defeating in the absence of the political and institutional conditions required for their effective implementation. What emerges from these experiences is that any one-dimensional view of development must be replaced by the understanding that there are multiple linkages and interactions in society and that bureaucracy is not a 'stand-alone' solution. The gain from the experiences of the journey of the concept of development administration should be to investigate these multiple linkages in order to understand the role of the bureaucracy, its strength and its autonomy in the act of governance.

Indian experience provides an interesting case of passing through the stage of development administration and now becoming the recipient of the various ideas assumed to have moved a predatory state into a developmental one. India sought to shape a developmental state through an ambitious strategy of economic planning, wherein the state was assigned a central role. An effort was made to give a certain amount of autonomy to economic decision-making by establishing the prestigious Planning Commission. The problem of development came to be evaluated in technical terms and was largely seen as a problem of correct policy formulation and design. The Nehru–Mahalanobis strategy that became the hallmark of the 1950s and

1960s was dominated by the discussion of prioritization of investment allocations, trade and industrial strategies, etc. As noted by many commentators, this was the time when development economics was coming into its own and the Indian experience had much to offer. It is not too much to say that the Indian development strategy was remarkable in its use of planning models, the sophisticated development which planning engendered, and the extensive utilization of such models with respect to formulation (Byres, 1997, p. 14).

The successive five-year plans took it for granted that their rationale would be accepted and that people would behave accordingly. If difficulties arose, they would be merely difficulties of implementation. The development policy design was regarded as technically correct, while failures were seen to be the result of social and political constraints and implementation. Less than a decade ago, it was being argued that the 'primary failure in several developing countries, including India, has been in implementation ...' (Jalan, 1991, p. 87). The technical argument was extended to implementation and the professional thrust of development administration immediately attracted the attention of Indian planners and policy makers. But more of this later.

The technical aura perceived around planning became possible by creating the Planning Commission as a unique institution away from the normal functioning of the government. It was a tribute to this uniqueness when critics called it a 'super cabinet'. The power of the Planning Commission flowed from Nehru's own patronage, a dependence that ironically also made it vulnerable and institutionally insecure. Economic development was entrusted by Nehru to a small group: over a decade, the membership of the Planning Commission was drawn from a pool of about 20 men (Khilnani, 1997, p. 81). Most were civil servants and some represented private interests too. Professional economists and technocrats very quickly came to dominate public discussion about India's economic development. The Planning Commission became the exclusive theatre where economic policy was formulated. The subject was taken away from the cabinet and parliament, which were merely informed of decisions taken by the small cohort of experts. Khilnani (ibid., p. 86) cites the Second Plan as an instance where political decisions were camouflaged in technical terms needed to insulate it from public deliberations. Since this plan entitled decisive rechannelling of investment towards heavy industry, there was a choice about consumption (less now for the promise of more later) that was undoubtedly a matter for public debate.

But even though the activities of the Planning Commission have left a lasting impression on India's development performance, its period of ascendancy was brief and did not last long after Nehru left the scene. The erosion of the role and status of the Planning Commission occurred soon after. Economic decision making began to shift towards the Finance Ministry and subsequent prime ministers did not raise its status or insulate it from governmental politics. As a matter of fact, it lost its pre-eminent position when the rupee was devalued in 1966 because the decision for doing so received severe criticism from both professionals and the political leadership. Institutionally, several steps were taken to redefine the position. Members of the Planning Commission were now to have fixed terms, unlike under Nehru when they enjoyed unlimited tenure. The cabinet secretary, who is the top civil servant of the country and had served as the secretary of the Commission, was detached from it. In addition, a prime minister's secretariat was created as an alternative adviser to the prime minister. This new office was headed by a senior civil servant who was a trained economist and more inclined towards the market mechanism. This was the beginning of the period when economic policy making became the arena of political battles that in the past had always been overwhelmed by Nehru's ideological certitude and political stature (Varshney, 1995, pp. 51–2).

This was also the period when the potential of being a strong state was seen in terms of the state's dominance in the economic sphere and its 'ideological advantage as the presumed defender of collective interests and socialist purposes and as the enemy of private and partial gains' (Rudolph and Rudolph, 1987, p. 13). The Rudolphs pointed out that the Indian state had sought, over the decades of the 1960s and 1970s, to insulate itself from the exigent pressure of a mobilized society and suggested that the Nehruvian state of the 1950s provided a credible if partial embodiment of relative autonomy. On the other hand, Myrdal (1972) explained the feeble development record of the Indian state by drawing a distinction between soft and strong states. He argued that if Indian poverty was to be overcome, a strong state was needed which could divest itself of the influence of special interests and enforce social discipline. The failure of effective structural changes in the Indian economy in the heyday of the Nehruvian state has been well documented. This has been described as the fundamental paradox of the Indian political economy: 'a commitment to radical social change and yet an equal determination to avoid a direct attack on existing structures' (Frankel, 1978, pp. 1–78).

The 'paradox' does not remain a paradox when state capability is seen as determined by pulls and pressures of various groups in society. State action does not emerge as a rational response to an economic situation by a unified, omnicompetent political institution. Rather, different groups of officials and/or parts of state compete over policy; in many instances their goals and interests can only be understood by reference to or interaction with non-state actors (Clark and Roy, 1997, p. 6). Conflict and contradictions among these actors will impinge on state policy. States have to be situated in their social setting and the reasons why individuals and groups respond differently to market signals and policy incentives have to be analysed and understood.

India inherited a colonial land settlement, which assigned ownership to rentier zamindars or cultivators (*ryots*) in return for the rent paid to the Raj. Economic power was widely dispersed and also entrenched in these propertied classes. Industry was at a nascent stage but powerful regionally based and family centred business houses had begun to emerge. In both the agricultural as well as the industrial sectors there were powerful individuals or groups who commanded significant economic power. This economic power relationship was defended by a powerful social order based on caste, family and region. The development strategy that was hammered out during the early years was one that kept these economic power equations in mind. Dominant caste groups and their relationships were also kept under consideration while framing policies. The major problems were those of very unequal distribution of landownership and very low levels of productivity. The power equations severely constrained and strictly circumscribed the capability of the state and its scope of action. In a much later explanation for the lack of investment in long-term growth, Bardhan (1984) suggested that politicians presided over a dominant coalition with three main elements: the industrial bourgeoisie, rich farmers and public sector employees. Each strived to maximize benefits from the development policies and the state was unable to rise above their interests or work for the society as a whole. Radical postures may have been taken but they could not be translated into action. What happened then was that the state was strong on regulatory law and weak on enforcement.

If these were the political conflicts which fractured the necessary support for industrialization and planned development, then Nehru had to look elsewhere to have his ideas translated into action. This task began to be increasingly entrusted to the civil service, even though Nehru had demanded a radical transformation of the ICS (Indian Civil Service) during the independence movement, and it had been left to Patel to argue for its place in the Constitution. The ICS was seen to represent state interests and to be relatively autonomous of local pulls and pressures. The doctrine of neutrality and impartiality was seen as its predominant behavioural trait, and it was assumed that its successor, moulded in the same tradition, would withstand the parochial pressures on the state. Together with Nehru, civil servants were the vanguard of the lobby for an industrial strategy, which sought to create and expand the public sector to run basic and heavy industry under the Second and Third Five-Year Plans. However, the national orientation and professional ethos soon lost their gloss because public sector undertakings could not be managed efficiently and profitably.

While the Indian bureaucracy is often cited as having Weberian characteristics, it is not known for creating sufficient state autonomy to pursue developmental interests. It has turned out to be a weak instrument of the state and the networks that it has created have usually been of a rent making variety. There is increasing evidence that the alliance between politicians and bureaucrats has been in the pursuit of mutual gain. The demands of career advancement are of paramount significance for a civil servant and an obliging politician is ready to do anything for a civil servant who bends rules to favour his political master. The close linkage of civil servants with caste or communal groups, business houses and the large farmer community has to be seen in this perspective of mutuality of interests (Bhambri, 1998). It is also not possible for the bureaucracy in the Indian situation to harmonize its interests with those of the private sector for an additional reason. For one thing, the private sector itself does not have identical interests and for another, the bureaucracy has grown on the belief that it is the only group that works in the public interest. It has not been easy for it to give up its self-perception of being the 'guardians' in the old British colonial sense. This has considerably restricted its initiative in mobilizing support for public policies and their implementation.

The Indian design of state intervention was usually engulfed by the characteristics of its larger administrative system, but a few successes in innovative institutional experiments occurred because they could move away from its stifling stranglehold. When India became independent, it was among the very few countries of the world that had a strong and effective bureaucratic machinery in place. As a matter of fact, the strength and coherence of its civil service was so striking that it was known as a steel frame. The Indian Administrative Service (IAS), created in the image of the ICS, was moulded as a monolithic instrument and an image of elitism was deliberately built in to provide a sense of separation from the common society. This was supported by frequent movement of officials from one position to another and a few people, whirled about by rapid transfers, were propelled by automatic promotions into higher positions exclusively reserved for them at all levels of government. On the way, they commanded handsome salaries and social status forever denied to others (Potter, 1986). The district collector was the head of the district and all other local offices were subservient to him. A direct line of command was established with central/state authorities and the district officer was recognized as the kingpin of the system. Vesting so much power in an individual also meant that higher levels of the government came to depend on him for all information and advice in matters pertaining to his local area. In the social context, he could be above local politics because of the prestige and status that came to him by being in the government hierarchy. Conversely, he could align himself with an individual or a group at the local level and wield considerable power himself or in conjunction with his ally.

The structure of the Indian administrative and civil service system has not changed much since colonial days. On the contrary, the political system has sustained it. A powerful bureaucracy and the structure existing prior to Independence have influenced the design of state intervention. However, faith in it has been so great that no new organization or institutional design could be put on the ground which did not take these factors into consideration. This pervasive influence was felt in institutions that sought autonomy from day-to-day government operations, but were gradually pushed into being semi-autonomous and then operationally came under the purview of politicians and administrators in the 'public interest'. Public sector manufacturing and service units were among the initial victims, but as the state expanded its role, institutions in education or health or rural development followed suit. The expectation that a bureaucracy would work in the public interest on its own has been belied. Just as it is necessary to analyse the concept of public interest, the instrument of fulfilling them also needs to be re-examined (Bjorkman, 1995).

It was not as if there was no concern expressed for poor administrative performance or for the inability of administration to respond adequately to the challenges of implementing development plans.

The first Five-Year Plan (1951–56) had set the tasks very clearly: 'From the maintenance of law and order and collection of revenue, the major emphasis now shifts to development of human and material resources and the elimination of poverty and want ... There is also a need for structural changes to raise the level of administration.' Administration came under scrutiny by many committees and the government demonstrated its commitment to administrative changes by accepting the offer of the Ford Foundation to bring in an American consultant, Paul Appleby. The thrust of development administration—of professionalism and behavioural change—was also accepted. Universities reoriented their teaching programmes, training institutions were strengthened and their number multiplied (Mathur, 1996). International assistance in sending civil servants abroad for training and reorientation was also accepted as part of the aid given for development projects. The Ford Foundation alone spent US$ 360,000 in grants and US$ 76,000 in providing funds to specialists and consultants to improve public administration in India during 1951–62 (Braibanti, 1966, p. 148).

The efforts at administrative reform were accompanied by reliance on the administrative system to bring about a change in rural society. Programmes to involve the people in making collective efforts for development usually resulted in domination by the administrative system, which suffocated people's participation. It had been hoped that the Community Development Programme would become a people's movement but it faded away leaving a legacy more of administration than of participation. Efforts at decentralization also suffered from a similar malaise and the ineffectiveness of panchayati raj (PR) institutions is well documented (Government of India, 1978). The three levels of panchayats from the district downwards were closely associated with local level administrators and government reports themselves reveal how this association led to obstacles in democratization and decentralization (Government of India, 1978). Bureaucrats were hesitant to part with power and colluded with local ruling groups in taking decisions. This picture was common to other institutions as well, such as those established to implement poverty alleviation programmes. The experience of panchayats in West Bengal is frequently cited as a contrast to this prevailing picture. It must be emphasized that this success stems from the political commitment of the state leadership, in making this level of government work effectively. The 73rd and 74th Amendments to the Constitution seek to advance the concept of self-governance by providing for regular elections, minimal suppression of PR bodies through an administrative fiat, and regular finances through statutory distribution by state finance commissions. The aim is to reduce the margin of political and administrative discretion and to allow the decentralized institutions to gather strength on the basis of people's involvement. The success of these amendments making decentralized structures part of the Constitution has yet to be seen—not only because they were only instituted in 1993, but also because the states have shown little evidence of implementing the requirement through their own statutes.

Another pillar of the earlier development strategy was the establishment of cooperative societies which were meant to serve the smaller asset holders in rural areas. Meant to be self-governing institutions where people came together to fulfill their economic needs, they have actually served the ambitions of local politicians and administrators. The legal framework envisaged in the Cooperative Societies Act throttled the growth of a movement and the government department of cooperative societies became an instrument for perpetuating the hegemony of the government and the bureaucracy (Shah, 1996). Rather than protecting cooperatives from petty sectional interests, the law in numerous instances has been unabashedly used by politicians and petty bureaucrats to stifle their growth by superseding elections to their boards for decades. There has been a strident demand for abolishing the very government department that was set up as the promotional agency (Jain and Coelho, 1996).

If little thought was given to structure state intervention to support panchayats or cooperative institutions, even less effort was made to ensure that the government's own institutional innovations in the rural development sector were embedded in a supportive environment. These institutions—like the Small Farmers Development Agency established in 1970, which was transformed into the District Rural Development Agency in 1979—were established with the aim of keeping them outside the normal bureaucratic framework so that the implementation of poverty alleviation programmes would be more effective. Government documents provided their rationale through phrases that would have one believe that it was ardently committed to decentralization, semiautonomous local organizations and local level planning for locally prioritized schemes of assistance to remove poverty. What happened? Effective decentralization did not take place, local accountability of these programmes was absent and the government stifled the operating agencies through its administrative policies (Mathur, 1995). These weaknesses were identified not only by academic researchers, but also by committees appointed by the government itself. Yet little was done. The urge for change to help rural communities and to create economic opportunities remained more in government documents than in reality. This account supports the view that there is greater effort in India to give *an appearance of a developmental state* than a commitment to create one. When institutions fail to perform, blame is laid at the door of rural society. Apparently, formal establishment of a public institution demonstrates state commitment to development and failure in its performance demonstrates weaknesses in society—illiteracy, backwardness, social conflicts, etc.

Clearly, state intervention was not designed in a way that development organizations could grow. The systems for economic planning and those for mobilizing financial resources tended to reinforce central tendencies of the entrenched administrative system. In a situation where a strong bureaucracy had sought to curb local initiative in order to gain social power and create a strong control and command system, the vastly expanded state intervention merely entangled individuals in increased socio-economic obligations towards the state. Autonomy without concomitant accountability meant bureaucratic licence and bureaucratic networks increasingly became opportunities of colluding for personal aggrandizement. A kind of dependency syndrome inhibited individuals and communities from taking social and economic initiatives; wherever such initiatives received state support but were left relatively alone, they have shown success. Dairy cooperatives in Gujarat and sugar cooperatives in Maharashtra come immediately to mind.

The perception that the state has the capability to provide a supportive environment to sustain and nurture local institutions does not emerge only from the experience of cooperatives in Gujarat and Maharashtra. Innovative institutions also appear in common property resource management. Evidence from fields as diverse as irrigation and forestry shows that user groups, when allowed to manage such resources, can exclude free riders, monitor the behaviour of their members, and enforce rules to sustain and maintain resources (Chambers et al., 1989; Ostrom, 1991; Poffenberger and McGean, 1996). In order to reduce conflicts between state agencies and user groups, joint forest management committees are being facilitated to respond to national needs and local management requirements. The national guideline to support such committees envisages people's involvement in the development and protection of forests. It states that one of the essential features of forest management is that the forest communities 'should be motivated to identify themselves with development and protection of forest from which they derive benefits' (Poffenberger and Singh, 1996, p. 62). West Bengal has taken a lead in the matter and has formulated an official programme providing legitimacy to grassroots resource management. Encouraged by the extensive and generally successful experiences of joint forest management in West Bengal, non-governmental organizations are attempting to spread the experiment elsewhere in the country. Through increasing dialogue between participating communities, non-governmental organizations and governmental agencies, new ideas are emerging and local groups are being encouraged to work for themselves and in the process help develop and manage local resources. These are hopeful signs, and greater support must be elicited from voluntary groups to accelerate this process.

The purpose of relating the Indian experience of development during the last 50 years was to focus on the issue of governance being articulated today. The 'success' of the early years of planning can be attributed to some extent to the consensus that had emerged during the national movement about the role of the state in development; it had therefore been possible to see the state as a powerful 'third actor'. But other powerful actors in society circumscribed its power. The inability to take them along led to a crisis and to the dismantling of the regime of planning. The introduction of economic reforms in a limited fashion shows the inability of the state to face the powerful social groups that influence public policy (Manor, 1995). While reform is in the air, precious little has been done to change or reform bureaucracy. It was the distortions produced by bureaucratic interventions that economic reforms sought to correct; yet it is precisely here that the state has not succeeded. Political action is needed to make the bureaucracy more accountable to the political system and to curb its dominance in the sphere that clearly should be democratic.

The thrust of development administration failed to energize Indian bureaucracy and one should be cautious about transplanting the experience of the East Asian tigers. The issue of distribution is a very important political issue in India and cannot be brushed aside in any discussion of development. When the East Asian countries started on their path of development, many of their equity concerns had already been resolved. Effective land reforms had taken place, there had been leavening in the assets of the private sector and literacy levels were much higher than what India has now reached after 50 years of independence. If there is lack of compatibility in the historical and socio-economic context, the nature and character of the bureaucracy is also different for the same reasons. The bureaucracy in India carried the heritage of colonial power and its concern was to maintain its role in the political system. It resisted any reforms that tended to whittle down its power and prestige. Without effective political control and social accountability, the bureaucracy used its autonomy to support the predatory forces in society.

In order to deepen democracy and create countervailing institutions that can strengthen civil society and counter bureaucratic influence as well, institutional pluralism needs to be promoted. We need to search for institutional alternatives and accept the idea that an array of diverse institutional managements are possible to respond to available opportunities. Cooperatives and joint committees between users and government and user associations are examples that provide opportunities for improved collective decision-making. We must build upon the common understanding and the shared experience of people in their particular circumstances. These may require changes in legal and contractual arrangements, explicit codification of rights as well as attendant obligations and these tasks should be high on the agenda of governance.

The main insight that emerges from this discussion is that the meaning of the notion of a strong state should not be limited to the institution of a strong bureaucracy alone. A high degree of bureaucratic autonomy and capacity may not necessarily lead to a developmental state because the bureaucracy may not be able to rise above its own interests. What is required is consent for policies pursued and legitimacy for mobilizing resources needed for future investments. This can come only through the strengthening of the democratic processes where there is negotiation and debate. Agreements arrived at in this way strengthen the capacity of the state to take strong decisions. Even within the neo-liberal agenda, the state needs to intervene to facilitate development, but the instruments of this intervention need not be the bureaucracy alone. A multiple institutional framework is needed and it must be recognized that there have been a host of other factors that have led the developmental states to fulfill their national goals.

REFERENCES

Amsden, A.H. (1989). *Asia's Next Giant: South Korea and Industrialization*. New York: Oxford University Press.

Bardhan, P.K. (Undated). (The Nature of Institutional Impediments to Economic Development). Mimeo.

Bardhan, P.K. (1984). *Political Economy of Development in India*. Oxford: Basil Blackwell.

Bhagwati, J.N. (1993). *India in Transition: Freeing the Economy*. Oxford: Clarendon Press.

Bhambri, C.P. (1998). 'Of a Partisan, Self-Serving Bureaucracy', *The Pioneer*, 23 September.

Bjorkman, J.W. (1995). 'Ethics and the Public Interest: Towards Understanding Public Choice in Developing Countries', *Indian Journal of Public Administration*, XLI(3): 275–95.

Braibanti, R. (1966). 'Transnational Inducement of Administrative Reform', in W.J. Siffin (ed.), *Approaches to Development Politics and Change*, pp. 133–84. New York: McGraw Hill.

Byres, T.J. (1997). *State, Development Planning and Liberalization*. New Delhi: Oxford University Press.

Chambers, R., N.C. Saxena and T. Shah (1989). *To the Hands of the Poor: Waters and Trees*. New Delhi: Oxford and IBH Publishers.

Clark, Cal and K.C. Roy. (1997). *Comparing Development Patterns in Asia*. London: Lynne Reinner.

Deyo, F.C. (1989). *Beneath the Miracle: Labour Subordination in the New Asian Industrialism*. Berkeley: University of California Press.

Dwivedi, O.P. and Keith M. Henderson (1990). *Public Administration in World Perspective*. Ames: Iowa State University Press.

Evans, Peter B. (1989). 'Predatory Development and other Apparatus: A Comparative Analysis of Third World State', *Sociological Forum*, 4:561–87.

Evans, Peter B, T. Skocpol and D. Reuschmeyer (1985). *Bringing the State Back In*, Cambridge: Cambridge University Press.

Frankel, Francine (1978). *India's Political Economy, 1947–77*. Princeton: Princeton University Press.

Gant, George (1979). *Development Administration: Concepts, Goals and Methods*. Madison: University of Wisconsin Press.

Government of India (1978). *Report of the Committee on Panchayati Raj Institutions*. New Delhi: Ministry of Agriculture and Irrigation.

Jain, L.C. and Karen Coelho (1996). *In the Wake of Freedom: India's Tryst with Cooperatives*. New Delhi: Concept Publishers.

Jalan B. (1991). *The Indian Economy: Problems and Prospects*. New Delhi: Viking Press.

Jayal, Niraja Gopal (1997). 'The Governance Agenda: Making Democratic Development Dispensable', *Economic and Political Weekly*, 36(8): 407–12.

Johnson, Chalmers (1982). *MITI and the Japanese Miracle: The Growth of Industrial Policy*. Stanford: Stanford University Press.

Khilnani, S. (1997). *The Idea of India*. London: Hamish Hamilton.

Leftwich, A. (1994). 'Governance, the State and the Politics of Development', *Development and Change*, 25: 263–85.

Manor, James (1995). 'The Political Sustainability of Economic Liberalization in India', in R. Cassen and Vijay Joshi (eds), *India: Future of Economic Reform*, pp. 341–63. New Delhi: Oxford University Press.

Mathur, Kuldeep (1995). 'Politics and Implementation of Integrated Rural Development Programmes', *Economic and Political Weekly*, 41 and 42: 2703–708.

—— (1996). 'Introduction', in K. Mathur (ed.), *Development Policy and Administration*, pp. 13–23. New Delhi: Sage Publications.

Myrdal, G. (1972). *The Asian Drama: An Inquiry into the Poverty of Nations*, Harmondsworth: Penguin.

Onis, Z. (1991). 'The Logic of the Developmentalist State', *Comparative Politics*, 24: 109–21.

Ostrom, E. (1991). *Governing the Commons: Evolution of Institutions for Collective Action*. Cambridge: Cambridge University Press.

Potter, David (1986). *India's Political Administrators*. New Delhi: Clarendon Press.

Poffenberger, M. and Betsy McGean (eds), (1996). *Village Voices, Forest Choices: Joint Forest Management in India*, New Delhi: Oxford University Press.

Poffenberger, M. and Chatrapati Singh (1996). 'Communities and the State: Reestablishing the Balance in Indian Forest Policy', in M. Poffenberger and Betsy McGean (eds), *Village Voices, Forest Choices: Joint Forest Management in India*. New Delhi: Oxford University Press.

Riggs, F.W. (1965). 'Bureaucrats and Political Development: A Paradoxical View', in J. La Palombara (ed.), *Bureaucracy and Political Development*, pp. 120–67. Princeton: Princeton University Press.

—— (1976). 'The Group and the Movement: Notes on Comparative and Development Administration', *Public Administration Review*, 36(6): 648–54.

—— (1998). 'Public Administration in America: Why Our Uniqueness is Exceptional and Important', *Public Administration Review*, 58(1): 22–31.

Rudolph, L.I. and S.H. Rudolph (1987). *In Pursuit of Lakshmi: The Political Economy of the Indian State*. Hyderabad: Orient Longman.

Shah, Tushaar (1996). 'Agriculture and Rural Development in the 1990s. Beyond Redesigning Relations between the State and Institutions of Development', in K. Mathur (ed.) *Development Policy and Administration*, pp. 85–125.

Skocpol, T. (1985). 'Bringing the State Back In: Strategies of Analysis in Current Research', in Peter B. Evans et al. (eds), *Bringing the State Back In*, pp. 3–37. Cambridge: Cambridge University Press.

Sorenson, George (1993). 'Democracy, Authoritarianism and State Strength', *European Journal of Development Research*, 5(1): 6–34.

United Nations (1975). *Development Administration: Current Approaches and Trends in Public Administration for National Development*. New York: Department of Economic and Social Affairs.

Varshney, A. (1995). *Democracy, Development and the Countryside: Urban–Rural Struggles in India*. Cambridge: Cambridge University Press.

Wade, R. (1990). *Governing the Market: Economic Theory and Role of Government in East Asian Industrialization*. Princeton: Princeton University Press.

CHAPTER SEVENTEEN

Human Rights Dimensions of Public Administration in India

Jaytilak Guha Roy

The late 20th century globalization has brought about a paradigm shift in the nature and character of the state and public administration from 'the traditional welfare administrative state to a corporate welfare state'.[1] Under the garb of promoting the cause of liberal democracy and human development, international and western aid-giving agencies, like World Bank, IMF, and OECD countries, seem to have been encroaching, not directly but indirectly, upon the sovereignty of the Third World countries, their right to development and forcing them to accept a revised version of the gospel of capitalism. Although, as of now, the impact of globalization and economic liberalization on the developing countries remains a mystery which would require some more time to unfold, at least an immediate outcome is distinctly visible to the extent that the theory and practice of public administration have suddenly been enriched with many new concepts or ideas—good governance, public service management, citizens' charter, reinventing government, ethical governance, contracting out public services, e-governance, to name a few.

Globalization and liberalization reinforced by information technology revolution have indeed been posing a major challenge to

[1] Ali Farazmand, 'Globalization and Public Administration', *Public Administration Review*, 59 (6), Nov.–Dec. 1999, p. 510.

Nordic countries and New Zealand are the best examples of 'Corporate Welfare States'. They are all market economies but their welfare measures cover their citizens from cradle to the grave (vide Address by R. Venkataraman, Former President of India on 'Governance in India: Today and Tomorrow' at IIPA, New Delhi, 18 October 2000).

developing countries as also providing new opportunities. However, for a developing country as ours, the unfortunate part of the ongoing process of globalization appears to be threatening since the agendas for economic and other reforms are likely to be imposed by international and Western donor agencies rather than adopted by choice in consonance with one's own national needs and interests. And herein lies the dilemma of the ongoing reform initiatives being faced by the planners and policy makers of the developing nations.

Origin and Implication of Current Discourse on Human Rights

After the end of the World War II, the United Nations was established in 1945 to fulfill the long-cherished aspirations of the world community for a world of peace, prosperity and happiness of all human beings, inhabiting any part of the world irrespective of race, region, religion, caste, creed, colour and community. Against the backdrop of the holocaust of World War II the birth of the United Nations marked the beginning of a new era of internationalization of human rights ideals and values with proclamation of the Universal Declaration of Human Rights (UDHR) by the UN General Assembly on the historic day of December 10, 1948. The UDHR is not just a declaration. It represents the collective wisdom of the world community to work together towards a world without injustice, indignity and ignorance; a world without cruelty and hunger.

On the contrary, human rights discourse in recent years owes its origin in the 1992 World Bank's document entitled *Governance and Development*. Traditionally, governance refers to forms of political system and the manner in which power is exercised in utilizing a country's economic and social resources for development.[2] Based on its lending experience in developing countries, the World Bank came to realize that 'good governance' was a concern worthy of attention in considering projects for assistance. Seven specific aspects of 'governance' were identified by the Bank and the Development Assistance Committee of the OECD. These were: (1) public sector management, (2) accountability, (3) legal and regulatory framework, (4) transparency and information, (5) human rights, (6) participatory approaches, and (7) military expenditure.[3]

---

[2] Mick Moore, 'Declining to Learn from the East: The World Bank on Governance and Development', *IDS Bulletin*, 24(1), 1993, p. 39.

[3] World Bank, *Governance and Development*, Washington, D.C., World Bank, 1992.

Donor agencies' attempt to prescribe an uniform model of governance seems to be too unrealistic to operationalize, in actual practice. In fact, governance, like democracy, observes a Western scholar very aptly, 'remains a particularly difficult variable to operationalize. At present "good governance" is seemingly defined in terms of a *checklist of criteria* ... that governance must broadly satisfy in order to justify receiving loans. However, it is not made explicit ... how they should be measured and compared. Governance is not, a *binary variable* and cannot be defined in terms of on/of/, or "present/absent" criteria'.[4]

Operational limitations apart, donor agencies' concern for human rights resulted in unnecessary proliferation of international human rights, the costs of which seem to be extremely unfair for the Third World nations. 'As rights-oriented agendas increasingly dominate the policies and budget of Western countries', observes a Western critique very poignantly, '*human-rights* activism has expanded to exert pressure on nations around the world to assure greater governmental and social compliance with Western *human rights* standards.' As this critique observes further, 'The unbridled growth of *human rights* accentuates differences among persons and groups, threatens internal order and social cohesion, and transforms nations into mere states. In the worst cases the uncontrolled growth of *rights*, like *cancer cells*, can kill the hosts that nurture them—and thereby kill themselves.'[5]

One may or may not agree with the above observations. Nevertheless, the fact remains that excessive emphasis on human rights by the donor agencies has backfired so much so that even the legitimate concern for human rights is now being looked upon with suspicion, and the concept of human rights is considered to be a Western or an alien concept by a large chunk of educated citizens including civil bureaucracy in our country.

CONCEPTUAL EVOLUTION OF HUMAN RIGHTS

The idea of human rights, in its present content and package, is a product of a long process of evolution. Essentially, human rights are an integral part of human life since the possession of these rights distinguishes human beings from other species. In all ages and in all

---

[4] Bob Currie, 'Governance, Democracy and Economic Adjustment in India: Concept and Empirical Problems', *Third World Quarterly*, 17(4), 1996 (emphasis added).

[5] John A. Gentry, 'The Cancer of Human Rights', *Washington Quarterly*, Autumn 1999, 22(4), p. 95.

forms of systems, there were oppressions of human beings by human beings which led to the struggles for restoration and protection of human rights. Thus, the concept of human rights is 'an idea with a history, an idea that changes in both content and social function.'[6]

Some western scholars have tried to distinguish 'three generations' of human rights.[7] The first generation refers to civil and political rights, commonly known as the 'classic' human rights. This generation was led by the classical as well as contemporary Western liberal scholars from John Stuart Mill to John Rawls who conceived civil and political rights as some kind of protection or safeguard against the state power. This generation was greatly influenced by the Magna Carta or the Great Charter of English Liberties granted by King John in 1215 under the threat of civil war, and the English Bill of Rights of 1689 which laid the foundation of parliamentary supremacy over the English Monarchy after the Glorious Revolution of 1688. This generation was rejuvenated and reinforced in the late 18th and the early 19th century with the American Declaration of Independence and French Declaration of the Rights of Man and the Citizen.

Civil and political rights, included such rights as the right to freedom of speech and expression, right to freedom of movement and right against arbitrary arrests which are even today considered as the essential safeguards for the citizens against arbitrary government or state power.

The post-colonial era witnessed the emergence of the second generation of human rights which was led by the political leaders and thinkers of developing nations who propagated the idea that economic, social and cultural rights were a prerequisite for the enjoyment of civil and political rights. This second category of rights *inter alia* include right against exploitation, right to work, shelter, food, social security, health care and education, the right to freedom of culture and religion.

The third generation of human rights was led by the scholars and thinkers of the Socialist and the Third World countries who conceived human right as the collective rights of a nation such as the right to development, the right to peace, the right to one's own

[6] Eugene Kamenka and Alice Erth-Soon Tay (eds), *Human Rights*, London, Edward Arnold, 1978, Introduction by Kamenka, p. vi.

[7] Cess Flinterman, 'Three Generation of Human Rights', in Jan Berting et al. (eds), *Human Rights in a Pluralistic World: Individuals to Collectivities*, Westport & London, Meckler, 1990, pp. 75–82; Peter R. Baehr, *The Role of Human Rights in Foreign Policy*, London, Macmillan, 1994.

natural resources and the right to one's own cultural heritage. In the contemporary context of globalization and economic liberalization, the collective right of a nation, especially the rights to protect environment and natural resources appear to be most significant for the survival of the developing nations against the economic imperialism of the multinational corporations having their origins in the developed nations.

The third generation of human rights also emphasized on the 'group rights', that is, rights of the weaker and vulnerable groups such as women, children, aged, minorities, refugees, prisoners, sex workers, etc.

The term 'generation' is somewhat misleading as it usually implies a succession of phenomena, whereby a new generation takes the place of the previous one. This is not so as far as the three 'generations' of human rights are concerned. On the contrary, as Baehr has rightly pointed out, 'the idea is rather that the three "generations" exist and should be respected simultaneously'.[8] In other words, this implies that the problem of generation gap does not arise in the case of human rights, as it often happens in the case of human beings.

FROM UNIVERSALITY TO PRACTICABILITY

The first two generation of human rights have been incorporated in the International Bill of Human Rights (IBHR) consisting of Universal Declaration of Human Rights (1948), International Covenant on Civil and Political Rights (1966) and International Covenant on Economic, Social and Cultural Rights (1966). With the subsequent reinforcement of the IBHR by several other instruments such as Convention on the Elimination of All Forms of Discrimination Against Women, Protocol relating to the Status of Refugees, the 1986 UN Declaration on Right to Development, and Convention on the Rights of the Child, the third generation of human rights has also been included in the UN agenda. In fact, the inclusion of target-group specific rights, e.g., women, children, refugees, in the UN agenda has resulted in the steady expansion and diversification of the domain of human rights.

One of the salient features of the IBHR is the recognition of human rights as universal moral rights, which are *indivisible, inalienable* and *inherent* in human dignity and existence. Another significant feature

[8] Peter R. Baehr, op cit., p. 8.

of the IBHR is that it lays down international human rights standards for the protection of all human beings throughout the world. Some are legally binding treaties, while others represent the non-binding declarations of the international community on the minimum standards which all states are morally obliged to observe. Human rights are, to quote the preamble of the UDHR, 'a common standard of achievement for all peoples and all nations'. These are why, the arguments of cultural specificities or civilizational specificities are increasingly being unacceptable to the world community. There is also a growing feeling that national boundaries are gradually disappearing as there is now a threshold level of human rights at the global level.

It must however be emphasized that even with the increasing acceptance of common minimum standards of human rights for all peoples and all nations, the practicability factors such as formulation and achievement of such standards cannot be ignored altogether. For instance, there is bound to be variations between a developed and a developing nation as also between an underdeveloped and a developing nation in setting benchmarks for assessing performance in regard to freedom from want and improvement in the standard of living of the downtrodden people. For, the minimum needs of a person pertaining to food, housing and livelihood are bound to vary in different nations with different stages of economic growth and human development. This relativity factor may also vary between the various groups of people even within a particular nation. Hence, the universality and practicability or relativity criteria need to be considered concurrently in setting minimum standards of human rights.

INDIA'S COMMITMENT TO HUMAN RIGHTS

India, being the motherland of one of the oldest civilizations of the world and the birthplace of diverse cultures and religions, has a very rich heritage of human rights ideals and values. Unfortunately, despite such a rich heritage, there had been barbaric societal violence against women, children and the so-called *untouchables* in our society since ancient times, and that too in the name of religion or *dharma*. However, the late 18th and early 19th centuries witnessed vibrant social reforms movements in Bengal and other parts of India against such societal violence. Later on, in the 20th century, when the nationalist movement became a mass movement under Gandhiji's leadership, social reform for preservation and promotion of human rights of the *harijans* and other vulnerable groups became an integral part of India's freedom struggle. The national movement led by Gandhi for various social causes like abolition of untouchability and *harijan's* rights for entry to temples were indeed very significant milestones in the annals of the human rights movement in modem India.

Dr B.R. Ambedkar who was one of the main architects of the Constitution of Republic India also cherished the ideals of human dignity and human development. It was a significant historical coincidence that around the time the Constituent Assembly of independent India was deliberating upon the Draft Constitution, the UN General Assembly was also drafting the UDHR. It was, therefore, quite natural that the ethos of our national liberation movement and the world community's concern for human rights were manifested in the framing of our Constitution. Hence, apart from the perambulatory promises for 'JUSTICE, LIBERTY, EQUALITY and FRATERNITY', the traditional civil and political rights or the first generation of human rights were incorporated as Fundamental Rights in Part III of the Constitution, while the second generation of human rights, that is social, economic and cultural rights were included in Part IV as Directive Principles of State Policy. Even the third generation of human rights, that is group rights found partial expression in some of the constitutional provisions such as abolition of the practice of untouchability (Article 17), prohibition of employment of children in factory or mine or in any other hazardous employment (Article 24), affirmative State action for the advancement of women and children (Article 15) and appointment of National Commission for Scheduled Castes and Scheduled Tribes (Article 338) and appointment of a Commission to investigate the conditions of socially and educationally backward classes (Article 340). In pursuance with these constitutional provisions a number of legislations were enacted by the central and state governments from time to time.

The exclusion of certain basic human rights such as the right to food, right to shelter, right to work and right to medical care from Part III of the Constitution, embodying justiciable Fundamental Rights had been criticized by some scholars and activists. Such exclusion, however, has to be viewed from the historical context of the time when the Constitution was framed. Perhaps, keeping in view the then socio-economic conditions of the Indian society after about two hundred years of colonial exploitation, the founding fathers of our Constitution might have thought that the inclusion of these basic human rights as fundamental rights would be futile at that particular juncture, and hence they considered it prudent to include them as Directive Principles of State Policy. Yet, they gave a mandate vide Article 37 that these principles, though not enforceable by any court, 'are nevertheless fundamental in the governance of the country and it shall be the duty of the State to apply these principles in making laws'. Therefore, the onus of our failure to provide these basic human rights to a large chunk of Indian people even more than five decades after Independence does not really lie with our Constitution makers but rather with the political authority and the governments of independent India. In the midst of this failure, it should not be forgotten that India, being a party to the IBHR and also a signatory to all the international human rights instruments, is legally and morally committed to ensure basic human rights for all its citizens. Hence, we as a nation, will have to find out the ways and means to fulfil our commitments to human rights.

TOWARDS HUMANE GOVERNANCE: ROLE AND RESPONSE OF SUPREME COURT

In a constitutional democracy as ours, judiciary is an important organ of the state for the enforcement of rights and realization of reliefs through remedial jurisprudence. The Supreme Court of India, being at the apex of judicial administration is 'the sentinel on qui-vive' or the custodian of the citizens' rights. If a citizen is aggrieved due to failure in the performance of duty by state agency and approaches the Supreme Court under Article 32 for the enforcement of a fundamental right, it is imperative for the apex court to act in aid of the citizen's right. Again Article 142 explicitly confers on the Supreme Court plenary powers for doing complete justice in any cause or matter before it. The phrase 'complete justice' used by our constitution makers needs to be understood in letter and spirit. It implies that at the end-point of dispensation of justice, the Supreme Court, as the court of last resort must exercise its power to do complete justice in every cause, if provisions of the existing law are not enough to achieve that result. Hence, it is the constitutional quest for justice which empowers the Supreme Court to reach and curb injustice perpetrated by any judicial, quasi-judicial or administrative body. The role, response and commitment of the Supreme Court, therefore, are of utmost importance for the preservation, protection and promotion of human rights in our country .

Since late 70s there has been a progressive trend of vigorous legal activism in certain areas concerning human rights. There are many instances where the Supreme Court played a creative or a catalytic role in its quest for justice which resulted in a vast expansion of the frontiers of public law and formulation of multi-dimensional legal strategies including public interest litigation (PIL) for providing access to justice as well as relief to large masses of people who were denied of their basic human rights and to whom constitutional guarantee of rights and freedom had no meaning. As a part of this enthusiastic judicial movement towards anti-poverty or people-oriented jurisprudence, the Supreme Court liberalized the traditional rule of *locus standi* in a series of cases[9] in order to liberate itself form the 'shackles of procedural limitations' and thereby to enable any public-spirited individual or social activist group to invoke the jurisdiction of the court or set the machinery of justice in motion by a letter, telegram or even a post card for enforcement of human rights, liberty and freedom of the poor masses who constitute the 'the low visibility area of humanity'. Article 226 of the Constitution had thus been held to be capable of ventilating 'collective or common grievances as distinguished from assertion of individual rights'.[10]

Judicial remedies had been attempted, even *suo moto*[11] by the Supreme Court, as in Asiad[12] and Salal Hydro-Electric Project.[13] Whereas in the first case, the Court appointed three ombudsmen to make periodical inspections of the sites of the construction work for the purpose of ascertaining whether the provision of beneficent labour laws such as the Minimum Wages Act, 1948, Equal Remuneration Act 1976, the Contract Labour (Regulation and Abolition) Act, 1938 were being carried out in respect of the workmen engaged in various Asiad Projects, the decision in the later case indicated the limitations of judicial remedies. As the court had observed in that case:

[9] *Mumabi Kamgar Sabha V. Abdulbhai*, AIR 1976 SC 1465; *Fertilizer Corporation Kamgar Union V. Union of India*, AIR 1981 SC 344; *S.P. Gupta V. Union of India*, AIR 1982 SC 149; *People's Union for Democratic Rights V. Union of India*, AIR 1982, SC 1473; *Bandhua Mukti Morcha V. Union of India*, (1984) 3 SCC 161; *Neeraja Chaudhury V. State of M.P.*, (1984) 3 SCC 243.

[10] Nair, M. Krishnan, 'Public Interest Litigation' *Cochin University Law Review*, VIII(4), December 1984, p. 452.

[11] Sukumaran, K., 'Judicial Remedies for People's Maladies', *Cochin University Law Reviews*, VIII(4), December 1984, p. 484.

[12] *Peoples Union for Democratic Rights V. Union of India*, AIR 1982 SC 1473.

[13] *Labourers Working on Sale Hydro-Electric Project V. State of Jammu and Kashmir*, AIR 1984 SC 117.

We are aware that the problem of child labour is a difficult problem and it is purely on account of economic reality that the parents often want their children to be employed in order to be able to make two ends meet ... it is not possible to prohibit child labour altogether, and in fact, any such move may not be socially or economically acceptable to large masses of people.[14]

Nevertheless, there are certain areas where the dynamic role of judicial remedies can hardly be ignored. Such a role, after *Batra I*,[15] for instance, imparted to the habeas corpus writ a versatile vitality and operational utility that made the healing presence of the law live up to its reputation of bastion of liberty even within the secrecy of the hidden cell in prison. Even in respect of prison labour, judicial remedy was made available to the prisoners as the Supreme Court directed the Government of Kerala to pay reasonable wages (Rs 8 per day) to them.[16] Problems relating to bonded labour and custodial violence were other areas which involved human rights violations and necessitated judicial remedies through PIL.[17] Judicial remedies in *Hussainara*[18] went to the extent of releasing nearly 20,000 undertrials languishing in jails of Bihar unnecessarily (in many cases) because of notorious delay' in investigations and trials and their inability to furnish necessary security for release on bail. 'It is a travesty of justice', as the court observed in this case, 'that many poor accused, little Indians are forced into long cellular servitude for little offences because the bail procedure is beyond their meagre means and trials do not commence and even if they do, they never conclude.'[19]

If the period between late 70s and late 80s witnessed legal activism directed towards redressal of plights of child labour and bonded labour, gender discrimination and injustices to women, victims of custodial violence and travesty of justice, the 90s experienced an increasing concern of legal activism towards the issues of good governance and clean environment. One of the positive achievements of legal activism has been to provide interim monetary relief to the victims of governmental action or inaction as well as administrative lawlessness.

In *Saheli V. Commissioner of Police, Delhi*,[20] the Supreme Court

[14] See Ibid., at p. 183, per Bhagwati, J.

[15] *Sunil Batra V. Delhi Administration*, AIR 1978 SC 1675, (197DI SCR 392).

[16] *In the matter of P.R.E. of Wages of prisoners*, AIR 1983 KER. 261.

[17] *Bhandhua Mukti Morcha V. Union of India*, (1984) 3 SCC 161: *Sheela Barse V. State of Maharashtra*, AIR 1983 SC 378.

[18] *Hussainara Khatoon V. State of Bihar*, AIR 1973 SC 1360.

[19] Ibid., at p.1361.

[20] AIR, 1990 SC 513.

directed the Delhi Administration to pay Rs 75,000 as damage to the parents of a child who died in police custody after being beaten and assaulted by police officials. The Delhi Administration was further directed to take appropriate steps to recover the amount or part thereof from the officer or officers who would be found responsible. These landmark directives of the apex court were a glaring instance of judicial creativity or innovativeness. For, under the common law system which we have inherited from our colonial masters and which remains operative in our country, the concept of individual accountability does not exist in public law pertaining to liability in tort. Our Supreme Court has in fact, borrowed this concept from the Continental Law System operative in France, Germany and some other continental countries and innovatively applied it in our legal system to ensure accountability of individual public functionary for abuse of authority or violation of citizens' rights.

Judicial creativity has resulted further in the reduction of the area of immunity and extension of the area of liability of public servants. In *Nilabati Behera (Smt.) V. State of Orissa*,[21] the Supreme Court, while ordering the State of Orissa to pay a sum of Rs 1,50,000 as compensation to the mother of the victim of custodial death, explicitly held: 'The defence of sovereign immunity being inapplicable, and alien to the concept of guarantee of fundamental rights, there can be no question of such a defence being available in the constitutional remedy'. The court further held that 'the purpose of public law is not only to civilize public power but also to assure the citizen that they live under legal system which aims to protect their interests and preserve their rights', and hence, 'the payment of compensation in such cases is not to be understood, as it is generally understood in a civil action for damages under the private law but in the broader sense of providing relief by an order of making "monetary amends", under the public law for the wrong done due to breach of public duty, of not protecting the fundamental rights of the citizen'.

In *N. Nagendra Rao & Co. V. State of A.P.*,[22] the Supreme Court further clarified the legal position concerning the applicability of the doctrine of sovereign immunity. As the court held: 'The demarcating line between sovereign and non-sovereign powers for which no rational basis survives has largely disappeared. Therefore, barring functions such as administration of justice, maintenance of law and order

---

[21] (1993) 2 SCC 746.
[22] (1994) 6 SCC 205.

and repression of crimes etc. which are among the primary and inalienable functions of a constitutional Government, the State can not claim any immunity.'

ROLE AND RESPONSE OF NHRC

The creation of the National Human Rights Commission (NHRC) under the Protection of Human Rights Act, 1993 marked the beginning of a new era of humane governance in India. It is true that the PoHR Act did not fulfil the long-cherished desires of human rights activists in our country primarily for the reason that it made the NHRC a recommendatory or advisory body. Even the Commission itself is aware of this fact which is evident from the following observation of the Commission in its 1997–98 Report:

It recalls only too well that at the time of its establishment, ... many were openly sceptical as to whether it (Statute of the Commission) provided a sound enough basis on which an effective national institution could be built. The Commission was not however deterred by this, even as it readily shared the view that weaknesses and ambiguities in its Statute would need to be remedied at the earliest, in the light of experience gained.[23]

Nevertheless, seven years after it was established, the NHRC has received popular recognition as an indispensable institution of governance due to its sincere and spontaneous efforts to maintain the standards of integrity, efficiency and probity and to ensure accountability and transparency in its functioning. Consequently, it now enjoys great moral authority and the responses to its recommendations by the concerned agencies of central and state governments are overwhelming. By and large, the commission's recommendations for the grant of immediate interim relief to the victims or the members of their families have been adhered to by the concerned governments or authorities, although this is not always so in case of its recommendations for departmental or criminal actions.

One of the significant achievements of the NHRC is to spread human rights literacy and awareness among various sections of society in pursuance with its statutory responsibilities. This is manifested in the dramatic rise in the number of complaints received by the Commission from 20,800 in 1996–97 to 36,800 in 1997–98, an increase of nearly 77 per cent. As per the Commission's latest Report (1998–99), tabled in the parliament, it received 40,723 complaints. The

[23] NHRC, *Annual Report* 1997–98, paras 17.4 and 17.5, p. 79.

Commission has also made commendable contribution in mobilizing and promoting human rights education not only for the students of various levels but also for police personnel, paramilitary and armed forces personnel and the functionaries of other government agencies at various levels. It has also been playing a supportive or complimentary role for the Supreme Court of India which resulted in the remittal by the court to the Commission of certain complex issues, having serious human rights implications such as the grave and persistent problem of bonded labour in the country, the allegations of deaths by starvation in the Koraput–Bolangir–Kalahandi districts of Orissa, and the proper running of the Protective Home for Women in Agra. The Commission has been playing the role of a catalyst in certain macro-areas concerning human rights, namely, rehabilitation of the people affected by the mega-dam projects such as Bagri Dam or Narmada Dam, abolition of bonded and child labour, rights of person with disabilities, human rights of the mentally ill and quality assurance in mental hospitals, abolition of manual scavenging, review of certain laws affecting human rights of the citizenry, implementation of international treaties and instruments of human rights, police and prison reforms, institutional changes in the legal system, quality of health services and protection of human rights and dignity of AIDS-affected patients and sex workers. All these are enough to contend that the prevailing notion that the NHRC is for police-bashing is a wrong notion.

The NHRC has evolved and practiced a new culture of governance by involving NGOs, educational and training institutions and individual activists in its efforts to protect and promote human rights particularly with respect to efforts to deal with child prostitution, child labour, bonded labour, iron deficiency among pregnant women, problems of the mentally disabled, prison reforms and rehabilitation of persons displaced by the construction of mega-dams. Being an important corrective institution of governance, the Commission has set a glaring example for other institutions of governance by inculcating and strengthening a new culture of cooperation and collaboration in governance.

As of now, the NHRC is handicapped on two accounts. Firstly, out of 29 states, State Human Rights Commissions have so far been set up in only seven states. What is even more disheartening, the State of Uttar Pradesh which accounted for 54 per cent of the total of 40,723 complaints received by the NHRC during the year 1998–99, is still without a state-level Human Rights Commission. Secondly, Human

Rights Courts at the district level as envisaged in the PoHR Act 1993 are yet to see the light of the day in any state of the Union of India. Despite these shortcomings, the Commission has been able to establish itself as a potential institution of humane governance. It is gratifying to note that in recognition of its laudable role in protection and promotion of human rights, the NHRC of India has for over the past three years, been serving as the Chair of the International Coordinating Committee of National Institutions for the Promotion and Protection of Human Rights.

REALIZING HUMAN RIGHTS THROUGH HUMAN DEVELOPMENT

The 21st century opens with new initiatives by poor and rich countries in fulfilling a long unfinished agenda of human rights and human development. It witnessed the convergence of human development and human rights in both concept and action. Thanks to the efforts of the United Nations, the human development index (HDI), constructed every year since 1980 to measure average achievements of different countries in basic human development in one simple composite index, has assumed new legitimacy. Consequently, there is now a growing acceptance of the fact that 'human development is essential for realizing human rights, and human rights are essential for full human development.' In other words, the nature of relationship between the two is like the oyster shells and the pearl where social development plays the role of oyster shells and human rights come out as pearls. As the UNDP's *Human Development Report 2000* has noted very poignantly:

Many countries—poor and rich—are already demonstrating a new dynamism in taking initiatives for human rights and human development. South Africa, since ending apartheid, has put human rights at the core of its development strategy, with the government establishing one of the world's most forward-looking structures of rights. In India, the world's largest democracy, the Supreme Court has insisted on the rights of all citizens to free education and basic health care. Europe is making human rights a key priority—as with the pioneering approaches of the Council of Europe and the European Court of Human Rights.[24]

In fact, current debates on human development and economic growth resulting from the UN initiatives in human development

[24] UNDP, *Human Development Report* 2000, Delhi, Oxford University Press, 2000, p. 1

have exposed the weaknesses of the earlier approaches to development, which laid emphasis on GNP as the development measure. The HDI is calculated using available international data on a wide array of indicators in diverse areas of human development such as life expectancy at birth, adult literacy, gross primary, secondary and tertiary enrolment ratios (calculated by dividing the number of children enrolled in each level of schooling by the number of children in the age group corresponding to that level), GDP per capita in terms of purchasing power parity (PPP) in US $. The emphasis on longevity in HDI emanates from the fact that 'longevity is itself an important means to other capabilities, since one does not have the freedom to do much unless one is alive'.[25] The HDI was subsequently reinforced with the introduction of the gender-related development index (GDI) and the gender-empowerment measure (GEM) in *Human Development Report 1995* as composite measures reflecting gender inequalities in human development and in economic and political opportunities, and the human poverty index (HPI) in *Human Development Report 1997*. While the HDI measures average achievements in basic dimensions of human development the HPI measures deprivations in those dimensions. Together, the HDI and the HPI provide a more comprehensive measure of human well-being than income or its lack.

THE GENDER QUESTION IN HUMAN DEVELOPMENT

Dr Mehbub ul Haq, the creator and chief architect of the *1995 UNDP Human Development Report* brought about the revolutionary change in the debate on gender relation in the world by analysing the core issues and asserting that, 'Human development, if not engendered, is fatally endangered.'

At that time Dr Haq wrote, 'It is quite clear that the 21st century will be a century of much greater gender equality than the world has ever seen before.' In fact, with the release of the 1995 UNDP Report, the gender debate experienced a paradigm shift: it is equality that is important and not only equity.[26] While the earlier *Reports on Human Development in South Asia 1997, 1998* and *1999* documented the magnitude of human deprivation in the region, the 2000 Report focuses on the disproportionate share of this burden of deprivation

---

[25] Ibid., p. 21.

[26] *Human Development in South Asia 2000: The Gender Question*, Oxford University Press, 2000, *Foreword*, p.v.

being borne by hapless women of South Asia. It also analyses gender-discriminatory practices in the legal, economic, political and social spheres, raises the issue of women's invisibility in economic and political spheres, and seeks to suggest institutional mechanism to bridge the prevalent gender gap in South Asia. Most significantly, it provides a comprehensive agenda for equality of women with men covering the areas of equality under the law, equality of access to capability building, equality of economic opportunity and equality in governance. In order to ensure significant change in public policy in favour of women, the 2000 Report focused on actions in at least the following five areas:

- The critical threshold of 33 per cent of seats must be reserved for women in all legislative, judiciary and executive bodies. In India, the introduction of Panchayatiraj has led to the participation of over a million women in local governments.
- Political parties should be legally required to reserve a minimum quota for women in party decision-making bodies and in giving party tickets for elections.
- The principle of affirmative action must be upheld in selecting women parliamentarians for powerful cabinet positions and in recruitment for the civil service.
- The capacity of women in governance structure, in all sectors and at all levels, should be enhanced through training and access to information.
- Gender sensitization training for male parliamentarians, judges, civil servants and members of local governments, is critically important for achieving gender equality in governance.[27]

IMPLICATIONS FOR PUBLIC ADMINISTRATION IN INDIA

The convergence of human development and human rights in both concept and action and the inclusion of the gender question in the agenda of human development have far-reaching implications for public administration in general. Such implications would differ among countries in accordance with the varying rate of advancement in human development. As per the 1998 data, India is placed at 128 among 174 countries in HDI, and at 108 among 143 countries in GDI ranking.[28] Hence, the challenges before the public administration in

[27] Ibid., p. 175.
[28] Supra, n. 24, Table II, p. 149 and Table VIII, p. 154.

India are stupendous and its tasks immense and multi-pronged. It needs to be reoriented on the following lines for realizing human rights and gender equality through human development:

1. Our policy makers must realize that poverty eradication is not only a development goal but also a major human rights challenge of the 21st century. For, a minimum standard of decent living, adequate nutrition, health care, education, employment and protection against calamities, are not just development goals—they are also human rights. To achieve these goals, it is not enough to formulate pro-poor economic and social policies and allocate funds for various programmes based on these policies. What seems to be much more important than these exercises is to ensure proper utilization of funds so that the benefits of economic and social development percolate down to the millions of poor people in our country.

2. Our public policy and programmes must recognize and address the foremost and formidable challenge to human development resulting from population explosion. As on March 1, 2001, India's population crossed the 1.02 billion mark constituting over 16 per cent of the world's population.

3. Our policy-making process needs to be transparent. As indicated in the UNDP's *Human Development Report 2000*, 'Economic policy-making behind closed doors violates the right to political participation—and is susceptible to the corrupting influences of political power and big money.'[29]

4. There is also need for transparency in governmental functioning. Our experiences with six states—Goa, Tamil Nadu, Rajasthan, Maharashtra, Karnataka and Madhya Pradesh—with their own law on the access to information, reveal that legislative guarantee of the right to freedom of information would not be of much help unless the public functionaries are sensitized, motivated and trained to accept the change towards openness and the citizens become aware and willing to play a more pro-active role with necessary intervention of the civil society organizations.

5. Accountability of public functionaries should be ensured at all levels of governmental system through appropriate legislative and administrative measures. It needs to be hardly emphasized that transparency and accountability would help in minimizing corruption in public life.

6. Public scrutiny and state accountability are complementary to

[29] Ibid., p. 8.

each other. Fortunately for India, we have a fairly open civil society and independent media. Yet, there is scope to institutionally strengthen our civil society organizations and the media.

7. It would be erroneous to contend that by playing creative and catalytic role, our superior courts are overstepping their limits to enter the realm of the executive. A large number of recent trend-setting rulings by the apex court on public interest issues reflect executive inactions and apathy rather than judicial activism or assertiveness. Hence, the role of higher judiciary needs to be considered in the correct perspective of our constitutional jurisprudence and the state of public administration in our country.

8. Human rights and human development cannot be realized without effective and meaningful linkages and collaboration between public service agencies and civil society organizations such as NGOs, workers and peasants organizations, women's groups, human rights, environmental and other activist groups. In the contemporary context of globalization and economic liberalization, partnership between government and industry not only in the economic sector but also in the social sector needs to be enhanced as well as strengthened.

9. It is necessary to ensure significant change in public policy in favour of women on the line of actions indicated in the 2000 UNDP Report on South Asia.

10. In order to minimize the propensity for state violation of human rights, the system of policing and police administration should be overlauled in such a manner as to ensure autonomy along with accountability of the police to the impartial external authority. Since Police is a State subject the recommendations of National Police Commission as well as the NHRC on police reforms deserve due consideration of the state governments. Likewise, reforms in prison administration should also receive adequate attention of the state governments.

11. Last but not the least, the NHRC should be strengthened with more statutory powers as required and adequate manpower and logistic support to enable it to discharge its duties and responsibilities more effectively as an institution of governance for protection and promotion of human rights in the country.

CONCLUDING OBSERVATIONS

If India as a free nation is yet far behind many other countries in achieving the goals of human development and human rights, it is not due to the poverty of ideas but for the poverty of actions. Way back in 1960, the Government of India's Administrative Reforms Commission (ARC) made valuable recommendations covering almost the entire gamut of what we now call good governance. Today, after over three decades since the submission of the voluminous reports by the ARC, the failure of our system of governance is primarily due to political and administrative inertia and inactions. If the current discourse on good governance can energize the political and societal conscience, it, will go a long way in achieving the goals of human rights and human development for the freedom, well-being and dignity of all people of India.

An Annotated Bibliography

Public Administration is constantly changing. The principal, if not the only, focus of traditional Public Administration was the rigid, rule-bound and hierarchic structure of governance with tangential reference to the socio-economic and political ambience. Under the impact of powerful domestic and international forces and new conceptualizations of administrative reality, the discipline today is more concerned about explaining diversity, complexity and interactivity. Globalization and opening up of the economy are perhaps the most significant inputs in radically restructuring the administration both in the developed and developing countries. To meaningfully articulate the changing nature of administration, the focus of the discipline has therefore been shifting more towards society and its exclusive character is no longer appreciated. The 1988 Minnowbrook Conference II is noteworthy in the development of theoretical literature in Public Administration. Most of the publications now reflect the changing perceptions of administration, which is both an outcome and response to a complex web of network involving state, society and market. Contemporary Public Administration is characterized by a recognition of multiple actors in public administration which has traditionally been the exclusive preserve of bureaucracy. The bibliography is by no means exhaustive. Since it is merely an attempt to comprehend the directions in the contemporary literature in Public Administration the well-known classical texts have deliberately been avoided unless they are absolutely crucial.

ADMINISTRATIVE THEORIES

For a detailed discussion of the major theories of Public Administration, the following articles and books are very useful: Woodrow

Wilson, 'The Study of Administration' in Dwight Waldo (ed.), *Ideas and Issues in Public Administration*, McGraw Hill, 1963; Besides, Arthur S Link (ed.), *The Papers of Woodrow Wilson* (vol. 7, 1890–92), published by the Princeton University Press, (New Jersey, 1968) is a good compilation of Wilson's work relevant to Public Administration at its inception as a specific field of enquiry. R. A. Dahl's 'The Science of Public Administration', published in *Public Administration Review* (vol. 7, no. 2, 1947) is a succinct discussion on the nature and scope of Public Administration. F. W. Taylor's *Scientific Management* (Harper and Row, New York, 1947 reprint) lays down the basic principles of what later became the Scientific Management School of Public Administration. Though brief, Dwight Waldo's 'What is Public Administration' in A. M. Willms and W. D. K. Kernaghan (ed.), *Public Administration in Canada: Selected Readings* (Methuen, London , 1968) is a very precise statement on the definition and characteristics of Public Administration as a field of study. Though dated, Leonard White's *Introduction to the Study of Public Administration* (Macmillan, New York, 1955) is one of the most comprehensive textbooks dealing with the growth of Public Administration as a separate discipline. Two volumes were produced in the 1970s striving to orient Public Administration toward Political Science. Edited by Frank Marini, the title of the first volume is *Toward a New Public Administration* (Chandler, New York, 1971) and the second volume was edited by Dwight Waldo with the title, *Public Administration in a Time of Turbulence* (Chandler, New York, 1971). Likewise, Kuldeep Mathur (ed.), *A Survey of Research in Public Administration, 1970–79* (Concept, New Delhi, 1986) is a fairly comprehensive survey of literature in Public Administration. In the introduction to this volume entitled 'Whither Public Administration?' Mathur has identified the areas which automatically fall under the Public Administration by critically defining the notion of 'public'. This idea was discussed in V. Jagannadham, 'Public Administration and the Citizen: How Far Public Administration Can be Public', *The Indian Journal of Public Administration* (June, 1978).

For a historical account of the growth of public administration in the context of western Europe, one of the most interesting works happens to be Ernest Barkar's, *The Development of Public Service in Western Europe, 1660–1930* (Oxford University Press, Oxford, 1944). For conceptual clarity, a combination of the following books will provide a fairly clear understanding of the subject and its theoretical foundations. One may begin with Richard J Stillman (ed.), *Public Administration: Concepts and Cases*, Houghton and Miffin, New York,

1996 (reprint). The other useful books are: John J. Corson and Joseph P. Harris, *Public Administration in Modern Society* (McGraw Hill, New York, 1963); Nicholas Henry, *Public Administration and Public Affairs* (Prentice-Hall of India, New Delhi, 1999); Nicos P. Mouzelis, *Organization and Bureaucracy: An Analysis of Modern Theories* (Routledge & Kegan Paul, London, 1975); Peter Self, *Administrative Theories and Politics: An Enquiry into the Structure and Processes of Modern Government* (George Allen & Unwin Ltd., London, 1972) and also by the same author, *Modern Theories of Government* (George Allen and Unwin, 1985). Michael W. Spicer's *The Constitution and Public Administration: A Conflict in World Views* (Georgetown University Press, Georgetown, 1995) deals with those questions that are raised if there is hardly or less correspondence between the Constitution and Public Administration. For a comprehensive account of the issues, relevant to a complex organisation, one of the frequently-cited works happens to be S. Clegg and D. Dunkerly (eds), *Critical Issues in Orgainsations*, Routledge and Kegan Paul, London, 1977. A fairly good account of the classical theories of organization, administration and public bureaucracy is available in Mohit Bhattacharya, *New Horizons of Public Administration*, Jawahar, New Delhi, 2000.

For a thorough discussion on the recent changes in Public Administration, see David John Farmar's *The Language of Public Administration: Bureaucracy, Modernity and Post-Modernity* (The University of Alabama Press, Tuscaloosa and London, 1995). The contradiction between bureaucracy and democracy has been adequately dealt with by Eva-Etzioni-Halevy in her *Bureaucracy and Democracy: A Political Dilemma* (Routledge and Kegan Paul, London, 1986). Similarly, Douglas Yates pursued an interesting line of argument highlighting the growing importance of bureaucratic culture in the US administration in his *Bureaucratic Democracy: The Search for Democracy and Efficiency in American Government* (Harvard University Press, Cambridge, 1982). The theme has recurred in a recently published article entitled 'The Big Question in a Democracy' by John Kirlin (*Public Administration Review*, September–October, 1996). An argument seeking to understand the role of bureaucratically controlled developmental state is found in Adrian Leftwich's 'Two Cheers for Democracy? Democracy and the Developmental State' in Adrian Leftwich (ed.), *Democracy and Development: Theory and Practice* (Polity Press, Cambridge, 1996, pp. 279–95).

Bureaucracy has traditionally been a pet theme for analysts seeking to grasp the growing complexity of Public Administration. Max

Weber's argument has clearly been spelt out in his 'Bureaucracy', published in H. H. Gerth and C. Wright Mills (ed.), *From Max Weber: Essays in Sociology* (Oxford University Press, Oxford, 1946). Also Max Weber, *Theory of Social and Economic Organization* (The Free Press, New York, 1964, reprint). Two classical studies on the modalities of decision making in complex organizations are (i) Herbert Simon, *Administrative Behaviour* (The Free Press, New York, 1945) and (ii) David Braybrooke and Charles Lindblom, *A Strategy of Decision: Policy Evaluation as a Social Process* (The Free Press, New York, 1963). Though drawn upon the structural functional logic, S. N. Eisenstadt interventions are theoretically enriching. S. N. Eisenstadt, 'Bureaucracy and Bureaucratisation', *Current Sociology* (vol. 7, 1958, pp. 99–164); as well his, 'Bureaucracy, Bureaucratisation and Debureaucratisation' in *Administrative Science Quarterly* (vol. 4, 1958, pp. 99–164). are very useful commentaries on social conditions under which bureaucratic organisations tend to usurp power in the name of efficient administration. Of the important theoretical interventions, the followings are significant: A. Downs, *Inside Bureaucracy* (Little Brown, Boston, 1967); Martin Albrow, *Bureaucracy* (Macmillan, London, 1978); Peter M. Blau, *Bureaucracy in Modern Society* (Random House, New York, 1956); Michael Crozier, *The Bureaucratic Phenomenon* (The University of Chicago Press, Chicago, 1964). The critical literature on the bureaucratic model of Max Weber is adequately developed. David Beetham, *Max Weber and the Theory of Modern Politics* (George Allen & Unwin, London, 1974); Alfred Diamant, 'The Bureaucratic Model: Max Weber Rejected, Rediscovered and Reformed' in Ferrel Heady and Sybil L. Stokes (eds), *Papers in Comparative Public Administration* (The University of Michigan Press, Ann Arbor, 1962); L. I. Rudolph and S. H. Rudolph, 'Authority and Power in Bureaucratic and Patrimonial Administration, *World Politics* (vol. 31, no. 2, January, 1979, pp. 195–227); For excellent review of literature on organisation theory, *Sociological Paradigms and Organisational Analysis* (N. H. Hienemann, Exeter, 1980) by Gibson Burrell and Gareth Morgan is fascinating. Similarly, Dwight Waldo's 'Organisation Theory: Revisiting the Elephant' (*Public Administration Review*, vol. 38, no. 6, November–December, 1978) is a powerful argument justifying further research in this area of Public Administration. K. J. Benson's 'Organisations: A Dialectical View' in *Administrative Science Quarterly* (vol. 22, no. 1, March, 1977) is an attempt to view organizations in their most complex form. Also relevant in this regard is Albert O. Hirrchman, 'The Search for Paradigms as a Hindrance to Understanding', *World Politics* (vol. 22, no. 3, March 1970). Goran Hyden has sought to explain the changes in the bureaucratic structure of administration in the 'Third World' countries in 'Democratization and Administration', published in Axel Hadenlus (ed.), *Democracy's Victory and Crisis* (Cambridge University Press, Cambridge, 1997). B. Guy Peters's *The Politics of Bureaucracy* (Longman, New York, 1984) is a useful commentary on the factors influencing the structure and functioning of bureaucracy. On the intricate role of politicians and bureaucrats in policy making, B. Guy Peters has made a useful contribution in 'Politicians and Bureaucrats in the Politics of Policy-Making', published in J. E. Lane (ed.), *Bureaucracy and Public Choice* (Sage, London, 1987, pp. 256–82). For a general discussion of the contemporary theories on organization, bureaucracy and administration, Mohit Bhattacharya's *Restructuring Public Administration: Essays in Rehabilitation* (Jawahar, New Delhi, 1999) is a competent and readily available work.

Despite Marx's tangential reference to bureaucracy while explaining the exploitative role of capitalism, literature on the Marxist approach to bureaucracy is plenty. Apart from *The Eighteenth Brumaire of Louis Bonaparte* by Karl Marx and Lenin's *The State and Revolution* that provide the basis of an alternative argument on the subject, the compilation by Martin Shaw, *Marxist Sociology Revisited* (Macmillan, London, 1985) is very comprehensive. A critical account of bureaucracy is available in Jon Pierre (ed.), *Bureaucracy in the Modern State: An Introduction to Comparative Public Administration* (Edward Elgar, England, 1995). Furthermore, Manuel Castells' *City, Class and Power* (Macmillan, London, 1978) and Cynthia Cockburn's *The Local State: Management of Cities and People* (Pluto Press, London, 1977) are fairly well-argued expositions of the Marxist position on the phenomenon. On urbanization, Manuel Castells' *The Urban Question: A Marxist Approach* (Edward Arnold, London, 1977) is theoretically stimulating. James O'Connor's *The Fiscal Crisis of the State* (St. Martin's Press, New York, 1973) provides a good account of the crisis of the liberal state from the Marxist point of view.

Decentralization is a significant theme in contemporary Public Administration. B. C. Smith's *Decentralization: The Territorial Dimension of the State* (Allen and Unwin, London, 1985) is a very thorough study of decentralization with reference to the major theoretical works. Similarly Gerry Stoker deals with the theories of local government and politics in his *The Politics of Local Government* (Macmillan, London, 1989). In his 'Decentralization as an Incentive Theme', published in *Oxford Review of Economic Policy* (vol. 3, no. 2, 1987), P. Salmon deals with the conceptual issues relating to the notion of decentralization. A critical study of local government in the context of structural adjustment programme is Allan Cochrane's *Whatever Happened to Local Government?* (Open University Press, Buckingham, 1993) and also, M. P. Smith, *City, State and Market: The Political Economy of Urban Society* (Blackwell, Oxford, 1988).

INDIAN BUREAUCRACY

Perhaps the best work on civil service in India during colonialism is Philip Woodruff's (the pen name of Philip Mason) three volume study entitled *The Men Who Ruled India* which was later compiled by the author himself in one volume with the same title and was published by Rupa, Calcutta, 1997 (reprint). In this genre also comes L. S. S. O'Malley's *The Indian Civil Service, 1601–1930*, John Murry, London, 1931. One of the pioneers of the study of bureaucracy in independent India is B. B. Mishra who in his *Government and Bureaucracy in India, 1947–1976* (Oxford University Press, Delhi, 1986) has graphically illustrated the rise and consolidation of Weberian bureaucracy with reference to India's immediate colonial past. His earlier study, *The Bureaucracy in India* (Oxford University Press, Delhi, 1977) is a well-argued effort tracing the rise of bureaucracy in the immediate colonial past. On the style, ethos and social bases of the Indian bureaucracy, David Potter's *India's Political Administrators, 1919–1983* (Clarendon Press, Oxford, 1986) is very useful. Some other works that deal with the bureaucracy in relation to the political system are Stanley J Heginbotham, *Cultures in Conflict: The Four Faces of the Indian Bureaucracy* (Columbia University Press, New York, 1975); Ralph Braibanti, *Asian Bureaucratic Systems Emergent from the British Imperial Tradition* (Duke University Press, Durham, 1985); Ashok Chanda, *Indian Administration* (Allen and Unwin, London, 1967); S. R. Maheshwari, *Indian Administrative System* (Jawahar, New Delhi, 1994) and also *Public Administration in India* by the same author (Macmillan, New Delhi, 2000) Kuldeep Mathur (ed.), *Development Policy and Administration* (Sage, New Delhi, 1996) is a compilation of articles dealing with the complex world of public administration in India with reference to the development policy, pursued assiduously by India's political leadership following decolonization. C. P. Bhambri's *Administrators in a Changing Society* (National Publishing House, Delhi, 1972) is an elaboration of an argument attributing the peculiar characteristics of Indian bureaucracy to specific socio-economic circumstances with links with India's colonial past. Similarly, the concept of representative bureaucracy has been related to the prevalent socio-economic milieu by Haridwar Rai and Sakendra Prasad in 'Indian Bureaucracy: A Case for Representativeness', published in *The Indian Journal of Public Administration* (vol. 19, no. 1, March, 1973). V. Subramaniam has sought to provide a theoretical index to the concept of 'representative bureaucracy' in his 'Representative Bureaucracy: A Reassessment', published in *American Political Science Review* (vol. 67, no. 4, December, 1967)

For a critical study of Indian bureaucracy in recent times, 'Evolving Trends in the Bureaucracy' by B. P. R. Vithal in Partha Chatterjee (ed.), *State and Politics in India* (Oxford University Press, Delhi, 1997) is a useful introduction to bureaucracy in its contemporary manifestation in India. Similarly, Anil Bhat's 'Colonial Bureaucratic Culture and Development Administration: Portrait of an Old-fashioned Indian Bureaucrat' (*Journal of Commonwealth and Comparative Politics*, vol. 17, no. 3, 1979) is a well-argued article showing the extent to which the colonial bureaucratic culture continues to remain a significant influence in Indian bureaucracy. A sharply critical account of the intimate linkage between bureaucracy and local political power is the essay by Jan Breman, 'I am the government Labour Officer ... : state protection for rural proletariat of South Gujrat' (*Economic and Political Weekly*, 15 June, 1985, pp. 1043–55). Though slightly dated, R. B. Jain dealt with the growing politicization of Indian bureaucracy in 'Politicization of Bureaucracy: A Framework for Comparative Assessment', *The Indian Journal of Public Administration* (vol. 20, no. 4, October–December, 1974). Based on the field data, Kuldeep Mathur identifies the historical roots of 'over-bureaucratization' that flourished in India in the aftermath of independence in his 'Bureaucracy in India: Development and Pursuit of Self-interest' (*Indian Journal of Public administration*, vol. 36, no. 4, 1991). The experience of a bureaucrat has been recorded by N. N. Vohra in 'The Rusting Steel Frame', published in V. N. Narayanan and Jyoti Sabharwal (eds), *India at 50s: Bliss of Hope and Burden of Reality* (Sterling Publishers, New Delhi, 1997, pp. 154–171). For a detailed description of India's bureaucracy in its contemporary manifestation *Annual Reports* (published by the Ministry of Personnel, Public Grievances and Pensions, Government of India) provide exhaustive data for further research in this area. Sudipta Kaviraj's essay entitled 'On the Crisis of Political Institutions in India' (*Contributions to Indian Sociology*, vol. 18, no. 2, pp. 223–43) is a balanced commentary on the growth of crucial political institutions, including bureaucracy, in India. Similarly, Ashis Nandy's 'The Political Culture of the Indian State' (*Daedalus*, vol. 118, no. 4, Fall, 1989, pp. 1–26) is a thought-provoking article seeking to link the emergence of a peculiar state structure with an equally peculiar political culture.

Bureaucracy continues to remain an important pillar of Indian state. There are major works on the Indian state with a substantial contribution to our understanding of the institutions holding the spirit and substance of the state. One of the first attempts made in this direction was Norman D. Palmar, *The Indian Political System* (Houghton Miffin, Boston, 1962), followed by W. H. Morris-Jones in his *The Government and Politics in India* (Hutchinson, London, 1964). The other works that deserve mention are *The Modernity of Tradition: Political Development in India* (Chicago University press, Chicago, 1967) by L. I. and S. H. Rudolph and *Politics in India* (Orient Longman, New Delhi, 1970) by Rajni Kothari. Achin Vanaik's *The Painful Transition: Bourgeois Democracy in India* (Verso, London, 1990) is one of most persuasive works on Indian state from the Marxist point of view. *In Pursuit of Lakshmi: The Political Economy of Indian State* (Orient Longman, New Delhi, 1987) by L. I. Rudolph and S. H. Rudolph is a powerful intervention in conceptualizing the growth of institutions, not always linked with the state–that has radically altered the character of the Indian state drawing traditionally upon Weberian hierarchy-based bureaucracy. Francine Frankel and M. S. A. Rao (eds), two volumes, *Dominance and State Power in India: Decline Of A Social Order* (Oxford University Press, Delhi, 1990) also identify the rise of a completely different socio-political system in India where the traditional bureaucracy had absolutely no role to play. Atul Kohli's *The State and Poverty in India: The Politics of Reform* (Cambridge University Press, Cambridge, 1987) is an adequately-documented study on rural government in India in the context of changes in the basic state structure in India. His later work, *Democracy and Discontent: India's Growing Crisis of Governability*, Cambridge University Press, Cambridge, 1992) is a further elaboration of an argument linking the crisis of administration with the democratic processes expanding the constituencies of politics. Similarly, Ayesha Jalal's comparative study of India, Pakistan and Bangladesh in her *Democracy and Authoritarianism in South Asia: A Comparative and Historical Perspective* is a persuasive comment on the strikingly different nature of bureaucracies in South Asian countries despite having exactly the same historical legacy.

The planning process is an important entry point to grasp the nature of the government in action. There is a significant amount of literature articulating the political foundations of India's economic policy as well as the role of bureaucracy in its most hegemonic form in shaping what finally emerges as five-year plans. For a general understanding of development planning that accounted for the growth of a specific type of bureaucracy the work by A Waterston, entitled *Development Planning: Lessons of Experience* (Johns Hopkins University, Baltimore, 1965) is a significant contribution. Though dated, Francine Frankel's *India's Political Economy, 1947–1977: The Gradual Revolution* (Oxford University Press, Delhi, 1978) is one of the first attempts to critically evaluate the planning process in the broad context of India's socio-political context where the colonial bureaucracy seems to have a significant sway in the policy making. Pranab Bardhan's *The Political Economy of Development in India* (Oxford University Press, Delhi, 1984) and Baldev Raj Nayar's *India's Mixed Economy: The Role of Ideology and Interests in Its Development* (Popular Prakashan, Bombay, 1989) are important works on the making of the development strategy in an environment where the Nehruvian 'socialist pattern of society' appeared to have struck roots. Though published in 1969, David Hirschmann's 'Development or Underdevelopment Administration: A Further Deadlock', published in *Development and Change* (vol. 12, no. 3, 1969, pp. 12–31) foresaw some of the problems, linked with overemphasis on the role of state in economic development.

POLICY STUDIES

Policies and policy making constitute an important area of research in Public Administration. Harold Lasswell explains policy approach to Public Administration in his 'The Policy Orientation', published in D. Lerner and H. Lasswell (eds), *The Policy Sciences* (Stanford University Press, Stanford, 1951). Y. Dror has dealt with public policy most extensively in his (i) *Public Policy Making Reexamined* (Chamber Publishers, Pennsylvania, 1968) that set the tenor of studies, based on the policy approach; (ii) *Design for Policy Sciences* (Elsevier, New York, 1971); and (iii) *Policymaking under Adversity* (Transaction Publications, New Brunswick, 1986). Martin Minogue's 'Theory and Practice in Public Policy and Administration' (*Policy and Politics*, vol. 11, no. 3, 1983) is a significant contribution to policy studies. Although the primary focus happens to be contemporary capitalism, Claus Offe's *Disorganised Capitalism: Contemporary Transformations of Work and Politics* (Polity Press, Cambridge, 1985) is a substantial work underlining the complexities of policy making under capitalism. For the beginners, *Public Administration and Policy Analysis* (Saxon House, Farnborough, 1979), provides useful insights. Christopher Ham and Michael Hill's *The Policy Process in the Modern Capitalist State* (Harvester Wheatsheaf, Hemel Hempstead, 1993), is a fairly balanced interpretation of the approaches on the subject. Furthermore, Thomas Dye's *Understanding Public Policy* (Prentice-Hall, New Jersey, 1972), is another benchmark study of policy making in the context of liberal democratic state. In his *The Policy-Making Process* (Prentice Hall, New Jersey, 1968), Charles Lindblom has most graphically illustrated the process of policy making underlining the significance of 'informal politics' in the so-called developed countries. L. M. Salmon's *Beyond Privatization: The Tools of Government Action* (Urbana Institute Press, Washington, 1989), documents the phases of the decision making process in a liberal democratic set-up. Public policy remains the underlying theme in W. N. Dunn's *Public Policy Analysis* (Prentice Hall, New York, 1981), and also Aaron Wildavsky's *Speaking Truth to Power: The Art and Craft of Policy Analysis* (Hill Ryerson, Toronto, 1981). A recent comprehensive account of the approaches to public policy is Helen Ingram and Sloven R Smith (eds), *Public Policy for Democracy* (Brooking Institute, New York, 1993). For a thorough study of the linkages between political theory and policy making, see R. E. Goodin, *Political Theory and Public Policy* (University of Chicago Press, Chicago, 1982). Similarly, *Models of Policy-Making* by L. Gunn and B Hogwood (Centre for the Study of Public Policy, University of Strathclyde, 1982) is a comprehensive study of various models of policy making.

HUMAN RIGHTS AND PUBLIC ADMINISTRATION

The major thrust in this sub field is on police and criminal justice administration. There are studies dealing with human rights *per se.* Maurice Cranston's *What are Human Rights?* (Taplinger, New York, 1973) is a serious effort at conceptualizing human rights with reference to basic features of what constitutes human rights. Cranston's *Human Rights Today* (Ampersand, London, 1962), an earlier version of this book, was published in 1962. Not only have these publications provided us with a relatively broad definition of human rights they are also readily available useful text books for the beginners as well. *Human Rights* by Scott Davidson (Oxford University Press, Oxford, 1993) is a full-fledged study of human rights focusing also on their violation both in the context of democratic and authoritarian polities. For a theoretical discussion, David Beetham's *Democracy and Human Rights* (Polity Press, Cambridge, 1999) is a very useful reference book. Also the book by Youcef Bouandel entitled *Human Rights and Comparative Politics* (Dartmouth, London, 1977) is a serious endeavour to grasp the concern for human rights from a Comparative Politics point of view. Similarly, *Democratization and the Protection of Human Rights: Challenges and Contradictions* by P. J. Campbell and K. Mohoney is a discussion linking the protection of human rights with the process of democratization. Nalini Ranjan's *Democracy and the Limits of Minority Rights* (Sage, New Delhi, 2002) is a further elaboration of this theme. Upendra Baxi's *Inhuman Wrongs and Human Rights: Unconventional Essays* (Har-Anand Publications, New Delhi, 1994) and *The Future of Human Rights* (Oxford University Press, New Delhi, 2001) are interesting compilations of articles dealing with situations where Human Rights become the first casualty without reasons or rhymes.

Police and Criminal Justice Administration

Public Administration literature on human rights largely concentrates on police and criminal administration. Carl Blockans' *The Idea of Police* (Sage, London, 1985) provides a well-documented history of the growth of police in Great Britain). Though dated George Barkley's *The Democratic Policeman* (Beacon Press, Boston, 1969) is one of the best books on the structural impediments on police in the western democratic polities. A recent attempt in conceptualizing the role of police more as an agent of the ruling authority is Kelly Anderson's *Police Brutality* (Lucent Books, San Diego, 1994).

P. S. Bawa's *Crime, the Citizen and the Police* (Rupa, Calcutta, 1986) is basically a narrative of the processes in which the role of citizens is as important as that of police in containing crimes in any society. This is also a good account of how the so-called 'Bobby Model' came to be widely accepted in England despite opposition from the aristocrats. David Bayley's *Police and Political Development in India* (Princeton University Press, New Jersey, 1969) is also a thorough study of how the Irish Constabulary was preferred by the colonial authority in India even when the Bobby Model made an impact in British society simply because of its effectiveness in containing those opposed to the British hegemony in Ireland. David Arnold's *Police Power and the Colonial Rule: Madras, 1869–1947* (Oxford University Press, Delhi,

1986) is an in-depth study of the emergence and consolidation of police in colonial Madras. Historical roots of Indian police have further been elaborated in Daili K. Das and Arvind Verma's 'The Armed Police in the British Colonial Tradition: The Indian Perspective' (*Policing: An International Journal of Police Strategies and Management*, vol. 21, no. 2, 1998). For an interesting discussion on the police in relation to the political system, see David H Bayley, 'The Police and the Political Order in India', *Asian Survey*, vol. 23, no. 4, April, 1983. The published *Reports of National Police Commission* by the Government of India provide interesting information on the functioning of Indian police.

GLOBALIZATION AND PUBLIC ADMINISTRATION

The 1992 World Bank Report is one of the most influential documents that radically altered the approaches to Public Administration. A clear description of 'globalization' and 'liberalization' is available in the report submitted by the UNCTAD's Secretary-General entitled *Globalization and Liberalization: Development in the Face of Two Powerful Currents*, 1996. One of the most recent attempts to conceptualize globalization is evident in Paul Streeton's 'Globalisation: Threat or Opportunity' in Paul Collins (ed.), *Public Administration in Development* (John Wiley & Sons, England, 2000, pp. 59–63). Amit Bhaduri and Deepak Nayyar's *The Intelligent Person's Guide to Liberalization* (Penguin, New Delhi, 1996) is a well-written text raising questions on the feasibility of liberalization as a strategy for the so-called developing countries. Raja J. Chelliah's *Essays in Fiscal and Financial Sector Reforms in India* (Oxford University Press, Delhi, 1999) is a specific study of the impact of liberalization on Indian economy in the 1990s. The special number on Liberalisation Policy and Social Concerns of *The Indian Journal of Public Administration* (vol. XLII, no. 3, July–September, 1996) has relevant articles. Arvind K. Sharma's 'People's Empowerment' in the above volume (pp. 235–44) has brought out the possible adverse impact on the people in the developing countries. Similarly, Mohit Bhattacharya's 'Rolling Back the State: Public Administration in the Age of Market Supremacy' (above volume, pp. 245–57) defends the utility of state especially in the social sector that will hardly attract private investment for obvious reasons.

Articulating the changes in public administration, *The Fifth Pay Commission Report* (Ministry of Finance, Government of India, 1997) provides clear directions to civil service reform. S. K. Das's *Civil*

Service Reform and Structural Adjustment (Oxford University Press, Delhi, 1998) is one of the first full-length studies of this phenomenon in the context of India. Drawing upon the 'rational choice' theory, Israel Arturo provides a theoretical basis of these obvious changes in public administration in his *Institutional Development: Incentives to Performance* (Johns Hopkins University, Baltimore, 1987). In his World Bank working paper, 'The Changing Role of the State: Institutional Dimension, Policy Research and External Affairs' (Country Economic Department, *The World Bank*, August, 1990) Arturo comments on the growing importance of globalization in radically altering the boundaries of the state in the so-called third world context. For a clear description of the limits of globalization, the volume edited by Robert Boyer and Daniel Drache is a useful collection. In fact, the title, *States against Markets: The Limits of Globalization* (Routledge, London, 1996) unambiguously suggests the direction of the volume. Gerald Caiden's 'Globalizing the Theory and Practice of Public Administration' in Jean-Claude Gracia Zamor and Renu Khator (eds) *Public Administration in the Global Village* (Praeger, Westport, CT, 1994, pp. 45–59) provides a clear glimpse of the changes in public administration in response to globalization. Milton Esman's 'The State, Government Bureaucracies and Their Alternatives' in Ali Farazmand (ed.), *Handbook of Comparative and Development Public Administration* (Marcel Dekker, New York, 2000) is both an elaboration of changes in civil service and also a search for alternatives within the prevalent sociopolitical international framework. Ali Farazmand's 'The New World Order and Global Public Administration', in Jean-Claude Gracia-Zamor and Renu Khator (eds), *Public Administration in the Global Village* (Praeger, Westpost, CT, 1994, pp. 62–81) is an endeavour to explore the new dimensions of public administration linking its articulation with the forces of globalization. This argument was developed further in his 'From Civil to Non-Civil Administration' (paper, presented at the 1997 American Society for Public Administration). That globalization is a unifying tendency is elaborated by Eric Welch and Wilson Wong in their 'Public Administration in a Global Context: Bridging the Gaps of Theory and Practice Between Western and Non-Western Nations', published in *Public Administration Review* (vol. 58, no. 1, 1998, pp. 40–9).

Public choice theory provides the most significant input to understand the changing nature of bureaucracy or civil service in response to the process of globalization. V. Ostrom's *The Intellectual Crisis in American Public Administration* (University of Alabama Press,

Tuscaloosa and London, 1974) is one of the first serious attempts to understand non-economic activity using the language and analytical tools of Economics. The other major theoretical works are William A. Niskanen, *Bureaucracy and Representative Government* (Aldine, Chicago, 1971); Mancur Olson Jr., *The Rise and Decline of Nations* (Yale University Press, New Heaven, 1982); Anne O. Krueger, *Political Economy of Policy Reform in Developing Countries* (MIT Press, Cambridge, 1993); J. E. Lane (ed.), *Bureaucracy and Public Choice* (Sage, London, 1987); Rober Bates, *Markets and States in Tropical Africa* (University of California Press, Berkeley, 1981); James M. Buchanan and Gordon Tullock, *The Calculus of Consent: Logical Foundations of Constitutional Democracy* (University of Michigan Press, Ann Arbor, 1962); Clifford S. Russell and Norman Nicholson (eds), *Public Choice and Rural Development* (Resources for the Future, Washington, D.C., 1981); Gordon Tullock, *The Politics of Bureaucracy* (Public Affairs Press, Washington, D.C., 1965); P. Dunleavy, *Democracy, Bureaucracy and Public Choice: Economic Explanations in Political Science* (Harvester Wheatsheaf, Hemel Hempstead, 1991).

Two new expressions now figure prominently in the lexicon of Public Administration underling its new perspectives. Reflective of the changes in public administration following globalization, New Public Management throws open those issues which are relevant to understand the new directions in governmental activities in both developed and developing countries. The Governance perspective is another seeking to articulate the governmental activities under the changed environment where government seems to be a peripheral actor in public administration. The thrust of the New Public Management and Governance has been toward a determined effort to implement the 3Es—efficiency, economy and effectiveness.

The theme paper entitled *Government in Transition—A New Paradigm in Public Administration*, circulated during the inaugural conference of the Commonwealth Association for Public Administration in 1995 identifies the distinctive features of New Public Management. The 1996 and 1997 World Bank Reports also provide significant inputs towards conceptualizing changes in public administration. While the 1996 *World Development Report: From Plan to Market* (Oxford University press, Oxford, 1996) indicates the growing importance of market the 1997 *World Development Report: The State in a Changing World* (Oxford University Press, Oxford, 1997) articulates the government activities in a new milieu. In *Reinventing Government: How the Entrepreneurial Spirit is Transforming the Public Sector* (Adison-Wesley,

Mass, 1992), D. Osborne and T. Gaebler coin a new term 'entre-preneurial government' to describe the new orientation of governments. For a very nuanced account of the growth of New Public Management one of the most impressive studies is P. Dunleavy and C Hood in 'From Old Public Administration to New Public Management', published in *Public Money and Management* (vol. 14 no. 3, 1994, pp. 9–16). Andrew Gray and Bill Jenkins have articulated their thought in 'From Public Administration to Public Management: Reassessing a Revolution', published in *Public Administration* (vol. 73, Spring, 1995, pp. 78–99). The idea was further elaborated by N. Denkin and K. Walsh in 'The Enabling State: The Role Of Markets And Contracts', published in *Public Administration* (vol. 14, 1996, pp. 33–48). One of the recently published comprehensive works is *The New Public Management in Action* by Ewan Ferlie and others (Oxford University Press, Oxford, 1996). That market may not always be a panacea is the basic theme, pursued by John B Goodman and Gary W. Loveman in 'Does Privatization Serve the Public Interest?', published in *Harvard Business Review* (November–December, 1991, pp. 27–38).This is the basic theme in Paul Streeton's 'Markets and States: Against Minimalism and Dichotomy', (*Political Economy Journal of India*, vol. 3, no. 1, 1995). This line of argument is pursued by P. Dunleavy in 'Explaining the Privatization Boom: Public Choice Versus Radical Approaches', *Public Administration* (vol. 64, no. 1, 1986). Similarly, Martin Minogue in 'Changing the State: Concepts and Practice in the Reform of the Public Sector', published in Martin Minogue et al. (ed.), *Beyond the New Public Management: Changing Ideas and Practices in Governance* (Edward Elgar, Cheltenham, 1998, pp. 17–37) has gone beyond what constitutes the fundamental principles of New Public Management. Ian Scott has shown the impact of New Public Management in the Asian context in his 'Changing Concepts of Decentralization: Old Public Administration and New Public Management in the Asian Context', published in *The Asian Journal of Public Administration* (vol. 18, no. 1, June, 1996, pp. 3–21). A critical assessment of the 'new world order' that emerged in the wake of globalization is made by Manfred Bienefeld in 'New World Order: Echoes of a New Imperialism' (*Third World Quarterly*, vol. 15, no. 1, 1994).

Governance is an equally significant perspective striving to grapple with the changed reality in public administration. An entire volume of *The Indian Journal of Public Administration* (vol. XLIV, No 3, July–September, 1998) has been devoted to deal with this new perspective where the boundary of government has been substantially shrunk. For conceptual clarity, the following two articles of the above volume of *The Indian Journal of Public Administration* deserve mention. O. P Dwivedi's 'Common Good and Good Governance' (pp. 253–64) and Mohit Bhattacharya's 'Conceptualising Good Governance' (pp. 289–96) have ably amplified the intricate dimensions of the perspective. The other very useful article is by Gerry Stoker entitled 'Governance as Theory: Five Propositions', published in *International Social Science Journal* (vol. 155, March, 1998, pp. 14–28). In the same volume of this journal, Bob Jessop's 'The Rise of Governance and the Risks of Failure: The Case of Economic Development' (pp. 29–47) is a critical assessment of this model. The other useful and serious interventions are (i) R Rhodes, 'The New Governance: Governing Without Governance', *Political Studies* (vol. 44, no. 3, 1996, pp. 652–67); (ii) Bob Jessop 'The Regulation Approach and Governance Theory: Alternative Perspectives on Economic and Political Change', *Economy and Society* (vol. 24, no. 3, 1995, pp. 307–33); (iii) J. Rosenau, 'Governance, Order and Change in World Politics' in J. Rosenau and E. O. Czempiel (eds), *Governance without Government: Order and Change in World Politics* (Cambridge University Press, Cambridge, 1992, pp. 1–30); (iv) B. Guy Peters, 'Models of Governance for the 1990s' in Donald F. Kitt and H Brinton Milward (eds), *The State of Public Management* (The Johns Hopkins University, Baltimore, 1996, pp. 15–43).

Feminist Perspective

The literature on the feminist perspective in Public Administration is scanty. However, there are attempts to articulate this relatively new dimension in recent researches. One may begin with the following writings: M. Butler, 'Early Liberal Roots of Feminism: John Locke and the Attack on Patriarchy', *American Political Science Review* (vol. 72, 1978, pp. 135–150); R. W. Bologh, *Love And Greatness: Max Weber and Masculine Thinking–A Feminist Inquiry*, Unwin Hymen, London, 1990; C. S. Aron, *Ladies and Gentlemen of the Civil Service: Middle Class Workers in Victorian America* (Oxford University Press, New York, 1987); C. Fox and C. E. Cochran, 'Discretionary Public Administration: Toward A Platonic Guardian Class' in H. Kass and B. Catron (ed.), *Images and Identities in Public Administration* (Sage, Newbury Park, 1990, pp. 87–112); S. Franzway, D. Court, and R. W. Connell, *Staking a Claim: Feminism, Bureaucracy and the State* (Allen and Unwin, Sydney, 1989); R. Pringle, 'Bureaucracy, Rationality and Sexuality:

The Case of Secretaries' in J. Hearn, Dl. Sheppard, P. Tancred-Sheriff and G. Burrell (eds), *The Sexuality of Organization* (Sage, London, 1989, pp. 158–77); Camilla Stivers, 'Toward a Feminist Theory of Public Administration', *Women and Politics* (vol. 10, no. 4, 1990, pp. 49–65); Stivers later developed her argument in the volume entitled *Gender Images in Public Administration: Legitimacy of the Administrative State*, Sage, Newbury park, 1993; For a gender perspective in Governance in India, D. Bandyopadhyay provides useful theoretical insight in his 'Gender and Governance in India' (*Economic and Political Weekly*, vol. 35, no. 31, July 29, 2000, pp. 2696–9).

Index